ESTUARY PEOPLE

Penclawdd 1900 to 1970

ANN ROBERTS

Published by the Author

Published in 2001 by
Ann Roberts
5 Amberley Drive, Langland
Swansea, SA3 4PJ
Telephone: (01792) 368148

A CIP catalogue record for this book is
available from the British Library.

ISBN 0-9540836-0-1

Printed and bound in Wales by
Dinefwr Press Ltd.
Rawlings Road, Llandybie
Carmarthenshire, SA18 3YD

For
Tina and Siân

Contents

Introduction 9

Acknowledgements 11

Chapter 1: The Village Stores 13

Chapter 2: Village Amenities 43

Chapter 3: Church and Chapels 82

Chapter 4: Working Underground 122

Chapter 5: Going 'Out the Sands' 155

Chapter 6: Penclawdd at War 183

Chapter 7: Women in the Forces 216

Chapter 8: Men in the Army 244

Chapter 9: Men in the Navy and Air Force 270

Chapter 10: Rugby and Music 305

Chapter 11: *Hiraeth* 347

Bibliography 372

Introduction

I was born in 1943 to Willie and Ilene Roberts. Being the daughter of *Willie Robert y Railway*, I was often referred to in the village as *Merch Willie Roberts y Railway* although I went into the public house only once – for a Band of Hope practice.

My aim has been to write of the years from 1900 to 1970. It was during the latter decade of this period, that, as in most villages, life in Penclawdd changed drastically with the introduction of television and cars, etc. However, I felt that in certain chapters, it was necessary to extend the year span.

My memories of living in Penclawdd – until 1966 – are vivid and happy. Those days have long gone, but I still feel nostalgia for this special village, straggling along the Llwchwr Estuary, and have endeavoured, with the help of friends, old and new, to recapture the unique privilege of living in Penclawdd.

Acknowledgements

I am indebted to Ann Hughes for proof-reading and encouraging me in my work, to Maureen Blyth and Ilene Foote for their help on 'Penclawdd matters', to Mary Howells for her Welsh translations, to my niece, Jemma Williams, for her excellent map, to Heather Holt for her expertise in publishing, to David Wibberly for his beautiful photography, to Jeff Carpenter for his understanding, and to Eddie John and the staff of Dinefwr Press for their help, guidance, and work, in producing this book.

I am grateful to my aunts, Win Walters and the late Marian Eaton, with whom I enjoyed talking over old times in the village.

I wish to thank the inhabitants of Penclawdd and area who gave me their stories and assistance – the late Beatrixe May (Beatie) Austin, Joan Callow, the late Mary Bennett, Maureen Blyth, Ethel Coghlan, Gwyneth Durban, Betty Edwards, Hilary Edwards, Morwyn Elliott, Ilene Foote, Myfanwy Gronow, Peggy Grove, Kathleen Guy, Nancy Guy, Gladys Harry, Mary Howells, Alison Jones, the late Annie Jones, Janet Jones, Marion Jones, Madie Jones, Peggy Jones, Winnie Jones, Gloria Lewis, Betty Lloyd, Maureen Mitchinson, Tegwedd Murley, Dulcie Nichols, the late Elaine Phillips, Vi Preston, Audrey Rees, Joyce Richards née Hodges, Joyce Richards née Howells, Kerri Shannon, Ruby Skinner, Daphne Smith, Lilian Thomas, Megan Thomas, Olive Thomas, Kathleen Trimm, Della Williams, Evan Melvyn (Mel) Austin, Harold Brenton, Jack (Cardi) Davies, Morlais Davies, the late John Elliott, Jacky Evans, the Reverend Terri Evans, Phil Foote, Morgan Guy, Arthur Harry, Arthur Hopkins, Jack Ian Hoppé, Cyril Howells, Leonard Howells, Davey John Hughes, Karl Jenkins, Idris Jones, Andrew Lewis, Ronnie Lloyd, the late Daniel McCarthy, Edgar Nurse, Dennis Parkhouse, Jeremy Parkhouse, Rudolph Ratti, the late Daniel Rees, George Rees, Griff Rees, Myrddin Rees, Denzil Sambrook, Furley Spanton, Gareth Small, Tony Small, Mark Thomas, Wynne Thomas, Ronald Tucker, the late Wilfred Tucker, Haydn Williams and the late John W. Williams. It was with great sadness that I heard of the passing away of friends.

I especially thank my cousin, Carolyn Williams. Together we discussed the possibility of a Penclawdd story, and it was with her help that the seed of 'Estuary People' was sown.

Mostly, I thank my daughters, Tina and Siân, for always 'being there' for me.

11

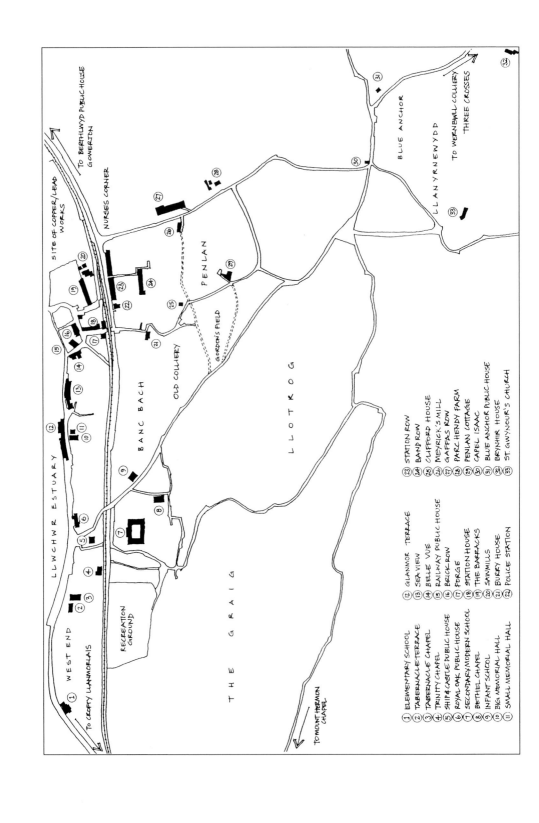

LLCHWR ESTUARY

WEST END

SITE OF COPPER/LEAD WORKS

TO CEFFY LLANMORLAIS

TO BERTHLWYD PUBLIC HOUSE
GOWERTON

NURSES CORNER

RECREATION GROUND

BANC BACH

PENLAN

OLD COLLIERY

GORDON'S FIELD

THE GRAIG

LLOTKOG

BLUE ANCHOR

LLANYRNEWYDD

TO WERNBWLL COLLIERY
THREE CROSSES

TO MOUNT HERMON CHAPEL

① ELEMENTARY SCHOOL
② TABERNACLE TERRACE
③ TABERNACLE CHAPEL
④ TRINITY CHAPEL
⑤ SHIP & CASTLE PUBLIC HOUSE
⑥ ROYAL OAK PUBLIC HOUSE
⑦ SECONDARY/MODERN SCHOOL
⑧ BETHEL CHAPEL
⑨ INFANT SCHOOL
⑩ BIG MEMORIAL HALL
⑪ SMALL MEMORIAL HALL

⑫ GLANMOR TERRACE
⑬ SEA VIEW
⑭ BELLE VUE
⑯ BRICK ROW
⑰ FORGE
⑱ STATION HOUSE
⑳ THE BARRACKS
㉑ SAWMILLS
㉒ BURRY HOUSE
⑮ RAILWAY PUBLIC HOUSE
㉒ POLICE STATION

㉓ STATION ROW
㉔ BAND ROW
㉕ CLIFFORD HOUSE
㉒ MEYRICK'S MILL
㉒ GAFFAS ROW
㉒ PARC HENDY FARM
㉕ PENLAN COTTAGE
㉚ CAPEL ISAAC
㉛ BLUE ANCHOR PUBLIC HOUSE
㉜ BRYNHIR HOUSE
㉝ ST GWYNOUR'S CHURCH

1

The Village Stores

Penclawdd is a long, narrow village, straggling for one and a half miles along the north coast of the Gower Peninsular in South Wales, squeezed between the Llwchwr Estuary to its north, and the fields of Parc Hendy Farm and the *Graig* (hill) to its south.

It entered the twentieth century as a thriving community. The eighteenth and nineteenth centuries had seen Penclawdd develop from a small rural village, to a busy industrial port. The rapid growth of the copper, silver, lead, tin-plate and brick industries in that period, had resulted in the increase of coal mining in the area, as coal was needed to assist the industries. In 1866, a railway line had been constructed from Gowerton (three miles east) to Penclawdd, to transport their products. By 1877, the line ran to Llanmorlais (one and a half miles west) and had been extended to passengers. The railway service enabled the existing cockle industry to expand further afield to the Rhondda Valley, Newport, Bristol and districts, thus accelerating its growth. By the early twentieth century, industry within Penclawdd had declined drastically. The metal works and many collieries had closed, but through the growth of many metal industries in nearby Gowerton and Gorseinon, and the opening of new collieries in and around them, and the Penclawdd area, employment remained plentiful.

Penclawdd, like almost every other community, had its class distinctions. There were a few landowners of small acreage, who assumed the position of 'squire'. The village had a 'middle-class' of preachers, clergymen, teachers, doctors, and those whose trade, craft, or business provided a moderate but stable income. There were a few local farmers, who owned or rented small farms that surrounded the village.

The majority of the inhabitants were manual workers who were employed in the collieries, industries and farms. Unique to the village were the cockle women, who through their own manual labour independently supplemented the family income.

The children of those who worked in industry and collieries usually found their future the same as their parents. Other families more financially secure, were able to support their children's higher education, enabling them to join the family business, or their further education, to enter a profession.

Crucial to village life was the role of the church and the chapels. They were the source of instruction in religion and wider reading, and the centres of social activity and musical entertainment.

When the Anglo-Normans invaded Gŵyr (Gower) in the twelfth century, they 'pushed' its Welsh-speaking inhabitants northeast as far as Subboscus – Penclawdd and district. As a result, Penclawdd, and to a lesser degree, Llanmorlais and Crofty, remained the only area of Gower, as we know it, where Welsh was spoken. However, the Anglo-Normans introduced the English language and so, in time, the inhabitants spoke both English and Welsh. Their Welsh was colloquial Welsh. The nonconformist ministers spoke pure Welsh, which was known as 'pulpit' Welsh.

Despite the class distinctions, Penclawdd was a closely integrated community of people who seemed proudly aware of inter-dependence.

Penclawdd had mushroomed into the largest village in the Gower Peninsular, its population having increased three-fold in the nineteenth century to three thousand, one hundred and forty-four. Its industries had provided employment for local men, but had also attracted a workforce from outside the village. Many came from Neath, the Swansea districts of Morriston, Llansamlet and Llangyfelach and a few from Gloucestershire, Somerset, Devon and Cornwall. Farm labourers earning meager wages migrated from the rural county of Carmarthenshire, and some immigrated to Penclawdd to escape the Irish Potato Famine of the 1840s.

The industrialists had built terraced properties to house their employees. Barracks Row, Brick Row, Blodwen Terrace, Station Row, Band Row and Gaffas' Row (for the senior workers, as the name implies) were situated in clusters around the works.

The seventeen houses of Barracks Row – the Barracks as they were known – were probably the oldest terraced properties in the village. They originated from the early nineteenth century, when they were built by the copper owners for their employees, parallel to and in close proximity to the copper works. The primitive, double storied, stone dwellings had irregular exterior wall surfaces, which were plastered following the contour of the stone, and lime washed pink. The backs of the properties had no doors simply one entrance at the front of each house.

On 4 June 1937, Ann Roberts, of the Railway public house, leased the properties from the owners, A. P. Lyons, F. P. Cheesman and F. J. Man, Trustees of the Benson Estate. The lease was to run for twenty-one years, commencing on 25 March 1937 for fifty pounds per annum. Three of the many conditions of the lease were as follows:

'Overhaul and put the demised premises into a good state of repair and condition.

Enclose the land included in the said demise at the rear of the said dwelling houses with a stone wall and rail not less then three feet six inches in height in the position indicated on the said plan in accordance with the specification supplied to the Lessee by the Lessors' Surveyor – for the purpose of forming a back yard and construct a wicket gate as access thereto through the existing stone wall between the demised premises and the station approach for the purpose of entering the said back yard only. [. . .]

Construct a back entrance to each of the said dwelling houses.'

The majority had one room downstairs and one room upstairs, but a few had the luxury of an additional small room at the back at ground floor level – known as the back-kitchen – and two bedrooms, one without a window.

A typical living room had a 'best side' housing a polished table, chairs and a sideboard, and a 'working side' comprising of a black leaded stove, a scrubbed wooden working table and a settee. The floor surface was bricks laid on earth. The hearth was made of two large flagstones.

Maureen Blyth, née James, lived in No. 10 during her childhood. "Worms used to come up between the bricks and the rugs used to become sodden with damp and quickly disintegrated. The walls were always wet. The houses had no running water but were all served by one outside water tap. A bowl and a metal jug of water were usually kept on a table in a pantry under the stairs. The water was used for drinking and cooking, etc."

Megan Thomas, née Rees, remembers how the primitive living conditions made household chores long and arduous. "In the winter, the water in the tap would freeze so we poured a kettle of boiling water over it to thaw it. I remember my mother scrubbing the floor on her hands and knees wearing a canvas apron. Washing took two days, but my mother considered herself fortunate, as she had a Dolly (mangle) to wring the clothes."

Some of Maureen's many memories of living in the Barracks are of hard work. "We were cleaning, cleaning, always cleaning. One of my many chores was to scrub the wooden lavatory seat and cut newspaper and thread it with string to hang behind the door. My mother would climb a ladder and paint the outside of our house, and some of the neighbours' houses as well."

As was the norm, in the majority of houses, before the installation of sewerage into the village in the 1960s, lavatories were at the bottom of

the gardens, but to the occupants of the Barracks, this caused more consternation than usual. Their gardens were at the front of the row, bordering
the railway line and adjacent main road, so the lavatories – built in pairs –
were in close proximity to passing traffic on rail and road. Maureen found
the situation embarrassing. "It was obvious that they were lavatories.
Everyone could see them. They were quite a distance from the houses as
the gardens were long. I was petrified, and I mean petrified to go there
in the night. I would run to the lavatory and bang the door shut, and then
run back to the house very quickly."

Despite the hardships, the young inhabitants of the Barracks, like most
village children of those times, experienced a carefree childhood. They
were allowed to wander around Penclawdd unsupervised by adults,
creating their own enjoyment. Saturdays, summer evenings, and school
holidays consisted of hour after hour of play, going home only to eat, and
sleep.

In Megan's early childhood, her teenage brother used to entertain his
friends with a portable gramophone. "When I was a little girl of about
seven, my brother, Willie, used to take the old gramophone with a horn
and wind up handle, out the marsh,[1] and he and his friends used to learn
to dance."

However, the Barracks was surrounded on three sides by, the railway
line, Bevan Brothers, Timber Merchants (known as the Sawmills), and
the treacherous Llwchwr Estuary, subjecting its children to many potential
dangers. In retrospect in later years, Maureen questioned her mother on
what seemed to have been a lack of parental concern for her safety. "I
asked my mother why had she allowed me to play out the marsh when
I couldn't swim. She said, 'You were all right. You always came home with
the first wave.'"

Maureen remembers playing with her friends in the timber sheds of
Bevan Brother with its many planks of timber precariously stacked high.
"I used to say to my mother later, "Mam, how am I still here today?"

Megan's brother, Ivor, was not so fortunate. "My brother's arm was run
over by a goods truck while he was playing on the railway line. He was
only eleven. We thought his future was going to be a problem, but he
learned to repair shoes with one hand. He was provided with an artificial
hand, but rarely used it. He covered his wrist with a sock. He was always
well-dressed, but he was unable to button his right shirt cuff. When he
went out, I used to help him put on his artificial hand and button his
cuff." Ivor repaired shoes in the back-kitchen of the house and later used
a shed in the garden. In the 1930s, when his family moved to Liverpool
House, at Station Corner, Ivor, with the help of his brother, Gomer, opened

a shoe shop with a shoe and boot repair service, in a front room of the premises.

Every year, a fair came to the village, parking on the site of the old copper works immediately behind the Barracks. Although it was only a small affair, with one roundabout and a few sideshows, the village children looked forward to it with great anticipation. Ivor used to repair shoes for the fair folk but his mother did not approve.

"The show people would come to the back window and shout, 'Ivor, are our shoes ready?'

My mother would say to him, 'Ivor. Don't you bring that showman to that window again.'"

By the 1940s, the postal address of Barracks Row had changed to Lead Works Row, but the properties were still referred to in the village as the Barracks. The inhabitants of the row do not seem to know why the name was changed, but it is possible that there was a stigma attached to the name Barracks. There is no doubt that many of its occupants did not want to be associated with the row. In her teenage days, Megan tried to hide the fact from her boyfriend. "When I was courting Glan, I'd never say that I lived in the Barracks. I'd wait for him to catch the bus home to Waun-arlwydd before I went home."

The houses were not of uniform size, and families often arranged, between themselves, to exchange properties to suit their individual needs.

In accordance with the conditions of the lease, Ann Roberts constructed a back entrance to each of the houses, and the tenants also improved their homes by installing windows in the bedrooms and cementing the floors, etc.

In 1941, two years after Megan married Glan Thomas, the couple occupied No. 15. "My mother had moved back to No. 1 from Liverpool House and said to us, 'Try and have a house near me.' We went to live in No. 15. We put a window in the bedroom, which was at the pine-end of the row. It had a beautiful view up the estuary. We put in a new floor and bought a red carpet. We had a big black stove, but I also had an oil stove to cook on. It was so cosy. I loved living there. We would sit out on the windowsills and talk. We didn't have a lot, but they were happy days. It was as if we were one big family."

The Barracks was condemned and demolished in the late 1950s. Many of its inhabitants were rehoused in Dunraven Close, which was purpose-built for them by Glamorgan County Council. They had mixed feelings about moving. Maureen's mother, Elizabeth Mary James, was adamant that she did not want to leave her home. Although Megan was happy there, she still looked forward to moving. "I was so excited about having a sink with running water." But now she feels, "My flat is modern but it is not the same living here as in the Barracks."

The burgeoning population instigated many villagers to open shops, which were run as family businesses by husbands, wives, sons and daughters. The majority of these were in the front rooms of their houses, but some properties were purpose-built as dwellings and stores combined under one roof.

D. Jenkins sold bread, confectionery, and fruit, in his shop in Compton House, situated at the entrance to Trinity Lane.

Morgan Morgans, known as Morgan Twice, a native of Carmarthenshire, lived with his wife Mary, and their children Annie May, David, Hannah Violet, and Lilian in Manchester House, which was situated adjacent to the Ship and Castle public house. Mary ran a grocery business from the premises, while Morgan Twice pursued his career as an insurance agent. By 1926, their daughter, Annie May, was in charge of the business.

William Guy, grocer, traded in the front room of Beach House, a few yards east of the Royal Oak public house. He also provided his customers with local cockles.

In 1901, about a hundred yards to the east, Rees Jeffreys built Westminster House with an adjacent stable. The premises had living accommodation

Rees Jeffreys in trap with son Glyn.

and also a shop area, which housed the sub-post office – Rees being the sub-postmaster – and a general stores. Rees delivered his wares to many areas of Gower in a horse-driven trap. His son, Glyn, delivered telegrams in North Gower – from Penclawdd to Landimore – on horseback. Glyn later married Jane Ann, and the couple went to live in Penlan Terrace. Although moving in the late 1920s with his wife and family back to live in Westminster House, Glyn did not follow in his father's footsteps, but worked as a fitter in a Gorseinon colliery. After Rees Jeffreys' retirement, the premises housed a chemist shop for some years.

Thomas Edward Booley, the proprietor of a confectionery and newspaper shop in the corner property of Belle Vue, opposite the Railway public house, was not the most popular shopkeeper in the village. He lived up to his name, as Win Walters, née Eaton, remembers. "He really was a bully. We were afraid to go into his shop to buy sweets." Booley also owned a bicycle and boot shop in the middle of the terrace.

Evan Morgan Rees, and his brother Gwyn, were the proprietors of the Emporium – a general stores and the largest shop in the village. Evan Morgan was in charge of the grocery department, while his brother, Gwyn, ran the haberdashery department. A partition separated the two areas. After Gwyn's death during the First World War, the haberdashery department was closed, and the partition removed. Later – Rees Jeffreys having retired as sub-postmaster in Westminster House – the area housed the sub-post office, with its own entrance. A large bakery was situated behind the shop, which supplied the villagers with excellent fresh bread daily.

Jonathan Morgan traded as a blacksmith, in the forge opposite the railway station. It seems Jonathan was a quick-tempered man, as Denzil Sambrook experienced. "I was passing the forge one day when Jonathan Morgan was shoeing a horse. He had the horse's rear leg between his legs, when the horse suddenly kicked up. Jonathan's temper was on a short fuse, and I was amazed to see him kick the horse, and it was a big horse too." The village children were under the impression that the water used for cooling the irons was a cure for warts. Daniel McCarthy swears that the twenty warts he had at one time on his hand were cured by this method.

Jane Davies had been widowed when her husband had been killed in a local industry. In the early 1920s, she bought the end building of Blodwen Terrace, next to the railway station, which was a private dwelling at the time. She extended the property to accommodate her family – W. Henry (always pronounced En-er-ee), Philip John, Lucy and Olwen. A large area of the ground floor was converted into a general stores, and named Gower Stores. It was an excellent shop, and one of the largest in the village, always retaining a high standard, and stocking a large variety of wares. Jane's son, Phillip John, and her daughter, Olwen, assisted her in the stores. When Olwen married David John Preston, the latter became manager of the stores. Jane's great niece, Marian Eaton, née Davies, has fond memories of visiting the shop. "I loved going to Aunty Jane's shop. David John Preston was a good man and an excellent worker. I shall never forget seeing boxes of biscuits in the shop for the first time. I had never seen biscuits in boxes before and immediately bought one. The accounts' area contained a very large ledger book about two feet long."

David John and Olwen had two children – Eurfryn and Lynda. Eurfryn assisted in the shop, eventually being in charge. When he married Vi, a native of Morriston, the couple 'lived above the shop'. Vi sometimes helped her husband. "I occasionally served in the shop. We used to sell the best of everything; the best butter, the best cheese and the best bacon – big sides of home-cured. A Mr. Hessletine from Sketty used to visit us. He was a traveller for Sharps tea – high-class tea."

Jane's sister-in-law, Elizabeth, opened a ladies' outfitters shop next door. It was also of a good standard and the two sisters were in strong competition. Elizabeth's daughters, Martha Jane and May, were employed as shop assistants. The stores became known locally as *Siop Jano's* (Jano's shop) – probably after Elizabeth's time.

William Rees, a native of Llanelli, Carmarthenshire, was proprietor of one of the oldest stores in the village. The shop was housed in Liverpool House, which was situated at Station Corner. William and his family lived on the premises. It was a general stores, selling groceries, glass, china and ironmongery, as well as being a drapers and outfitters. When William's wife died in childbirth, Laura, a native of the village, went to live in Liverpool House to look after him and his family. She married Gwilym, one of the youngest sons, who later inherited the business from his father. Gwilym was no businessman, and preferred to be in the Railway public house drinking with the commercial travellers, leaving the shop and his children in the care of his wife. He often came home drunk, and Laura became increasingly annoyed and exasperated by her husband's behaviour. Their daughter, Megan, remembers her mother relating those times. "My mother couldn't stand the drinking and so left him in Liverpool House and went, with my brothers and sisters, to live in No. 14, The Barracks." Eventually, Gwilym, realizing the error of his ways, gave the business to his brother, Richard (Dick), and went to work in Gowerton Steelworks. His actions redeemed his wife's respect, and she invited him back into the 'family fold'. They extended their family to eight children. Dick's son, Evan Grey succeeded his father as proprietor of the shop.

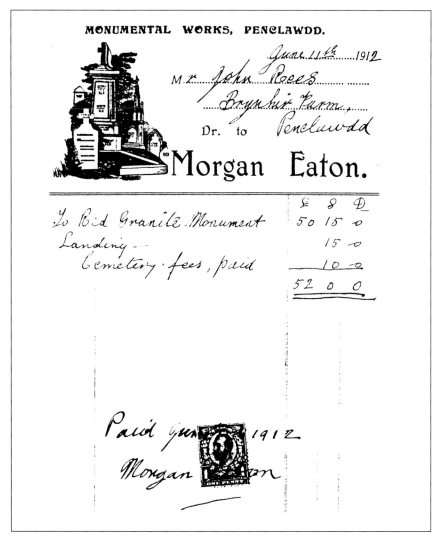

Receipt of gravestone for Catherine Rees, first wife of Johnny the Blue.
Died 6.7.1911, aged thirty-four years.

Morgan Eaton was the village's monumental mason, operating from a zinc shed situated in a field next to Band Row. The field belonged to his older brother, Henry Eaton, of Clifford House, Penlan, who allowed Morgan the use of the field rent-free. It was a fair arrangement as Henry, being the oldest son, had been the sole inheritor of the estate after their parent's death.

Edgar Nurse, accompanied by two of his brothers, came to South Wales from Gloucestershire, in the early 1880s. His brothers found work in Llanelli. Edgar, an experienced pickler in the tin-plate industry, found employment in Penclawdd Tin-plate Works, and bought the east-end property of Station Row, for seventy pounds. He became known in the village as Nurse the Pickler.

On his retirement from the tin-plate industry, Edgar rented the field behind his house, where he grew and harvested hay and kept a few horses. He also established himself as a coal merchant, delivering his merchandise in a horse-drawn dray. He was later joined in the business by his son Stanley, and bought a hard-wheeled Dennis lorry. Edgar erected a petrol pump in the garden, at the side of his property, to fuel the vehicle. The pump attracted the village children, and Edgar, finding them a nuisance, discouraged them with, "Go away! This is Nurse's corner." Henceforth, the area became known as Nurses Corner, and is still called so today. While delivering coal to Blue Anchor in his dray, his horse kicked his leg. The ensuing wound eventually caused his death.

Stanley's son, Edgar – named after his grandfather – now living in the family home, recalls his father's unfortunate premature death, also through an accident. "My father got killed in Llanrhidian when I was only four. He liked his couple of pints. He and Freddie Bennett had been drinking at the Dolphin pub in Llanrhidian. My father was pranking about, and jumped on the lorry's bonnet. The lorry went over the edge of the mound near the main road, and my father toppled off. The lorry went over his chest. It happened on the Friday, and he lived until the Sunday. My mother was widowed, with five children under four years of age. We relied on, 'Uncle Sam' – parish relief – and hand down clothes. It was hard on my mother. My grandmother took one of the twins to live with her down The Wern, in Llanmorlais."

Mary Ann Thomas, née Evans, sister of Danna Evans (confectioner), was anxious to establish a business with the one hundred pounds profit that she had received from a season of cockle selling in Newport. Her husband, David – a man of small stature, known as *Davey Bach* (small David) – wanted to open a pub. Mary Ann, conscious of the fact that her husband was 'fond of the drink' knew that his plan would spell certain disaster, and had no intention of complying with his wishes. Instead, she opened a grocery business in the front parlour of their house in the Old Colliery.[2] It prospered, and a larger premises was soon needed. Mary Ann built a shop nearby, and its success enabled her to build a large house for herself, her husband, and their seven children – John, Cassie, Lilian, Evan, Mary, Ann and Willie – opposite their existing home.

Assisted by her young son, Evan, Mary Ann worked extremely hard in her business. Her customers were inhabitants of Penclawdd, The Wern, Three Crosses and the Gower Peninsular. Mary Ann employed a daily housekeeper to help run her home and also a woman who came every six months to mend clothes. The part-time employee brought her own sleeping mattress, and stayed until all the mending was completed.

Mary Ann had a stable near Wernbwll Colliery, where she kept horses and passenger brakes. She hired out the horse-drawn brakes, which were driven by Evan. The latter's daughter, Marion (Jones), remembers her father relating his experiences. "My father, when only nine years old, used to drive six or eight men at a time around the Gower pubs, to go 'on the merry'. On one occasion, the horse went wild and kicked and kicked. My father eventually discovered that the shafts were rubbing the poor horse's sides. On another occasion, he was coming home from Park-mill one dark winter's night, when the candles in the brake's candle lamps burned out. He went into Kilfrough Manor that was then occupied by Admiral Heneage. There was a ball being held there that night. At the front door, he met a tall elegant man, with golden hair, and a yellow beard. He said to my father, 'What do you want young lad?' My father replied that he wanted candles for his lamps. He was taken through the ballroom. It was a magnificent place, with many chandeliers. The men were dressed either in military uniform or black evening dress, and the women, dressed in colourful ball gowns, were like flowers."

Marion says of her grandmother, "All her children adored her. She was a very strong character, and a shrewd business woman." *Davey Bach* worked spasmodically in a local colliery, and spent many hours in the local pubs. Consequently, he was of little help to his wife, in the business, or the home. The poet, tramp and author, W. H. Davies (1871-1940), often visited *Davey Bach*. The two men would sit on a bench outside the shop and exchange limericks. They were oblivious of time, a subject W. H. Davies addressed in his poem, 'Leisure' (*Songs of Praise*. 1911):

'What is this life, if full of care,
We have no time to stand and stare?

No time to stand beneath the boughs,
And stare as long as sheep and cows.

No time to see, when woods we pass,
Where squirrels hide their nuts in grass.

No time to see, in broad daylight,
Streams full of stars like skies at night.

No time to turn at Beauty's glance,
And watch her feet, how they can dance.

No time to wait till her mouth can
Enrich that smile her eyes began.

A poor life this if, full of care,
We have no time to stand and stare.'

"Meanwhile," says Marion, "My grandmother was working her little head off in the shop. When anyone inquired of my grandfather's health, he would reply, 'I'm in the pink, but I'll soon be in the Blue.'(Blue Anchor public house).

One day, after my grandfather had been drinking, he threw a cup at my grandmother, which cut her face and drew blood. My father was so annoyed that he hit him, but immediately retreated into the nearest hayrick, where he spent the night."

Mary Ann made plans to expand her business. She intended opening a bakery next to her shop, and hired a chef. However, she experienced a vicious pain once a month which used to incapacitate her, and so she decided to seek medical advice. She discovered she had an internal problem and was to have an operation. She walked barefoot to Swansea, carrying her shoes. She washed her feet at the stream at *Olchfa* (washing place), donned her shoes, and continued walking to Swansea.[3] After completing her business at the wholesaler, she admitted herself to Swansea General Hospital. Mary Ann died of blood poisoning a few days after her operation. She was forty-two years of age. On the evening before her death, she had been visited by her husband. The medical profession were then of the opinion that the consumption of cold liquids was fatal to patients with high temperatures. Mary Ann had begged and begged her husband for water, and eventually *Davey Bach* had given her a small drink of lemonade. He blamed himself for her death for many proceeding years.

Their son, John, and his wife Ceinwen, became the proprietors of the business, which they ran successfully for many years. John was known as John Mary Ann, and on becoming a shop proprietor, John the Shop.

Win Walters remembers the shops providing the villagers with a Chocolate Club. "An employee of a shop, I can't remember which one, collected contributions from each house, and at Christmas, we had a box of King George chocolates. We had few luxuries in those days, but when we did have them, they were a real treat."

Before the Gowerton-Penclawdd road was constructed in 1921 to 1923, Penclawdd had no bus service, and the majority of the provisions, groceries, etc. came to the village either by train, or by horse-drawn vehicles on the Penclawdd-Three Crosses road. Lipton's grocery firm delivered provisions to the many grocery stores in Penclawd by a horse-drawn wagon, with a tarpaulin top. Wilfred Tucker, who lived in Blue Anchor until the age of sixteen, remembers the deliveries. "One day, we heard one hell of a crash at the bottom of the very steep hill by the Blue Anchor Inn. Its garden contained two huge trees. The brakes of the wagon had failed, and the poor horse hit the first of the trees and was killed instantly. The wagon tipped over. I had mother's apron on – the old-fashioned kind – at the time. The contents of the wagon – jam and tea, etc. – tipped over the bank. We had a 'field day' helping ourselves.

Liptons had a commercial traveller who cycled to his work in the village. The poor man had to walk with his bike up the hill to Three Crosses on his homeward journey. In fact, I never saw him on his bike. Even down in the village on the flat road, he pushed it along by the side of him. We kids used to make fun of him."

George Rees remembers the Liptons' representative. "You could order anything from him. I remember my father buying a bike with three speeds and a step at the back, for five shillings. He called it Mary Betsy. My mother bought a stove. The goods were delivered in a cleaned out cattle lorry, belonging to Grove's of Gower."

Ben-y-Saer.

Benjamin Thomas, Sea View, was known as *Ben-y-Saer* (Ben the carpenter). He was also the local undertaker. Benjamin's house and business premises were on the sea front near the Memorial Halls. He and his wife had three sons, Benjamin (Ben), Frank, William G. and Griffith Edgar, and three daughters, Elizabeth (Lizzie), Margaret Ann (Mag) and Sarah (Sal). After their school days, William and Benjamin joined their father in the business. Lizzie's daughter, Marian, who lived with her grandfather during her childhood, often reminisces of those times. "We knew immediately when someone had died in Penclawdd, as we would hear them coming around the back of our house to fetch a board for the body. My grandfather would then make a coffin for the deceased. Mrs. Roberts, who lived on the *Graig*, was called day or night to lie out the body for the fee of two shillings and six pence."

As the population increased, more shops were opened or inherited by sons and daughters, and some changed ownership and trade. They provided excellent comprehensive shopping for the villagers with a reliable delivery service. By 1926, the following shops existed in close proximity along the narrow straggling village:

Grocers: Mrs. Ann Banfield, Mill Street.
Mrs. Margaret Jane Brenton, West End.
Mrs. Ann Dark, Station Row.
Mrs. Jane Davies and Son, Gower Stores, Blodwen Terrace (next to the railway station).
Ivor Fry, 20 Station Road.
William Francis.
John Howells, Blue Anchor.
Frank Lewis, Sea View Stores.
Miss Annie May Morgans, Manchester House.
Evan Grey Rees, Liverpool House.
Evan Morgan Rees, Emporium – also baker.
Tom (Major) Rees (near the Old Council Houses).
David (*Davey Bach*) and Mary Ann Thomas, Old Colliery.
Walter and Co.
Misses M. A. (dressmaker) & M. E. Williams. (Opposite the Mill House, which they inherited from their mother, Catherine Williams).

Confectioners: Robert John Davies (next to the forge).
Ebenezer Evans.
Daniel Jenkins, Beach House – also sold fruit, cream cakes and laverbread.
Daniel (Dana) Evans – also sold fruit and had a tearoom in the middle room of his premises. It was also rented by the Swansea dentist, Stammers Alabaster, on Fridays as a dental surgery.
Mrs. Hannah Thomas, West End.

Butchers: George Francis, Station Row.
Thomas Henry Thomas, West End.
Mrs. Harriet Howells.

Tailors: David Austin.
Joseph Gronow.
David Dixon Jones, Blodwen Terrace.

Drapers:	Robert Davies (to become *Siop Jano's*).
	Miss Mary Elizabeth Owen, Belle Vue.
Boot Makers:	David Evans, 1 Blodwen Terrace.
	Thomas Oswald Griffiths (in-between the forge and the Emporium).
Fried Fish:	Owen Evans, Compton House (at entrance to Trinity Lane).
	George Harry, Station Road.
	William James Howell, The Central Bar, Glanmor Terrace.
	John Rees.
Hairdressers:	William Howells (*Wil y Barbwr* – Wil the Barber, Station Road).
	Arthur James Jenkins, Sea View (son of Reverend A. T. Jenkins, Bethel Chapel).
Station Master:	Isaac D. Jones.

Ben-y-Saer retired, and his son, Ben, continued trading as carpenter and undertaker. Lizzie's husband, William Henry Davies, building contractor, constructed a pair of semidetached houses both named The Croft, in Banc Bach. *Ben-y-Saer* took up residence in No. 1, The Croft, with his daughter Sal, and her husband Frank, and Henry William and Lizzie lived in No. 2, The Croft, with their children Marian and Francis (Sis). *Ben-y-Saer* loved to sit in the front room of his home and watch the schoolchildren play in the Infant School, situated opposite. The children grew to love him, his long white beard instigating them to nickname him, 'Father Christmas'.

Midland Bank Limited had a sub-branch in a front room of Liverpool House and opened weekly, Monday 10.45 a.m. to 12.15 p.m. and Lloyds Bank's sub-branch, next to Ratti's Ice-Cream Parlour in Belle Vue, opened weekly, Tuesday 11 a.m. to 2.15 p.m.

Visiting dentists provided a dental service. Stammers Alabaster, a Swansea dentist held his surgery in Daniel Evans' premises on Fridays and Austin Jenkins, a Gowerton dentist, held his surgery on Thursdays 2 p.m. to 6 p.m.

Ceinwen Ellicott opened a grocery shop on the Trumpic Road.[4]

Maggie May Davies had a fish and chip shop in-between the forge and the Emporium.

Arthur James Jenkins was the son of the Reverend A. T. Jenkins. His barber and hairdresser shop at Sea View was a centre for many interesting discussions. Mel Austin enjoyed the experience. "I used to love going to Arthur James' shop to have my hair cut. He lost a leg in an accident. He

would sum up his customers, and then he would start them off by introducing a subject that they would be interested in. All in the shop would
become involved in deep discussions – politics, sport, etc. During the
Second World War years, he displayed in his shop window, photographs
of all the boys and girls in the village who were in the forces."

In 1928, Morgan John Rees rented the business premises in Westminster
House, where he traded as a grocer. He inherited beautiful narrow,
rosewood, glass-fronted wall cases from the chemist – who had traded
there previously – where he displayed small items such as herbs and
spices. During the Second World War years, he employed Freda, daughter
of Glyn Jeffreys. Amongst her many duties, Freda was in charge of the
ration books. Morgan John's son, Cliff, sometimes served in the shop
during his teenage years. He used to wait on the seawall opposite the
shop to meet Audrey, Glyn Jeffreys' oldest daughter, when she came
home from Gowerton County School. Love blossomed, and in 1941,
Cliff and Audrey married but were soon to be separated, when Cliff
joined the Royal Artillery Regiment. After the war, Cliff attended Greggs'
Secretarial College, where he studied shorthand and typing, having no
intention of working in his father's shop. However, his father found
difficulty in trading on his own and so Cliff, having no alternative,
decided to work with his father. Later, on Morgan John's retirement,
Cliff and Audrey took over the running of shop with the help of a few
errand boys. On Cliff's illness in 1973, the store closed, and the premises'
use as a business terminated.

The village boasted another barber and hairdresser. *Wil y Barbwr* (Wil
the barber) was also a miner in Wernbwll Colliery. He was one of the
fortunate survivors of the colliery explosion in 1929. After the disaster, he
decided to leave his employment, close his hairdressing business, and
open a fruit, vegetable and wet fish shop. He traded in the premises of his
hairdressing business – a small wooden extension that he had built onto
the pine-end of his house, Harlech, at Station Corner.

His son, Cyril, remembers the shop. "My father bought a Morris Cowley
van and sold his produce around Gower, as well as in the shop. Every
Tuesday and Thursday morning, he was up at five, and by seven, he was
at Swansea Docks buying his fish. The depression was bad then. He
allowed his customers to buy his produce and pay later. One Bank Holiday
Monday, he took our family to Oxwich in his van. He left my older brother,
John, in charge of the shop with the warning not to give tick to anybody.
A woman came in and begged John for food, as she had nothing in the
house to give her family. John filled her bag and never had a penny for
it. He had a row from my father when he came home for giving the

woman too much, but not for giving her tick. My father had a weakness. He couldn't refuse anybody who was in need, and as long as they owed him ten shillings, and paid him five shillings, he didn't mind. When he finished trading in about 1938, there was a list of people who owed him money.

He also made ice-cream. My mother boiled the milk – which was bought from the Hendy Farm – and then added the cream and ice-cream powder. The mixture was poured into the tub of the ice-cream machine, which was kept in the lean-to at the back of the house. Three of us would take it in turns to turn the handle for two hours. It was very tiring. The mixture was left overnight to cool. When my father bought his fish at the docks, he also bought blocks of ice to keep the ice-cream and the fish cold. The ice was wrapped in hessian potato sacks, and kept under the floor of the lean-to, which was accessible from the coal shed behind. If my father ran out of ice, although in competition, Mr. Ratti would be more than happy to sell my father some. The ice-cream was sold in the shop, and my brother, Mydrim, also sold it around the houses of the village, in a small handcart.

After my father closed his shop, he went prospecting for coal near the North Gower Road. He cycled there, and back, everyday, but didn't have a penny for it. My father was in the venture with four other men – Danna Merthyr, Will Davies the Ship, Robert Howells and my father's brother, Walter. The four put money in to buy equipment, etc., but my father was working his share in. They prospected for two years without success. They then prospected at the old Western Colliery in the west-end of the village, but only had a small success there."

Cyril's family was experiencing the grim economic climate of the country at the time. The return of the Labour Government in 1929 (without a working majority) was soon followed by an economic crisis, which was part of a world depression, sparked off by the sudden and violent collapse of the New York Stock Market. This was the result of the wild speculative boom by American businessmen disintegrating, bringing in its train, widespread bankruptcies and suicides. Frantic withdrawals of short overseas loans by the American speculators led to a slump spreading across the world. Mass unemployment in the USA was followed by a rapid rise in Britain, of already high unemployment figures. On the government front, a business expert, Sir George May, head of the Prudential Insurance Company, was chosen as the best man to advise the government on how to cope with financial crises. Unemployment benefit went down from seventeen shillings to fifteen shillings and threepence for an adult man, and his wife's allowance from nine shillings to eight shillings. Only the children's allowance of two shillings was untouched, but all those who were in work had to pay weekly contributions from wages which were lamentably low. It was, however, the application of the means test, which was the most inhuman aspect of these savage economy measures. After receiving twenty-six weeks benefit, claimants were subjected to a searching and humiliating means test into their private affairs, before they could receive any further payments, which were called 'transitional benefits'. These payments would be made from a special grant from the treasury, but paid through the Labour Exchange. This examination of resources would be carried out by a local public assistance committee, with salaried officials. All family circumstance would be investigated and then scales of relief would be recommended to the Employment Exchange for payment.

Many men who had never been near the Poor Law and had paid years of contributions, now had to undergo a searching means test. Relief scales varied widely and added to the distress. Some were as low as ten shillings for a man and wife. Added hardship and humiliation were caused by the applicaion of a household means test, by which all the resources of the family were added up, and deducted from the recommended payment. Questions to the householders would include inquiries about the source of items of furniture and clothes. The possession of a piano was always a source of suspicion. This means test was, in some cases, the cause of a loss of transitional benefit.

Cyril recalls, "They were hard times between the wars. My four brothers were working in Fairwood Tin Works, in Gowerton. There was no work there in the summer months, so they picked potatoes in Gower. They went down on Sunday night in readiness to work on Monday morning, and returned home on Saturday afternoon. They were down there again on Sunday night. They didn't get paid, only had their food provided. Neither was my father getting paid in his coal venture. We were subjected to the means test. My father applied for a new permit, but when Burgess came and saw furniture in our house, he said we couldn't have any money. The parlour was empty. We didn't even have a carpet in it. My Uncle Walter kept a few bikes and my father tried to help him a bit."

Cyril's uncle, Walter Howells, was a miner in Wernbwll Colliery. He had silicosis and appreciated that the end of his working life in the colliery was imminent. He decided to establish a business in the village in readiness for his retirement. Through unforeseen circumstances, his daughter, Myfanwy, and her husband, Haydn Gronow took over the running of the shop after his death.

Myfanwy recalls, "My father opened his shop in 1929, eight years before he left employment in the colliery at the age of forty-four. Years after leaving the colliery, he was the first person to be granted a lawful compensation for his silicosis. He received four hundred pounds.

He was good with his hands and repaired watches and umbrellas – six pence for a new watch winder, six pence for a new umbrella steel, and nine pence for two steels. We don't have that service today. If an umbrella breaks, we have to throw it away. My father rented the front room of the Emporium premises from Mrs. Daisy Rees, Newton House. My father stocked a few bikes, which he kept in the room above the Emporium shop. He later rented a room behind his shop for the bikes, from Mrs. Rees' son, David.

I was working in an office in Swansea. My grandmother fell and broke her hip, so I left my work and came home to look after her. She died in 1939, and I returned to my office. My father then was taken ill, and I came home again. He died unexpectedly at the age of fifty-five and I was left to run the shop. My younger brother, Aneurin, was employed by the government and working in Malvern during the war. I assumed that when the war finished he would take over the running of the shop, so I continued working there as opposed to returning to my office. When my brother was demobbed, he was disinterested in the shop, as, compared to his research work during the war years, I'm sure he must have thought that running a shop would be boring.

My husband, Haydn, came home from the air force in 1946 where he had trained as an electrician. My brothers persuaded him to run the shop, which we ran mainly as an electrical shop. I had a brass and iron scales on which I weighed leather and nails for repairing shoes – people used to repair their own in those days – and carbide for bicycle lamps. The scales' weights were made of brass and iron. They had to be checked every year by the Weights and Measures. The latter used to come to the Ship and Castle public house, and Bob the Cockney, the town crier, used to take the weights there for us. I still have the scales today and use it for cooking.

In 1958, on the day of Alfryn Jones' funeral, we moved to the larger premises on the sea front when Frank Lewis' grocery business finished there.

Haydn and I have been very happy, but it wasn't really our calling. You have to be a certain type to cope with cutthroat business, and we weren't."

When Walter Howells rented the room in the Emporium premises that had previously housed the sub-post office, the latter had been relocated. Its sub-postmistress, Mrs. Rees, had met and nursed her husband, a native of Penclawdd, during the First World War years. Mr. Rees' war injuries had resulted in his being unable to work. After the war, he had returned, with his wife to Penclawdd, and Mrs. Rees had opened a sub-post office in the front room of London House, a property belonging to her husband's family. In 1939, Mrs. Rees moved her business to a purpose-built post office, with living premises behind, next to Beach House. In 1951, she sold her property to the Cooperative Society. A telephone exchange also operated from the building.

The first cinema in the village was owned by Frank Hayward – cinematography proprietor. It was housed in a zinc and wood lean-to at the back of Tom Booley's bicycle shop in Belle Vue, and contained about fifty hard wooden seats. Griff Rees spent many happy hours there. "It only had silent films. It was before the time of talkies. Mr. Hayward's wife played appropriate music on the piano to accompany the film during the performance. Mr. Hayward was in charge of sound effects. Thunder and lightning were simulated by pounding metal sheets, and the sound of rain was produced by throwing rice on metal sheets. It was very effective and worked well. I used to go with my mother and grandmother. My grandmother could not see so my mother used to read the subtitles out to her."

In 1929, the silent films suddenly found themselves redundant with the arrival of the talkies – heralding the golden age of the cinema. Cinemas were built in suburbia and towns, with names such as, the Odeon in Sketty, and the Plaza in Swansea. Penclawdd had its own cinema, simply called the Pictures.

In 1921, Penclawdd Miners' Welfare Committee had erected two halls of corrugated zinc, on The Pond,[5] in memory of the men of the village who had been killed in the First World War. Many miners had lost their peers during the war. The Committee later operated as the Welfare Committee and raised funds to create facilities for the village. Its trustees were represented from each religious denomination in the village – Olly Fry (St. Gwynour's Church), Henry Davies (Tabernacle), Olly Rees (Bethel), and Mr. Davies (Baptist). In the 1930s, the larger of the two Memorial Halls was converted into a cinema, and although less salubrious than those purposely built, was frequented and loved by villagers of all ages. Griff Rees remembers its maiden performance being 'All quite on the Western Front'. The building's outer frame of corrugated iron provided the cinema with excellent acoustics.

Its manager, Mr. Becket, took his job very seriously, and conducted a quiet and well-behaved audience, who respected him highly. From 1942, Ilene Foote, née Humphries, was greatly involved in the running of the cinema, working as bookkeeper, typist and cashier. "When I started, my salary was just over one pound a week and when I finished in the late 1950s, it had increased to two pounds and nineteen shillings. Saturday morning seats cost six pence. At the two evening performances, the wooden front seats cost one shilling and the back comfortable seats, known as 'the plush' cost one shilling and nine pence. Our local policeman, Sergeant Lord, took an active interest in the smooth running of the cinema. He stood at the door checking that all who entered had tickets, which he ripped in half on their entry. One evening he had another appointment and he asked me to, 'Cut the tickets Ilene until I come back.' I considered it a great honour that he trusted me to do so."

Jane Ann Jeffreys treated herself and her daughters, Audrey, Freda, and Norma to a cinema visit once a week. "Every Monday, when I came home from Gowerton County School, Mamma would have been washing since early morning with a washing tub and a scrubbing board. She would then start ironing. Afterwards, Mamma, Freda, Norma and I would go to the Pictures. The performance over, we would cross the road to Jim's fish and chip shop, which was directly opposite. Supper was ready." Audrey particularly remembers one Monday evening when the shop was extremely busy and Jim was being pressurized by a customer. "Jim was standing behind the counter, all hot and bothered, conscious of all these people waiting for fish and chips. David Jenkins, Dai Jinks as he was known, was in the queue and becoming a bit restless. He asked Jim how long the chips were going to be. Jim must have really been in a bad mood, as he answered that some were going to be this long, measuring an inch in the air between fingers, and that some were going to be that long, measuring three inches. After Jim's sharp retort, his customers waited patiently for their fish and chips in silence."

Jim installed two billiard tables and a table tennis table in an upstairs room of his shop premises, and consequently, it became a popular meeting place of the village youths. He also ran a car-hiring service. His son, John William, was betrothed to Marion, granddaughter of *Davey Bach* and Mary Ann Thomas. John William had taught his fiancée to drive. Marion chauffeured Jim's car free of charge as, considering herself part of the family, and also enjoying driving, she drove as a hobby. However, one incident remains in her memory. "We received a message informing us that Ann Roberts, landlady of the Railway Inn, wanted to go to Blue Anchor. I asked Jim how much should I charge her. He replied, 'Don't charge her anything.' I took her to Blue Anchor and she gave me half-a-crown saying to me, 'You must have that.' It was a solid bit of money in those days. When I arrived back at the shop, and showed Jim my half-a-crown, damn me, he took it."

The profits from the cinema provided the Welfare Committee with a reliable income. Once a year the Committee also had a large contribution from the Drama Week held in the Big Memorial Hall, and later in the larger hall of the Secondary Modern School. During the first week of

January, seven three-act plays – four in the English and three in the Welsh language – of an extremely high standard, were performed by visiting companies from Swansea, Llanelli, Bristol and the South Wales Valleys, etc. They were adjudicated by famous people such as the actor Clifford Evans. A prize was awarded for the best English play, the best Welsh play, the best actor, and the best actress. Tickets were 'like gold' and were ordered months in advance.

Ratti's Ice-Cream Parlour was much frequented by the youngsters of the village. In 1911, at the age of fourteen years, Ernest Ratti left his native Italy, unaccompanied, to seek a new life in Wales. His family owned a small farm. It was expected of him, being the oldest son, to leave home to earn his living, and if possible, send money to his parents. He arrived in Llandybie with no knowledge of either the English or the Welsh language. Undeterred by the language barrier, he soon found employment in a fish and chip shop in Pontarddulais. His oldest son, Rudolph, has great respect for his late father. "I can remember him telling me that all he did, day in and day out, was to peel potatoes. There were no machines in those days.

Then the 1914-18 War came. The Italians were our allies and my father went to the forces.

He came to Penclawdd in his early twenties, and after courting Annie Collins for about three years, at the age of twenty-seven, married her on 4th March 1924. My father was a Catholic and the ceremony took place in Aberavon Catholic Church. They had four children – Perine, Michael, John and me.

Tom Booley had closed his bicycle shop in Belle Vue by then, and my father rented the front room of the premises and opened an Ice-Cream Parlour. We lived at the back of the premises and on the first floor. Only a curtain separated Frank Hayward's cinema from the kitchen, and when a breeze blew the curtain, we would be immediately transported from the kitchen to the cinema. When the cinema closed, my father bought the whole premises, and later, when I was about eleven, the house next door as well.

Both my parents had tremendous qualities, but my father had particularly high principles. He and Mr. Hughes, minister of Bethel Chapel, were great friends. The minister used to call in the shop twice every week to see my father. I can remember Mr. Hughes saying to me, 'You're father's knowledge of the Bible is fantastic.'

I replied, 'I can understand that as not one night goes by without his reading the Bible.' My father attended neither church nor chapel, but perhaps if a Catholic Church had been nearer – the nearest was in Gorseinon – he would probably have attended early mass. Unlike most Catholic men, he didn't force my mother, or us as children, to join the Catholic faith. He insisted on getting married in a Catholic Church, but my mother remained a Baptist all her life, as did we children.

When as a child, I read the popular comics of the time – 'Dandy' and 'Beano' – my father used to say to me, 'Why don't you read a good book. You will learn from it.' He could speak six languages – German, French, Spanish, Portuguese, English and Welsh – apart from his native tongue. He spoke Welsh better than English. My father did my French homework. He thought he was helping, but he couldn't sit the exam for me. Mr. John, my French teacher, commented, 'You're exams results are nothing like your homework.' I had to admit to the truth.

My father was also a clever craftsman. He built many of the sheds that the cockle-gathering families of the village favoured to live in, usually in the gardens behind their houses. He made a black oak bedroom suite for my parent's bedroom. He made *gambos* (drays) for the farmers, and even made the wheels. He drove a horse and cart, the latter he made himself. He also had a great control over horses – a Horse Whisperer. Some years after the war, my mother took my brothers, John and Michael, to visit my father's mother in Italy. My mother was shown an outside stove, and was told with the help of a neighbour who knew a little English, 'Your husband made that before he went away on his fourteenth birthday, and it is working now as good as it ever has.' Penclawdd winters were not nearly as harsh as my father had experienced as a child in his native Graparella La Val in northern Italy. One of his chores was to collect wood for the stoves in winter.

I used to go to Caerau Farm – on the way to Three Crossses – owned by Bertie Thomas' parents, to buy milk for my father to make ice-cream. It was hard work going up the hill, but I used to fly down with the milk cans over the handlebars of my bike. I often lost all the milk by the time I arrived home.

The shop hours were extremely long. My father would even open the shop on Christmas Day if a villager required something."

Elizabeth Mary Smith, daughter of Bob the Cockney, washed Mr. Ratti's white working coats for two shilling and six pence a line-full. The shop premises had no back garden so Elizabeth May hung the washing on a long line on the *Scêr* (the shoreline behind the sea wall) near the Railway public house.

Rudolph spent many summers with his mother in Port Eynon. "My mother rented the old lifeboat house in Port Eynon, where she ran a tearoom and a small shop in the summer months. My Aunty Florence, Rosie Fry and Megan Rees used to help her. The living quarters were far superior to our old quarters behind the shop in Penclawdd. The old launching pad was still there. I had a skeleton of an old pram that I used as a go-cart, and a lovely little Pom dog. I can see him now. When the tide was in, I sat him on my lap, and down we'd go into the tide. My mother was convinced the dog didn't like the game, but I disagreed with her, as he always came back for more.

I attended the local school in Port Eynon. My teacher was Marian Eaton, Miss Davies as she then was, from Penclawdd. She was an excellent teacher, and the school was very successful in the eleven plus examination. The pupils of each year were divided into sections, and all were taught in the same classroom. It was always very orderly, and I can't recall any fighting. It was obvious that the people of Port Eynon took to Miss Davies."

Rudolph remembers being told of his maternal grandfather's extraordinary escapade. "My grandfather, Isaac Collins, was a Catholic of Irish extraction. As soon as my mother was 'on the way', he ran away to the army, and changed his name from Collins to Collier. Why he did this I do not know. It was just one of those things. My grandmother was unable to trace him, and after a while, she was told to assume that he was dead. She remarried a gentleman called Will Morgan, and they had three daughters – Mary, Evelyn and Florence – and a son, Will. They also brought up a cousin of my mother's called Lizzy Ann Collins.

Will Morgan was crossing the gate opposite John Harry's shop at Nurses Corner one day, going shooting. The gun was loaded. It shouldn't have been, but people take chances. He stumbled and the gun went off and killed him.

My grandfather was demobbed after about twenty-one years' service in the army. He made inquiries about my grandmother, and discovered that she had remarried, but was widowed. He returned to Penclawdd, and he and my grandmother got back together again.

My grandfather was a character, no two ways about it. They kept him on at the Mountain Colliery until he was seventy, as he was such an excellent worker. When I used to go to Mrs. Evans' boot shop at No. 1, Blodwen Terrace, she used to say to me, 'Your grandfather was the handsomest man that ever walked the roads of Penclawdd.'"

Shops continued to open, close and change ownership as the population of Penclawdd increased to four thousand, five hundred and twenty-seven in 1951.

Siriol Francis bought Annie May Morgans' premises where he opened a chemist shop and also lived with his family. Ior Evans traded as wet fish merchant and greengrocer in the front room of Beach House. Henry Hopkins opened a grocery stores in Glanmor Terrace.

In 1951, Olive and Ambrose Thomas came to live in Penclawdd to open a post office in The Poplars, Sea View, the premises that had previously housed Arthur James Jenkins' barbershop. Olive was a native of The Hafod, Swansea, and Ambrose of Fforestfach, Swansea.

Living in close proximity to Ben Thomas (Undertaker)'s shed, Olive remembers being conscious of its distinctive smells. "Ben, *Ben-y-Saer's* son, who was then married and living in Gowerton, came to work in the shed next to our house every day. I can remember smelling the pitch that he used to seal the coffins. He used to make a fire out of the wood shavings from the coffins and melt the pitch on it in a round saucepan. He had a box of ribbons – black and mauve.

Our house was called The Poplars because there was a row of poplar trees by the side of the property, de-marking the western boundary of the Benson Estate, from the Dunraven Estate. In about 1955, we were unfortunately forced to fell the last of the trees, as it was rotten.

Everybody used to congregate in the post office, especially Mondays and pension days – Thursdays. It was a focal point in the village. Doctor Thomas lived in Gwernffrwd, but had his surgery in Beach House. He spent a lot of time in the post office. I can remember one Thursday Ivor Parkhouse was in the post office, sitting on the chair in the corner. Someone said to him, 'What's the matter Ivor? You're looking a bit down today.'

David Huton (present postman), Olive Thomas (postmistress),
Gwyn Howells (past postman).

'Ai,' he said, 'there's no bugger here to talk to.'

My husband wasn't really fit enough to help me as he had a heart complaint. As a baby, our younger son, Mark, used to be in a high chair with me, behind the counter. He was always in the post office. He listened to everything that went on, and got to know all my customers.

All the men were keen gardeners, and they'd be in the throes of it before Easter. They would all have set their gardens by Good Friday but if they hadn't, well, that was it."

On her retirement in 1997, Olive bought the old post office building, next to Beach House, that by then had been converted to a private dwelling. She says of her time as postmistress, "I spent fifty-one years in post office service, and forty-six of those in Penclawdd. The only thing that I miss, is the company in the post office. I don't miss the work, but I do miss the company."

John Willie Morris traded as confectioner in the front room of a house in the middle of Sea View. The village youths had the use of a table tennis table in a shed behind the shop. Miss Owen retired, and Mrs. Morgan took over her drapery business. David Rees, son of E. M. Rees, became proprietor of the Emporium after his father's tragic death. He was an excellent baker, and won many awards for his high standard of bread. Dan Dalimore became the village ironmonger, trading in the middle premises of Blodwen Terrace where David Dixon Jones had once had his tailor's shop. Mr. and Mrs. Morgan opened a greengrocer and wet fish shop in-between the Emporium and Robert John Davies' confectionery shop. Megan Oats acquired Liverpool House and opened a drapery shop. Midland Bank Limited moved to Glanmor Terrace and the Rees family moved back to the Barracks, with the exception of Ivor, who moved his business to Danna Evans' old premises. William and Lona Howells traded as butchers in Station Road when George Francis retired. After Nurse the Pickler's death in 1929, John Harry, who lived in Blue Anchor, erected a wooden shed in the former's garden, and traded as general stores and hairdresser.

The women of Penclawdd were very dress conscious. The village shops were inadequate in supplying clothes for special occasions, such as the *Gymanfa Ganu* (singing festivals) and so their apparels were usually bought in the town of Swansea, nine miles east of Penclawdd.

Before the Second World War, Swansea boasted a wealth of excellent departmental stores. Ben Evans was the largest, which Ilene Roberts, née Eaton, used to say was "just like Selfridges, in London's Oxford Street." David Evans was situated opposite Ben Evans, Lewis Lewis in High Street, and Edwards, a high class drapers store, was situated at the junction of

Oxford Street and Waterloo Street. Sydney Heath, Theopholus and Moriarty also sold ladies clothing of a high standard.

Lizzie Thomas, daughter of *Ben-y-Saer*, spent many happy years before she married Henry William Davies, being employed as an assistant in Edwards. She enjoyed her work and the camaraderie of her colleagues immensely. The girls stayed in a hostel in Swansea during the week, travelling home after work on Saturdays and returning to Swansea on Monday mornings. These circumstances gave them the advantage over the girls working in the village in having the opportunity to frequent the Grand and Empire Theatres.

Milk was not bought in shops, but delivered by the village's much-loved milkman, Gwyn the Milk, or Gwyn the Mill, so called because he lived in Mill House. He had inherited the property, Meyrick's Mill, from his father, Tom Harry. It had originally been the flourmill for the locality. Gwyn possessed a faithful horse, Tom, and two cows; one named Rhoda after Rhoda Eaton from whom he rented a field, and the other Maureen, after his niece. He had a dog named Peter, and also numerous cats, but the most important was Willie, who used to follow him everyday to the field in front of Clifford House, Penlan, where he brought Rhoda and Maureen to graze.

Gwyn spent all day delivering milk on his milk float, pulled by his faithful horse, Tom. The inhabitants of Penlan were fortunate in living near his home, as they received first delivery, but many villagers were not so lucky. Gwyn was in no hurry to deliver his milk, making it a daylong task. He never passed the Railway public house without stopping for liquid refreshment, and as the years rolled by, the stops became longer. Tom was used to this 'port of call', and waited patiently outside. In the summer months, the milk on the float gradually curdled in the heat. When the villagers to the west of the Railway public house received their milk in late afternoon, it was usually unusable, but they never complained. Some overcame the problem by also buying milk from a reliable milkman living in Crofty. When Maureen Blyth asked her mother why she bought stale milk from Gwyn, her mother replied, "We can't see him out of a job."

Gwyn loved all his animals, but his love for Tom knew no bounds. Willie Roberts gave Gwyn a warm winter overcoat that he no longer needed. When a little later he asked Gwyn if the coat was suitable, Gwyn informed him, "Well Willie, I have given the coat to Tommy, as his need was greater than mine."

However, when Andrew Lewis gave Gwyn his coat, the reverse happened. "I had a nice fawn duffel coat. It was still in very good condition but my wife, Gloria, and I decided to give it to Gwyn to put on Tommy.

After a few weeks, not having seen the coat on the horse, Gloria said to Gwyn, 'You know that duffel coat we gave to Tommy. Well, we haven't seen it on him.'

'Oh no gel,' he said. 'I've got that on the bed.'"

In his youth, Gwyn had attended a Veterinary College in Bristol, with the attention of becoming a veterinary surgeon. Unfortunately, before he qualified, his father and two uncles died, forcing Gwyn to terminate his studies and return to Penclawdd to run the family butchery business. He had acquired a great knowledge of horses, and the cockle women often asked him to cure their horses' maladies – colic, etc.

Gwyn delivered milk in a large metal container from which he poured the milk into jugs, provided by his customers. It was a common sight to see milk churns containing local farmers' milk on wooden stands in 'pick-up' points on the Gowerton-Penclawdd road, waiting collection from the Milk Marketing Board.

Later, as stated in the new laws, Gwyn sent all his milk to the Milk Marketing Board to be sterilized, and in return received bottled milk. These he kept in Nant Cedi stream that flowed northward from the *Cwm* (valley) under his house, to the Llwchwr Estuary. The locals of Penlan thought that inevitably progress had caught up with Gwyn when, one day, they heard that he had installed a new dairy. Andrew Lewis, who lives in Penlan, used to call for a pint of milk on his way home from work. He remembers

Gwyn the Mill or Gwyn the Milk.

the dairy well. "We used to buy a pint every day from Gwyn to keep him going, but we also used to buy from Davies'. Gwyn's dairy was a grey cement walled room with a perforated water hose hung by nails around the ceiling. The water sprayed from the holes over the milk bottles underneath. The tap was on the far wall of the dairy so to get milk you had to put your coat collar up and blindly fiddle around to turn off the tap, trying to avoid being soaked. You grabbed a milk bottle, turned the tap on and ran out as quickly as you could. But you came out soaking wet with a milk bottle in your hand. It was Gwyn's cooling system: a leap into the future." Gwyn was very proud of his dairy.

Gwyn's love of animals equalled his love of children, and he exercised endless patience on their behalf. He grew hay in Gordon's Field in Penlan, where George Edward Gordon's drive had once ran through. The local children spent many happy hours 'helping' Gwyn gather his harvest, playing hide and seek among the haystacks, and riding with him on the hay-filled *gambo* back to the Mill.

In the middle of the field's south boundary hedge stood a turnstile, known as the Cuckoo Stile. It was a magical place. Because of its geographical situation, sounds made on the spot echoed with incredible clarity around Penlan. It was a popular hobby amongst the village children to stand at the stile and shout 'cuckoo', and in the school holidays, the sound of the cuckoo resounded continually in the summer air. In the late 1960s, the building of the Pen-y-Lan housing estate in the field eradicated the echo. Part of the turnstile is still there, but the cuckoo has flown away.

NOTES

1. Marsh: Early in the twentieth century, spartina grass was planted on Whiteford Sands to consolidate the sand dunes. The grass rapidly spread eastwards forming a thick carpet of short marsh grass along the estuary shoreline.
2. The Old Colliery: A small area of Penclawdd where Penclawdd Colliery had existed.
3. A ritual that Mary Ann was used to having been a cockle woman. (See Chapter 4, p. 169.)
4. Trumpic: Corruption of turnpike. In 1706 Parliament sanctioned the first Turnpike Trust. Such a trust comprised of a group of local men who were keen to improve a stretch of road in their locality. They were usually motivated by self-interest rather than wishing to provide a service to the community. Once such a group had decided to form a trust they had to apply to Parliament to obtain an Act giving them the legal right to proceed. The Act empowered the trustees to raise turnpike gates along the nominated road and to collect tolls to help pay for repairs. They also had to appoint a surveyor, a clerk and a treasurer. The trustees usually took out a loan of money to pay for the trust's legal fees, the building the toll-keeper's house and the cost of the initial work required to bring the road up to standard. The tolls that were collected from the travellers had to pay for a variety of expenses such the interest on the loan and the salaries of the officials. Only after these expenses had been met was anything spent on maintaining the road. The Act was only to last for 21 years, when the trust was obliged to apply for a renewal. David Taylor, *Mastering Economic and Social History. Macmillan Master Series* (Houndmills, Basingstoke, Hampshire, RG21 2XS, and London. 1988), pp. 126-127
5. The Pond: A pond had once existed a few yards west of Sea View. The area is still known by some villagers as, 'The Pond'.

2

Village Amenities

Penclawdd had most of the amenities that its inhabitants required, and within walking distance of their homes.

Doctor David Jones Hughes, M.B., succeeded Doctor Richard James Isaac, L.R.C.P., S.E., L.E.P., S.G., as village general practitioner at the turn of the twentieth century. He was to be Penclawdd's highly respected doctor for the whole of the first half of the century. Doctor Hughes was a surgeon, and also medical officer and public vaccinator of North District Gower Union,[1] as had been his predecessor.

Vida, Dr. Hughes, Della, Carys.

He lived with his three daughters, Carys, Vida and Della in Burry House, a large house at the station corner of Penclawdd. The property brought peace and tranquillity to that busy area of the village. On the grassy banks underneath the majestic trees in front of the house, drifts of daffodils flowered in the spring. The beautifully tended lawns swept down to the front gate, bordering the drive to the house. As was the norm in those days, the surgery, waiting room and dispensary were all in the house, a far cry from the smart impersonal medical centres of today. As was often the practice, the Doctor dispensed his own drugs. In those pre-National Health Service days,[2] all working men contributed to a weekly fund run by Doctor Hughes to cover costs of medical care. They usually had a private insurance policy also. Parents paid for their children while they were school pupils.

Doctor Hughes was a diligent practitioner. Being always 'on call' he worked long unsociable hours. He made several visits to his patients until he was satisfied that they were fully recovered. Wilfred Tucker says of him, "He thought of himself last. I remember when I was young, a fellow from Blue Anchor telling me that he had occasion to call Doctor Hughes out at twelve o'clock midnight for a sick relative. Not having a phone, the fellow went personally to Doctor Hughes' house to ask him for his help. When he arrived home, the Doctor was already there. He had come by foot."

The villagers are of the opinion that the Doctor was extremely talented in his profession and could have furthered his career in qualifying as a specialist. Gladys Harry, née Rees, remembers her father's thoughts on the subject. "My father said that Doctor Hughes would have been an excellent bone specialist. There was no plaster in those days, but nobody had a creak after he set a bone."

On some occasions, the Doctor was forced to operate on his patients in extremely primitive conditions. Morgan John Rees was dangerously ill with a neglected rupture. The family called Doctor Hughes who came immediately. Time being of the essence, he performed an emergency operation using the family kitchen table as an operating table. Morgan John survived the operation, and with the help of a support truss, lived into old age. Doctor Hughes was also the village dentist, extracting teeth without the aid of anaesthetic. However, it was not only human teeth that he took out, a fact which sisters, Audrey and Freda Jeffreys, discovered. Audrey remembers, "One dark winter's night – there were no street lights in Penclawdd then – we were walking down Penlan Hill behind the Doctor's house, when suddenly a huge white thing appeared on the wall, with a large binding around its head. We were really scared and started to run like mad. We realized later that the apparition was Doctor Hughes' dog. He had a smooth white coat like a pig, and the bandage around his jaw and head was the result of teeth extractions performed by his master." The dog – Bonzo – was regarded in the village as a force to be reckoned with. Marion Jones remembers the incident that preceded the teeth extractions. "The dog used to go to my grandparents' house. They respected him, but never spoke to him, and kept well away when he entered. This particular day, he picked up a joint of meat and walked away with it. They just let him go. They didn't tell the Doctor but he got to know of it and as a result took out some of the dog's teeth. But of course, it was rumoured in the village that Doctor Hughes had taken out all his teeth."

The Doctor organized, and lectured to an ambulance class in the village. Gladys Harry remembers her father was a pupil in the class. "He taught my father all he knew, and my father was a very good ambulance man."

David Henry Rees, an employee of Elba Colliery, Gowerton, was one

Penclawdd Ambulance Class in front of Burry House.
Back row, left to right: David Henry (Dai Staff) Rees, Walter Howells, Ben Griffiths,
Jim Davies, Griff Guy, William Howells.
Front row, left to right: Walter Tucker, ? Davies, G. E. Gordon, Mary Jane Gordon,
Doctor Hughes, John Howells.

of the fortunate survivors of the 1905 colliery disaster. When interviewed by a local newspaper reporter, he stated that he would like to thank Doctor Hughes of Penclawdd, for his splendid exertions in helping the injured, and for not having spared himself in the least. Twenty-four years later, another colliery disaster occurred in Wernbwll Colliery, Penclawdd. It was reported in 'The Cambrian' newspaper on Friday 29 November 1929, 'Doctor Hughes, Penclawdd, and Doctor Thomas, Gowerton, rendered yeoman service in the medical attention to the badly gassed and injured colliers.' Doctor Hughes attended the funerals' of the Penclawdd miners.

The Doctor had no time for dishonesty, and so was unpopular with the men in the village who tried to obtain sick papers from him without due cause. Dulcie Nichols, née Evans, often visited the Doctor's house where her aunt, Miriam, worked as housekeeper. "He did not like malingerers. He gave sick papers to those who genuinely needed them, but not if he thought they were 'swinging the leg'. But we women used to like going to him because he used to tease us and call us *Bach i* (Little one)."

Doctor Hughes was aided by his equally hard-working nurse, Nurse Elizabeth Harris. She was nurse and midwife delivering the babies in Penclawdd in what were often adverse conditions. Gwyneth Durban, née Barnfield, says of her, "She was fastidiously clean and always wore starched garments. She used to live next door to our family in Mill Street. She born three thousand babies."

Carys, Vida and Della often assisted their father in his work. Dulcie remembers Vida's nerve being tested when a patient needed medical attention after accidentally severing a little finger. "She was great while Doctor treated and bandaged the hand, but when she threw the used water away, and saw the finger floating in it, Vida passed out."

Doctor Hughes' earliest form of transport was a horse, later being replaced by a bike, and eventually one of the first cars in the village. It was an early Ford model known as Tin Lizzy. In 1926, Ruben Hodges was employed as chauffeur and gardener. He sometimes helped to dispense drugs, having a first-aid certificate, which sufficed. Cars were not as comfortable as they are today. Carys Hughes related to her good friend Ilene Roberts, of Clifford House, Penlan, that hot water bottles were essential in the unheated car on their annual pilgrimage to Aberystwyth to visit her mother's grave. They probably went during the one-week-a-year's holiday that the Doctor allowed himself and his staff.

Ruben Hodges used to visit his family in his native Hereford with his wife, and daughter, Joyce. The latter remembers the holidays well. "My father travelled by motorbike and I rode in the sidecar. My Mother went by train with the cases. My father stayed for the week, but we stayed for a

Ruben Hodges.

month. It was always cherry picking time. We used to sort the black cherries from the white cherries."

Doctor Hughes kept himself apart from the villagers, never socializing and was considered an enigma. He had an impressive wine cellar, unheard of in Penclawdd at that time. His eating habits were strict, and he ate very little. His diet consisted of an abundance of fruit and home-made bread, always eaten at least three days after being baked by his housekeeper. She dutifully carried out all the many household duties. Win Walters says of her, "His housekeeper Miriam was a marvel. She did everything."

The sitting room of Burry House contained magnificent furniture, intricately carved with animals' heads, which Miriam diligently cleaned with a toothbrush. She also looked after Doctor Hughes' personal appearance, making sure he was always well-groomed. He favoured a Norfolk Jacket, which was a fashionable garment of the time. Miriam often went down on her hands and knees to polish his shoes. Her niece says of her, "She was a great admirer of his. She would tell him off in no uncertain terms, but no one else could say a word against him. If he had a case of someone being seriously ill, she would hear him walking at night in his bedroom, praying for guidance before visiting the patient in the early hours of that morning." He was evidently a man of great faith, and did not reserve his prayers only for the seriously ill. Ilene Foote recalls that Doctor Hughes always prayed on his hands and knees outside the bedroom door of a mother whose baby he was about to deliver.

His ideas were sometimes controversial. In the diphtheria epidemic of the early 1940s, it seems that he encouraged parents to keep their children at home, and to dose them with liquid paraffin. He was opposed by the rest of the medical profession, who thought the disease could be treated most effectively in hospital. Doctor Owen, a Gowerton doctor, reported Doctor Hughes to the Medical Board, but it seems no action was taken.

However, Ilene Foote remembers, "I was one of the fifty-four diphtheria patients in Garn Goch Fever Hospital in 1941, the year that the retail centre of Swansea was blitzed."

The Doctor was twice widowed, both his wives having died in childbirth. Miriam mothered his daughters, especially Carys, who used to call her Milam. She was regarded by Doctor Hughes and his daughters as family, rather than employee, being guest of honour at the daughters' weddings.

Burry House was rented from Jonathan Morgan, the village blacksmith. It is believed by the villagers that Jonathan Morgan had no wish to sell the property.

Doctor Hughes passed away in retirement in 1952.

Penclawdd boasted its own town crier. Robert Smith nicknamed Bob the Cockney – a prominent village character – originated from London's East End. He lived with his wife, Sarah, and their five children, Sarah Ann, Elizabeth Mary, William John and twins Calvin and Luther (known as the Childs) in a small terraced house on the *Graig*. Bob was provided with a cap, tunic and bell, the latter being kept under the bar shelf in the Royal Oak public house. As town crier, he proclaimed local news and forthcoming events in the village, such as carnivals, etc. He also worked as a railway porter, and delivered parcels in a small hand pushed cart from the train, to their relevant destinations. He was always prepared to undertake odd jobs and errands for a small fee. The family lived a meagre existence. They would buy one quarter of a pound of butter or one candle at a time from nearby Mary Ann Thomas' grocery shop. One day, Bob called in the Royal Oak on his way home from a visit to Tom Henry Thomas, the butcher in West End, with a sack over his shoulder,

Robert Smith – Bob the Cockney.

Sarah Smith.

looking very pleased with himself. Wilfred Tucker was serving behind the bar at the time. "He wanted half a pint. It was not often that he could afford a pint. I asked him what was in the sack. He showed me its contents – a sheep's head. How old it was I do not know. When I asked him what he was going to do with it, he told me that his Mrs. would boil it, and make a nice broth. That was the way they lived." Sarah Smith lived to be one hundred and one and a half years of age, being the first centenarian inhabitant of Penclawdd.

Carl Gustav Pamp, nicknamed Mr. Pop, a native of Sweden and an ex-sailor, is a much talked-about village character. It seems that he never recovered his land legs as Wilfred Tucker remembers. "He used to be a seaman. He never sat when he came into the Royal Oak. He would stand and sway back and forth all the time."

He greatly intrigued Glenys Harry, and her friend Ilene Davies, on a homeward journey from school. "Ilene and I were coming home from school one day when we saw Mr. Pamp sitting by the railway sleepers – it was before the sea wall was built. Mr. Pamp was always immaculately dressed in a black coat, grey and white trousers, and a bowler hat. It was a red-hot day and Mr. Pamp had taken off his coat. To our amazement he wasn't wearing a shirt, only a white bib, a stiff collar and a dickey bow. Although young, we knew that it was not right. I told my mother when I got home, but she didn't like it, and my father was even worse. 'You shouldn't be saying things like that,' he told me.

I insisted, 'But he didn't have a shirt on.'

'Well he probably had his reasons,' my father said. 'He might have been hot.'"

It seems that the Swedish sailor never completely mastered the English language as Glenys remembers. "On a warm evening when passing you on the road he would say, 'Good evening. It's very closed.'"

Pamp, Robert Brynley Austin, son of David Evan and Elizabeth Ann Austin, tenants of the Ship and Castle public house and a few other local men formed the Penclawdd Motor Company. They bought a charabanc, which was affectionately named The Queen of Penclawdd, and ran a bus service for local excursions such as Sunday School and rugby trips. It was garaged on the sea front near the Railway public house.

Pamp, a mechanical enthusiast, made a contraption, which had a Ford engine, seats, a tarpaulin canopy and solid rubber wheels. He provided a taxi service for the village men, transporting them to and from their work in the neigbouring areas. Before 1925, the Gowerton – Penclawdd road had been cut but not surfaced. Coupled with the fact that Pamp's vehicle had solid wheels, the journeys were extremely uncomfortable. Wilfred Tucker took advantage of this service when he worked in Gowerton Tin-plate Works. "When I was working mornings, I'd go over to his house at five o'clock – he lived near the Royal Oak. He'd drive the lorry out and shout to his sister-in-law Edith, 'Edin,' he couldn't say Edith, 'jump in and put foot on brake' which she did while he closed the garage door. I used to travel with John Brown, who was well over six-foot tall. The road was very bumpy and John's head would keep hitting the tarpaulin top of the lorry. He was a half-soaked fellow, and he'd say to Mr. Pamp, 'Take your time *wus*.'[3]

Mr. Pamp would reply, 'I can't help it. The road is bad.' And it was bad too."

By 1925, the road was surfaced. It had been necessary to terminate 'Rights of Way' that were used by local farmers to graze their animals on the marsh across the path of the proposed road. A bridge was constructed over the road to give the coal trams of Berthlwyd Colliery access to the railway line.

The South Wales Transport Company ran the first public bus transport service from Penclawdd to Swansea via Gowerton and Waunarlwydd. Messrs. Theopholus Johns and Williams of Gorseinon provided a service from Penclawdd to Pontarddulais via Gowerton and Gorseinon, which they called The Enterprise. Police Superintendent Smith, of Gowerton, had been appointed Inspector of hackney carriages for the district on January 1924. The Bluebird Buses, run by Walby, were established, and the Vanguard Bus Company, already running in Gower, extended its services to Penclawdd. The United Welsh travelled to Swansea via Gowerton, Dunvant and Killay.

During the years 1925 to 1927, a road was constructed from Penclawdd to Llanrhidian, eliminating the problem of road flooding on the existing marsh road from Crofy to Llanrhidian. Again, the road was cut through and not surfaced until a later date when the bus services were extended to Llangennith and Llanmadoc via Llanrhidian.

Of the variant bus services at the villagers' disposal, there was one that became loved by all – the Parkhouse Bus. Robert Parkhouse emigrated from Devon to Penclawdd in the late nineteenth century. In the 1910s, he bought a horse and cart and delivered coal from the local collieries to the homes of the villagers. He was later joined by four of his sons, Ernie, Sidney, Jimmy and Ivor and together they established the firm of Parkhouse and Sons. They quickly expanded the coal business and also started trading as haulage contracts, eventually owning twelve tip-up lorries.

The firm then decided to run a private bus transport service, which became very successful. Parkhouse and Sons initially used the filled-in land that was once the site of the reservoir for the old copper works at Nurses Corner, for their depot. The latter was later transferred to the site of the old colliery at Berthlwyd. The firm installed a petrol pump – pumped by hand – to fuel their vehicles, at Hendy Road, where their office is today.

Their fleet of fifteen buses, double and single deckers, were hired for village trips – church, chapel, darts, football, etc. Parkhouse and Sons also had a contract to transport pupils to and from the local schools. Many of them lived in remote areas of Gower, and rather than leave the children at the bus stops, the drivers took them safely to their homes. Sidney's son, Dennis, remembers his father working long hours driving the buses. "I can remember my father going off seven days a week. For example, if he went to Stratford, he'd be up at five in the morning, and not back until two the next morning. It was a long journey in those days before the building of motorways."

In the late 1960s, the South Wales Transport Company was reimbursed by the government, and consequently reduced its contract price. Parkhouse and Sons was unable to compete and lost the contract. Dennis talks of the disappointment. "Once we lost the school contract we were unable to keep our bus service going as it was our 'bread and butter'. We were unable to keep going on occasional trips."

Dennis recalls, as a child, accompanying his father in the lorries during the Second World War years. "During the war, we delivered cockles in our tip-up lorries to High Street Station, in Swansea, for the cockle women. The cockles were wheeled to the trains in trolleys. From there, the cockles would go to Bristol, etc. Although the Germans would be bombing, it wouldn't deter the cockle women, but we'd go home as quickly as we could.

There was a large gun near our depot at Berthlwyd, as it was feared that the Germans would come up the Llwchwr Estuary. When the gun was fired in practices, a red flag was flown on the marsh opposite Berthlwyd, and at Crofty, to warn the cockle women. They became friendly with Frankie Howard, who was stationed on the Point. After the war, they went to London to see him. He was busy and said that he was unable to see anybody. The cockle women sent him the message, 'The red flag is up' and he came out to see them in a flash – or so the story goes.

My father had taxis during the war. He used to take the cockle women to sell their cockles to the Carmarthenshire farmers. The cockle women were paid in kind – butter, bacon, etc. They became nervous of being in possession of the black-market produce and sent my father to collect them on his own. He was coming home one day with butter hidden behind the headlights, and the back of the taxi full of pork, etc. covered by a sheet. A policeman stopped him in Carmarthen and asked him what he had under the sheet. My father said, 'Ten pounds of butter, two sides of pork.'

The policeman told him, 'Pull the other leg. Bugger off,' and off my father went. He was also paid in kind himself and would come home with best butter, bacon, etc."

After leaving school, Dennis worked for the family firm on the 'coal side' of the business. "Delivering coal kept us very fit. It really toughened us and we never had colds. We'd go out at seven in the morning, and not be home until perhaps seven in the night. Most mornings, the lorry seats would be full of water, and you'd squelch down on them. The coir coal bags were thick, and always wet, and so, very heavy. The leather back shields were worn to prevent the wet going through onto your back. Your back became like iron. Everything was done by hand. I think that's why Welsh rugby players aren't so good today. They are no longer colliers and steelworkers, etc. I would go home and have a warm shower followed by a cold shower until my body was frozen. I felt so good afterwards. Even now I can go out in the winter without a jacket."

On analyzing the wind swept sand on Whiteford Sands, Llanmadoc, in the mid-1950s, it was discovered that it was salt-free. At the time, there was no restriction on the removal of beach sand, and Parkhouse and Sons removed hundreds of tons. It was mixed with other salt-free sand and used in the building of the foundations of Trostre Steelworks in Llanelli, as it produced extremely strong, durable cement.

The firm bought the rights of the land in Swansea Valley,[4] the site of the heavy industries of the eighteenth and nineteenth centuries – copper, iron, steel, etc. The hardcore of the old buildings was removed and sold to construct motorways. The ash was screened and filtered to surface tennis courts, and was also used in the building of local minor roads. Parkhouse and Sons constructed the roads to Llanmadoc and Llangennith beaches, and undertook road works for Gower farmers.

Over the years, Parkhouse and Sons has provided employment for many men – as many as thirty-five at one time. Dennis remembers, "A lot of people worked for us, on the coal and on the buses. They'd start with us, and then have a good job in a factory, and leave, but others would take their place. There was a constant flow." Mrs. Megan Morris, a native of the village, was employed as secretary by the firm during the Second World War, and today still works happily in their office in Hendy Road.

In 1926, Penclawdd had its first purpose-built police station situated opposite the railway station. It was manned by Peter Thomas – sergeant – and his two constables. By the 1930s, the force was reduced to one sergeant – Sergeant Lord – who had been transferred from Port Eynon. He worked long hours, unassisted, and without transport. Sergeant Lord took an active interest in village life, especially sport. He was a keen cricketer and had been a member of Gowerton Cricket Club when stationed there. He befriended Wilfred Tucker, who was conscious of his long working hours. "When I worked in the steelworks in Gowerton, I had a frying pan made out of steel for my mother to cook welsh cakes, which of course I had not paid for. I cycled home with the pan under my coat, tied with cord around my neck. At half past one in the morning, while I was cycling past the post office, Sergeant Lord stepped out and stopped me. This bloody thing was like a weight around my neck, and I tried not to look uncomfortable, but it was getting heavier by the minute. He wanted to know where I had been, but once he recognized me, he told me to cycle on. I was so glad to see him go."

The sergeant did not always receive the respect that he deserved. A story in the village relates so: 'One day, Sergeant Lord tried in vain to detain a man on the sea shore whom he thought was stealing a fishing boat. He shouted to him, "Ai, Lord here!"

The man replied, "Well, I'm Jesus Christ. Bugger off," and rowed away.'

On his retirement, Sergeant Lord bought a house in Blodwen Terrace. He walked daily to Mrs. Harry's newsagent shop to buy his paper. He often used to see Wilfred Tucker who lived next to the shop, and always voiced the same sentiment; "Wilfred, this road gets longer every day."

In true Welsh tradition, Penclawdd had many public houses, but after the closure of the Glan-y-Môr, in the 1910s, only the Ship and Castle, the Royal Oak, the Railway and the Blue Anchor, remained.

Wilfred Tucker remembers a beer delivery to the village. "Swansea United Breweries Beer was delivered to Penclawdd on a four-wheeled dray, drawn by two large shire horses. It had a regular driver who looked like King Edward the Seventh, but he had ginger hair and a ginger beard. We used to call him George the Pop. As a child, living in Blue Anchor, I remember this particular day. He had been delivering beer to the pubs in the village, as all except the Royal Oak served Swansea United Beer. On his homeward journey, by the Blue Anchor pub, one of the horses fell. When George the Pop opened the horse's harness to help him to his feet, the animal kicked his hand, and as a result, the top half of the driver's fingers were severed, and hung off his hand by their skin. He eventually got the horse to his feet, but it was necessary to borrow an extra horse from Mr. Beynon, in nearby Blaen Cedi Farm, to draw the dray up the hill. I don't know what happened to his hand as I was too interested in the horses."

At the turn of the twentieth century, the tenants of the Ship and Castle – known locally as the Ship – were David Evan and his wife, Elizabeth. They lived on the premises with their eleven children, Robert Brinley, Sarah Ellen, Daniel Thomas, Margaret Ann, David Amrose, Elizabeth Jane, Luther Rees, Joseph, Mary Catherine, Beatrice May and Evan John.

The Ship was demolished and rebuilt in the 1930s. The Austin family lived in the back of the original building while the new one was being built, and occupied the new premises on completion.

Not many women frequented the public houses as it was not considered 'the done thing', and those that did, were considered rather common. The few that ignored local criticism, congregated out of the public view in the 'snug' in the Ship, where they drank lemon dash (shandy) and the occasional whisky with lemonade. The men used the public bar, where they drank ale or neat spirits.

It was common practice in many villages for the public houses to be used as meeting places for clubs and societies. Penclawdd was no exception.

The Friendly Society, the Order of Foresters Club, used the Ship as their headquarters. 'Before the introduction of National Insurance in 1911, Friendly Societies provided a workman with protection against unemployment and sickness. They catered mainly for the skilled workers, and worked on a contributory bases. The workman paid weekly contributions to the society, who, in turn, paid benefits – unemployment benefits, sickness benefits, pensions and Death Gratuities – to the workman. The Friendly Societies provided social occasions and friendship. The origins of this type of society were to be found in the medieval Guild system. When the Guilds declined, Friendly Societies took over their role. They had branches (or lodges) nationwide. Usually there was a certain amount of pomp and ceremony – new members were sworn in. The President wore a chain of office and strict secrecy was upheld about the affairs of individual members. Friendly Societies stayed a force until the Welfare State schemes were introduced, and now their role is very much a supporting one.'[5]

In the 1930s, the village Youth Club held meetings on a Saturday night in the Ship and the Royal Oak. They took the form of discussion groups chaired by Vernwy Davies, a local teacher. John and Dulcie Nichols were staunch members. "We had great topical discussions of the day, for example, Russia and its new policy. We were very serious, although only about fourteen years of age at the time. We used to have some marvellous Saturday evenings. After the discussions, we would play table tennis and then the customers would all partake in singing and playing all sorts of musical instruments, even tin whistles."

The Rugby and Cricket Clubs held their business and social functions at the Ship. The Rugby Club had the use of two rooms for changing purposes, one for the home team, and one for the away team. The tension between the two teams was so high before a match that the publican and his wife forbade the players to meet inside the pub. After the match, however, all were friends, whoever won, and the two teams would congregate inside for sandwiches and copious amounts of beer.

On the marriage of Margaret Ann (Maggie) – the oldest daughter of the Austin family – to Evan John, the couple occupied and ran the Dolphin Inn in Llanrhidian. Beatrixe May, known as Beatie, now aged ninety-one, the youngest and only surviving sibling of the Austin family, remembers visiting her sister and family with her mother, in the horse and trap owned by the Ship. Before the building of the New Road, in 1925 to 1927, between Penclawdd and Llanrhidian, the only road was the marsh road. "On high tides, we had to wait in my Uncle Joe's house in Crofty for the tide to go out so that we could cross Crofty River."

Beatie recalls working hard in helping her parents run the Ship. "I used to chalk the front step very early every morning, and in winter, by candlelight. After every rugby match, I used to fill the tubs with hot water for the players to wash in, and also make sandwiches for them. My mother was very strict. Her word was law." Beatie also served behind the bar but she disliked this task. "I did not enjoy it. I wasn't fond of the drinking. I did not like that part of it." Beatie found alternative employment as deputy cook in Penclawdd Secondary Modern School where she worked for many happy years until she was forced to retire through ill health.

Evan Melvyn (Mel), son of Luther Rees Austin, enjoyed visiting his

Beatie Austin.

grandmother at the Ship. "The Ship has been rugby for as long as I can remember. I used to go there when I was a little boy, to visit my grandmother. I didn't know much about rugby then. I used to see the men drinking beer, and I wanted the same. My grandmother used to try and give me pop, but I wouldn't have it. I wanted beer from the barrel. She would give me a tot of beer. It was only a mouthful but it satisfied me."

When the Austin family lived in the Ship, the licensing laws forbade the opening of public houses on Sundays, which was stipulated in the Welsh Sunday Closing Act of 1881. It seems Elizabeth Austin anticipated the laws changing in the future as her daughter, Beatie, remembers her mother saying, "When that day comes I will walk out." She did not have to carry out her threat, as she retired as landlady before Sunday opening became legal again. David Evan and Elizabeth Austin bought a field next to Tabernacle Chapel, where they built an attractive terrace of houses known as Tabernacle Terrace, in anticipation of their retirement. The end house was to be theirs and the others for various members of their family. On completion of the terrace, they placed the houses for rental on the understanding that the tenants were to vacate the premises when the members of the Austin family were ready to occupy them. David Evan died before retiring. After her days at the Ship, Elizabeth moved to Tabernacle Terrace with her unmarried daughters, Beatie and Cassie (Mary Catherine).

Elizabeth Jane proceeded her mother as landlady of the ship.

In 1923, Edgar, an ex-miner of the Western Colliery, and his wife, Carrie, moved with their children, Wilfred, Phyllis, Ray and Morley from their cottage in Blue Anchor to live in the Royal Oak, on the sea front, as tenant publicans. Like her fellow publicans, Elizabeth Austin, and Ann Roberts of the Railway, Carrie Tucker was very strict, and took no nonsense from her customers. The Royal Oak, the only public house in Penclawdd that sold Hancock's beer, was also the only public house in Gower to have a delivery service of Hancock's beer flagons. Wilfred Tucker left his employment at Gowerton Tin-plate Works to help his parents run the Royal Oak. His first job was to deliver beer flagons to regular customers living in Gower and to the farmers at harvest time. For about three years, he delivered the quart flagons of beer in a horse and float.

The Royal Oak had a single licence – a licence to sell beer only. A double licence – a licence allowing the sale of spirits, wine and beer – was difficult to obtain, and it was not until 1961 that the Royal Oak acquired same. When Edgar informed the brewery of his impending retirement, they suggested that he requested a double licence, as they felt sure he would be granted one. He complied with their wishes, and was successful. However, Wilfred remembers that the customers did not suffer because of the single licence. "But that does not mean to say that the odd glass of whisky was not served when requested. Father always kept a bottle or two out of sight."

Although Carrie had plenty of beer on hand, she loved making home-

Edgar Tucker.

57

Edgar Tucker.

made wine. "My mother would make wine out of anything. One day I was sent to buy stone-less raisins and a Gower farmer provided her with wheat. She told me she was going to make wine. The liquor prepared, and strained for fermentation, she threw the unwanted raisins into the chickens' run. Father arose the following morning and went to see if the chickens had laid any eggs. When he came back he said to my mother, 'Carrie, there's something wrong with the chickens. They're all lying down on their backs with their legs sticking up in the air. I think they're dead.' When my mother started laughing, he told her to stop laughing, as it was not a laughing matter. We went to see the chickens. They were all drunk. They had eaten the raisins and had fallen off their perches. They struggled to walk for the next twenty-four hours, but afterwards, they did well, and laid regularly."

It was not only the chickens of the Royal Oak that suffered the after-effects of home-made wine. One Christmas Eve, Wilfred, and his wife, Elsie, visited their friend Annie Roberts, of Sunny View. "Annie gave me a whole tumbler full of elderberry wine and I was foolish enough to drink it all. I had promised the caretaker, David Rees (*Dai Puss*) to ring the church bell on Christmas morning for the eight o'clock service. After ringing the bell,

I went for a walk down the *Cwm*, as I did not feel very well. I met Willie Roberts on the way home. He asked me why I had not rung the bell that morning. He said that he was in church at five to eight and had not heard it. I know that I did ring the bell, but as to what time, I do not know to this day."

The Railway, in the centre of the village, was also a well-patronized public house. The original public house – the Oddfellows Arms – was situated at the south end of Benson Street. It was demolished in 1877 by the Llanelli Railway and Dock Company (LRDC) for further development of the railway line westwards from Penclawdd Station to Llanmorlais. The site of the Oddfellows Arms had been purchased from Stanley Benson, a prominent industrialist and landowner in Penclawdd. In 1885, the public house was rebuilt on its present site, renamed the Railway Hotel, but referred to as the Railway.

At the turn of the twentieth century, John Roberts, and his wife Ann, took over its tenancy. They lived on the premises with their four sons, Wendall, Randall, Harry and William. Their youngest son, William, was known *as Willie Roberts y Railway* (Willie Roberts the Railway). Ann Roberts was always referred to as *Mrs. Roberts y Railway* (Mrs. Roberts the Railway) and never Ann. She often physically threw out customers who used unacceptable language or overindulged in alcohol. Marian Eaton says of her, "She was bigger, stronger, more physically determined and more damned sure of herself than any other woman in Penclawdd at that time. By God she was. She took no nonsense from those boys (her customers). She was an excellent organizer and very much in charge of the pub. She always stood erect and her upright stance enhanced her unfailingly well-groomed appearance." Megan Thomas remembers taking the family's rent to their landlady at the Railway. "She was very bossy and upright, like a sergeant major. She reminded me of Queen Mary, but my mother thought the world of her."

Beatie Austin remembers the excellent system that the three public houses organized to keep law and order in their

Mrs. Roberts y Railway on right with her good friend Miss Owen (draper).

establishments. "If any one in the Railway had a drop too much to drink, the message would come down to the Royal Oak and to the Ship. The landladies would be waiting for them, and say, 'These can't come in. These had enough,' and wouldn't serve them of course. The landladies took the lead, as the male customers would hit a man, but never a woman. No man would risk earning the very bad reputation in the village of having hit a woman." However, the three landladies were very strong characters, and greatly respected, so would have been obeyed despite their gender.

As a child, Daniel Rees, a great friend of Willie Roberts, spent many happy hours in the Railway. "It was a good public house, selling beer and spirits. They were measured in pewter measures. Beer was a penny-half-penny a pint, and thrupence a quart. Spirits were six pence a measure. Mrs. Roberts was a good worker. She very rarely went out of the Railway, but John Roberts used to go out. He never wore a hat. He had a large goiter at the back of his neck. The doctor did not want to touch it and told him to leave it alone."

The slate system of payment was used in the public house, the men paying their debts when they received their wages on Fridays. Daniel remembers John Roberts' kindness. "The tin works was losing money and

The Railway's pewter measures – a quart measure and spirit measures.

the government decided to close it. The men didn't have any money. They were poor dabs. They would say to John Roberts, 'Can I have a pint of beer. I'm very sorry but I haven't any money.'

He'd say to them. 'You sit down. I'll bring you a pint.' He was a very kind man. Some of the men from the tin-plate works went to work in the collieries, but many went away. They went far, far away." Before becoming a publican, John Roberts had worked in the tin-plate industry, and so was probably sympathetic to the workers' plight.

The Oddfellows Club – a Friendly Society – met in the clubroom of the Railway.

In 1923, the Colliers Arms – a freehouse – was owned by John Davies. It was frequented by the miners of Berthlwyd Collieries, hence its name. Sometime after this date, possibly after the colliery closure, it became known as the Berthlwyd Inn. It served Rogers beer, which was a Bristol ale. Although geographically nearer Penclawdd than Gowerton, it was in the village of Gowerton, but was popular amongst the inhabitants of Penclawdd.

The Workingmen's Club was housed in the premises that was previously Thomas Booley's shop, at the corner of Belle Vue. The main attraction of the Club was its licensing laws, which were more relaxed than those of the public houses, allowing Sunday opening. It was also run on a co-operative system, with no profit, and so as a result, the beer was cheaper than in the public houses. In the early 1950s the Club moved to Burry House. It closed in the mid-1970s.

The Recobites was the third club in the village, but unlike the Order of Foresters and the Oddfellows Club, its members were against alcoholic drink, and so did not meet in a public house. Its secretary, Dan Jenkins, father of Gwynfor, was an insurance agent, based in Swansea.

Dan Jenkins, George Edward Gordon, mining engineer, and William Jenkins, music teacher caught the nine o'clock morning train to Swansea to their respective occupations. They were referred to in the village as the 'city gents'.

The game of quoits was a very popular sport in the village. Most of the Gower villages had a quoit team, and all belonged to the Gower Quoit League. The matches were highly competitive, and organized within the league. Wilfred Tucker enjoyed the game. "Penclawdd had a large pitch of four beds situated in Station Road opposite the railway station. Within the grassed area, four quoit beds of about one yard square, and regulation feet apart, were cut out. They were filled with yellow clay, which was gathered locally, and edged with wooden strips. A steel peg was placed in the centre of each bed. The purpose of the game was to throw the quoit – a two to three pound steel wedge shaped oval disc with a flat bottom – at the peg. The nearest quoit to the peg won the game. Two beds were used per match. The players stood at the edge of one bed and threw their quoits to the other bed. When all quoits were thrown, that bed then became the throwing point. The beds were prepared before each match. It was important that the clay was of the right consistency; too soft and it would splatter over the spectators; too hard and the quoit would shoot off the bed. If a thrown quoit struck a stationery one, it would shoot out like a bullet. It was wise to stay clear of them. They were made of steel and shone like silver. They had to be 'up to the mark'."

With the building of the police station, the quoit beds were abandoned. If possible, the local public houses made their own quoit pitches, and selected teams to represent their establishments. George Edward Gordon, being a mining engineer, was an influential figure in the local mining industry. He often played the game at the Ship. The occasion usually attracted many locals, as all the men, especially the miners, were anxious to flatter Gordon. Griff Rees was often one of the competitors. "Mr. Gordon would quoit, and if he hit the peg, there was some clapping. We would shout, 'Good quoit Mr. Gordon!' You could hear the clapping across the estuary in Llanelli." Consequently, it became a popular saying in the village. When one did a deed exceedingly well, one was congratulated with, "Good quoit Mr. Gordon!"

The children of the village played their own version of the game with improvisation. Wilfred Tucker played on a grassy bank near the Blue Anchor public house. "As kids we made our own beds on a bank by the Blue (Anchor). We had the time of our lives, but we used horse shoes as we couldn't afford quoits."

A carnival was held in Penclawdd every year at the Rec. (recreation ground) behind Tabernacle Chapel. Prior to the day, a Carnival Queen, Rose Queen and Fairy Queen were chosen from the village girls, and it was considered a great honour to be crowned Queen. Many competitions were organised. The greasy pole was a great attraction. Any competitor who could cross a greased pole without falling off, won a prize. The grand finale of the carnival was the donkey derby. There was no shortage of donkeys in the village. Tegwedd Murley, née Davies, became famous for winning the event. "I used to borrow my auntie's donkey, Jack. The race was a very serious thing. I won the race in Swansea, Upper Killay and Penclawdd in three consecutive years, and I still have the cups. The owner of the Tivoli Cinema in Gowerton had a wild horse. Anyone who could stay on him for three minutes had a prize. Ernie Parkhouse and I were the only ones who could."

Tegwedd Murley, née Davies, on Jack. Champion Donkey Derby Winner.

The first electricity supply in Penclawdd was generated from a power-house at Berthlwyd, providing electricity for D. D. Williams' collieries – Wernbwll and Caereithin. An electricity line was installed from Wernbwll Colliery to the Blue Anchor public house, Brynhir House, Brynhir Farm and St. Gwynour's Church, Llanyrnewydd, providing them with electricity. The church congregation always knew when the trammers were working, as the lights in the church would dim.

When the South Wales Electrical Power Distribution Company installed electricity in the village in 1932 to 1933, *Willie Roberts y Railway*, a self-employed, qualified electrical engineer, helped by his young assistant, Daniel McCarthy, installed electricity in many houses in the village. A central ceiling light, operated by a wall switch, was fitted in each room, and one plug in the kitchen, for a fee of five pounds and ten shillings. Morwyn Elliott, née Roberts, remembers her mother deciding to have electricity installed in their house saying, "Let's get Willie Roberts to do it."

Daniel enjoyed his two years working with Willie. "When I left school at fourteen my first job was in Bevan Brothers Sawmills. It was hard work carrying the timber into the workshop, and I only earned ten shilling a week. My working day was half-past seven in the morning to four o'clock in the afternoon. My mother was concerned about my working so hard for only ten shilling, so I left the sawmills, and went to work with Willie when I was sixteen.

I enjoyed my time with him. He was easy to work with and good company. There were no problems. It was a pleasure to work with him. He was courting Ilene Eaton then, and married late.

I can vividly remember Willie treating me to a soccer match at the Vetch in Swansea. After the game, when he went for a pint, I had to wait outside, as I was underage. Licensing laws were very strict then.

Willie's equipment was kept in a storehouse, where the beer was kept, behind the Railway where he lived. I used to go down to the Railway in the mornings about nine o'clock, and wait for Will – he didn't start too early – and off we'd go for the day.

We went to Parkmill by bike to wire the police station. Buses were few and not convenient to South Gower. We carried our equipment in bags hung on the bikes. I don't know how we managed to carry all our gear. We usually had to push our bikes up the hills. The electrical wires were coated in lead and so the drums of cables were extremely heavy. Willie allowed me to have the discarded lead that coated the wires. When I had about twenty pounds, I used to take it to Fred Owen, the scrap merchant in Gowerton and had quite a good price for it. I didn't have a set wage, but Willie gave me what he could – a couple of pounds – after wiring each house. A house was wired for about five or six pounds.

I was living in Mill Street then. We wired all the houses in the street including ours. We were wiring Elsie and Muriel Fry's parent's house in Station Road. A hole had to be made in the ceiling to wire upstairs. Willie accidentally cut through into part of the chimney breast, and soot came down all over him. He was covered in it. He laughed, but it frightened him really. The job was sometimes tedious and frustrating, but I never heard him revert to one swear word. I respected him for that. He never lost his temper and was refined in every way. He was a wonderful chap. We connected the electricity in the church from the colliery to the main electricity supply. Willie wouldn't accept any money for the work.

When I became competent at wiring houses, at twelve o'clock I wouldn't see Willie. He would have gone to the nearest pub. In the meantime, I would have done a good bit of work but I didn't mind. I was not to have a pint with him until years later when I bumped into him in the Royal Oak in Penclawdd.

Ivor Morgan was the other electrical contractor in the village. He had an apprentice called Charles Lewis, who later went to America. Some people went to Ivor Morgan thinking him better, but Willie was very capable and did a good job.

I learned a lot from him. When my parents and older sister, Annie and her husband Dan, went to live in a pair of semidetached houses in Penlan, I wired the houses as they were being built. Willie used say, 'Any problems let me know and I'll come over.' He used to come and check every now and then to see if all was well.

My experience with him helped me greatly when I was in the navy in the Second World War. I was conscripted in 1940, and one of the first questions I was asked was, 'What trade would you like?'

'Electricity,' I replied, and went to the torpedo department which included electricity. I also used to mend fuses and replace lamps, etc. on the ships. Fuses were more frequent on ships because of the water, than in buildings on dry land. A sailor from Penllergaer and I used to run the SRE (Speaker System).

After the war, I met up with Willie again when I went to work in the ICI in Waunarlwydd. He was an electrical foreman there."

After electricity had been installed in the village, a female employee of the electricity board demonstrated the use of electric cookers in the church hall. However, electricity was not an immediate success with all the villagers. Many women still used their familiar oil stoves rather than buy a new electrical cooker. Ilene Foot remembers an elderly villager saying, "Let's light the light (oil lamp) and spite the electric."

Although electricity for general use was installed in the village in 1932 to 1933, many inhabitants did not have it installed in their homes immediately as Wilfred Tucker confirms. "It was the Saturday night of the Penclawdd Carnival, and the place (the Royal Oak) was heaving. Every inch of the house was packed, and I had put a few friends from work in the kitchen. Suddenly, low and behold, every light in the house went out and there was a panic. Mother slammed the till shut and stood in front of it. We were generating our own light. We eventually discovered that someone had put a brush handle behind the pipe that was carrying the carbide into the house thus cutting off the supply from the generator. We improvised with candles that night, but it was not long before my parent had electricity installed."

As in all Wales, the village children's education improved greatly during the first half of the twentieth century.

Until 1870, the government took very little responsibility for education.

Schools were set up by individuals, industrialists – for the children of their employees – or by organizations such as churches and chapels. The Church Schools were known as National Schools and the Chapel Schools as British Schools.

Until the first half of the eighteenth century, most people in Penclawdd were illiterate. It was not until 1741-1742, when Griffith Jones' Circulating School was operating at Llanyrnewydd – attended by one hundred and twenty pupils – was the situation alleviated. Griffiths Jones was born in Pen-boyr, Cardiganshire, in 1683. He was ordained in the Anglican Church, became a curate in Laugharne, Carmarthenshire, and later took up the living of Llanddowror in the same county. His opening a school in Llanddowror to inculcate Anglican doctrine instigated him to establish a network of schools across Wales. The schools, run by itinerant teachers, were free. 'The major expense was for teachers, though poorly paid, and the money came mainly from English subscribers who were provided with an annual report, Welsh Piety. [. . .] The schools were normally held for some three months in the period from September to May when there was least pressure on an agricultural population. The schoolmaster, provided with his itinerary by Griffith Jones, completed his assignment in one area, in church, chapel or house, then moved on, but schools often returned to different parts of parishes at regular intervals. During the day, the schoolmaster would teach children to read from the Book of Common Prayer and the Bible. [. . .] In the evenings, adults were taught along similar lines.'[6]

After Griffith Jones' death, Madam Bevan, of Laugharne, took over the patronage, and held a school in Penclawdd in 1767 with thirty-seven pupils.

In the late eighteenth century, John Gronow, a native of Anglesey, came to Swansea to work in the copper works. There, he met, and married, Elizabeth Jones. The couple took up residence in a thatched cottage in Penclawdd, situated at the foot of the *Graig*. Both were able to read and write – some accomplishment for the working class of the time. Elizabeth decided to address the problem of illiteracy in the village, and established a school in her home. Teaching was a difficult task, as books were rare and expensive. However, she kept her school for many years, and in time, her daughters, Margaret and Susan, carried on her good work. The school became known as Sue Gronow's School. Wilfred Tucker remembers his father, Edgar, reminiscing of his time as a pupil there. "My father went to Sue Gronow's School – a Dame School – at the foot of the *Graig*. He paid her tuppence a week." One of Sue Gronow's punishments for her pupils' disobedience was to tie them to her apron strings. Wherever she went, the culprit had to follow.

In 1843, a Church School was established at Banc Bach under the patronage of Starling Benson, owner of the copper works in Penclawdd. It was later to come under the National Schools movement.

The last headmaster of the school was John Brown. David Jones, who attended the school at the time, had fond memories of him. "I attended the National School on Banc Bach. The headmaster was Mr. Brown, an Irishman from Northern Ireland: short of stature and slightly lame, a man greatly beloved by all his pupils. Portions of scripture and a prayer were read before the session opened, and a hymn sung. One of his favourites was 'A Day's March Nearer Home'. [. . .] The school was void of any pictures save here and there a map on the walls."[7]

In 1870, the government accepted the problem of universal primary education and passed the Elementary Education Act. The whole country was divided into School Board areas, in each of which the School Boards were made the authorities of elementary education. The ratepayers of the district elected the members of the School Board who were employed to levy an education rate of up to three pence in the pound.

1874 saw the building of a new Board School in the west-end of Penclawdd. The National School records of 21 July of that year noted, 'It is to be hoped that the new school buildings may be completed soon, and the present school transferred to them with as little delay as possible.'

A School Board of seven members was formed in 1875. The Reverent John Thomas, of Trinity Chapel, Penclawdd, was appointed Clerk to the Board, and Daniel Collins was the School Board Officer. The new Board School opened on August 1875 to accommodate four hundred pupils of mixed sex, both infant and junior.

John Brown, headmaster of the National School was appointed headmaster of the Board School. On 30 June 1876, the annual HMI's (His Majesty's Inspectors') report stated that, 'The school has been transferred to new and spacious premises at the opposite end of the village since August last, and the attendance has more than trebled. Making due allowance for this great increase and for the extra work which it has entailed, the state of the school reflects credit upon the master (John Brown) and his assistant (Jacob Cocker).'

Mundella's Act of 1880 made schooling compulsory, by forcing School Boards and Attendance Committees to make bylaws to compel attendance.

On 1 September 1884, Seth Prothero Jones was appointed headmaster of the school. He served the needs of his pupils diligently for many years. It was not an easy task, and he was presented with many problems during his years of office.

Most of the village gardens had fruit trees, bearing fruit with great abundance. But it was a well-known fact that stealing fruit from another's garden was far more fun than picking freely from one's own. As George Edward Gordon was a manager of the school, his garden was a prime target. 'Having had complaints of about four boys stealing pears from Mr. Gordon's garden, I spoke seriously to the school upon theft and honesty.'[8]

The Act of 1891 gave parents the right to demand free schooling for their children.

In 1893, an Act was passed fixing the school-leaving age at eleven years, which in 1899 was raised to twelve years.

Balfor's Education Act of 1902 abolished all Board Schools, bringing the schools in control of the County and Borough Councils. They were renamed Public Elementary Schools. Penclawdd School's records of 30 September 1903 stated, 'This is the last day to be under the management of the Llanrhidian Higher School Board and on 1 October they recorded, 'From this day, the school will be managed by the Glamorgan County Council's Education Committee.' The Act also gave the councils responsibility for technical schools and colleges (formerly run by the counties) and teacher-training colleges.

Absenteeism was a constant predicament for Seth Jones. He reported on 3 April 1903, 'A considerable improvement has taken place during the past year in the school work, but the attendance is still unsatisfactory.'

At the reopening of the school on 4 January 1904, after the Christmas holidays, he was a little encouraged. 'Reopened with a good attendance. This may be due partly to the fact that Mr. G. E. Gordon, one of our local managers, has promised a medal each for all scholars who will make a full attendance during the year 1904. Self has also promised rewards for full attendance, excepting in absences through illness or other unavoidable circumstances to be certified in every case.'[9]

The master decided to gave his pupils a half-day holiday on the annual anniversaries of the local chapels – Tabernacle, Bethel and Trinity – as most of the children attended the anniversary services.

The annual Gowerton Fair proved too great an attraction to be missed by the pupils, and again on these occasions, the school was closed in the afternoon.

On 22 November 1904, Gordon kept his promise and distributed valuable silver medals to seventeen children who had made a full attendance since 1 January of that year. The headmaster also kept his word. The next day, he gave all his pupils Christmas cards, and commended them for the improved attendance during the year, and exhorted them to improve it still more the next year, again promising medals for full attendance.

However, the children were not always to blame for their absence from school. Many parents thought education unimportant, and considered their children more usefully employed at home, helping with family chores – taking a midday meal to their fathers at the local works, cleaning, looking after younger brothers and sisters, etc. 'Several boys did not return to school after play time this afternoon. Punished same. It seems that some of them are encouraged by their parents to try to come home sooner than usual on Fridays. Many ask leave, but this is not granted, hence truancy.'[10]

In the early years of the twentieth century, Daniel Rees, now one hundred years of age, lived in the Llotrog area of the village, and attended the Elementary School. "I had to go to school every day, but sometimes I used to mitch (stay away) from school to pick blackberries. My teacher, Mr. Jenkins, used to give me a caning on my hand. He was a hard man. He was a very hard man."

Laura Rees often persuaded her daughter to take days off from school. "My mother would often say, 'Don't go to school today Megan, deliver the rent to *Mrs. Roberts y Railway*, clean upstairs, clean the brass rods on the stairs.' I was always cleaning instead of going to school." Megan was determined to give her own daughter the schooling that she had missed, and was ecstatic when in the early 1950s, her daughter, Jean, passed the scholarship examination to attend Gowerton Grammar School. "I was so happy and excited when my daughter passed the scholarship, that I cried with joy."

On some occasions, school closure was forced by epidemics as opposed to outside distractions. On 17 July 1903 it was reported, 'School closed 'By order' through Epidemic (measles).' On 29 April 1904, the school closed again due to an epidemic of scarlet fever. It was reopened on the following 30 May, but not before the building was disinfected.

During their preschool days, the majority of the village children's first language was Welsh. The Elementary School taught in the medium of the English language – a legacy of the Welsh Not.[11] Daniel Rees' first language was Welsh. "I was brought up by my parents to speak Welsh and I learned my English when I went to school." By 17 February 1905, Welsh was introduced into the school when the headmaster requested his teachers to 'cherish Welsh recitation of verses and poetry.' On 15 March of that year, Welsh lessons commenced in the school. 'Welsh taken as a class subject to be taught on Wednesdays, 10.30 to 11.00 and 2.40 to 3.20, and on Fridays, 9.30 to 9.45 and 3.40 to 4.20.'[12] By 1906, it was recorded, 'Special attention paid by self to the teachers' efforts to teach Welsh, advocated more translation from and to.'[13]

Teaching methods were far removed from those of today. The headmaster reported on 8 July 1904, 'Made special examination of the penmanship in each class this week. Teachers own handwriting on blackboard noticed. Urged all teachers to give more mental arithmetic and expression of children's own thoughts.'

Seth Jones took every opportunity to evoke his pupils' interest. 'A lady missionary from India (the wife of Reverend W. R. James) visited the school this morning and I asked her to give a short address on the children of India, which she did most interestingly.'[14] G. E. Gordon was invited to the school to give a talk on the comparison between schools in Wales, and in Canada and the United States of America, after he had recently visited the latter two countries.

A system of employing pupil teachers was practised at the school. On 27 July 1906, Evan Wendall Roberts, the oldest son of John and Ann Roberts, tenants of the Railway, was appointed pupil teacher for two years. He was seventeen years of age. However, it seems that Wendall was not happy in his position, as the headmaster found on one occasion that he 'could not get Wendall Roberts to Standard Four today. Too shy and unprepared.'[15] The pupil teacher left the school before completing his two-year contract, but he continued his own education to qualify as an architect.

By 1904, it was recognised that the school was too small. In the HMI's report of 7 April 1904, it was written, 'The classrooms are crowded and some of the teachers therefore work under a disadvantage. [. . .] The question of accommodation here should be carefully considered. It is perhaps desirable that a new Infant School should be built in a more central position. These premises could then be devoted entirely to the use of the older children, and opportunity would be offered for the improvement of the lighting, etc. and of the furniture. The Board of Education will hope to learn in due course the intentions of the Local Education Authority with regard to the premises.' On 1 November 1904, there were as many as seventy-three pupils in one class. It was often necessary to use the lobbies as classrooms to accommodate all the children. But it was not until 1910 that a new school was built at Banc Bach for infant pupils only. Henceforth, the Elementary School became known as the Old School.

The Infant School was to accommodate one hundred and fifty children. On May 23 of that year, Miss Janet Walker – certified teacher – was appointed headmistress. She had been in charge of the Infant Department at the Elementary School since 26 November 1901. Her staff consisted of Annie Evans, Hannah Violet Morgans, Laura Thomas, a supplementary teacher, and Lilian Mary Morgans, a student teacher.

However, the Infant School – the New School as it was referred to locally

Penclawdd Infant School.

– failed to solve the problem of overcrowding. By 22 July, the average number of children in attendance per week was one hundred and seventy. On the following 19 September, Janet Walker received instructions to exclude all children under five years of age from the school. The reason was explained in the HMI's report for 1909 to 1910. 'The new premises are conveniently arranged, but it is a pity that the needs of the locality have been underestimated. The babies' room is greatly overcrowded. Children under five should be excluded or another classroom should be built. The room mentioned above is not properly furnished.' It was not until 21 July 1924 that children under five years of age were readmitted to the school.

In June 1911, the school closed for a week to allow the pupils to enjoy the coronation celebrations of King Edward VII and Queen Alexandra. 'There will be no school during the whole of next week, it being Coronation Week. Children will assemble here next Thursday to receive flags and medals before taking part in the procession. Afterwards, there will be tea and sports, etc.'[16] A holiday was given on 12 July for Investiture Day.

In the New School's formative years, language continued to be an issue, as it was in the Old School. The HMI's Report for 1913 stated, 'Welsh, in the form of recitation, singing, and conversational lessons is taken, but the language might still receive greater prominence. Only one of the teachers is capable of conducting the conversation lessons with ease, but the other members of the staff are making commendable efforts to perfect their knowledge of the language.' Seven years later the HMI reported, 'The instruction is given almost wholly in Welsh, and very good progress is being made.'

Epidemics were still rife, and in 1920, from 21 May to 7 June, the school was closed owing to a serious epidemic of measles. Four years later, scarlet fever forced school closure from 20 October to 10 November.

Only the privileged few in the village became teachers, and as a result, were highly regarded. Janet Walker lodged in Clifford House, Penlan, with Henry and Rhoda Eaton and their children, Ilene, George and Winifred. The headmistress mystified Wilfred Tucker during his first months at the school. "Miss Walker always wore a net around her neck with two silver blobs either side. I used to wonder how she could be alive with something sticking through her neck, which I assumed was joining the metal blobs. It took me months to discover that she wore a metal neck support discreetly hidden by the net, which was attached to the metal blobs."

Janet Walker returned to her native Devon, and on 30 August 1915, Miss J. Blodwen Jenkins commenced duties as head teacher of the school.

One of her pupils was Marian Eaton. The latter often relates the tale of when her teacher, Hannah Violet Morgans, instructed her to go on an important errand. "Miss Morgans was the daughter of Mary Morgans, grocer, and Morgan Twice, a deacon in Tabernacle Chapel. One day she called me to the front of the class and said, 'I want you to go to my house to fetch something for me, but if you open it something terrible will happen to you. Do not talk to anyone and come straight back.' I went to the shop behind the Royal Oak Inn where Miss Morgans lived with her

Hannah Violet Morgans' class.
Marion Eaton, née Davies – middle row, fifth from left.

parents, and handed the envelope given me to Mrs. Morgans. I was given another envelope in return. Miss Morgans had so emphasized that I was not to open the envelope that my curiosity got the better of me. I opened it on the way back to school and found her false teeth in it. I had such a fright that I nearly dropped them. Thank God I didn't. I quickly tried to reseal the envelope hoping that she would not notice that I had disobeyed her orders. But when I returned to school, she knew immediately what had happened by my inadequate resealing of the envelope. She looked sternly at me and said, 'I thought you said you were not going to open this?' Although I was only about six years of age at the time, I shall never forget that incident."

Marian continued her education at Gowerton County School and qualified in the teaching profession at Bangor Training College. She comments on her career, "I never thought of being anything else but a teacher."

Wales' patron *Dewi Sant* (Saint David) has always been widely acknowledged in Wales on 1 March – *Dydd Dewi Sant* (Saint David's Day). Young girls wear the national costume adorned with a daffodil, and boys sport a leek, usually the largest they can find. Both the daffodil and the leek are national emblems. On the morning of 1 March 1935, under the headship of Miss I. Mary Price, the first concert was held in the school to celebrate the occasion. It was followed by the usual half-day holiday. The concerts became an annual event in the calendar of the school and were attended by the pupils' parents.

On 12 May 1937, the pupils were treated to a tea at the school to celebrate the coronation of King George V and Queen Mary. Each child was presented with a mug given by Glamorgan Education Committee.

Language at the school continued to be a problem in this village where both English and Welsh were spoken. The HMI's Report for 1939 reads, 'The main task of an Infant School is to help the pupils to gain control of the 'mother tongue' as a medium of expression. Welsh is the language of this school. The pupils have a very undesirable habit of mixing English words and phrases with their speech. This serious fault should be checked from the outset, and the children should be guided and trained by well-planned oral work, and by good example from the teachers, away from this adulteration of language. Every lesson should be a lesson in good Welsh.'

In 1889, the Welsh Intermediate Education Act was passed allowing local authorities to set up County Schools, also known as Intermediate Schools, which could educate pupils up to the age of eighteen. There were scholarships to be won for free education at the schools or entrance examinations, when, if passed, granted education for a small fee. By 1911, an examinations of the Central Welsh Board could be sat for the examinations of the Central Board Junior and Senior Certificates.

In 1897, a County School for male and female pupils was built at Gowerton, which served all the Gower Peninsular, including Penclawdd. There was also fee-paying Secretarial Colleges in Swansea – Clevedon College, Greggs School and Clarks College.

The high cost of the fees of these colleges rarely made attendance by the village children possible. Neither were many parents in the village financially secure enough to support their children's attendance at Gowerton County School, even if the scholarship or entrance examinations were passed. Books, uniforms and train fares were expensive. Moreover, parents often needed their children's working wage to supplement the family finances.

After 1918, children of these circumstances continued attending the Elementary School until the raised school leaving age of fourteen, but did not enter the scholarship class or try the scholarship examination.

In 1926, a government committee – the Haddow Committee – reported on the system of state education. It suggested an examination at the age of eleven for all children and the setting up of a new kind of secondary school for the children who did not then pass on to County or Grammar School. During the years of the Second World War, a Secondary Modern School was built in Penclawdd behind the Ship. This school was then called the New School, and the Infant School was referred to by its correct name.

Betty Edwards lived in Oldwalls, Llanrhidian. She attended Gowerton County School, lodging at Gowerton during the week and coming home at weekends. The journey was long as the train from Gowerton only ran as far as Llanmorlais and so Betty had to be transported by her family or friends to and from the train. At high tides, the road from Llanmorlais to Llanrhidian flooded, and so on her homeward journey, Betty sometimes caught the train to Killay and then travelled by bus along the North Gower Road to Llanrhidian. After completing three years at the school, her friends with whom she lodged decided to terminate their education. Although Betty's parents gave their consent for her to stay at school to gain her certificate, she thought she would be lonely lodging on her own, and so left school and helped her parents on the family farm.

R. A. Butler was responsible for the 1944 Act, which raised the school leaving age to fifteen (achieved in 1947) and also for abolishing fee-paying for County (Grammar) Schools.

Elaine Phillips, née Jones, a native of Penlan, was a pupil at Gowerton County School and a student at Barry Teachers' Training College. She commenced her teaching profession in Wolverhampton. Three years later, she returned to Penclawdd, and spent five years as a supply teacher in the area.

"I started teaching in Penclawdd Junior School in March 1947. It was a marvellous school to work in – a happy place. The staff got on so well together. My headmaster, Gwynfor Jenkins, came to the school in the late 1940s from Penclawdd Secondary Modern School. He was an excellent headmaster – a good administrator – and very supportive of his staff.

Thanks to Mrs. Rees, the cook, the pupils and staff were provided with wonderful school dinners. Mrs. Rees took endless trouble. She often made pancakes and Welsh cakes for the one hundred and eighty pupils. The meals were extremely palatable – rich beef casseroles, treacle puddings, spotted dicks, etc. – and there was never any waste. She was a wonderful cook, and a wonderful lady, but time was not of the essence to her. I'd be on dinner duty, and the children would be waiting for their pudding,

Penclawdd Junior School teaching and kitchen staff in front of school 1949-50.
Back row, left to right: Mary Jenkins, Falmai Jones, Ivor Davies, Betty Rees, Elaine Jones.
Front row, left to right: Miss Howell, Esther Rees, Gwynfor Jenkins, Miss Howells

but then Mrs. Rees would be taking it out of the oven. I often used to go around into the kitchen and help serve.

My first class was Standard Four. I had about thirty-six pupils, one of which was Janice Jenkins. The next year – with Mair Davies and Jennifer Lord, etc. – was one of the two very good classes that I taught. The other class – with Janet Davies, Mary Jones, Hilary Durban, etc. – I taught for two years from 1951 to 1953. They were all good children and a high percentage passed the scholarship exam."

Standard One had been taught by Miss Howell and Standard Two by Miss Howells for a number of years. Both were incompetent teachers, but Miss Howells of Standard Two was also extremely lazy. Her idea of teaching mathematics was to chalk the problems with their answers on the blackboard. English lessons took the form of the best reader in the class reading a story while Miss Howells slept peacefully having organised another pupil to pick her grey hairs off her cardigan.

In September 1951, the situation was addressed when Gwen Jenkins replaced Miss Howells, Standard Two, but the unfortunate pupils of the two previous years – Hilary Durban's, etc. class – then in Standard Three, had, in a sense, lost two years of schooling. Gwynfor Jenkins decided to move Elaine, whom he obviously thought an excellent teacher, from Standard Four to Standard Three, to, as Elaine puts it, "knock them into shape." It was a hard task, but she has fond memories of the time.

"I didn't have a great deal of help in the way of books. They were free, but there was no library in the school. I made ink out of ink powder and water, which I poured into the china inkwells in each pupil's desk. The children used pens with primitive scratchy nibs, and the ink stained their fingers and clothes. Biros were a wonderful invention. The rooms were extremely cold in winter, only having one coal fire and a very large chimney that absorbed most of the heat.

I was a strict disciplinarian. My pupils had to sit and listen. I can remember one girl being unhappy when I first taught her, and I learned that she voiced her thoughts to her mother, but a month later, she would have nothing said against me. Children will take advantage of a weak teacher. I think they like discipline and to know their boundaries. Ex-pupils often say to me, 'I can remember you giving me a clip,' but they all talk to me, so I couldn't have been as bad as all that.

In those days, the parents supported the teacher. When children complained at home of having a row in school, they would be asked, 'Well, what did you do wrong?' Today it is often the case that when children complain to their parents, the parents go to school and reprimand the teacher.

Penclawdd Junior School Standard 4, 1953.
Back row, left to right: John Guy, Michael Brenton, Peter Thomas, Brian Murley, Huw Thomas,
Howard Tucker, Spencer Davies, Howard Stock, Malcolm Alden.
Middle row, left to right: Norman Alden, Dewi Thomas, Wendy Jones, Muriel Sutton, Kathleen
Bennett, Joyce Howells, Mary Jones, Olwen Perkins, Ann Roberts, Jeffrey Rees, Jeffrey Nichols.
Front row, left to right: Bethan Evans, Nest Hughes, Hilary Durban, Pauline Gunnell,
Janet Davies, Betty Adlam, Margaret Davies, Ann Hughes, Jill Fisher, Daphne Rees,
Marion Lane, Mair Roberts. On left: Gwynfor Jenkins, Headmaster. On right: Elaine Jones.

Penclawdd Junior School teaching staff in front of school September 1951.
Back row, left to right: Emrys Jenkins, Gwen Jenkins, Ivor Davies, Mr. Arthur.
Front row, left to right: Elaine Jones, Gwynfor Jenkins, Miss Howell.

I never used a cane although it was permissible in those days. I'd give my pupils a smack or a shake, but I was conscious of my quick temper and was afraid that if I had a cane, I might damage. One day I was in such a temper with one boy who had been very disruptive in class. I'd had enough of his bad behaviour. I put him to stand in front of the class and I walked to the back of the room with my hands held tightly behind my back while I gave him such a talking to. I don't believe that a cane is necessary for staff, but I think the headmaster should have one, more as a deterrent than anything else.

Mr. Jenkins was a character – a kindly man – but he had little discipline. The latter came from the teachers. I used to preach to my pupils, 'In my classroom I'm the boss. You do as I say.' One day, when Mr. Jenkins was in my room, I requested some exercise books. He told David Davies to go and wait for the books outside his room. The child didn't move, but looked at me, and it was not until I nodded my head, did he go. Mr. Jenkins didn't like that.

It is not knowledge that makes a good teacher. Teaching is an art; some have it, and some don't. It also involves hard work. People used to say to me that I was a good teacher. 'No,' I used to say, 'I'm not a good teacher. When I'm in my classroom, I work very hard.'

At the end of the year, Gwynfor decided that I should move with my class to Standard Four. He told me to keep it a secret from my pupils until last minute. They kept asking me, 'Who is going to teach us in Standard Four Miss?'

I kept saying, 'I don't know.' When I eventually told them at the end of the year that I was to be their teacher again, they were so pleased."

Elaine was in an unusual position in that two of her colleagues – Gwynfor Jenkins and Ivor Davies – had been on the teaching staff when she had been a pupil at the school. "Our headmaster, Mr. Gilbert James, was a brilliant mathematician and often took Mr. Jenkins' class – the scholarship class – in the afternoons. Ivor Davies taught the fourteen year-old boys who had not tried scholarship – the tough nuts. I was scared stiff of him. When I joined the staff, he immediately started referring to me as Miss Jones, while Mr. Jenkins continued to call me Elaine, even in front of my class sometimes.

Ivor Davies was a disappointed man. When I stared teaching in Penclawdd School, he was temporary headmaster and hoped to get the headship. However, Gwynfor Jenkins was appointed. Ivor Davies also acted as temporary head in Llanmorlais Junior School and unfortunately he was again disappointed in not obtaining the headship. He had been a pupil teacher in Penclawdd School, but had never attended college, and so was unqualified. Gwynfor, on the other hand, had been a pupil teacher, but had also qualified in college.

Ivor Davies was a very strict disciplinarian with no sense of humour. It was almost a military discipline. He was not popular with his pupils but it was not his fault. He was an only child and had experienced an extremely harsh upbringing, especially by his father. It seems he had been subjected to little affection and support at home. He was discouraged to mix with others, and so friendships came uneasily to him. He never married. He lived in Penuel then – about a mile and a half west of Penclawdd – and walked to and from school each day. I remember his telling me of how he took a cold bath every morning, a self-afflicted penance in those times of extremely cold winters. Neither did he experience the luxury of a bathroom. His bath was taken in a tin tub. He was quite a good-looking man, but he wore the same double-breasted navy pin strip suit every day without fail. I think it stood up on its own when he took it off. He always wore boots, never shoes.

When I was about thirteen, Mr. Williams, minister of Tabernacle Chapel, organised operettas, which were held in the cinema building, with an entrance fee of thrupence. They were great and of a high standard. Vera Rees was usually in the cast. There was so much talent in the village and Mr. Williams took advantage of it, but for some reason, Ivor Davies always thought himself better than anyone else.

When I joined the staff, Ivor Davies was teaching Standard Five – the scholarship class. He seemed to believe in all work and no play and often curtailed his pupils' playtimes. When he was in his room, the children were afraid to move, but when he left, it was hullabaloo. I often had to go in to restore order. My discipline was different. I strove for good behaviour from my pupils at all times, in and out of my presence.

I tried hard to liaise with Ivor Davies on teaching methods, but without success. He was very dogmatic and thought it unimportant. It was a shame, as inevitably, the children were confused when he taught different methods than did I. I remember Ioan Thomas – a brilliant boy – questioning me on a mathematical problem that he thought he was unable to solve. I explained to him that it was a familiar problem to him, but it was the unfamiliar method taught by his teacher that had confused him. When Ivor Davies was on yard duty, he lined the children and instructed them on breathing exercises – breath in, breath out. He always held his cane half-hidden up the back of his jacket. He was invited to give a talk to the Womens Institute. He talked on breathing in and breathing out, and I had to give the vote of thanks.

I did not agree with Ivor Davies' teaching methods but neither do I agree with today's. Too much authority has been taken away from teaching staff. I believe in a happy medium – discipline but also relaxation.

One afternoon a week, in the spring and summer terms, I used to take my pupils on rambles over the *Graig*. I gave them nature talks and they picked wild flowers for the classroom. The *Graig* was very beautiful and unspoilt in those days, and it was the highlight of the week for the children.

I left Penclawdd School when my eldest son Lynn was born in 1958. Seven years later, after I had had my second son, Kerri, I was asked if I'd return to replace Miss Howell, who had had an accident. At the time, all the teachers living in Penclawdd were working. I taught there for a while and then spent three years teaching in Penclawdd Infant School. I didn't like teaching the younger age group and when Gwen Jenkins was appointed headmistress on Miss Gwynne's retirement, I was fortunate in replacing Gwen in the Old School. However, the new position of deputy head was introduced and I was last in and so first out of the school. I spent the last fifteen years of my teaching career in Gowerton Junior School, but I always think of Penclawdd as 'my school'. I was so very happy there."

When the comprehensive system was introduced in the area in 1974, the Secondary Modern School was used for the first year of secondary education. By 1991, the Comprehensive School at Gowerton had been greatly enlarged, and the old Secondary Modern School building housed Penclawdd Infant and Junior Schools. The Infant School building became Penclawdd Community Centre, and the Old School was demolished, its site now being part of the Greenacres private housing estate.

In 1966, the school leaving age reached sixteen years. It remains so today.

A considerable number of Penclawdd's inhabitants joined the teaching profession, and a concentration of them lived in Penlan. They were, George and Ilene Eaton, William Jenkins, his nephew and nieces, John, Lavinia and Gwen Jenkins, Dilys Davies and her sister, Blodwen, Elaine Jones, Nancy Francis and her brother John, and Henry and Margaret Davies' children, Morien, Prothero, Vernwy and Mary. In fact, one or more of the children in nearly every house in Penlan, became teachers. The majority taught in schools in Penclawdd, and a few were employed in the teaching profession in neighbouring towns and villages.

NOTES

1. In 1834 the Poor Law Amendment Act was passed. Its main objects were to abolish outdoor relief for the able-bodied workers and their families and to compel them to enter the workhouses where their lot was to be harder than that of the lowest paid labourer not on relief. The idea was to make the workhouse a feared institution so that the able-bodied would apply for relief only as a last resort. Parishes were to be grouped into unions in which workhouses would be set up to form Poor Law Unions governed by an elected Board of Guardians. The guardians had to be ratepayers who were elected by other ratepayers with a property qualification. Responsible to each Guardian was a salaried Clerk. Each union employed staff of Relieving Officers, District Medical Officers, a Workhouse Master and Matron with their staff as well as Assistant Overseers for each parish who were paid to collect the rates. The work of the Board of Guardians was closely supervised by the Central Authority – The Poor Law Commissions – to be replaced in 1847 by the Poor Law Board. The local unions were Llanelli, Swansea and Gower. Swansea Workhouse was in Mount Pleasant, Swansea (built 1860) and the Gower Workhouse in Penmaen (built 1861). Penclawdd was in the North District of the Gower Union.
2. The National Health Service was introduced on 5 July 1948 by Welsh MP Aneurin Bevan. A 1948 leaflet explaining the new NHS was issued. 'It will provide you with all medical, dental, and nursing care. Everyone – rich of poor, man, woman or child – can use it or any part of it. There are no charges, except for a few special items. There are no insurance qualifications. But it is not a 'charity'. You are all paying for it, mainly as taxpayers, and it will relieve your money worries in time of illness'.
3. A corruption of *Gwas* (Welsh for servant). A village endearment.
4. Now the site of Swansea Enterprise Park.
5. David Taylor. *Mastering Economic and Social History*. Macmillan Master Series. Houdsmills, Basingstoke, Hampshire, England, pp. 405-407.
6. Gareth Elwyn Jones, *Modern Wales. A Concise History c.1485-1979* (Cambridge 1984), p. 144.
7. *Gower Journal Volume 17*, p. 51.
8. *Penclawdd Elementary School Report. 19 November 1894.*
9. *Ibid 4 January 1904.*
10. *Ibid 9 November 1906.*
11. The Welsh Not was a plaque containing the words 'I will not speak Welsh' (or similar) attached to string and placed around the neck of the offending pupil who spoke in that language. As the day progressed, the plaque was passed on as in a game of 'tag' to subsequent offenders. The last culprit of the day was punished.
12. *Penclawdd School Report 15 March 1905.*
13. *Ibid 18 September 1906.*
14. *Ibid 8 July 1904.*
15. *Ibid 13 October 1906.*
16. *Ibid 16 June, 1911.*

3

Church and Chapels

Sunday was a special day in the village and was revered as the Sabbath. Shops, public houses and the local cinema were closed, and only essential work was undertaken inside and outside the homes. The church and chapels were attended regularly by the majority. All respectable people went to church or chapel and those who did not attend were considered not so.

Before the nineteenth century, the Established Church was the only place of worship in Penclawdd. The church of Llanyrnewydd,[1] situated on a height to the south of the village, was dedicated to St. Gwynour, after a Breton saint – St. Eneaour. The church was completely rebuilt in the Early English style in 1850, on the site of an old Chapel of Ease to

St. Gwynour's Church, Llanyrnewydd.

Llanrhidian Church. It was opened and consecrated for divine service on 17 December 1850, by the Bishop of St. David's, and the petition of consecration stated, 'that the old chapel of Ease of Llanyrnewydd alias Penclawdd in the parish of Llanrhidian had become dilapidated and unfit for use and that a new chapel had been erected on or near the site of an old one.'

'The total cost of rebuilding the church amounted to seven hundred pounds of which three hundred was raised by subscription. The remaining four hundred was paid by Philip Evans, churchwarden, of Brynhir House. The Incorporated Church Building Society refused its aid towards the building cost because Evans had neglected to apply for a grant before erecting the church despite the fact that it was substantially built with the best materials [. . .] The church possesses a remarkable silver double-beaker chalice that belongs to the Cromwellian period and bears the hallmark of 1657. The chalice was originally two secular wine cups joined together at the base, so that when one is used as a drinking vessel the other acts as the support. It has been referred to as the 'Leper' cup of Llanyrnewydd. It is inscribed: 'Lanynewir Chappell 1677'.[2]

During the late nineteenth and early twentieth centuries, St. Gwynour's Church experienced great benefactors in George and Charlotte Jane Baker Haynes. The couple had proceeded Evans as owners of Brynhir House. George Baker Haynes was a well-known Swansea solicitor and probably the richest man in Penclawdd at the time. He owned much property in the area and was known locally as Squire Haynes. His residence was a large imposing house, by Penclawdd standards, with magnificent views over St. Gwynour's Church to the distant Whiteford Sands and Llwchwr Estuary.

Born in Swansea in 1831, he would have been one of the few inhabitants of the village to be working in Swansea. He started his career as a clerk to solicitor Charles Collins of 5 Fisher Street, Swansea. His activities in Swansea and the surrounding area were varied and many. He was Freeman of the town of Swansea, Clerk to Swansea Union of Guardians,[3] on the West Glamorgan Agricultural Society, Superintendent Registrar, on the Swansea School Board and on the Committee of Swansea Infirmary. In 1860, he became Sergeant of the Fourth Glamorgan Rifles, Lieutenant seven years later, and by 1868, was Captain at the age of thirty-seven years.

Baker Haynes was highly respected by the locals, especially amongst the church congregation. Willie Roberts, a loyal church member, used to speak of him with great reverence. "He was a real gent," he used to say. The Squire and his wife attended church regularly and involved them-

Golden Jubilee Cup.

selves in church life giving generously of their time and money. The following article was published in 'The Cambrian' newspaper:

'PENCLAWDD – The Queen's Jubilee was honoured in this quiet village on Monday, the 20th inst. by a Church Boundary School Treat, under the superintendence of Mrs. C. Morris, the Lodge. The following ladies officiated at the tables: Mrs. Bond, Rheanfawr; Mrs. Jones, Benson Street; Mrs. John Aberkedy; Mrs. Davies, Blue Anchor; Mrs. Ford, Mrs. Prince, Llanmorlais; Mrs. Dr. Jones, Mrs. Lewis, Mrs. Jeffreys, Miss Ford, Mrs. Jones, Cae Ebol. Tea and cake was served to about 200 children and adults. At 4.30 the Sunday School formed in a procession and marched to a field kindly lent by Mr. D. Rees, Brynhir Farm, where they indulged in various games. Mr. & Mrs. G. B. Haynes had provided a good assortment of Jubilee prizes, and 160 very useful articles had been carefully laid in bran tubs by Mrs. Haynes, that each Sunday School attendant may be safe of one prize. One orange and bun were given afterwards, and at the close a Jubilee cup ordered for the occasion was handed to each scholar by the Curate, inscribed thus:- Llanyrnewydd Church Sunday School Jubilee Treat, 20th June, 1887. Queen Victoria born May 24th 1819 ascended the Throne 20th June 1837; may God preserve her. Mr. G. B. Haynes proposed a vote of thanks to Mrs. Morris, the Lodge, and all others who had taken part in the day's proceedings for their labour of love; also to Mrs. G. Birbell and Mr. C. Morris, Lower Tin-plate Works; Mr. W. Leys Phillips, M. A. Bedford; Mr. Stodhart, London; and Mrs. Ror Dimrant etc. for subscribing so liberally towards the treat, without whose aid it could not be carried out on so large a scale. He also made a very appropriate reference to our beloved Queen.'

In 1889, a portion of ground was given to the church by Baker Haynes. It was used to extend the existing churchyard and was consecrated by the Bishop of St. David's on 27 November 1890.

Wilfred Tucker has childhood memories of him. "I can't remember much about him because I was young when he died, but whenever I hear his name mentioned, I see him walking to church wearing knicker bockers, thick grey socks and a grey belted jacket. He always carried a little nut stick. He used to visit the poor and sick locally and in Gower. I think of him as a Guardian." Mr. and Mrs. Baker Haynes were privileged in having their own locked cupboard in front of their pew in which to keep their church books. Every year, Baker Haynes presented each Sunday School pupil with a book, appropriate to his or her age.

As a young girl, Mary Bennett, née Rees, living in nearby Llotrog, used to sell locally caught fish to the Brynhir household. "Mrs. Haynes was lovely. She always had a cup of tea and a piece of cake for me. A small little woman she was."

In her latter years, Charlotte Jane appeared rarely apart from church attendance. Wilfred Tucker confirms, "I went to the house quite regularly, especially on New Year's Day." It was a village custom to sing door to door on New Year's Day morning until midday. The carol never varied. Wilfred Tucker sang its English version:

> 'Happy New Year to you all,
> In this house so great and small,
> Can you hear me when I call,
> Happy New Year to you all.'

"We always went to the back door. Miss Evans, the housekeeper, would ask us into the kitchen. It had a large settle and a huge cage hanging from the ceiling with a parrot in it. Mrs. Haynes was always in bed. She had an electric bell at the bottom of the stairs that she rang for attention by pressing a bell by the side of her bed. The only time I saw her was when she was wheeled to church in a large wicker chair by her gardener and handyman, Mr. Finch. How they managed to get up that hill I do not know."

In 1917, Baker Haynes died, aged eighty-six years, and was laid to rest in St. Gwynour's churchyard in front of the east window.

His wife continued to live in Brynhir House, faithfully served by Mary Thomas, who lived in nearby Caerau Farm. Her support of the church never waned. Wilfred Tucker remembers her generosity. "The churchyard was an oval walled area surrounding the church in the centre of the field then owned by Mrs. Baker Haynes. In about 1920, she summoned my father, Edgar Tucker, Mr. Evans the curate, and Graham Anderson, a churchwarden, to her bedside, and asked them in turn what they could see out of the window overlooking the church. Mr. Evans and Graham Anderson both answered that they could see a beautiful view. My father, Edgar, as she referred to him, seemed to give her the answer she required. He said that the contour of the wall of the churchyard was in exact symmetry with the boundary of the field. 'This is correct,' she said. 'I'll give the whole field to the church on the proviso that you never alter the symmetry of the new wall.'"

In 1922, Charlotte Jane Baker Haynes died with no issue and was laid to rest with her husband. In 1935, the Mothers' Union and friends of the

Baker Haynes' were to provide the church with a carved oak reredos and panelling in memory of the couple.

The established firm of solicitors Strike and Bellingham, 29 Fisher Street, Swansea was instructed by the vendors, the executors of Charlotte Jane Baker Haynes' will to auction the whole estate with auctioneer John M. Leeder and Son, 46 Waterloo Street, Swansea. It consisted of about 320 acres including, Brynhir House, Pencaerfenny Farm, Brynhir Farm, Brynhir Cottage (The Lodge), accommodation lands, 3 small holdings including Cold Harbour Farm and Cerrigman Farm, 2 detached houses including Pen-y-Graig, the freehold of the Blue Anchor public house and many freehold ground rents.

John Rees, who lived in the nearby Blue Anchor public house, bought its freehold, and also Brynhir House and the field in front of the house. The Parochial Church Council, needing a vicarage for their imminent new vicar, bought Brynhir Cottage. A little later, the church, realising that it was unsuitable for their purpose, being too small, agreed with John Rees to exchange properties, but the latter kept the field. So for the first time, Brynhir House became a vicarage. When the Parochial Church Council took possession of the property, Wilfred Tucker's uncle was made caretaker until the house was occupied by the new vicar. He found many photographs and postcards from friends of Mr. and Mrs. Baker Haynes in the South of France and Biarritz. The couple obviously had another life outside Penclawdd.

1924 saw Penclawdd and Gwernffrwd became a separate parish when St. Gwynour's and St. David's Churches received their own vicar on 28 August of that year. The Reverend D. Thomas was inducted as the first vicar of the new parish by the Bishop of the Diocese. Previously, the Chapel of Ease at Llanyrnewydd was served by the vicar of Llanrhidian Church, Penclawdd being in the Higher Division of the Parish of Llanrhidian.

Wilfred Tucker remembers much confusion over the churchyard. "It was decided that the churchyard was too large, and against the late Mrs. Haynes' wishes, the south side was sold to the farmer who owned the adjacent land. Unfortunately, there was some confusion when the boundary was fenced. The farmer insisted that he owned the drive to the church. It transpired that he was correct as when Mrs. Haynes had sold her land to the Parochial Church Council, the plans had been drawn incorrectly. The church bought the drive back from the farmer. It was a joke, but it was an expensive joke as fifty pounds was a lot of money at the time, which was the price we had to pay." The new churchyard was formally opened by Miss Alice Morgan of Caswell in August 1929.

George Edward Gordon was also a prominent figure in the church. He lived with his wife, Mary Jane, and her niece, Miss Maud Jones, in Penlan Cottage, Penlan. A highly respected mining engineer and owning a considerable amount of land in Penclawdd, he was considered quite a wealthy man in this village of manual workers. He was referred to locally as Squire Gordon – a title that he loved and encouraged. He was deeply involved in local activities. He was elected onto the Board of the Gower Union Guardians[4] at the end of the nineteenth century and his wife followed suit on 5 May 1908. He was Chairman of the very active Tabernacle Chapel Choir, JP, Gower District Councillor, and Chairman of the Council in 1918.

Penlan Cottage was approached by a private driveway, through a beautiful avenue of horse chestnut trees from the Trumpic Road. Until 1923-24, it was the only carriageway to Penlan and it was necessary for the other occupants of the hamlet to obtain Gordon's permission for its use. It was more than often refused. George Eaton, who lived in Clifford House, two hundred yards north of Penlan Cottage, used to laboriously transport one hundred weight of coal at a time, on a donkey, up the very steep Penlan Hill from the main road – one of the many occasions when permission was not granted.

On 7 November 1923, a Deputation consisting of Messrs Walter Tucker, Jonathan Morgan and William Jenkins, representing the Penlan residents appeared before the Roads and Bridges Committee of the Gower District Council to call attention to the great inconvenience and difficulties experienced by Penlan residents through the lack of a proper cartway leading to Penlan.

On 17 November, the same Committee decided that a new road be constructed over land forming part of Parc Hendy Farm joining up two existing roads giving Penlan a cartway. The owners of the farm, Messrs. Richards and John Rees, had consented in writing to sell the necessary land for the sum of one hundred and fifty pounds. The road was constructed but not surfaced until years later. George Rees lived near the road in *Cwrt-y-Felin* (Mill Court). "The road was made of black ash. It was not tarred until much later. My mother used to stop us using the road as it made our stockings dirty, and made us walk down Penlan Hill instead. For some unknown reason, hundreds of hedgehogs used to gravitate to the road. I have never seen so many hedgehogs."

On 15 December, the Committee requested Gordon to replace the stile situated at the one end of the public footpath, which crossed his property from the Old Colliery to Penlan, with a wicket gate, which would be more convenient for the residents. Gordon refused and eventually on 2 January 1924, the Committee insisted that iron swing gates be erected at either end of the footpath at the expense of the Gower District Council or the Parish Council.

On 4 February 1925, Gordon again came into conflict with the Committee by refusing to dismantle a barbed wire fence that he had erected along side the above mentioned path. He was informed that the fence was a nuisance caused to a highway or footpath and therefore a violation of the Barbed Wire Act of 1893. After much disagreement, Gordon eventually consented, and the fence was disassembled.

Win Walters, sister of George Eaton, says of him, "Mr. Gordon loved his position of power and as a result was not well-liked in Penlan, but the family mixed little with the local inhabitants. He kept cows on his land at Penlan, which surrounded his house. I used to go to Mr. and Mrs. Gordon's house to buy milk. The large kitchen had a red quarry tiled floor where the servants ate, while the owners ate in the breakfast room. Mrs. Gordon used to skim the milk in front of me, keeping the cream for the household, before selling it to me. She was a semi-invalid and always wore a flannel around her head to try to ease the pain of neuralgia. She occa-sionally came to Clifford House to visit my mother, Rhoda Eaton. She always wore a cloak, never a coat."

Elaine Phillips' grandmother, Margaret Jane Jones, was employed by Mr. and Mrs. Gordon. Elaine talks of the time. "My grandmother laundered and ironed for the Gordons for one shilling a week. It was hard work then with irons to be heated on the fire and starched wingback collars to launder and iron. My grandfather had an accident and was confined to bed for three years before he died. His colleagues had a whip-round for him. Mr. Gordon took charge of the money saying that my mother was too young to be in control of it and that my grandmother, not being able to read or write, was not capable. My grandmother couldn't read or write it was true, but she wouldn't be diddled and was more than capable of looking after the money. The Gordons thought they were better than anyone else in the village."

Daniel McCarthy recalls, "Mr. Gordon had a beautiful horse. He came around the houses in the village driving his horse and trap collecting his rent. He drove it himself wearing a top hat. He was a real toff."

Mary Rees also sold her fish at Penlan Cottage. "I used to go to Mr. and Mrs. Gordon's house if I had mullet, Dover soles, or salmon bass. They paid me one shilling a pound for them. I was always asked by Mrs. Gordon to clean the fish for her, which I had been taught to do by my mother. One day Mrs. Gordon said, 'You must call me Mum.'

When I went home and told my mother that I had to call Mrs. Gordon Mum, my mother said, 'You go and tell her that you've only got one mum, and that's me.' Mrs. Gordon always wore a white cap on her head. No doubt she wanted me to bow to her but I wouldn't do that. Gordon was alright, but I can remember him telling his wife to remember that I was working class."

Mary Jane Gordon was not popular among the children of the village. On New Year's Day morning, when carols were sung from door to door, it was hoped that the dignitaries of the village would contribute more pennies then the other households. This was not the case at the Gordon's residence. Marian Eaton remembers the occasions, "Being Welsh speaking we sang our carols in Welsh:

> 'Blwyddyn Newydd dda i chwi,
> Ac i bawb sydd yn y tŷ,
> Dyna yw fy nymuniad i,
> Blwyddyn Newydd dda i chwi.'

Which translates as:

'Happy New Year to you,
All people in the house,
This is my wish for you,
Happy New Year to you.'

We always went to the Gordon's but we never had a penny. Nobody else had a penny from Mrs. Gordon either. We never saw her. The door would open and close. It was a pity as Gordon was not a bad old chap on the whole. The men seemed to like him but they did not know his wife or want to know her. She wouldn't have anything to do with Penclawdd people and was rarely seen in the village. Local social visits were rare at their home. She was a failure in every way."

George Rees' sister, Glenys Harry, remembers her in a completely different light. "Mr. Gordon was a terror and his niece, May Jones was even worse, but Mrs. Gordon was an angel. I remember her well. My oldest brother, Aneurin, used to shop for her. He could never remember the name of Mazawati tea, which he used to buy in the Emporium, so my father used to write it down for him. He couldn't do any wrong in Mrs. Gordon's eyes. One day he scalded his foot. It was snowing heavily and I was outside making snowballs when I saw Mrs. Gordon walking up the hill to our house. I rushed in to tell my mother, but she told me, 'Don't be so silly,' but I knew it was her because she was wearing her cloak. She rarely went out of her house, but she ventured out in all that snow to see Aneurin, and bring him goodies. She loved him. One day, an incident occurred that proved her affection for him. It became a famous family story. Prothero Davies, who lived next door to Mr. and Mrs. Gordon, bet Aneurin that his Bantam cockerel would make mincemeat of Mrs. Gordon's Plymouth Rock cockerel. The fight took place and Prothero's cockerel won. They were vicious birds. May Jones was furious with Aneurin and wanted to call the police, but Mrs. Gordon said, 'No, no. The hens hated that cockerel. He was a very bad husband and they banded together and killed him.'

Mr. Gordon was more generous in his younger days. It was a high day and holiday when hay was gathered in Mr. Gordon's field. Even May Jones was human then. All the men not at work, and the children of Penlan, helped Mr. Gordon harvest his meadow. Summers were summers then. The harvest over, he rewarded them with a tea of sandwiches and cakes in the corner of the field in the afternoon.

On the western corner of his property, near the Trumpic Road, was a triangular field of fir trees – a rare sight in Penclawdd. My friend Ilene, and I, used to love wondering in the field with its beautiful smell of fir. We used to pick the fir cones and put them on the windowsills of our homes. We believed that if the cones opened it would be fine, and if they stayed closed, it would rain. Every Christmas, Mr. Gordon presented Llanyrnewydd Church, Capel Isaac and the Infant School with a large tree."

Gossip was created in Penlan when Gordon went on a cruise with his niece. Win Walters remembers, "When they returned, May Jones reigned supreme in the household. We questioned 'what happened on the cruise?'"

In the coal strike of 1915, coal was outcropping in Baker Haynes' field next to St. Gwynour's Church. Wilfred Tucker comments on Gordon's alertness to any connection with the local coal industry. "Father went to get coal as we had none for the house. Mr. Gordon got to know of it and it was stopped. Mr. Gordon had informed Mr. Haynes."

Gordon took and active interest in St. Gwynour's Church, which he attended regularly as a churchwarden. He was also its treasurer for a while. He had his own oak chair at the back of the church where the font is now situated. Wilfred Tucker recalls, "Every Whitsun Monday, sports were held in the field to the south of the churchyard. Mr. Gordon always had his pockets full of pennies. We'd have tea in the church hall and then we'd all traipse up to the field to have games. Mr. Gordon used to stand on the bank by the style. Someone always had a bat and ball and whoever caught the ball would have a penny from Mr. Gordon. Mr. Gordon was alright, but I never saw Mrs. Gordon." Win Walters also remembers the sports. "Mr. Gordon would throw sweets on the field and we would rush to pick them up. Sweets were not wrapped in those days and animals had been grazing in the field. What a thought! It would not be allowed today."

At the end of the church's financial year, each member of the congregation's yearly contribution was listed in financial merit and displayed at the back of the church. Gordon headed the list every year. Edgar Tucker, publican of the Royal Oak was anxious to introduce the envelope system for church collections, but Gordon was against it thinking it too much of a chapel custom. Eventually the system was adopted. At the end of the first year of the new system, the list was produced in the vestry in the presence of Gordon. Edgar Tucker's name was top of the list. Gordon questioned the list's accuracy and on having an answer in the affirmative, quickly made up the difference in the amount between his contribution and Edgar Tucker's plus a little extra so that his name was again head of the list.

One October afternoon, Win Walters remembers her mother, Rhoda Eaton, coming home from decorating the church for the Harvest Festival with dramatic news told her by Mrs. Thomas, the vicar's wife. "Mr. Gordon has lost every halfpenny of his money." Tegwedd Murley can remember her father, John Pugh Davies, relating how, at the time, he saw Gordon crying on the train from Swansea to Penclawdd and expressing his feeling of sympathy for him. It seems that Gordon had experienced financial disaster, and it was believed in the village that he had been declared bankrupt. He suffered a nervous breakdown, and it is possible that he never recovered from the shock as he died soon afterwards on 19 August 1929, at seventy-three years of age. He was not buried at St. Gwynour's Church where he had been such a loyal servant, but at St. Rhidian's Church, Llanrhidian, where many generations of the Gordon family lie buried.

Margaret Maud Sambrook, née Rees, had been in service in Penlan Cottage. Her son, Denzil, can remember his mother's kindness to Mary Jane Gordon in her time of need. "I can remember Mrs. Gordon – after Mr. Gordon's death – being in such dire financial straits that my mother used to make apple tarts, etc. for me to take down to old Mrs. Gordon. What a change of events isn't it. Mother was in service with them and they were good to her. That is why my mother repaid them. Mrs. Gordon was a small little woman, but she used to frighten me."

Gwyneth Durban remembers living near them. "Mr. Gordon had died by the time we came to live in Penlan from Mill Street, in 1932. Mrs. Gordon still lived in Penlan Cottage with her niece. They were the *crachach* (snobs) of the village. We used to bow to them. Mrs. Gordon used to drive in her carriage and pair dressed in a beautiful mauve taffeta dress to Penmaen Workhouse, where she was a governor or something."

The Reverend D. Thomas was succeeded by the Reverend Ben Evans in 1937. On the latter's retirement in 1954, the Reverend M. W. Davies became the parish's vicar the following year.

After M. W. Davies retired in 1972, the Church Governing Body decided that for numerous reasons, Brynhir House was unsuitable as a vicarage. It was sold, and a smaller, more modern house was purchased on the New Road in Crofty. Brynhir House reverted to a private dwelling, and renamed Tanglewood.

'The nonconformist denominations came into being from the seventeenth century onwards as a result of differing theological interpretations of scripture and consequently of worship and church government. The main seventeenth century sects in England were the Baptists, Presbyterians and Independents, together with the much smaller Society of Friends or Quakers. Most of these sects played a part in the religious history of Wales, although the principal ones were the Baptists and Independents. The eighteenth century saw the rise of Methodism, which broke from the Established Church and in turn split into several divisions, the two most important being Wesleyan and Calvinistic Methodism. In Wales, the Calvinistic Methodists later became the Presbyterian Church of Wales.

Baptist churches are generally self-governing within a Baptist Union. There are separate Baptist Unions for English and Welsh speaking congregations.

Welsh Independent chapels have for the most part remained separate from the English-based Congregational Union and the United Reformed Church (created in 1972 from a union of English Congregational and Presbyterian churches). They belong to a loose association, the Union of Welsh Independents (*Annibynwyr*).

The history of nonconformity in Wales is one of steady growth in the eighteenth century and explosive expansion in the nineteenth, with communities having at least one chapel, often several vying for prominence in inter-denominational rivalry. Baptist and Independent congregations are self-governing, whereas the Wesleyan Methodist and Welsh Presbyterian churches have a central administration.[5]

The first Baptist church in Wales was established at Ilston, on the Gower Peninsula, in 1649, by John Miles, and his fellow worker, Thomas Proud. But its life span was short, and the end of the century saw its demise.

In 1807, Joseph Harris (Gomer), a prophet of the Baptist faith, erected a chapel high on a hill between Penclawdd and Llanmorlais, with spectacular views over the Llwchwr Estuary to the opposite coastline. It was named Mount Hermon. The site had been the Sunday meeting place of the youth of the area, where they had congregated 'to desecrate the Lord's Day'. The building became a shipping mark for sailors, guiding

Mount Hermon Chapel. Built 1807.

them to the safety of Penclawdd Docks. Ronnie Lloyd, a staunch member of Trinity Chapel and its secretary for many years, acknowledges that it had not only been the geographical position of the chapel that had guided. "It put many people on course – on their sea voyages and on their spiritual path of life."

23 December 1817 saw Mount Hermon received its own ordained minister, David Thomas, a native of Waunelyndaf, Carmarthenshire. Six years later, Penclawdd Copper Works stopped – a common occurrence in its interrupted life – and many of the chapel members were forced to move from the area to seek employment elsewhere. As a result, the congregation diminished drastically, and David Thomas moved to Salem Chapel in Llangyfelach. He continued, with the help of Daniel Davies, a Swansea minister, to administer communion at Mount Hermon until 1836, when, suffering from a severe loss of voice, retired.

John Williams, who had come to Penclawdd in 1836 to run a day school at the chapel at Mount Hermon, was ordained in 17/18 October 1837. He continued teaching his young pupils as well as ministering to the spiritual needs of his congregation. On 24 November 1839, he married Susannah Lewis, a widow of considerable means. He acquired yet another occupation when he and his wife opened a general store in Penclawdd.

In about 1862, Mr. Stock, a dedicated Baptist, came with his family from Bristol to Penclawdd, as supervisor and director of the lead works, which had been converted from the copper works. An industrial boom ensued and wages soared. It was beneficial for the employees of the works to support the same chapel as their employer, and so consequently, Mount Hermon's congregation increased. The chapel's new wealth encouraged the members to renovate the chapel. The pulpit was replaced from the side to the end of the building[6] and new seats were positioned to face the rostrum.

But members began to realize that Mount Hermon was not conveniently situated for either its members in Crofty, Llanmorlais or Penclawdd. They were fortunate in receiving a gift of land in the centre of Penclawdd from their minister, which was part of the plot he had purchased to build his store and house. Trinity Chapel was opened in 26/27 November 1867.

Trinity Chapel. Built 1867.

The industrial boom continued in Penclawdd, and the chapel received another bonus. At the end of 1871 and the beginning of 1872, John Glyn Thomas of Maes-y-cwmmer, and his company, opened a tin-plate works in the village, he being its manager and a shareholder. Thomas and his parents took up residence in Burry House, and were active members of Trinity. Again the membership of the chapel increased. Thomas and his parents moved at a later date to Llangennech.

In 1872, John Williams resigned his ministry under the deep conviction that he could not do justice to both chapel and his business. A tablet was erected in his memory on the wall behind the pulpit.

> 'He was an earnest Christian and truly faithful to his ministry for 37 years. 'He being dead yet speaketh'. This tablet was erected by his numerous friends as a lasting record of the generosity of his heart and life.'

John Thomas, a young student from Pontypool College became minister of Trinity in 1874. By 1883, the strength of the chapel was at its zenith. The membership reached two hundred and its Sunday School pupils totalled two hundred and ninety-three: the maximum in the history of the chapel. However, in 1885, the tin-plate works closed for two years during which time, as at the closure of the copper works, many villagers moved away from the village to find alternative employment. The congregation suffered drastically, dwindling to almost half its size. Nevertheless, John Thomas served his members faithfully with an evangelist sincerity, and greatly involved himself in the politics, philanthropy, education and religion of the area. He was Chairman and later Clerk of the School Board, and secretary of West Glamorgan Baptist Association for many years.

The members of Trinity Chapel living in Crofty and Llanmorlais – deciding that travelling to Penclawdd was inconvenient – erected a schoolroom at Llanmorlais where Sunday School and the occasional service was held. The building was named Tirzah and was completed in 1905. The majority of the members in this area spoke English. One of John Thomas' last public duties was presiding at the opening services in May 1906. He died the next month, and was sorely missed. A tablet of white marble was erected in Trinity Chapel in his memory.

The Reverend Richards became minister of Trinity Chapel after John Thomas' death. Beatie Austin of the Ship and Castle public house was very friendly with his daughter, Nest. They were inseparable and both were known as 'Me and Nest'. Unfortunately, the Reverend Richards' stay in the village came to an unexpected and abrupt end. He lost his reputation in the village, but accepted his blame, and was forced to leave the ministry. Beatie Austin remembers sadly, "That was the one that caused the trouble. He went with another woman you see. This girl from the village was going there to clean, as his wife wasn't very well. She had a baby by him. He retired from the church and went away to live. I used to visit them but I was a bit young to know what had happened."

In January 1931, the trustees of Tirzah Chapel, Llanmorlais, approved that Tirzah should carry on as a body entirely on its own, as an English

Baptist Assembly. In October 1945, D. J. Jones of Soar Baptist Chapel, Llwynhendy, was ordained and became Tirzah's first minister.

The two chapels decided to hold an anniversary service at Mount Hermon, on the last Sunday in August. It became traditional for each chapel to choose the visiting minister on alternative years. The selected ministers deemed it a great honour to be chosen. Comments Ronnie Lloyd, "If a minister was invited, he's made it. He'd hit the jackpot. An introductory service was held for him on the Saturday evening, and on the Sunday, he preached at morning, afternoon and evening services. The quality of the preaching was such that it attracted a huge congregation rendering the chapel too small to accommodate all. So, given the weather, the services were held on the opposite side of the lane on the grassy slope of the *Graig*. Good ministers were popular and in great demand, so they had to be invited well in advance of the day. They were the big names in the ministry. A Baptist service concentrates on the sermon. The sermon is what it is all about. The last preacher at Mount Hermon was Menai Jones from Pontarddulais. He was an outstanding preacher. I can see him now even with my eyes closed. He was of a stocky physique. At the service we were too many for the chapel, but not quite enough to warrant going on the *Graig*, so the service was held in the graveyard. The minister stood on the doorstep and the congregation sat on the graves. Before he started the service he said, 'This may appear to be a put-up job but I assure you that it is not. I did not know when I came here that this would be my pulpit and the graves your pews, but this is my text already prepared, 'I know that my redeemer liveth'. During these outside services, the singing of the hymns was unaccompanied, but we were used to this, as Herman Chapel had no organ, no electricity and no heating. The walls – undecorated – were of grey cement plaster. Only the window frames were painted. The floor was sloping from the back and the seats were very narrow. It was not a comfortable place to sit. Apart from the quality of the preacher, there was no fear of going to sleep."

When Ronnie became friendly with Betty, the latter was not committed to any particular denomination and so joined Ronnie in his place of worship. Betty remembers, "I was brought up in the church as my father was church. When about twelve, I accompanied my friend to Bethel. I had not been confirmed in the church and had not become a member of Bethel. I was a free agent." Ronnie adds, "Betty was ripe for the picking and I picked her.

In Trinity Chapel, the Baptismal Pool is situated in-between the pulpit and the *Sêt Fawr* (Big Seat) – the seat where the deacons sit. It's about three-feet deep at the base of three steps. At the service, when we are submerged backward by the minister, the women wear white robes weighted at the hem and the men wear grey trousers and white shirts. Betty and I were baptized together on the same night when I was about twenty-five years of age. It was a tremendous sensation as far as I was concerned. Due to the pressure on my spinal cord over the years, I was unable to put my bare feet on cold surfaces without experiencing a reflex in my back, and my legs would go from under me. My mother was worried about my Baptism and so was I. The stone steps to the Baptismal well were cold and so was the water. I could have become a member without 'going through the water' but I wouldn't have it. Before the day of my Baptism, I experimented by putting my feet several times in a bowl of cold water, but everytime my legs went from under me. Anyway, on the day, my foot touched the cold step and nothing happened. I went into the water and again nothing happened. I went through perfectly. I couldn't believe it. When I returned home I put a foot in cold water and my feet went from under me again.

In 1884, my grandfather, who faithfully attended Trinity, went to the chapel to see a baptismal service. After the service, the minister invited anyone present to be baptized. My grandfather took advantage of the offer. At the time, he was living in a house attached to Hermon Chapel. He walked home in wet clothes over the *Graig*, which was covered in snow. On his arrival home, his clothes must have been frozen stiff. When he told his mother of his baptism he said that, 'the joy on her face was wonderful to see.' He survived the experience without having a sniffle."

After the last residential minister, Tom James, a native of Llanelli, left Trinity in 1937, the members relied on visiting ministers for many years.

Ronnie and Betty entertained the visiting ministers of Trinity Chapel in their cottage in Llotrog for lunch and tea on many Sundays. Ronnie has great admiration for them. "When they were in our home, their words made an even greater impression on us than in chapel. They were very ordinary, but great men."

Trinity services were originally conducted in the medium of the Welsh language, but gradually, as the older members died and the younger non-Welsh-speaking members joined, English was introduced into the services.

In 1813, Lady Barham, daughter of Admiral Sir Charles Middleton, First Lord of the Admiralty in Pitt's ministry, discovered Swansea accidentally when delayed there en route to her daughter's home in Somerset. During her stay, she became acquainted with the Reverend Kemp, minister of the Countess of Huntington Burrow Chapel, in Swansea. Lady Barham accompanied the Reverend Kemp on his frequent preaching visits to Gower. She was horrified to learn of the spiritual destitution of its people.

Nine months later she returned, and rented a beautiful Georgian house known as Fairy Hill, in Renolston, from the Stouthall Estate. Within nine years she had established six chapels in Gower. They were:

Bethesda	Burry Green	1814
Bethel	Penclawdd	1816
Trinity	Cheriton	1816
Paraclete	Newton	1818
Emmanuel	Pilton Green	1821
Mount Pisgah	Ilston	1822

Having no inclination to any particular denomination during her early years in Gower, she took the advice of Reverend Kept and arranged for her chapels to be officiated by ministers of the Welsh Calvinistic Methodist Faith. Rees Jones, of Llanfwrog, Angelsey, was stationed in Penclawdd in 1816. A year later, William Griffith commenced his ministry in Gower. Through the diligent work of the two ministers, a flourishing Cause was established in the village.

However, in 1821, Lady Barham decided to sever her connections with the Methodists. She wished her steward, William Hamilton, to be ordained, but as he did not comply with the Calvinistic Methodist ruling of having passed as a minister for the probationary five years, her wish was not granted.

The circumstance had little effect on the members of Bethel until a few years after Lady Barham's death in 1823. Rees Jones died in 1829, and on the appointment of his replacement, Reverend Peter Griffith, Llanrwst, of the Independent denomination, many chapel members seceded.

The 'split' rendered the membership of Bethel extremely weak, and the Reverent Griffiths' work did not prosper. He remained for just over a year before retiring to Llanrwst.

Mr. William Lewis, from Carmarthen College, succeeded Peter Griffiths. The former preached to a depressingly small congregation, and soon moved to Gloucestershire, where he died.

The Cause became so low, that the chapel was forced to close for a number of years.

It was reopened in 1839, under the ministry of the Reverend John Evans, minister of Three Crosses. Some of the villagers, who had been members in Three Crosses for many years, joined the flock at Bethel, and by 1848, the membership was about one hundred, enough to necessitate a gallery and new seating in the chapel. John Evans worked diligently in both Bethel, and Three Crosses, with a great amount of success, until his death in 1856.

In 1858, the Reverend J. Lloyd Jones, of St. David's, was called to minister both chapels. 1870 saw Bethel being restored and repaired as new, at a cost of five hundred pounds. The number of members at this time was one hundred and twenty-three. In 1884 a schoolroom – Capel Isaac – was erected in Blue Anchor. The Reverend Jones did not confine his work to Three Crosses and Penclawdd: he was also the Bishop of the area.

Reverend A. J. Jenkins (1846-1924).

The Reverend A. J. Jenkins came to Penclawdd as minister of Bethel Chapel on 23 September 1894. He had spent the preceding sixteen years as pastor of Trerhondda, Ferndale. Prior to becoming a minister, he had worked in various professions in turn – as a pupil teacher, a surveyor and a merchant. Initially, he lived in Barham House – attached to the back of the chapel – which had been built by Lady Barham, and later, in The Lodge, a large house in The Park area of Penclawdd, behind the Ship. In 1910, the members rebuild their chapel, on a larger and grander scale, on the site of the original building. When the Reverend A. J. Jenkins died in 1924, at the age of seventy-eight years, after a long and painful illness, he had served the chapel faithfully for thirty years and had been a minister for fifty years. The minister's burial at Parc Hendy Cemetery took place amid manifestations of great sorrow. The solemn cortege was one of the largest ever witnessed in the district, and was a representation of all classes of the community around. An article in a local newspaper paid tribute to him:

> 'Inflexible in his determination having once made up his mind, he was a formidable antagonist and fearless, yet the embodiment of sympathy and tenderness. When taking leave of his loved ones, he

Bethel Chapel. Rebuilt 1910.

remarked that, "It was only the old house that was being beaten and battered, but the tenant was perfectly safe."'

He was survived by his widow, Mary, and their three sons and four daughters.

1927 saw the commencement of the ministry of the Reverend Richards, who was renowned for his excellent sermons of a modern approach to religion. Their popularity filled the chapel to capacity, even attracting church members. On the first Sunday of every month, the minister shortened his sermon, and afterwards, invited the congregation to question it. The chapel had an even bigger congregation on these Sundays. Extra chairs were places in the aisle and even the foyer was full. Inhabitants from outside the village attended, sometimes hiring special buses to transport them. College lecturers as well as a professor from Aberystwyth University, who lived in the village, were usually in the congregation asking in-depth questions. Says Jack (Cardi) Davies "I couldn't understand some of the questions as they were so deep." The Reverend Richards taught Jack and his friends in Sunday School. Each week, the lessons, conducted in Welsh, followed the same pattern. A pupil was chosen by the minister to read a passage from the Bible. He then questioned each member of the class on the reading. The lesson was concluded by the Reverend's comments on his pupils' answers. Jack is full of admiration for his teacher. "He remembered everything each one of us said. He was a great thinker, and in my opinion, a genius. It was a great honour, and privilege, to have been his pupil in Sunday School." However, Reverend Richards, aware of his weaknesses, was known to include the words in his sermons, "Don't do as I do, do as I say." It was with great sadness that the villagers of all denominations saw the premature departure of the minister. The strong rumour that he had fathered an illegitimate child by a village girl was too unacceptable for his continued stay in the village, and he left in 1931. His brilliant ministry had lasted only four years.

The ministers' Religious Instruction is illustrated in a letter written by the Reverend Henry Hughes, who was appointed minister of Bethel Chapel in 1935, after the Reverend Richard's unfortunate departure. It reads:

'Bugeifa
Penclawdd, Swansea.
August 1944

Dear friends,

Thank you for your letters. I am glad that these news-sheets are acceptable, and that they help you to think about the highest and best things in life. One of you has asked me to explain the meaning of one aspect of the life and death of Jesus, for her own benefit as well as for the benefit of a circle of friends. This is what she says in her letter. "We know that He died to save us, but what we tried to fathom was, to save us from what"?

Well now, let us begin by stating that Jesus lived and died to save us from sin, 'the blood of Jesus Christ his Son cleanseth us from all sin' (1 John L7) The essence of sin is selfishness

It begins in a desire to serve God. That is what the Prodigal Son did when he asked to be independent of his father and went off to a far country, making himself a separated, isolated unit instead of helping his brother and father to till the farm. He wanted to enjoy himself regardless of everybody else, he wanted to live solely for the gratification of his own desires and impulses. Jesus came to show us a way of life which would free us from this sort of self-ishness, which is the root of all evil. 'God made you,' he said, 'and set you in the world to cooperate with Him in the working of His plan.' He shows us what He wants us to do; the motive behind all our actions must not be a desire to serve our own interests, but a desire to serve God and our fellowmen.

You know that acts are not good or bad in themselves. It depends upon the intention or motive in which they are done whether they become good or bad. The motive is the soul of an act. I read these words once, "Imagine to yourself a Red Indian in a wood with a little child on his knees, and he is cutting it with a sharp knife because it satisfies his lust to see the writhing agony of the child's limbs. His motive is cruelty. But then turn in your imagination to the operating theatre of some great surgeon and watch him doing the same thing. He too has a child on the operating table, and is making (perhaps) the very same cuts in the child's limbs. But his action is good, because his motive is to free the child from some disease of deformity, to liberate it into a fuller life. His motive is not selfish lust but a desire to cooperate with God to help the child." Jesus Christ in His life and death reveals the will of God, and shows by His example how we may cooperate with it. If we follow Him, if we allow His Spirit to rule our hearts, then we shall be freed from the motive of selfishness, which is the beginning of all evil. Jesus lived and died to save us from this.

I can only touch upon this aspect of the question here, but I hope that the above will shed some light upon the matter.

Y Golofn Gymreig

Daeth Adroddiad Eglwys Bethel am 1943 allan beth amser yn ôl. Bwriedais grybwyll amdani yn fy llythyr diweddaf ond nid oedd lle. Dyma i chwi rhai ffeithiau ohono – Rhif yr aelodau 477. Casgliad wythnosol yr aelodau £873.

Mewn llaw ddiwedd y flwyddyn £331. Gwelwch oddi wrth y ffigurau hyn ein bod yn ariannol o leiaf yn dal ein tir yn dda.

(Bethel Chapel report, 1943, was published some time ago. My intention was to refer to it in my last letter, but there was no room. Here are some details.
Number of members 477
Weekly contributions of members £873.
In hand at the end of the year £331.
It is evident from these figures that we are financially secure, at least holding ground well.)

Worth remembering.

Every man has a weak side. Every wise man knows where it is and will be sure to keep a double guard there.

Reverend Henry Hughes.

Please inform of any change of address.

With very best wishes,
Henry Hughes, (Minister)'

Reverend Hughes, a young man of twenty-one years of age, came from Penmaenmawr, in North Wales. A few years after his arrival, a manse was built in front of the chapel where he lived with his wife and in time, three daughters, Siân, Nest and Meinir. He was to serve his members faithfully for forty years. The Reverend Hughes was greatly loved and respected by the members of Bethel, and all who were acquainted with him. Joyce Richards, née Hodges, and her family – members of St. Gwynour's Church – who lived in Manchester House, were neighbours of the minister. She says of him, "He was a good neighbour, and a real gentleman. He used to visit everyone. His members went to Bethel Chapel for God, and also for him." The Reverend Hughes was rewarded for his kindness and diligence to his members, both spiritually, and materialistically, as he expressed during a local wedding:

'Wedding celebrations, silver wedding celebrations and golden wedding celebrations, when you work in a community like this you serve them the best you possibly can. But of course you are blessed to. Their attitude towards you and very often their courage and bravery under difficult circumstances inspire you to go on. I know these people very well. The land doesn't choose the hillside where it is born and the flower doesn't choose the place where it blossoms. And just like the flowers, love too has a way of coming through.'

In its formative years, the chapel's services and teachings were conducted in the medium of the Welsh language. Gradually, with the influx of English-speaking people through the metal industries, English was introduced.

Nevertheless, Welsh remained the prominent language. The Reverend Hughes compromised by conducting his sermons in half-English and half-Welsh.

When members of Bethel Chapel of the Calvinistic Methodist Cause seceded in 1829, they were without a place of worship and so met at various venues in the village – The White House Inn, The Great House farmhouse, Mount Hermon Chapel and different dwelling houses. Sometimes, through lack of suitable buildings, meetings were held outside at Ship Banc, in front of the Ship.

Eventually, the first Tabernacle Chapel of the Calvinistic Methodist Faith was opened on 3 June 1836, near the site of the present chapel. In 1844, members of the Cause living west of Penclawdd opened their own chapel, Penuel, on a hill behind Llanmorlais. William Williams of Penllyn, near Cowbridge, was chosen as pastor in charge of both chapels and was stationed at Penclawdd. William Williams was not to be ordained until four years later.

In 1851, he left the village to become pastor of Bethany Chapel, Swansea and was succeeded by Reverend Charles Bowen. Unfortunately, the young man died three years later at thirty-one years of age. He was followed in quick succession by David Saunders in 1856, Watkin Williams in 1857, and Thomas John in 1861.

Penclawdd lost a stalwart of Methodism on the death of the Reverend Williams Griffiths in 1861. Although he had spent thirty-six years of his ministry at Bethesda Chapel in Burry Green, he had taken a personal interest in the Cause at Penclawdd. He had become known as the Apostle of Gower, and in a sense was the founder of Methodism in Gower.

At this time, the membership of Tabernacle had slowly increased to about sixty members.

In 1864, the Reverend Morris Morgan was chosen as pastor. The industries in Penclawdd were at their zenith and were attracting people from outside the area in great numbers. Consequently, as in all places of worship in the village, there was a marked increase in the membership of Tabernacle. By 1866, it had increased to one hundred and nine. In the same year, Penuel was extended and a year later a new Tabernacle was completed on the site of the present chapel.

The industries prospered in the village and in 1876, four years after the Reverend W. D. Williams succeeded Morris Morgan, the congregation at Tabernacle exceeded four hundred in number, while the Sunday School was attended by one hundred and fifty-five scholars and fourteen teachers. The Reverend W. D. Williams had by this time been relieved of the care of Penuel which henceforth shared the ministry with Old Walls, Llan-rhidian. Consequently, he was able to devote greater attention to the Cause at Crofty.

The Reverend Hugh P. James' ministry saw the building of Zoer Chapel in Crofty in 1884. It was to be rebuilt in 1906, and three years later was to cease to be a branch of the Cause at Penclawdd.

Reverend D. M. Davies.

In 1888, the Reverend David Morgan Davies was invited to include Taber-nacle Chapel in his pas-torate of Penuel and Old Walls. His ministry saw the Friends of Tabernacle organize the building of a vestry in 1892. It was erected onto the back of the chapel.

Despite the gradual demise of the industries in the village at the end of the nineteenth century, the membership of the chapel, which had decreased to one hundred and forty five in 1888, increased to three hundred and forty seven in 1909. Many members felt that a new and better chapel should be built. A building fund was established and immediately a sum of over seven hundred pounds was raised. During construction, the Reverend D. M. Davies visited the chapel daily. When completion was imminent, the minister was on holiday in Llanwrtyd Wells. Sadly, he died there on 20 May 1911 and was never to see or preach in the new chapel.

The beautiful new Tabernacle, with a spire, was opened in 1911, and has become a landmark in the west-end of the village. The building, plus its organ, reached a total cost of five thousand and four hundred pounds. The chapel was to strive to reduce the debt for many proceeding years.

Tabernacle Chapel. Built 1911.

In May 1914, the Reverend Rhys Griffith Davies came to Tabernacle Chapel from Pontarddulais. In 1922, the minister christened Ronald Tucker, a dedicated Christian and staunch member of Tabernacle. But Ronald has not always respected the ministry and has vague memories of being severely reprimanded for his behaviour in chapel. "When I was young, I used to go to chapel with my Aunty Lil Guy and her friend, Gracie. Like most of the other women in the village, my mother stayed home to cook the Sunday dinner. Lil was only a few years older then me and so like a sister. One Sunday, when I was about four, Lil was unable to go to chapel and so Gracie took me. After the service, Mr. Davies said good morning to all the members. He said to me, 'Good morning Ronald.'

'Go on, you bugger you,' I said to him. Gracie was furious and vowed that she would never take me to chapel again without my Aunty Lil. I remember Mr. Davies better when, after his retirement to Sketty, he returned once a year to preach at Tabernacle.

Mr. W. E. Williams came in November 1928 when I was in the Infant School. He was a very caring, loving man. Like the other ministers in the village, he knew everybody. There were no cars and everybody walked and met and talked on the road. In the summer, some of the members of Tabernacle used to go for a walk up the *Graig* on fine Sunday evenings instead of attending chapel. It used to upset Mr. Williams and he used to say to his congregation, 'Well, well. All my work has been in vain,' and the tears would run down his face. Those who had gone for a walk would be told how they had upset Mr. Williams and the next Sunday the chapel would be full again. He took an active part in the Band of Hopes (operettas). He would occasionally help with the singing during rehearsals, but about a month before the performance, he would come regularly and 'put the polish on it'." Reverend W. E. Williams was a widower when he retired. He was proceeded by Reverend Thomas, a married man with no children. Reverend Williams, having lived in the manse for over twenty years, regarded it as his home and expressed a wish to continue residing there saying, "It's a big manse. Mr. and Mrs. Thomas are only two, and only one room I want." But it was of no avail. He vacated, moved to a cottage in Blue Anchor and the Reverend and Mrs. Thomas took up residence in the manse.

Throughout its history, Tabernacle has successfully provided for its mixed congregation of English and Welsh-speaking members by introducing both languages into each service, but with a prominence in English. Ronald Tucker remembers his father relating a tale that emphasized the difficulties in having a bilingual congregation. "He told me of a Gower man – called Mr. Beynon I think – who used to come to Tabernacle in his horse and cart. There was no Welsh spoken in Gower. All the ministers knew Mr. Beynon as he attended regularly. The man was hard of hearing and used a horn. When the various ministers had finished their preaching in English, they'd look up at him and say, 'There you are. You've had your lot now in English. I'm going on to Welsh so put your horn down and go to sleep.' So he'd put his horn down and go fast asleep."

The Reverend Lent, a Loughor minister, preached as visiting minister in Tabernacle Chapel for over forty years. He insisted on preaching in the Welsh language. After his retirement, he requested to preach in the chapel but was told he would only be invited if he preached in English. This he consented to. Ronald Tucker was in the congregation. "It was one of the finest sermons that I ever heard. His Welsh sermons had been wasted for forty years on most of the members of Tabernacle. We paid him about ten shilling for the day."

There was a great divide between the Established Church and the nonconformist chapels, and little integration existed between their members. The Reverend Ben Evans was particularly strict on the subject. In 1939, he was invited to the wedding of George Eaton a member of St. Gwynour's Church, and Marian Davies, a member of Tabernacle Chapel. As the ceremony took place in Tabernacle Chapel, he refused to enter the building, and stayed outside during the service. However, a harmony has existed at all times amongst the various nonconformist chapels in the village.

The latter stressed theology and the careful reading of the Bible. Ministers were highly regarded and had a vast knowledge of the Bible. They were often actors and exhibitionists, talents they put to good use when in the pulpit. The sermon was an extremely important part of the service. It was discussed in great depth amongst the chapel members after the service, in groups outside the chapels, and as they walked home together. During weekdays, the previous Sunday's sermon of each minister was retold and discussed amongst the members of all non-conformist denominations during their working hours, in the collieries and industries.

Deacons (Independents and Baptists) and Elders (Presbyterians-Calvinistic Methodists) played an extremely important roll in chapel life. Their duty, which was voluntary, involved the smooth running and maintenance of the chapel. They were held in high esteem by the ministers and members. To be elected deacon was a great honour – the accolade of confidence, trust, and appreciation. During the services, they sat in the *Sêt Fawr* immediately in front of, and facing, the pulpit.

All full members of the chapels were eligible for election, but it was not until the 1980s that female members were elected in Penclawdd. Only full members had the right to vote, which was by secret ballot. They chose those whom they considered to be good-living people, with the qualities of organization and reliability. Each denomination had its own rules.

Trinity's minister and existing deacons were asked, by the members, if more deacons were needed, and how many. A meeting was called in January to discuss same, and any other matters arising. One of the main stipulations asked of the candidates was that they be regular attendants of chapel services, prayer meetings and Fellowship. Voting took place by secret ballot in the chapel. Previous to the voting, those unable to attend were given the opportunity to vote at home. Each candidate had to obtain a seventy-five percent vote by the members. If this was unattained, voting was postponed until the next year.

No higher authority was involved in the election of deacons in Bethel Chapel. The deacons, unless choosing to resign, were deacons for life. Cyril Howells, when elected, was not happy initially. "I wasn't chosen to be a deacon because of my knowledge of the Scriptures. I have not been a great reader of them, as has my wife, Mary. I didn't feel I qualified to be a deacon, but Mr. Hughes assured me that the chapel needed people that could 'lend a hand'. I installed the central heating in the vestry. I charged nothing for my labour. I can't understand anybody taking money out of the chapel." Mary refers to her knowledge of the Scriptures on the subject. "The disciples themselves were a bunch of tradesmen and not academics."

The Presbyterians had a more complicated system. Members were given the opportunity to elect elders at least once in every seven years. The chosen candidates presented themselves to Presbytery (church court) to be conferred with regarding their background and religious experience, and in the Scriptures and the history and organisation of the Connexion. If Presbytery was satisfied with them, they were later ordained at an open meeting by the Moderator of the Association.

For no particular reason, there was a concentration of deacons living in Penlan. The two prominent families – Jenkins and Davies – boasted many deacons between them. Audrey Rees, née Jeffreys, who lived in Penlan until the age of seven years, was always aware of its theological aura. "Penlan was a fascinating place. It used to remind me of Jerusalem on a hill. One had to climb a hill whichever way one went there from the village. Most of the men living there were chapel deacons. It was always so peaceful up there. It was the quietness of it. There was no traffic: not a car in sight. Nobody had a car then and everybody walked everywhere. The only sound would be the birds. All that peace combined with those chapel goers. My uncles, William and Tom Jenkins were deacons, and all the Davieses were deacons, at Tabernacle Chapel. My Uncle William was a musical composer, music teacher, and choirmaster and organist of Tabernacle Chapel. He attended its morning, afternoon and evening services. I used to ask him how he managed to walk up and down the steep Trumpic Hill six times every Sunday. 'The secret is' he used to say, 'don't talk. Save your breath. Don't talk to anyone when walking up the hill.'"

Before the introduction of cars, funerals were grand affairs for the moneyed families of the area. Rabbi Bynon was a wealthy Gwernffrwd farmer. His granddaughter, Win Walters, remembers his funeral in Llangennith Church. "In 1919, at the age of seven, I attended the funeral with my parents, sister, Ilene, and brother, George. I was dressed in a grey coat and hat. All the adults were in black attire, the ladies wearing black veils over their faces. The funeral firm of Bullins, Dillwyn Street, Swansea was hired, which provided horse-drawn carriages and a large black hearse. The magnificent horses were draped with black ribbons and black tassels over their ears, befitting the occasion. We drove slowly from the farm at Gwernffrwd, through the narrow Gower lanes to Llangennith Church. The procession was quite spectacular."

If the family of the deceased had little money, the coffin was carried from the house to the place of rest. If a long distance was involved, it was carried in relays by a small team of bearers. Bullins also hired horse-drawn wedding carriages. Manure was smelt strongly in the vicinity of the firm's premises in Swansea.

The custom of Bidding Weddings as practised in Gower, survived until the beginning of the twentieth century. Some days before the ceremony, the Bidder, carrying a staff adorned with red, white, and blue ribbon, walked the neighbourhood. With a suitable Bidding Rhyme, he invited friends to the wedding ceremony, wedding breakfast and to give or 'heave' a contribution towards setting up the young couple as man and wife. To 'heave' meant that, if invited guests were unable to make an outright gift, they could make a contribution either in money or in kind. A record was kept of their contribution so that when any member of the donor's family was married, the recipients were expected to make a return gift of equal value.

Phil Tanner, a native of Llangennith, was one of the last Bidders in Gower. A rhyme used by him reads as follows:

'I'm a messenger to you and to the whole house in general,
To invite you to the wedding of Morgan Eynon and Nancy Hopkins,
The wedding, which will be next Thursday fortnight,
The wedding house will be the Ship Inn, Port Eynon,
Where the brides will take breakfast on plenty of good bread, butter
    and cheese,
Walk to Port Eynon Church to get married, back and take dinner,
And then I'll see if I can get you some good tin meat and some good
    attendance.
And whatever you wish to give at the dinner table the brides will
    be thankful for.
There will be a fiddle in attendance, for there'll be plenty of
Music there, and dancing if you'll come and dance,
There'll be fiddlers fifers drummers and the devil don't know what
    beside,
I don't know what.
There'll be plenty of drinkables there, so they tell me, but that
I haven't tasted.
And if you'll come to the wedding
I'll do all that lie in my power that evening if required
To get you a sweetheart apiece, if I don't get drunk:
But the brides is wishful you should come or send.'[7]

The bride and bridegroom were referred to collectively as 'brides'.

After the ceremony at church or chapel, the wedding party walked to the wedding house. The latter was any convenient building such as a church hall, vestry, inn, barn, etc. A fiddler headed the procession followed by the 'brides' and guests. Ropes held by local children were stretched across their path, halting them on route, and not allowing them to proceed until coins were thrown to the children.

After the formality of the breakfast was over, the 'house' was open to all and sundry. There was plenty to eat and drink at a cost, the profits going to the benefit of the married couple. The tin meat mentioned in the rhyme was traditional fare at the weddings. Mutton and vegetable pie, encased in pastry, was made in large tins and baked in local ovens.

Marion Jones remembers hearing of her aunt, Elizabeth Jane Francis' marriage to Thomas Rees, during the years of the First World War. It seems it was the last Bidding Wedding in Penclawdd. "The Breakfast was held in the vestry of Bethel Chapel. The pies – *Bwyd Mewn Tin* (food in a tin) – were made of lamb and pastry crust. They were cooked in large tins and were absolutely delicious. Nearly everyone in the village attended. Perhaps a small gift or half-a-crown were given to the couple for the privilege of attending. It was a 'bone of contention' with my father (Evan Thomas), that he had been to loads of Bidding Weddings and so had bid many present, but by the time of his marriage, the custom of Bidding Weddings had ceased." Bob the Cockney, Penclawdd's town crier, was probably Penclawdd's Bidder.

Wilfred Tucker, on marrying Elsie, broke with tradition in getting married in St. Gwynour's Church on a Sunday. He was anxious for his parents to attend their wedding, which was only possible on a Sunday, being the only day that their public house, the Royal Oak, was closed. Accompanied by Elsie, Wilfred Tucker went to the vicarage to ask the Reverend Ben Evans for permission to be married on a Sunday. He was rewarded for his bravery by permission being granted. Says Wilfred, "I didn't expect it, because he was a stickler and everything had to go by the book. It happened to be Easter Sunday. As the wedding service followed the morning service, the congregation of about two hundred, always large on Easter Sunday morning in those days, remained, and so as a result, the church was packed out for our wedding on that Easter Sunday morning of 1939."

Organised trips were always a great favourite with the members, church and chapels alike. A few family firms in the village ran a horse and brake hiring service – Tom Harry Mill Farm, Griffiths Band Row, and D. Leyshon – which were hired for the occasion. Parkmill, situated on the south of the Gower Peninsular, was a popular venue for the church trips. Wilfred Tucker enjoyed the treat. "It was a great day out. I remember one particular outing. It was raining. It was absolutely pouring. There were a number of brakes in the party. The curate at the time was D. Rees Enoch. The horses jibbed halfway across Fairwood Common, what was the cause I do not know, but they played pop. Cassie Thomas, later of Brynhir Lodge, was sitting in the front. It frightened her so much that she started crying and could not be consoled. We did manage to get to Parkmill eventually. The destination was a café, with a building in the garden, which served teas for large parties, now the site of Shepherds shop.

On another occasion, sports were organised in Park Lebroes Valley, in Parkmill. It was arranged that we travelled by the Vanguard Bus Company, a Swansea firm. The bus came as far as Brynhir Lodge, but no further, as if it came down the steep hill, it would not be able to go back up. All the families, including about a dozen (twelve) kids, walked up the steep hill to catch the bus. The Vanguard Buses were used to transport produce to Gower as well as passengers. The roofs of the buses where the produce was transported were made of wooden slats, with a rail around the edge to ensure their safe transport. A steel ladder was attached outside the back of the bus to enable the bus driver to reach the roof. The adults sat in the bus while we kids sat on the wooden slated roof, our feet against the railings. We were all quite young. I don't think it would be allowed today." George Eaton suffered so acutely from travel sickness that he couldn't even travel in a horse and brake, and so walked behind it on the church trips.

The church and chapels were an extremely important part of village life, providing a wealth of musical and social entertainment. Band of Hopes, plays, Christmas and Whitsun teas, whist drives, trips and bazaars were enjoyed by all denominations. The church boasted a strong Mothers Union Group and the Sunday School pupils performed nativity plays in the church at Christmas. The chapels organised concerts and oratorios of an extremely high standard, when local and visiting artists were invited. A well-known dignitary from the village such as G. E. Gordon, or Doctor Hughes, was invited as chief guest. *Eisteddfodau* (competitions) and penny readings were held for the children.

The Temperance Movement of the 1880s considered alcohol and drunkenness and consequently public houses a great evil, which undermined the Christian way of life. Temperance Hymns were composed to illustrate its message:

⚜ Tabernacle Chapel, Penclawdd. ⚜

A GRAND
Evening Concert
WILL BE HELD AT THE ABOVE PLACE
ON SATURDAY, NOV. 7TH, 1908
When Handel's Sacred Oratorio:

"The MESSIAH,"

WILL BEPERFORMED BY
✤ THE TABERNACE CHOIR. ✤

Chairman = G. E. Gordon, Esq., J.P., Penclawdd.

DOORS OPEN AT 6.45
TO COMMENCE AT 7.15 *Reserved Seat (No. 2) - 4/-*

'The Messiah' ticket.

'There is color in the wine glass,
There is fire beneath its crest:
There are sparkles in the goblet,
Gems of light made manifest,
But the hue is red infernal,
Hot with food for mad desire,
Every sparkle is a demon,
Gladly leaping in the fire.

There is laughter where they revel,
In their wild and drunken glee,
But 'tis cold, and false, and hollow,
Born for woe and misery:
Friendship form'd by wine is fleeting,
Love abhors its unchaste light;
Nothing born of wine is lasting,
With its sparkles joy takes flight. [. . .]

Minds of might and brilliant genius,
Which with light refulgent shone,

Now are dark, and lost and shatter'd,
And their strength and power gone;
Forms of bright majestic beauty,
Which a-mid our circles trod,
Now beneath the ground are resting,
Lost to us and lost to God.'

Words by E. Z. C. Judson. Music by J. R. Thomas.

The Movement led to the Welsh Sunday closing Act of 1881, which closed public houses in Wales on Sundays. The Movement called on the young to renounce alcoholism. Members visited schools to guide the children in the right direction. Win Walters remembers one of their talks. "They gave us a lecture on the greater nutritional value of milk compared to that of alcohol. It didn't mean a thing to me, as social drinking was not popular in homes at the time. All I was used to was a bottle of Sanatagen Wine at Christmas." The Band of Hope operettas were legacies of the movement, and were performed by members of the church and chapels for many years. They were extremely popular with players and audience alike.

In the first week of February 1949, St. Gwynour's Church performed its first operetta, 'Princess of Poppyland'. Gloria Lewis, née Morris, was its eponymous heroine. "I was fifteen years of age. Unlike the children who attended the chapels, it was the first time I had done anything on stage, and I was scared stiff. The chapels had been performing Band of Hopes for years, and also the *Gymanfa Ganu* gave their

Left to right: Harry Hayward – Chaplain, Gloria Lewis, née Morris – Princess of Poppyland, Doug Morgan – King.

children the opportunity to recite etc. in front of an audience. After Sunday School, I practised with Mrs. Evans the Railway who accompanied me on the piano. I also practised with Hilda Davies. The Band of Hope was her first public appearance as a pianist, and she later became church organist. It so happened that the dress I had worn for the previous Harvest Festival was red, and so it was suitable to wear as Princess of Poppyland, the operetta's theme colours being red and white. I wore silver shoes. The young dancing girls, organized by Mrs. Thomas, wore red and white dresses, and carried garlands adorned with red and white poppies. Ronnie Lloyd was the prince, Harry Hayward the chaplain, and Doug Morgan, the king. The musical score was written in tonic sol-fa. We practiced in the church hall and the operetta was performed in the Big Memorial Hall. I can remember walking down Penlan Hill in my thin dress through the snow."

The Reverend Ben Evans entered the following article in the March edition of the church magazine:

'Operetta – We offer our grateful thanks and sincere congratulations to the producer, Mr. D. W. Bidder, performers and helpers, who were responsible for the excellent performances of the Operetta, 'Princess of Poppyland'. The excellence of the production provoked a wealth of laudatory remarks from the three chairmen and their remarks were re-echoed by the large attendances which gathered from far and near.'

Gloria continues, "I took the principal part in the following three operettas performed by the Church – 'Pearl the Fisher Maiden', 'Zurika the Gypsy Maid' and 'Snow White'. My aunt, Gwyneth Durban, sewed my dresses for these parts, and also for the dancing girls. I retired from the stage when I left Gowerton Grammar School and started working in the bank, and Janice Stock took over the principal role."

Trinity held its annual concert on the night of the full moon in November. The same format was practised each year. Visiting artists – base baritone, tenor, soprano and contralto were invited. They were often winners of the Welsh National Eisteddfod held on the previous August. One year, the chapel was fortunate in obtaining the famous tenor opera singer, Stuart Burrows. The same format was followed each year. The first half consisted of a quartet by the four artists, proceeded by a solo from each. In the second half, the artists were coaxed into performing encores. The concert was terminated with another quartet.

On Good Friday afternoons and evenings, each chapel performed a one-act play – in the medium of the English language – in the Big Memorial Hall. The proceeds contributed towards the upkeep of the cemetery.

Eisteddfodau were held in the chapels when local school children of all denominations competed in writing essays, reciting and many musical events. At the age of about eight years, Gwyneth Durban and her older sister Elsie, having entered their essays under nom de plumes at day school, attended the *Eisteddfod* at Tabernacle Chapel on Christmas night with their mother Lizzann Barnfield, née McCarthy. The latter had been brought up in the Calvinistic Methodist Faith. She was the daughter of Cornelius McCarthy who had emigrated from Ireland to Penclawdd during the Irish potato famine of the 1840s and had found work in a local colliery. He had married Ann Morgan, a native of the village and daughter of a staunch Calvinistic Methodist family. Cornelius involved himself in village life and often entertained the wedding guests with his fiddle at the Bidding Weddings. At the age of twenty-one years, Lizzann had married Joseph Henry Barnfield, the son of Edward Barnfield. The latter had moved to Penclawdd from Cheltenham in 1876 to work on the construction of the Board School in the west-end of Penclawdd. He had married Ann Eaton, a local girl, and settled in the village. He was a staunch supporter of the Established Church and strongly against nonconformism. Gwyneth and Elsie were taken to the *Eisteddfod* on the condition that it was not mentioned to their paternal grandfather. "When we used to go to Tabernacle Chapel, Mam used to tell us not to tell *Dad-cu* (grandfather) Barnfield as he would be very angry. Mam loved going to Tabernacle, her heart was there, but she was loyal to Dad and went to church with him.

When the winners of the essay were announced – Mistletoe and Felix – we said to Mam, 'That's us.'

A whisper went around the congregation, '*Pwy ydyn nhw*? (Who are they?). Oh! The church girls have won.' I was so proud that I had done as well as Elsie, my older sister. When my turn came to go to the pulpit to collect my prize I was very nervous, as we were not allowed to go into the pulpit in church. My mother told me to go and I received a little silk purse hung around my neck by a ribbon. It had twopence in it."

Win Walters still vividly remembers Mary Tucker, née Guy, reciting the same poem with great fervour at each *Eisteddfod*:

'Tell me not in mournful numbers
Life is but an empty dream,
Because it is the soul of slumbers,

And things are not what they do seem.
Life is real, life is earnest,
And the grave is not the goal. [. . .]'

Mary was a serious competitor in the village *Eisteddfodau* and those in the vicinity. After her son Ronald was born, she competed only occasionally, but she told her son of her experiences. "My mother was a champion reciter. She would win at both the Tabernacle and the Bethel *Eisteddfodau*. On one occasion, she was unexpectedly beaten by Enos Guy. My grandfather was a collier in the Western Colliery. Enos was working with him as his 'boy' – his helper. All helpers were called 'boys' irrespective of their age. Somebody had told my grandfather that the adjudicator, Mr. Brainwater from Gorseinon, had been invited to tea at Enos' house on the day of the *Eisteddfod*. My grandfather had a very quick temper. On the following Monday morning he was on the coal in the tophole. When Enos joined him, my grandfather punched Enos all the way down the tophole. Enos proved his guilt by never asking my grandfather the reason for the assault."

Bethel and Tabernacle chapels held *Cwrdde Mawr* (Big Meetings) three times every year. These were very important in the chapel calendar. A visiting minister was invited to partake in a weekend of intensive services, Saturday night, Sunday morning, Sunday afternoon when Sunday School was cancelled, and Sunday evenings.

Each chapel held a half-yearly anniversary service. Bethel's was held in March and September, Tabernacle's in June and December, and Baptist's in July and January. At these services, each chapel was eager to introduce their preachers to the other denomination. On the anniversary day, one of the other two chapels closed. Two ministers were invited. One preached in the morning and one in the afternoon. In the evening, one of the ministers preached at the chapel holding its anniversary and the other preacher at the chapel that chose to open. When the lead works was operating in the village, the employees working on night shift attended the evening service in their working clothes – an unusual occurrence as 'Sunday Best' was always worn to chapel. However, the men often became so absorbed in the sermon that they failed to attend work that night. It became increasingly difficult to obtain good preachers and gradually the custom ceased.

The highlights of the year were the *Gymanfa Ganu*. They were held in Bethel Chapel on Whit Sunday and Tabernacle on Whit Tuesday. Trinity Chapel's was held on alternative years on Easter Monday in conjunction with Bethesda Chapel (Gowerton) and Zion Chapel (Waunarlwydd). All denominations held a tea and sports for their Sunday School pupils on Whit Monday.

Penclawdd has always been a village of immense musical talent and interest. The hymns to be sung at the *Gymanfa Ganu* were practised months before the forthcoming events – after Sunday evening service in Bethel and Tabernacle and also on weekday evenings.

During the late 1940s and 1950s, the pupils of the Junior School were taught the hymns in school hours, by their headmaster, Gwynfor Jenkins, who belonged to one of the great musical families of the village. During the *Gymanfa Ganau*, the hymns were sung with great confidence and *hwyl* (enthusiasm) reaching a crescendo by the evenings, the last verse of a hymn and sometimes, every verse of a hymn, repeated three times. These singing festivals were one of the few occasions when church members attended the chapels.

Olive Thomas, Penclawdd's postmistress from 1951 to 1995, remembers other preparations for Whitsun. "The week before, lime would be bought from Gowerton Steelworks and all the stone walls in the front of Sea View and the walls dividing the houses would be lime washed for Whitsun.

Whit Monday Walk, Bethel Chapel.

The two cottages behind the post office would have their cottage walls whitened as well as the garden walls."

The Whit Monday teas were the highlight amongst the Sunday School pupils and were looked forward to eagerly. Excitement reached fever pitch on Whit Sunday night when the new frock bought especially for the occasion was checked and white shoes were blancoed.[8] Win Walters comments "We did not need take drugs to be on a high. All we had to do was blanco our shoes." The nonconformists congregated on the Ship Banc and walked in procession easterly through the village behind their individual banners to the square outside the church hall. Here they formed an orderly circle and sang favourite appropriate hymns with great gusto. They then returned to the Ship Banc, sang more hymns and dispersed to their various halls for tea followed by sports in the nearby recreation ground. St. Gwynour's Sunday School pupils met at the church for a short service, which was followed by a procession behind their banner to the square outside the church hall. Here they also sang hymns followed by tea in the hall and sports in outside venues that varied over the years: the field south of the church and the field in front of Clifford House, Penlan, or, if raining, in the church hall.

Olive Thomas and her husband, Ambrose attended different chapels. "I was Baptist and Ambrose was Bethel. I didn't speak Welsh, and Bethel was nearly all Welsh then, while Baptist was mostly English. Ambrose walked with the Bethel, and the boys and I walked with the Baptist. But, Ambrose always came to the Baptist for tea. We used to have some fun in the vestry and tease him that our teas must be better than Bethel's. We used to buy big slabs of plain, seed and cherry cake from the Emporium. It was lovely. I used to go to the Emporium after Whitsun and ask Mr. Rees for a pound of the same cake that he had made for the Whitsun teas. But it never tasted the same, and although Mr. Rees assured me that it was the same recipe, I never believed him.

The roads had always been tarred and the girls used to get tar on their socks. The teenagers couldn't have their teas quickly enough so that they could go to the Pictures."

One's clothes worn on these religious festivals were of great consequence. It has always been said of the women of Penclawdd, "They know how to dress." The female members of the congregation, young and old, had new outfits – sometimes one for each service – and much thought, time, and money were spent in purchasing them. All walked to church and chapel in those days, and looked forward eagerly to viewing the other's splendour, as every year, the standard remained extremely high.

George and Marian Eaton's daughter, Carolyn Williams, who lived in Neath, stayed Whit Week with her great aunt, Sal Francis, in The Croft, Banc Bach. "Yes I remember *Gymanfa Ganu* at Whitsun. I remember it everytime there's a space of time of immense family importance, filled with high emotion – the morning of a wedding, Christening, Christmas Eve, Christmas morning, my children's birthdays.

I know I learnt that feeling, getting ready in the back bedroom of The Croft, my aunt's house, looking up at Bethel, in the morning sun. My mother was trying to wash my face and hands, again, with water from a huge floral jug, while the rest of the visiting family buzzed around in preparation. Was I two or three years old? My first *Gymanfa*? My dress was blue and white, smocked, with white bird buttons and two rows of white rick-rack around the hem. My shoes were blue with silver buckles. I dressed my doll in the complete outfit long after I'd outgrown it. I came to learn that everyone's outfit was always selected for the perfection of the style, material, and colour match of hat, gloves, shoes and handbag. It was not just outdoor smart – it was Ceremonial dressing.

As years went by, I learnt the tunes and the words: '*R'wyn canu fel cân a'r aderyn*', 'Onwards, forwards, rally round the banner', '*Aberystwyth*', '*Calon Lân*', '*Trewen*' – mostly in minor keys, all in tonic sol-fa.

But the Dressing! It was a main topic of conversation. What year was I all in champagne? What year coral? What year did the person, judged by my mother, the worst dressed, sing in mauve? What year did my mother wear the best, i.e. the largest hat – black and cream in many tiers of feathers?

My father missed so much, and spared himself so much. He was from Gower. He was a member of the church. He couldn't speak Welsh and he couldn't sing. He stayed at home to chop the mint for our roast lamb dinner. He'd send us off and welcome us back with, 'You all look wonderful,' holding the 'Daily Herald' or a book of poems.

With all the hats and shoes, blackcurrant tarts, kisses and hugs and endless conversation, and games up apples trees, I know for me it's the 'singing' that 'will never be done'.

NOTES

1. Llanyrnewydd: From the seventeenth century word Llannynwere.
2. Geoffrey R. Orrin, *The Gower Churches*. Swansea, The Rural Deanery of West Gower 1979, pp. 56-57.
3. See footnote 1, chapter 2.
4. *Ibid*.
5. Kim Collis MA DAS. *A guide to the collections*. The West Glamorgan Archive Service. (1998), p. 80.
6. It had originally been the norm when building chapels to site the pulpit on the side of the building
7. *Gower Journal, Volume 1*, pp. 22-23
8. Blancoed: Whitened with a white paste.

4

Working Underground

Coal has been mined in the north of the Gower Peninsula and the land surrounding the head of the Llwchwr Estuary for centuries. The earliest record of mining in Gower was in the mid-thirteenth century. In the sixteenth century, there were mines at Llanrhidian, Landimore and Weobley. Some belonged to Neath Abbey, while others were under lay-ownership.

Sir Richard Mansel operated the colliery at The Wern, Llanrhidian until circa 1686 to 1687, when two thousand tons of coal was exported. Before 1730, Mathew Price was developing mines under the salt marshes of Llanrhidian. In 1730, Sir Richard Mansel granted a lease to Robert Popkin, of Fforest, Pontarddulais, to work coal mines in Llanrhidian Parish, and to Gabriel Powell to work Llanmorlais coal works. A lease from Sir Richard Mansel enabled Gabriel Powell to export his coal from Salthouse Pill in Crofty. At the beginning of the eighteenth century, Sir Humphrey Mackworth took up a coal-mining lease at Penclawdd and in the glebe land at Loughor. In 1730, Thomas Popkin took a lease of coal mines in the Parish of Loughor.

Much of the coal was exported to Cornwall and Ireland, but home use increased as timber sources declined.

This area was on the edge of the South Wales coalfield where the coal was nearest the surface. It was the largest continuous coalfield in Britain, covering nearly one thousand square miles. It contained three main types of coal. Anthracite was found in its deep ranges, with the highest carbon content. These coals were not suitable for burning in an open grate or in steam boilers but ideal for use in central heating boilers. Steam coals occurred in its deep and middle ranges. The best steam coals burned with little smoke and gave a bright hot open fire. They were used in the steam boilers of ships and railway engines. Bituminous coals were found quite close to the surface and were used for burning in open grates, for manu-facturing gas and smelting metals.

The most common form of mining in the mid-nineteenth century in South Wales was the driving of drift mines. A passage was made into the hillside to reach the deepest coal seam. Drifts were known as levels or slants depending on the angle they had to be driven to reach the coal seam. At approximately ninety degrees to the slants, other levels about nine-feet wide were set each about forty to sixty yards apart. From these, topholes (vertical passages) were made to the next level, fourteen yards apart and about nine-foot wide. Crossings for ventilation purposes about seven-foot wide were made across the topholes.

The advantage of the slants to the coal owners were that they were inexpensive compared to the sinking of deep mines. They could be abandoned once any problems like flooding, gas or roof falls occurred and new ones could be fairly quickly and cheaply opened to replace them.

There were two main methods of mining coal – 'pillar and stall' and 'longwalls'. The former was the most commonly used in South Wales in the mid-nineteenth century, and a modification of this method was used in Penclawdd (known as the 'tophole' system). It was practically the only system suitable for seams dipping at an angle greater then twenty to thirty degrees. It was also the most appropriate for mining underneath valuable surface buildings, where there was a risk of flooding the mine with water through fissures in the rocks overhead, or when working beneath the river or the sea.

The topholes were the chambers in which the colliers worked, cutting the coal. Every ten yards approximately, pillars about thirty-foot square were left standing to bear the roof weight. At one time it was the practice to extract the pillars many years after they were formed. It was later found that by working them off as soon as possible after they were formed and before the roof weight had time to settle down and crush the pillars, a greater percentage of coal could be obtained. Moreover, if the pillars were left too long, ventilation became increasingly difficult, falls took place in the walls, and there was continuous danger of the pillars sinking into the soft yielding material of the floor or roof.

The seams were worked entirely by hand, with the aid of shotfiring the coal from the topholes. The coal was cast into trough shaped iron sheets, laid in the topholes, down which it slid to the bottom of the topholes. Barriers were placed across the bottom of the topholes to prevent the coal running into the levels. There, the trammers lifted the barriers and scooped the coal into the trams. At the headings (at the end of the slants), the coal was in piles on even ground, and so had to be shoveled into the trams. The trammers took the full trams to a double parting close to the slant, in readiness for the hauliers to collect. The hauliers' guided the horses along the level, stopping at each tophole for the trammers to unhitch an empty tram to fill with coal. On the return journey, the horses stopped at the topholes to receive full trams of coal from the trammers.

The 'longwall' method replaced 'pillar and stall' in most South Wales mines in the late nineteenth century. By this method the whole coalface could be worked at once. Pit props replaced the pillars. It increased the speed of the coal produced with a consequent increase in profits.

In Penclawdd, however, only 'pillar and stall' or 'tophole' was used because of the lie of the coal.

The majority of the colliery owners did not own the coal. The land above and below ground and the coal seams usually belonged to the landlords. The colliery owners leased the mineral rights of the land from them and bought the equipment and erected the buildings for their collieries.

Under the terms of such leases, the landlords received three types of payment from the colliery owners.

1. Rent for use of the surface or ground on which the colliery with its buildings and rubbish tips was situated. The rent was an annual sum, generally for a term of years.
2. Royalty for the removal of minerals from underneath the surface of the land usually calculated on a charge per ton of coal raised.
3. Wayleaves for right of way, which was a tonnage charge on the conveyance of material:

Individuals with quite modest amounts of money could set up as colliery owners as not much capital was needed to start mining operations.

By the late nineteenth century, limited liability companies[1] became the main type of colliery concern. Although these companies issued shares to raise their capital, most of the shares were held by the directors, who were in effect the owners. Very few of these shares were offered to the general public so ownership was in few hands.

In 1872, by an act of parliament, it became law for managers to undergo proper training to achieve a manager's certificate, and the same Act laid down the duties of managers and other officials:

1. He has the responsible charge and direction of the mine.
2. He has the control of all the officers and of all other persons employed in or about the mine.
3. He shall lay out the ventilation of the mine.

Under managers assisted managers and had special responsibilities for safety in the mine and the way miners carried out their work. Overmen took special responsibility for certain areas of the mine. Firemen had to have special qualifications in safety regulation. They were employed to carry out safety inspections, especially to detect the presence of gas.

The Mines Act passed in parliament in 1842 stated that no women or boys (under 10) were to be employed underground. However, the collieries of Penclawdd never employed female workers, as the local women thought gathering the cockle harvest of the Llwchwr Estuary a far healthier and more independent occupation. The majority of the male population in Penclawdd worked in the collieries and the metal industries.

Penclawdd and its surrounding area were underlain by rich seams of coal. However, these seams presented problems when worked. They sloped northwards at a steep angle creating a drainage problem and consequently were extremely wet and prone to flooding. Faulting was also acute. Because of these complications, the coal seams could not be worked profitably for any distance, so large-scale workings were not a viable financial proposition. Most of the collieries had short or interrupted lives.

By the late eighteenth century, a copper works was operating in Penclawdd. It was easier and more economical to bring copper to coal than vice versa and Penclawdd, with its proximity to a good coal supply, as well as having an adequate port, was in a suitable position. The copper works was converted into a lead works in the nineteenth century. In 1872, Mr. John Glyn Thomas erected a tin-plate works next to the lead works. Growth of these metal industries, which needed coal, and the continuing need for coal for domestic use, halted its export from Penclawdd, and consequently, more small collieries were opened in and around the village. Many of these were served by private sidings or tramway connections to the railway, including the Elba, Alltwen, The Drive, Beaufort, Caereithin, Wernbwll, Penlan and New Penlan, New Lynch Upper and Lower Llanmorlais, Cwm Vale and Morlais Vale Collieries. The Drive and New Lynch sidings were particularly noteworthy, each being about half a mile in length.

By the turn of the twentieth century, the metal industries in Penclawdd had closed, but the growth of metal works in nearby Gowerton and Gorseinon, and their surrounding districts, ensured the continuous need for the supply of coal locally.

The tin-plate industry came to Gorseinon in 1881 and was expanded in 1885 by the Lewis family (William, and his sons, David William Rufus, and Thomas). This was the Gorseinon Tin-plate Works (the old works). The Grovesend Tin-plate Works were set up in 1886, which combined with the steelworks in 1904. In 1897, the Lewis family built the Bryngwyn Steelworks. The Elba Steelworks, Fairwood Tin-plate Works, and Gowerton Foundry were also operating and the last of the tin-plate works – the Mardy Tin-plate Co. – was started in Gowerton in 1910.

The Elba Colliery, Gowerton, was situated within a mile to the southwest of the village of Gowerton, about two and a half miles east of Penclawdd. The first reference to the Elba Colliery appeared in the list of Mines 1881 as the Elba Main, the property of A. Ll. Pearse and Company. Like many collieries in the area it had an interrupted working life. It was abandoned in February 1886 when A. Ll. Pearse was known to have been bankrupt. In 1888, the colliery was worked by Wright, Butler and Company. In about 1902, it was taken over by Messrs Baldwins Limited.

One hundred men were employed to raise over one hundred tons of its bituminous coal a day, its output being used in the firm's Elba Steelworks in nearby Gowerton. It was on the southern outcrop of a seam locally known as the Three feet, which, together with the Six feet and Five feet above, and the Two feet below, had been worked in the neighbourhood for many years. It was worked by means of slants and the 'pillar and stall' method.

The colliery employed men from the surrounding areas of Gowerton and Three Crosses, but the majority of its employees lived in Penclawdd. They walked to their work, three miles being a most acceptable walking distance in those days.

On Friday, 20 January 1905, about forty-eight men reported for night shift duty, arriving at 5.00 p.m., earlier than other days, as Friday was payday. All gathered to descend the slant as usual, but one, George Rees of Penclawdd, had a premonition of impending doom, instigated by a recent dream. Although he voiced his fears to his work mates, all miners carried on regardless. Between 12.30 a.m. and 1.00 a.m. an explosion of gas occurred in the Six feet seam in the lowest heading to the west known as No. 7 heading. The uninjured men hurried to the surface, assisting injured men to safety en route. Herbert Griffiths (manager) was summoned and was soon on the scene. He entered Slant Three where three burned bodies were seen immediately. A fall was discovered and gangs sent to remove it, but being ten to twelve yards in length, it was estimated that it would take eighteen to twenty-four hours to clear.

Where possible, injured men were helped to the surface and taken to the carpenter's shed. The bodies of the dead men were laid in an office building. Doctor Abel Davies and Doctor Hughes of Penclawdd arrived soon after being informed of the accident, and gave all assistance to the injured men in the shed, and also to the injured still in the slant. The men's worse injuries were horrific burns from coal gas. The miners were taken to their homes by horse-drawn cabs, where trained nurses were instructed by the doctors to continue vigilance and medication. George Williams, a young boy of fourteen years, died en route home. He had been working at the colliery for only three weeks before his premature death.

The Loughor Rescue Brigade.

On a roll call of employees, all but three were accounted for, and it was assumed that the unfortunate men were underneath the fall. Their bodies were eventually brought up to the surface. Some of the injured died in their beds at home, bringing the final fatalities to eleven. They were:

Alec Ogilvie, Gowerton. Single. Trammer. Aged twenty years.
William Bowen, Three Crosses. Single. Coal shifter. Aged seventeen
    years.
William Davies, Penlan, Penclawdd. Married. Collier. Aged fifty-
    nine years.
Tom Pratt, Penclawdd. Coal shifter. Aged nineteen years.
Edward Rees, Penclawdd. Collier. Aged twenty-six years.
David Davies, Penclawdd. Married. Collier. Aged twenty-six years.
George Williams, Penclawdd. Single. Door boy. Aged fourteen years.
David J. Rees, Three Crosses. Single. Trammer. Aged twenty-one
    years.

George Rees, Penclawdd. Single. Trammer. Aged twenty-three years.
W. H. Morgan, Penclawdd. Single. Trammer. Aged eighteen years.
John Long, Three Crosses. Married. Repairer. Aged forty-five years.

The seven injured men were:

Thomas Bevan, Cefnstelle. Married. Slightly burned.
David Edwards, Three Crosses. Married. Slightly burned.
D. Ogilvie, Gowerton. Slight burns.
J. Davies, Penclawdd.
John Austin, Three Crosses.
Henry Rees, Penclawdd. Married.

Seven out of the eleven fatalities were natives of Penclawdd, and apart from Tom Pratt, were members of Bethel Chapel. On the Sunday after the accident, the Reverend A. T. Jenkins, minister of Bethel Chapel, was so overcome with emotion, that he turned his service into one of prayer. The village of Penclawdd was in great shock and deep mourning. The following week saw a succession of seven funerals. The six funerals at the cemetery were officiated by the Reverend A. T. Jenkins (Bethel) and the Reverend D. M. Davies (Tabernacle). Tom Pratt was laid to rest in the churchyard of St. Gwynour's Church.

Penclawdd Elementary School was closed on 25 January for the funeral of three of the miners, and on the following day, for four further victims. On 27 January, there was a 'reduced attendance owing to the gloom and sorrow caused by the Elba Explosion.'[2] Mr. E. J. Long, a teacher on the staff of the school, was absent all the week as his father, John Long, lay seriously ill suffering from severe burns. The teacher did not return to school on 30 January, as his father had died the previous Friday evening. The school closed again on 31 January for the funeral. *Ben-y-Saer* undertook the funeral arrangements.

A group of mining officials examined the district underground where the explosion had occurred. They came to the conclusion that a 'blower' (a pocket of gas) must have been struck near the fault. George Edward Gordon, mining engineer, examined the area and gave his official report. He thought that the explosion was due to excess gas caused by disturbed ground.

John Williams, the Miners' Agent, advised the relatives of the deceased to place a claim under the Workmens' Compensation Act. The assurance company – Injured Provident Clerks Insurance Society – accepted the views of colliery management and independent colliery officials that an accident had taken place, and compensation was paid as follows:

For widows or families that had been totally dependant on the deceased, two hundred and sixty pounds.

For widows or families that had been partially dependant on the deceased, eighty pounds.

The injured miners were paid a sum for loss of work.

As a result of the explosion, the colliery was abandoned by Baldwins in 1905, and plans were filed with the Abandoned Mines Office at the Home Office. In 1906, the Elba Colliery Company and later, in 1910, the Elba Colliery Company (1910) Ltd. tried unsuccessfully to run the colliery as a going concern. In 1913, the Elba Colliery Company (1910) went into voluntary liquidation and the Elba Colliery finally closed.

Today, the only evidence that remains of the colliery is the ivy-clad ruins of the tower, and the offices and carpenter's shed, in a small wood south of the Gowerton-Penclawdd road, a few yards west of the Pont-y-Cob Road to Loughor.

The Welsh poet, Vernon Watkins (1906-1967), describes the experiences of a young boy 'working underground', in his poem, 'The Collier':

'A coloured coat I was given to wear
Where the lights of the rough land shone.
Still jealous of my favour
The tall black hills looked on.

They dipped my coat in the blood of a kid
And they cast me down a pit,
And although I crossed with stranger
There was no way up from it.

Soon as I went from the County School
I worked in a shaft. Said Jim,
'You will get your chain of gold, my lad,
But not for a likely time.'

And one said, 'Jack was not raised up
When the wind blew out the light
Though he interpreted their dreams
And guessed their fears by night.'

And Tom, he shivered his leper's lamp
For the stain that round him grew;
And I hear mouths pray in the after-damp
When the picks would not break through.

They changed works there in darknesss
And still through my head they run,
And white on my limbs is the linen sheet
And gold on my neck the sun.'

George Edward Gordon was a prominent figure in the mining industry of Penclawdd and its surrounding area. In 1898, Mr. and Mrs. G. E. Gordon cut the soil for the sinking of Penlan Colliery[3] with a beautiful ceremonial spade which had a silver blade and ebony handle.

In the early 1900s, he was mainly responsible for securing the Workmans' Train Service from Llanmorlais to the colliery in Clyne Valley. In 1907, in appreciation, he was presented with an illustrated address:

'We, the undersigned, on behalf of a committee formed to get a special Workmans' Train Service between Penlan, Llanmorlais and the Clyne Colliery, hereby beg to present you with this token of our high appreciation of the service you so kindly rendered in securing this long felt necessity.

We feel we should have been utterly unable to succeed in this matter without your guidance and assistance and we readily admit that the practical part we took was very insignificant with that so effectively performed by you.

Your well-known kindness and affability have secured you a wide circle of friends amongst the influential businessmen of Swansea and neighbourhood, therefore in leaving the matter mainly with you, we felt that we were adopting the best possible course in this, giving greater freedom to your mature experience to accomplish the desired object.

Not only do we as a Committee feel our indebtedness to you, but all the inhabitants of the village concerned join in this expression of gratitude, for the Train Service secured has proved a great and well appreciated conveyance.

Having been the recipients of many other kindness from your ever ready and generous hands, the more heartily do we beg your kind acceptance of this Address.

Invoking the richest blessings of Providence on all such kind actions,

We are Sir, yours sincerely,

John Jenkins, Chairman.
John Rees, Treasurer
Richand Lewis, Secretary.   December 1907

Gordon became famous for his maps of the South Wales coalfield. In 1897, he produced a large map illustrating the South Wales coalfield with its collieries and railways. In 1905, he issued an up-to-date version including the metal industries with their owners' names. The map was updated again in 1921.

Up to the end of the nineteenth century, the Liberal Party had totally dominated Welsh politics, but the beginning of the twentieth century saw the formation of the Labour Party. After a ballot of miners in 1908, their union, the South Wales Miners Federation (SWMF) decided to affiliate to the New Party.

In the Gower Rural District Council elections of May 1919, the successful councillor was to become an alderman. Gordon, who had been a Liberal councillor for many years, stood for re-election. His neighbour, W. Henry Davies – weigher, secretary of the SWMF, and a popular figure in Caereithin and Wernbwll Collieries – stood against him as Labour candidate. Most villagers assumed that Gordon would be re-elected as he had served long-term as a councillor and had been Chairman of the Gower District Council the year previous to the election. It seems that Gordon did not share their confidence, as he approached his opponent requesting him to stand down at this election, and make the way clear for himself to become alderman. He suggested that W. Henry Davies could have his turn another time. His opponent obviously ignored the request, as he was the successful candidate. Gordon was greatly affected by his defeat. Wilfred Tucker remembers his reaction. "Mr. Gordon never stood for council again. He was so dis-appointed at having missed the chance of becoming an alderman and thus a councillor for life." The election result seems to have instigated Gordon's retirement from numerous activities, for example, his resignation from the Board of Gower Union Guardians. His wife, however, remained involved with the Board until she moved to Porthcawl in the early 1930s, after his death in 1929.

In 1922, the death of John Gower-Williams,[4] Labour MP for Gower, which included Penclawdd, created a bye-election. Julian Grenfell, Labour candidate, won the seat. Marian Eaton remembers canvassing with her father Henry William Davies, agent for Julian Grenfell, by taking papers around the houses in the village. "We did not argue on doorsteps. Politics were not discussed much but the villagers were very serious in their political beliefs and actions." Gower remained a labour stronghold for many years.

1924 saw the first Labour-Liberal coalition government in Britain, with Ramsey MacDonald as the first Labour Prime Minister.

In 1913, the South Wales coal industry reached its zenith with a coal output of fifty-six million, eight hundred and thirty thousand, and seventy-two tons, but as a consequence of the 1914-18 War, the 1920 figure of coal production was ten million tons lower.

During the war there was a high demand for Welsh steam coal for the navy, but, as miners were conscripted into the armed forces there was a shortage of manpower to produce the coal needed. The SWMF thought that the country's great need for coal, coupled with their strong belief that the colliery owners were making record profits, put the miners in a strong bargaining position for higher wages. The colliery owners refused the miners' demand for a new wage agreement in July 1915 and consequently two hundred thousand South Wales miners went on strike. The miners were opposed by, the colliery owners, the government, and even the Miners Federation of Great Britain, who believed that a strike would stop the coal supply to the navy. The Welshman, David Lloyd George, Liberal Member of Parliament and Minister of Munitions, settled the strike on the government's behalf, granting the SWMF most of its demands. To ensure that the coal supply to the navy was secure, the government took control of the South Wales coalfield in 1916 and a year later, the British coalfield.

At the end of the war, a Royal Commission, which had been set up to decide on the future of the coal industry, issued a report in 1919 in favour of nationalization.

However, in 1921, the government decided to return the control of the industry to the colliery owners. The latter decided that the miners wage rate had increased in excess during government control and demanded that the miners accept lower wages or be unemployed. 1 April 1921 was the start of a three-month lock out[5] of one million miners in Britain who refused to accept the new terms.

As in the whole of the South Wales coalfield area, with so many of its males employed in the coal industry, the 1921 coal strike greatly affected the families of Penclawdd. The miners and their wives used ingenuity and sheer determination to support their families in these extremely difficult times. David Henry Rees, an inhabitant of Penlan, was known locally as Dai Staff, as his father was from Staffordshire. He was a miner in Caereithin Colliery, Three Crosses, and father of seven small children. He decided to take advantage of the work available in the construction of the Gowerton-Penclawdd road that was being made at that time. He bought a horse and cart and became self-employed in helping transport material for the making of the road. His wife, Marged May, gathered cockles and travelled twice a week, by train to Swansea. She walked across the Ha'penny Bridge[6] over the River Tawe to St. Thomas in east Swansea, where she sold her cockles and garden produce of fruit and vegetable door to door. She returned home on the 2.30 p.m. 'Relish Train'.

During the strike, 'soup kitchens' were organized in the Small Memorial Hall where daily meals were provided for the children of the miners. Vegetables, meat and bread, etc. were contributed by local farmers and village shopkeepers. David Henry Rees' son, Griff, enjoyed the meals. "I used to go to the Small Hall with my brothers and sisters. The weather was very warm. The potatoes and swedes were boiled in large cauldrons on a fire outside the Hall. Inside, where we ate the meal, the meat and gravy was cooked. Although on strike, my father was earning good money on the road and us kids were eating in the 'soup kitchen', but my father did contribute to them."

As did many shopkeepers, E. M. Rees cooperated with the villagers by introducing the slate system for payment in his Emporium shop, the debts to be settled after the strike. But even after the strike was over, if debts were not paid he still did not demand money. Some he received and some he did not.

By the end of June of that year, the SWMF accepted defeat, not having received the promised support of the Transport Workers and the Railwaymen. The miners returned to work under the colliery owners' terms.

The largest and most successful coal seams in Penclawdd were the Penlan and Penclawdd seams. They followed the same line, the Penlan seam being above the Penclawdd seam. The latter was known as the Big Vein, and was considered by the local miners to have, 'the best coal in the world'. They were worked separately by means of slants from the surface in Caereithin and Wernbwll Collieries where the 'pillar and stall' or 'tophole' method of mining was used.

Caereithin Colliery was owned by D. D. (Danny) Williams, which he had inherited from his father. The manager was John Phillips and the under manager, Olly Rees. It was situated about two miles southeast of Penclawdd, near Three Crosses.

Jack Davies joined the payroll of Caereithin Colliery in June 1922, at the age of seventeen and a half years. He is a native of Cardiganshire, hence his nickname, Jack Cardi. He comes from a seafaring background, his father and two brothers having been in the navy. "My father was serving on the ship Majestic at the turn of the twentieth century. I can remember his suits, one of white and one of navy." Jack's ambition was to join the navy, but fate intervened. Instead of a life on the open seas, he worked underground in the collieries of Penclawdd and area.

After leaving school at fourteen years of age, Jack laboured on a local farm. He earned nine pounds per annum and when he left three and a half years later was earning sixteen pounds per annum. "I was working on a farm and saw no future in it. I was working twelve hours a day, seven days a week with no holidays apart from a half-day off twice a year. My father died when I was about ten years of age and my mother was left with five children. My mother had eight shillings a week on parish relief. She was a very proud woman. She took in washing, and charged two shillings for a large basketful of clothes, washed, ironed and aired. I wanted to work to be off her hands."

Jack and his friend, Ben Morris, decided to better their employment. They travelled together by the Great Western Railway to Gowerton. They hired a room for the night in the Commercial Inn, situated in close proximity to the station. The two boys were in unknown territory. At the inn they met John Culli, who helped them find employment. "John Culli told us that they were looking for men in Caereithin Colliery, Penclawdd. He had a slight speech impediment and when he said Penclawdd we thought he had said Porthcawl. 'Oh!' We thought, 'Porthcawl would be a lovely place to work.' He directed us along the Gowerton-Penclawdd road, which was under construction at the time. We reached the Berthlwyd pub and asked if we were on the right road to Porthcawl. We were told that we were going the wrong way. When we discovered that we were in Penclawdd we realized our mistake, but it did not matter. We were directed to the colliery yard and office which were near the pub, where, after being asked many questions about our previous employment, we were given work in Caereithin Colliery, to start that very night."

Jack's first job was labouring at night, packing the wall where the coal had been drawn. "It was quite a good job and I didn't mind the work, but I had no interest in being underground. I hated every minute of it. I wanted to be at sea." Jack worked six nights a week and was paid an extra shift for working nights. "I earned two pounds fifteen shillings a week. It was a fortune. I didn't have much money to spare as I was paying one pound five shillings for food and lodgings with Mr. and Mrs. Aires, who lived in the Old Council Houses. They were good people. I stayed there until I married."

Soon after Jack commenced work, he experienced three frightening incidents that he was to remember for the rest of his life. Willie Haynes, an employee of the colliery, had served his country in the army during the First World War. When in action on the Adriatic coast of Italy, he was bitten on the back of his head by a mosquito. A large lump ensued which failed to subside. He was also suffering from shell shock. His mental health was seriously affected, manifesting in violent fits, demonstrating great physical strength. Fortunately he hurt no one, but Jack remembers the witnessing of these attacks being an extremely frightening experience. While working a night shift, Jack happened to be in close proximity to Willie in the level. Without warning, Willie suddenly swung from the bars at the roof of the level and hurled himself at Jack's throat. "He was a heavy man, about three times my weight, and he had me down flat on the floor. I said, 'What are you doing Willie?' He immediately released me, but seemed puzzled and unaware of his actions."

A few nights later, Jack and seven of his colleges were taking their food break. "We were sitting in a row on a tree stump in the level. Willie suddenly appeared with a hatchet and the look in his eyes was terrible. He placed the blade near each of our faces in turn, and then threw it into a nearby tophole. A haulier emerged from the tophole guiding his horse. Willie threw himself at the animal, knocking him down on his side. He then grabbed the horse and put him back on his feet. Such was the strength of the man when he was in that state. We were shaking like leaves." Jack has great admiration for Johnny Rees the fireman on duty at the time. "He told the men to go back to work and stayed with Willie until the end of the shift. Willie never worked underground again."

Jack felt inferior to a certain group of young men working in the colliery who were going to night school to improve their education. He admits that when in school he neglected his education and blames only himself. "I met some of the finest boys that you could hope to meet when I worked in Caereithin Colliery. They were studying at night school and eventually all left the mine to better careers elsewhere." One of the group studied theology, and became vicar of St. Paul's Church, Sketty, Swansea. Thomas Dalimore went to night school, and also studied correspondence courses. He left mining to join the teaching profession.

Jack soon accompanied them to night school, where he studied mining and marine engineering, as he still hoped to join the navy. "I was always good at mathematics, especially mental arithmetic. The classes, run by the local authority, were held in Penclawdd Elementary School and Gowerton County School. I was taught by Mr. James of Gowerton. He was a wonderful teacher." Jack studied for five years and obtained his fireman's certificate. There was no vacancy for a fireman in the colliery at the time, so Jack became a shotfirer.[7]

Miners were renowned for their deep discussions on many subjects but mainly politics and religion. These usually occurred when they sat together during their twenty-minute food breaks, which they could take at their own convenience. The colliers choose the period immediately after shotfiring, while they waited for the smoke to disperse, and the dust to settle. After

Jack shotfired the coal, he hurried to listen to their debates. "I always tried to get back to listen to them. Most of the colliers were members of Bethel Chapel. Mr. Richards, the minister of the chapel in the late 1920s, was an outstanding preacher and teacher. They discussed religion and politics. They discussed everything. Politics was number one subject except on Mondays. It was always religion on Mondays when they used to pull Mr. Richards' sermon to pieces. It was politics the rest of the week, especially if there was an election pending. They were very strongly politically minded in their labour beliefs.

I went to night school, chapel service and Sunday School with the crowd I worked with and so greatly admired." Jack was employed in Caereithin Colliery until it closed in the late 1930s.

By the early 1920s, the coal industry throughout Britain was on the decline but it was more marked in South Wales. Part of the reason for the diminishing production of coal in all coalfields was that oil, being cheaper, cleaner and easier to handle had started being used. The main contributing factor as to why the South Wales coalfield suffered more than other coalfields was its geological difficulties, which resulted in coal mining being more expensive.

In this time of crises, the large colliery companies were able to survive more easily than the smaller companies, as they were often not totally dependent on the coal industry. The owners believed that the problem was the high cost of coal production, which was caused by the short hours and high wages of the miners. In 1925, all colliery owners asked their miners to accept cuts in wages and an extra hour on their working day. The miners refused. The Miners Federation of Great Britain, under the leadership of A. J. Cook, fought the proposal with the slogan, 'Not an hour on the day. Not a penny off the pay'. On 30 April 1926, the miners who refused to accept the colliery owners' terms were locked-out of work, and the British coalfield came to a stop. On 3 May 1926, they were joined by all trade unionists and a General Strike in Britain ensued. After nine days, the Trade Union Congress called off the General Strike, and the miners fought on alone.

Jack Davies stayed in Penclawdd for a short time. "I thought the strike wouldn't last long, so I stayed in Penclawdd for about two weeks. I then realized that it was going to carry on for quite a while, so I decided to go back to Cardigan. I bought a second hand bike for two pounds from Rufus Harris. Two of my friends accompanied me to Carmarthen. There we had a cup of tea together and I went to Cardigan, and they went back to Penclawdd." There was little work in Cardigan and Jack was soon short of money. "I had a few odd jobs in Cardigan but one day I only had a penny in my pocket. I said to one of my friends, 'I'll toss you up for a penny.' Woodbines were tuppence a packet. Up went the penny and I lost the toss. I didn't have a smoke that day."

As in the miners' strike of 1921, David Henry Rees used his horse and cart to work on road construction – the Penclawdd-Llanrhidian road. 'Soup kitchens' were organized in the Small Memorial Hall and the shopkeepers cooperated with the villagers again. At the end of the year, the strike ended when starvation drove the miners back to work defeated.

As all mining families, David Henry Rees and his family experienced hardship in the coal strikes, but the late 1920s brought more bad luck and even greater financial difficulties. David Henry originally worked as a collier,[8] but at the age of nineteen, he qualified as a fireman. While examining by hand a shot that had failed to ignite, it exploded and blew off all the fingers of his right hand. As a result, his hand was amputated. His sole compensation was twelve pounds to buy an artificial hand. When he recovered, he was capable only of light work, and was re-employed for a short time as a pump man. His son, George, has much admiration for him. "I can't remember my father with two hands. He never wore his artificial hand, and found a metal hook more useful. When he worked as a pump man, I used to take his dinners to him on a covered plate. When he left the colliery, he used to cut a four-acre field in the west-end of Penclawdd and cut the railway bank from the White Gates (half a mile west of Gowerton) to Penclawdd."

David Henry was invalidated out of work for many months. His son, Griff, reminisces. "We were seven children and although my mother went 'out the sands' and sold fruit and vegetables from our garden to help family finances, we still had to go on the parish relief. The office was near the Infant School. Every Thursday, we went to the office where we were given a voucher to exchange at a shop to the value of one pound. We were subjected to the means test. A man called Burgess visited us from Dunvant to take away our furniture, and sell it, but we didn't have the money for it. Our neighbours, Mr. Rees of the Emporium shop, and his wife Daisy, who owned our house, were very kind to us. They stored our furniture when a visit from Burgess was expected, and as a result, we managed to keep all our possessions. Our landlords did not expect rent to be paid until my father was back in work. In my opinion, they were the finest people in Penclawdd. They were good to everyone."

David Henry was a talented musician, and his accident greatly curtailed his playing of the many instruments he enjoyed. His daughter, Glenys, remembers the accident. "My father was a clever musician and played the flute, the cornet, the organ, the piano and the fiddle. My mother used to say that he made the fiddle sing. He used play it at weddings, as was the custom then. After the accident, he could still manage to play the piano and the organ with one hand."

On 24 November 1922, the sale took place between vendors, Herbert Davies Evans the Younger of Lampeter, Cardigan, Elizabeth Edith Morgan, 2 Florence Road, Southsea, Southampton and John Norton, 54 Queen Anne's Gate, Westminster and the New Berthlwyd Gas Coal Company, purchasers of land – part of Blaen Cedi Farm, Penclawdd – for three hundred pounds. On 29 November of the same year, the Company bought adjoining land from Sir Robert Armine Morris, Sketty Park, Swansea, for five hundred and twenty-eight pounds and ten shillings.

In 1923, the Company opened Wernbwll Colliery on their newly acquired land.

Slants were opened into the Penlan and Penclawdd seams, which were worked separately. John Phillips, Gowerton, was the manager, W. J. Hughes the under manager, and Llewellyn Thomas, the overman. The total number of persons employed below ground on three shifts was one hundred and sixty men.

In 1929-30 the Company was made into a limited company and renamed Berthlwyd Colliery Limited. On 16 February 1931, the latter was to buy more adjoining land from John Bevan, Cheriton House, Cheriton, Glamorgan, for one hundred and thirty pounds. The directors of the Company were D. D. Williams, who already owned Caereithin Colliery, G. Thomas, and the secretary, W. H. Edwards.

Wernbwll was one of the most successful collieries in Penclawdd, enjoying a continuous output of coal throughout its working life. The majority of its employees lived in Penclawdd, and the rest in Three Crosses, and west of Penclawdd – Llanmorlais, Crofty, and Llanrhidian.

On Thursday, 28 November 1929, a disaster occurred in the colliery that shocked and deeply saddened the occupants of these villages. At about seven o'clock, when the men working on the afternoon shift were about to take their meal break, an explosion occurred at No. 13 level of the West District, resulting in the loss of seven lives.

The first intimation of the disaster came from the engine man below, who indicated to the surface that an explosion had occurred. The owner and management were immediately informed by telephone and quickly arrived on the scene. D. D. Williams, John Phillips, W. J. Hughes and Llewellyn Thomas descended to No. 13 level where they immediately discovered the two bodies of William Arnold Bennett and Henry Griffiths, but the presence of afterdamp[9] prevented them continuing further into the level. The Loughor Rescue Brigade, assisted by breathing apparatus, took over the task, and eventually recovered the bodies of Thomas Luther Hughes, Thomas Henry Harry, Edwin Harry, David Davies and Thomas Jones, at about two o'clock on the Friday morning. T. L. Hughes, T. H. Harry, E. Harry, and D. Davies were working in the topholes. It seems that they had abandoned their tools and clothing in the vain attempt to reach the surface and safety. They reached No. 13 level where they were overcome and fatally poisoned by afterdamp. Thomas Jones worked in the main slant but happened to be at No. 13 level at the time of the explosion, seeking timber. Lewis and Griffiths were colliers working with the boring machine at the heading at the end of the slant. The machine wasn't working properly and Lewis volunteered to go out to turn on more blast. The action saved his life. He miraculously escaped with only a cut on his nose, minor cuts by gravel, and stupefied by gas. He went out eighty or ninety yards to turn on more blast, (compressed air), leaving his partner boring. The following article appeared in 'The Cambrian' newspaper on Friday, 29 November:

'The only way I am alive now is because I went out to turn on some more blast for the machine. Griffiths was my partner. I left him at the machine boring, and the others were cutting coal at the tophole. We could not see them. [. . .] I was blown down and I could feel myself being knocked back and forward just like as if I was in the middle of the storm, or as if I was on the waves of the sea. [. . .] I could feel myself being blown against the side blown every shape I was by the force of the explosion and when I stopped I was twenty to thirty yards away, close to number fourteen slant, my lamp out still hanging onto my coat. [. . .] I must have been there a quarter of an hour when I could hear voices quite dim. It turned out to be Francis and the others from No. 14 and keeping my face down to the track we managed to get out somehow, but if the machine was working properly, I would have been there with Griffiths instead.'

As in the previous colliery disaster at Elba, Gowerton, Doctor Hughes, of Penclawdd, was soon on the scene and with Doctor Thomas, of Gowerton, gave all the possible assistance to the injured men. Arthur Williams, Three Crosses and Andrew Gwyther, Tycoch, Swansea, were taken to Swansea Hospital where they were detained with burns and shock. Mr. John Phillips, manager, Llewellyn Thomas, Penclawdd, David Lewis,

Victoria Road, Penclawdd, John Sambrook, Blue Anchor Terrace, Penclawdd and John Francis, Benson Terrace, Penclawdd suffered from afterdamp. The fatalities were:

> T. Luther Hughes, Penclawdd, aged thirty-two years,
> Edwin Harry, Llanmorlais, aged sixty-one years,
> David Davies, Penclawdd, aged thirty-four years,
> Henry Griffiths, Penclawdd, aged thirty-four years,
> Thomas Jones, Three Crosses, aged fifty-four years,
> Thomas H. Harry, Penclawdd, aged thirty-three years,
> W. Arnold Bennett, Llanrhidian, aged twenty-nine years.

The proximity of Penclawdd, Three Crosses Llanmorlais and Llanrhidian resulted in many inter-marriages between the villages. Consequently, many families were in mourning. 'The Cambrian' newspaper reported:

> 'Though the death roll is seven, forty homes in Penclawdd have been plunged in sorrow. [. . .] One father and son were killed.'

F. H. Wynne, Majesty's Deputy Chief Inspector of Mines undertook a formal investigation under section 83 of the Coal Mines Act 1911 into the causes and circumstances of the explosion on 18 and 19 February and 18 and 19 March 1930 at the Llewellyn Hall, Swansea. His report to E. Shinwell Esq., Secretary for Mines at the Mines Department, Millbank London stated that there was considerable divergence of opinion among the witnesses called by the owner of the mine as to the cause and place of the explosion. John Phillips, manager, felt that the naked flame of an acetylene lamp in tophole 1, was the source of the ignition. D. L. Davies, Miners Agent, thought that the ignition of coal dust was the reason, and took place between 1 and 2 tophole. Messrs. Lea, Waldin and Finney, H. M. Inspectors of Mines, thought that the initiating cause was an accumulation of firedamp[10] between 1 and 2 topholes. F. H. Wynne was of the opinion that a flame of an ignited acetylene lamp ignited a mixture of firedamp and air, which exploded between 1 and 2 topholes.

An inquest had been held by the Swansea County Coroner, C. J. C. Wilson, at Penclawdd on 14 and 15 January, 1930, at the conclusion of which the jury had brought in a verdict as follows:

> 'That the death in each case was due to carbon monoxide poisoning.
> That the explosion took place in the vicinity of No. 1 tophole.
> That the nature of the explosion was unknown.
> That no one was responsible and that there was no negligence.'

The part of the seam in which the explosion occurred was abandoned after the disaster and would have consequently filled with water. Work was started in an alternative area of the seam.

Two years later, undeterred by the disaster, David Henry Rees' son, Griff, started working in the colliery. He was so anxious to commence his mining career that he left school illegally before his fourteenth birthday, on 16 January, and as a result, was summonsed. The amount of the summons exceeded his weekly wage of fourteen shillings. Later in the New Year, he was legitimately on the payroll, and started work on the oil drams on the surface – referred to by the miners as 'on the bank'.

The miners divided the managers into two categories: the pub managers – the men who frequented the pubs, and the chapel managers – the men who frequented the chapels. John Phillips was in the latter category. Griff Rees comments of him, "He was a tidy chap, but he was a godly man and we had to be careful not to swear in front of him."

Griff had the additional job of supplying the miners, and the manager, with their daily supplies of cigarettes and tobacco. The Blue Anchor public house (the Blue) was situated about one hundred yards north of the colliery. "On the morning shift, as soon as smoke was seen coming out of the chimney of the Blue, I would be sent down to buy cigarettes and tobacco for the men working on the surface (smoking was prohibited underground), and for Mr. Phillips, the colliery manager. Johnny Rees – known as Johnny the Blue – and his wife, Catherine, would be having their breakfast. I'd be given the thickest ham sandwich that was possible to get my mouth around. Johnny would have the same, his moustache dripping with grease as he ate. I was too young to drink alcohol, but sometimes Johnny would give me a small glass of beer, but was always careful to make sure that I was not drunk going back to my work.

Johnny ran a slate system of payment for the miners. All purchase prices were put on the slate, and no money exchanged hands until payday on the following Friday. Woodbine cigarettes were tuppence a packet, and Player cigarettes, six pence a packet. Phillips smoked Franklin Strong tobacco in his pipe, and his son, Arnold, was a 'Players man'." On the Friday of his first week, all the men gave Griff money to clear their debts on the slate, with the exception of the manager. Johnny instructed Griff, "When you go back, ask Phillips when is he going to pay me for his bacco (tobacco)?" Griff agonized over his predicament. "It was difficult for me to have to tell the manager to pay his debt. I was between the devil and the deep blue sea. I didn't want to offend Johnny, but I was afraid to tell the manager, as he might give me the sack." Griff decided to remain silent on the subject.

Wernbwll Colliery, waiting to go down.

Back row, left to right: Idwal Davies, George Brown.
Front row, left to right: Griff Rees, Ernie Dallimore.

On his next visit to the Blue to fetch the men's daily requirements, Johnny inquired of him if he had asked Phillips for his money. Griff replied evasively, "No Johnny, I have not seen him."

"Well," said Johnny, "What do you mean you have not seen him. Who is this bacco for?"

Griff was left no alternative, and on returning to the colliery, plucked up courage and informed Phillips, "Johnny the Blue wants to know when you are going to pay for your tobacco."

Phillips replied, "When you go to the Blue tomorrow morning, tell Johnny that I am going to pay for my tobacco when Danny (Daniel, Johnny's son) pays me for the coal that he is taking off the trams."

When Griff gave Johnny, Phillips' message, Johnny never again asked Phillips for payment for his tobacco, and Daniel continued taking coal from the trams.

After a morning shift, the men would take it in turns to help themselves to a bag of coal from the trams and exchange it at the Blue for a packet of cigarettes or half a pint of beer. All concerned were aware of the situation but turned a blind eye. It was 'perks of the job'. Says Griff, "Damn, Johnny had a stack of coal. He had more coal than the colliery."

Before the introduction of the pit baths in the 1950s, the miners were unable to bath until at home, usually in a tin tub in front of the kitchen fire. A plan was devised advantageous to the miners of the nearby Wernbwll and Caereithin Collieries, and this enterprising landlord. Johnny built a shed on his land near the Blue where the miners could meet for a welcome drink, and sometimes collect their weekly wage immediately after completing an arduous shift underground. Wynne Thomas, of Parc Hendy Farm, remembers the shed. "It had wooden benches, wooden tables and a stove in the corner. Everything was very functional. They worked in gangs in the collieries. On Fridays, payday, one man would have the money and they'd share it out there and drink Johnny's beer."

Johnny overcame the problem of Sunday closing. On Sunday mornings, and again in the evenings, the pub regulars converged from different directions, and congregated under hedges and bushes in a field next to the grounds of the Blue. Here Johnny had previously placed glasses and beer flagons. The men drank undisturbed until twelve o'clock midday, and returned in the evening to partake again. Says Wilfred Tucker, "On a Monday morning, we kids would go round the field and we used to help ourselves to the glasses before Johnny collected them. This was a regular event each week. Johnny was clever. They were not drinking on his property. They were not even in his garden. If anyone of authority poked their nose in they would have had a hell of a job to make anything stick on Johnny. Clever!"

Johnny had another 'card up his sleeve'. One Sunday, a group of men finished their supply of beer. When one of the miners – Graham – went into the Blue to fetch more supplies, he was seen by the local policeman, Sergeant Lord. The latter was walking in the *Cwm* nearby. Graham was summoned to the magistrates' court in Gowerton. In his defence, he stated that he was going into the Blue to fetch beer that he had bought the previous day – Saturday – and not to buy beer. He was found not guilty. The magistrate reprimanded Sergeant Lord with, "Don't you have any better work to do than to watch people drinking?" Griff remember that Sergeant Lord was 'very cut up about it'. It so happened that the magistrate was a close relation of Johnny's.

Griff was happy working on the surface. "We had lots of fun working 'on the bank', but at the age of sixteen, I went to work underground, as the rate was higher. The standard dress was an old pair of trousers, shirt, waistcoat, jacket and a flat cap. Moleskin trousers became the rage. They were very expensive, but very hard-wearing, and would last forever. Only the colliers could afford to buy them as they were on a higher wage than the rest of the men. My father owned a pair."

Griff became a trammer. "There was a depth of two foot of water on the floor of the levels. Our leather boots were not waterproof, and the water would come over the tops of our boots. When we bought a new pair of boots, which happened quite often, as they did not last long, our first job was to make holes in the uppers, so that the water would then run out through the holes that we had made.

The pitched topholes where the colliers worked were dry, but they had to travel through the wet levels to their work. To prevent working with wet feet, they walked in parallel pairs along the tramlines in the levels, balancing themselves by placing their arms around the others' shoulders."

Griff later worked underground as a haulier, guiding the horses as they pulled the trams of coal. It was a job he loved. Wernbwll Colliery had fourteen horses. A machine was situated on the bank and another at the outlet at Berthlwyd. When six trams were full of coal, they were pulled up to the bank by the machine situated there. When twenty full trams had collected on the surface they were driven down the underground tramline known as the 'horseway' to the outlet at Berthlwyd. They were driven down by the machine on the bank, and pulled out by the machine at Berthlwyd. The trams crossed the Gowerton-Penclawdd road by bridge to the railway line, where the coal was loaded into train trucks to be transported to its destination. The engines and powerhouse were driven by steam from boilers fired by coal. Tall chimney stacks channeled away excess steam. The miners manning the boilers were called stokers.

As it was difficult and stressful for the horses to be taken down the slant to where they worked, they remained underground, living in stables and coming to the surface only during the miners' holiday – Stop Fortnight.[11] The horses were well looked after by Twm, who was in charge of them. Each horse was to work only half a shift at a time, the hauliers having to change horses mid-shift. Says Griff, "After completing a shift, Twm would view the horses all over, and if there was a mark on them, God help you. If he discovered that a horse was worked a whole shift, the man responsible would have the sack. The horses were extremely important in the running of the colliery, and if there was a fall underground, the first question the management asked was, 'How is the horse?' and not, 'How is the man?' He could get plenty of good men, but not plenty of good horses. A trained horse was a valuable asset. The horses could sense an impending fall of stone, and stopped immediately. They saved many miners' lives. The horses knew when the end of a shift was near. If a collier wanted another dram (corruption of tram), you would have a job to take that horse in. He knew that it was time to go. There was no need to look at the clock. The horses would not tolerate abuse from the men. If you were nasty to them they'd get you. They'd ram you against the wall. They'd get you. But if you treated them properly, when they came to know you, well, they'd do anything for you. There would be no need to shout at them. They always knew what to do, and did it properly. We had a large garden with lots of apple trees. I used to take pockets of apples for the horses. When I approached the stables, they used to neigh a greeting. They would not pass my coat, which was hanging up while I worked, until I had given them an apple." A Pit Ponies Protection Society existed which constantly tried to improve the pit ponies' lot. On 15 July 1929, the following article featured in the 'South Wales Daily Post' newspaper:

'The Pit Ponies Protection Society whose president is Sir Robert Gower, OBE, MP, has recently issued an appeal for support to carry through a new piece of legislation relating to pit ponies.

Among the suggested resolutions which would alleviate the lot of the pit ponies are the following:

That a limit should be placed to the number of years pit ponies should work, and that they should be taken care of afterwards.

Determined efforts should be made to introduce modes of mechanical haulage, that pit ponies should work under improved conditions.'

The wet dark conditions of the collieries were a perfect habitat for rats and mice. They also had access to an abundant supply of the horses' feed of corn and chaff. Wernbwll was infested by hundreds of rats. The horses' feed was supplied by nearby Berthlwyd Farm, the property of Danny Williams the colliery owner. Each day, fresh supplies of corn and chaff were delivered to the stables in empty beer casks. Although the casks were covered, the tap holes provided easy entry for the rats. Before filling the horses' large leather feed bags, the hauliers first pounded the casks to frighten out the rats. When the hauliers ate, the horses were fed. Again the bags were pounded. Says Griff "The rats sat on the support timbers, watching us, their tails hanging down in rows behind the beams. Fortunately, they were frequently run over by the trams, keeping their numbers in control to a certain extent."

Miners worked on a piecework basis, wages being determined by individual effort. Griff was in favour of this method of payment. "I was much happier working piecework than the later method of a set amount per hour. If you worked hard, you received the money that you deserved, and did not 'carry' those who slacked in their work." Each collier had his own tram to fill with coal. When full, the trams were guided over the weighbridge. Ivor David checked their weight for the colliery records, and W. Henry Davies checked their weight to calculate the colliers' wages. The latter was known as 'Father' by the men, as he looked after their interests.

There were many strict rules in the mines that occasionally the men attempted to break, usually unsuccessfully. It was known that miners took short cuts filling the trams, supplementing a small amount of coal with rubbish. Spot checks were undertaken, and if rubbish found, the responsible miner was taken off work for a time in relation to the amount of rubbish in his tram.

Large electrically operated fans drew the air down into the topholes, to circulate and prevent the accumulation of gas in them. Dan, an electrician, and Will Smith were badly burned when a small explosion occurred while they were working in the topholes. Compensation was not easily given. On this occasion, smoking was suspected, and the area was brushed and the contents sieved. As a result, matchsticks and cigarette stubs were discovered, and so it was assumed that the men had been smoking. It was stated that the men had endangered themselves, and so received no compensation.

When the colliery closed for two weeks in the summer, the seven-day-a-week workers, who carried out essential duty, worked every day, and had no official days off. They were the engine drivers, the men stoking boilers and the pump men. It was imperative that the pump worked continuously. They worked a system between them to ensure that they sometimes had a Sunday off from work. They worked 'doublers' (two consecutive shifts), their own shift, and the shift of the relieving pump man. The system seemed to work well, and was accepted by the management. On a Sunday, when the colliery was closed, the management arranged for a young miner to accompany the pump man in the case of an emergency, when the young lad could run for help if necessary.

D. D. Williams seems to have been well-liked by his employees. Griff says of him, "We saw a lot of Danny Williams. He was a nice chap. When we had our annual trip, Danny Williams was invited as guest of honour." The trips included a visit to Liverpool the year of the opening of the tunnel under the Mersey, from Liverpool to Birkenhead, London and tea at a Lyons Corner House, Bristol Zoo and Cardiff. When at Cardiff, Griff and his friend lost the bus home. Fortunately, Griff had ten shillings in his pocket, which sufficed to buy a bus ticket each to Swansea for the stranded miners. They walked from Swansea to Penclawdd, arriving home with the milkman.

While working at the colliery, Griff was courting Edith Standard, of Alltwen, Gowerton. "After visiting Edith in Gowerton, I'd walk as far as Berthlwyd. There, I'd jump on a dram and travel underground and come out by the Blue. It was much quicker than walking up the hill. My brother-in-law, Willie Maggie May (Willie, husband of Maggie May) was a rider (operating the trams)."

Edith lived with her parents in Alltwen Farm, near the site of the old Alltwen Colliery, about half a mile east of the site of the old Elba Colliery. Edith's father made good use of the old Alltwen Colliery's disused slant by growing mushrooms – the dark damp conditions being perfect the purpose.

In 1939, Griff married Edith. Griff disputes Johnny the Blue's village reputation of being ungenerous. "He was kind to me. On our wedding day, he took us to Swansea in his car to get married. On the way home, he stopped the car outside the Commercial Inn in Gowerton. My wife stayed in the car while Johnny, my father, her father and I went in for a drink."

Johnny and Doctor Hughes were the first villagers to own a car. Johnny had a large Overlander, which he garaged in the grounds of the Blue. Wilfred Tucker recalls. "I can remember his garage being built in the garden in front of the Blue. A garage being built in Penclawdd was something new at the time."

The workings of the colliery went east to Berthlwyd, north into the

Llwchwr Estuary and west as far as Tabernacle Chapel. Here, the workings west, terminated, as the owners were afraid of endangering the foundations of the chapel. Consequently, Penclawdd now sits on a labyrinth of colliery workings.

In the late 1930s, problems arose in the colliery. The ventilation deteriorated as the levels were worked further and further from the colliery's main slant openings, resulting in less and less oxygen in the slants. Moreover, the coal seams were grossly depleted, and so the management decided to close the colliery.

Tragically, Sid James was killed by a rock fall on the last colliery working-shift on the first Thursday in September 1937, the day of the Gower Agricultural Show.

Wernbwll Colliery had provided the miners of Penclawdd and district with continuous work with good wages for fourteen years. Griff bemoans the demise of the colliery. "It was a sad day for Penclawdd when Wernbwll closed. It was a good colliery."

In 1939, the Company went into voluntary liquidation, and the most successful and last colliery in Penclawdd closed, terminating the mining industry in the village.

In 1989, Don Howells erected a plaque in memory of the miners who lost their lives in Wernbwll Colliery during its working life, on the site of the old colliery, adjacent to the Penclawdd-Three Crosses road.

Today, the only remaining evidence of the colliery is a small mound of stones that was once the engine house, in a field behind the Blue, where the sheep of Parc Hendy Farm grace peacefully. The entrances to the slants are barely visible in the *Cwm* below, and the colliery's old workings are a safe haven for the many families of local foxes.

> 'There are countless tons of rock above the head,
> And gases wait in secret corners for a spark;
> And his lamp shows dimly in the dust.
> His leather belt is warm and moist with sweat,
> And he crouches against the hanging coal,
> And the pick swings to and fro,
> And many beads of salty sweat play about his lips
> And trickle down the blackened skin
> To the hairy tangle on the chest.
> The rats squeak and scamper among the unused props,
> And the fungus waxes strong.'[12]

Griff was only unemployed for a few days before commencing work in

Broadoak Colliery in Loughor. Broadoak was an old colliery sunk before 1870. It was a pit colliery that had a remarkable double-beam, steam-winding engine, which worked until the colliery closed in 1948. The pit was not deep, but the slants at the bottom continued further downwards. The method of decent was outdated, and Griff was nervous during his first few days there. "I had never been down a pit before. The cages had wooden shaft guides as opposed to the later rope guides. As the pit shaft bent, so did the wooden shaft. When I reached the bend, I nearly fell over, and I thought my days had come, but I soon got used to it."

Griff worked as a haulier, a job that was familiar to him. The horses were taken underground and brought to the surface each working shift. Each haulier worked his own horse, and both travelled in individual cages. The same procedure operated on each shift. The horses were guided into a line where they patiently awaited their turn. When the haulier went down the shaft in his cage, the horse entered the next cage without assistance, following his haulier down the shaft. They came up to the surface likewise.

Griff was informed that Broadoak Colliery had an uncontrollable horse that all the hauliers found impossible to handle. Griff recognized the horse as Bwlla, one that he had worked in Wernbwll Colliery. "I told them that he was one of the best horses you could wish to have. They were amazed that I could handle him. He was the only horse I came across that would drink underground water. All the other horses were provided with fresh tap water, that was taken underground in casks, and then given to them in buckets."

Griff cycled to work via the Pont-y-Cob Road over the marsh. At high tide, the road flooded, and so the longer route had to be taken through Gowerton and Gorseinon. Griff experienced the continuing decline of the coal industry while working in Broadoak Colliery. "There were slack times in the 1930s, but Wernbwll Colliery always worked. I never lost a shift during the six years that I worked there. The Penlan and Penclawdd seams had excellent coal. The Morlais Colliery in Gorseinon used Wernbwll steam coal for their boilers, and the manager and under manager used its house coal for their own domestic use. When I was in my teens, I earned seven pounds an hour in Wernbwll, but when I married at twenty-one years of age, I was only earning two pounds eight shillings an hour in Broadoak."

Broadoak sounded a siren to warn of no work on the following shift, which could be heard across the Llwchwr Estuary in Penclawdd. It was a consideration which prevented the miners travelling unnecessarily to the colliery. The number of shifts worked per week varied, and the miners were gradually 'drawn out' (made redundant). Says Griff. "It was a case of last in first out. I was last in and so was unemployed again."

At the outbreak of war in 1939, both Jack Davies and Griff Rees were working in Mountain Colliery, Gorseinon. Coal was desperately needed in the war years for ships and industries connected with the war effort. When war was declared, Jack immediately volunteered for the navy, thinking that at last his ambition would be fulfilled, but when the authorities discovered that he was a miner, he was told to go back to work.

Horses were not used in Mountain Colliery, so Griff had new employment. His first job was riding the trams, but because of the required increase in coal production, he became a collier. Large disasters were infrequent occurrences in the collieries, but individual accidents happened often. Griff recalls, "I saw some bad accidents in the Mountain Colliery. I was pretty lucky myself. I never broke a bone. The only accident I had was a cut to my face and eye. I happened to be on the spot when there was a nasty accident. Emrys Davies, an overman, had a habit of walking under the pit cages as they went up and down, instead of using the sidewalk. One day he misjudged a cage. He thought it was going up but in fact it was coming down. It came down on top of him, and crushed him to death. We were all there, and watching helplessly. He was such a nice man."

The conscription of many miners into the armed forces had depleted the manpower in the industry. There was a particular shortage of boys. Before the war, many parents had encouraged their children to secure occupation with more regular wage, and attractive conditions. Recruiting problems had increased since the start of the war due to rival attraction presented by the RAF and war factories. Major Thomas had been an active member of the Territorial Army in the First World War, and in the interwar years. He had encouraged the young men in the colliery to join the Territorial Army, succeeding with all but three – Griff Rees, Mervyn Dalimore and Edgar Thomas. The young men in the Territorial Army were immediately enlisted at the outbreak of war. Griff remembers, "Major Thomas had all the youngsters in the Terris, and when war broke out, the only youngsters left in the colliery were Mervyn, Edgar and me."

In 1942, the government adopted two new measures to increase manpower. In May, it was decided that seven thousand miners be brought back to the collieries from the armed forces and an additional four thousand from industries and Civil Defence. In September, it was decided that all men between eighteen and twenty-five years of age, who were eligible for military service, should be given the option of volunteering for colliery work instead. Despite the recall of miners, the manpower declined through more men leaving the collieries through sickness, etc., than receiving new recruits. One of the most damning indictment of conditions in the industry was illustrated by thousands of men, who given the choice between conscripting into the services or the mines, choose the services. The fact that the government advocated colliery work as a patriotic act had little effect.

In 1943, Ernest Bevin, minister of employment, introduced a drastic and controversial scheme. One out of every ten men conscripted for active service was conscripted for the collieries instead – their names being determined by a ballot system. Consequently, young men from varying walks of life became miners.

They started training in the newly opened Oakdale Colliery Training Centre on 13 January 1944 and the first group of Bevin Boys, as they were known, went down the mines on 21 February 1944.

Experienced colliers were put in charge of the Bevin Boys, for a three-month training period and were given extra wages for the task. Griff Rees trained three of them. "We were given one shilling and six pence extra to train the boys. Some boys quickly learned to work in small groups on their own, but others would never have made colliers. I trained a young lad from Cardigan, called John Lloyd. He was an orphan who had been brought up by his uncle, a shoemaker. He was a good worker. Gareth Bevan from Penyrheol was another good one. After a month to six weeks, he was as good as myself, so I shared my extra money with him."

It was debatable as to whether or not the Bevin Boys were of benefit to the coal industry. The responsibility of the colliers for teaching and safeguarding their inexperienced trainees must have impaired their own work. Griff experienced the problem. "Some boys were a waste of time. They would play about instead of working, and in fact, were a liability to the collier. Wherever I went, the Bevin Boy had to be with me. But on the whole, the scheme was pretty good, as we were desperate for more labour during the war years."

Griff's younger brother, George, was in the first group of Bevin Boys to work in a colliery. "When I was very young, I worked in The Hills Farm, off the North Gower Road. I didn't like working there, and asked my father if I could leave. He said, 'You've got to stay there because that woman is going to be ill.' She was expecting. Pregnancy was a top secret in those days. They thought I didn't know, but I did, as I had seen my sister, Maggie May, in the same way. The woman had gone to work there as a servant. I remember my Uncle Walter explaining to me why she was in that condition: 'She walked into the wrong room one night.'

I left school at fourteen, in 1939, and worked at first as tea boy to the men building Penclawdd Secondary Modern School. I can remember, when working there, seeing one of our fighter planes fighting a German plane over the estuary near Whiteford Point Lighthouse. After thirteen weeks, I went to work in Gowerton Steelworks.

I was called up for the army at seventeen and a half. I signed on at the YMCA in Swansea. I passed A1 but was instructed to report to Oakdale Colliery Training Centre as a Bevin Boy. They gave me a pass one-way, and I never had a pass home during my four-week training there. I went with five shillings in my pocket and was paid two shillings a week. I could not afford to go home.

I did my training with Bevin Boys from all walks of life – banks, shops, etc. The English boys were very sociable. There were more boys afraid of the colliery than of the army, especially the boys from London.

At the colliery, there was an old seam that had finished being worked, by the side of a working seam. The former was used for our training. I was one of the first Bevin Boys to go underground. I accepted it, as I had to go somewhere – the army or the colliery. They found digs for us. I lodged in Newbridge-on-Usk.

After my training I didn't have a pass to go home, but a pass to a colliery near Resolven. I was disappointed, as there were so many collieries near home that I could have worked in. I was paid two pounds ten shillings a week, and spent twenty-five shillings on lodgings. I worked on the coal with a collier. He used to watch me – keep an eye on me all the time. It was a two-foot seam, and we worked lying on our sides. You get used to it. I had never been underground before, and had no idea what it would be like. If a collier had a good week, he would give me five shillings. I think that I was the only Bevin Boy there.

After I had been working there for about twelve months, I injured my finger. I went home to see Doctor Hughes who signed me off work for a couple of weeks. While at home, my father helped me obtain a transfer to No. 3 Colliery, at Garn Goch, which was managed and owned by Danny Williams. Before becoming a Bevin Boy, I had done a bit of bricklaying while working with my older brother, Aneurin. At No. 3, I did a bit of everything, including walling.

I worked over my time in the colliery to the end of 1948. My last job was building pillars. I asked if I could do a bit of bricklaying on the surface. I would have stayed on if they had agreed, but they didn't, so I left and went to work in Gowerton Steelworks."

The Bevin Boys were demobbed from the mines in 1947. Some stayed in the collieries, but many went back to their previous employment or found better work.

One of the Bevin Boys' main criticism of the scheme was the lack of recognition they received for their war effort – a recognition they felt would have been acknowledged had they served their country in the armed forces.

After the war, Griff worked in Morlais Colliery, in Llangennech, where the miners conversed in the Welsh language. Griff could understand Welsh, but speak little. He found this disconcerting at first, but he soon became competent enough in speaking Welsh to converse freely with his work mates.

During the 1950s, pit baths were introduced, which enabled miners to bath and change into clean dry clothing at the collieries, before their homeward journey. Griff comments. "It was one of the best things that ever happened. Our wet trousers would freeze in the cold weather, while cycling home or waiting for buses." His daughter Daphne was also relieved. "I can remember my father coming home from work filthy dirty, and the tin bath in front of the fire. We children were banished upstairs until he finished his bath."

Griff was a popular figure in the colliery, and his work mates gave him a good 'send off' when he retired in 1979. "They thought the world of me. On my last working shift, before retiring, the local pub in Llangennech that we went to, opened especially for us at five-thirty in the morning. We all went to the pub straight from the night shift. By nine o'clock in the morning, one would think it was a Saturday night. Bill's wife phoned the colliery to ask if they knew where he was. When he got home, she asked him where he had been all that time. He said 'Oh *aisht*! (be quiet). You should be glad to see me. I was all but under a fall.' He was all but under a fall in the pub."

Griff comments on his career in the colliery. "The men all worked together and we were never on our own. I thoroughly enjoyed myself, but my favourite job was a haulier, driving the horses. I was a miner all my working life, and I'd do it all again."

Jack went to work in Mountain Colliery on a temporary basis, as it was inconveniently situated from home. The management persuaded him to stay until a replacement was found. Jack worked there until he retired on 30 June 1966.

NOTES

1. Limited liability company: Where the liability (or responsibility) of a shareholder in a company for its operations is limited to the number of shares held.
2. *Penclawdd Elementary School Report*, 27 January 1905.
3. Now the site of Penmorfa Housing Estate at the east-end of the village.
4 John Gower-Williams, Labour MP for Gower 1906-1922: He was a miner from the age of twelve to twenty years, Miners' Agent for the Western Mines Association for twenty years, Baptist minister, Lecturer in economics, Welsh poet, JP for Glamorganshire and Governor of the University of Wales.
5. Lock out: Where employers refuse work to those who are not prepared to accept the terms of employment offered.
6. When a bridge was constructed over the River Tawe, a toll of a half-penny was introduced. The toll was abolished in 1889 but the bridge was still known as the Halfpenny Bridge for many years.
7. A shotfirer placed the explosives in the coal holes bored by the colliers.
8. Collier: The collier cut or hewed the coal.
9. Afterdamp: A non-flammable heavy gas carbon dioxide left after an explosion in a coalmine.
10. Firedamp: A natural gas highly explosive when mixed with air then called firedamp. Coal gas contains a large proportion of methane.
11. The miners were awarded two weeks holiday without pay every summer. This period was known as Stop Fortnight and was an integral part of Welsh culture. Thousands of miners and their families flocked to the popular seaside resorts of Porthcawl and Barry Island. The Gower Peninsular was also a popular venue for caravan holidays.
12. Idris Jones. *Gwalia Deserta*.

5

Going 'Out the Sands'

Penclawdd was an unusual industrial and mining community in that the wives of the miners and the metal workers had their own occupation. Few stayed at home to keep house. While their husbands worked in the collieries and industries, the women gathered the cockles[1] and mussels[2] of the Llwchwr Estuary, supplementing their husbands' salaries, simultaneously being housewives and mothers. In few other Welsh villages did women work so physically hard for so many years.

As in most villages, the inhabitants grew garden produce – fruit, vegetables and flowers – for their own use. In Penclawdd, the cockle women's husbands usually produced surplus to family requirements for their wives to sell in addition to their cockles. Little poverty existed in the village. Disabling injuries were common in the mines and local heavy industries, but if invalided out of their work, if physically possible, the men changed their careers to cockle and mussel gathering, or fishing. They sometimes worked the estuary as well as their full-time employment.

Cockle gathering has existed in the Llwchwr Estuary since prehistoric times. Cockleshells have been found in hedgerows, caves and churchyards.

It would have been impossible to be unaware of the cockle industry in Penclawdd, which has made the village famous. There were cockleshells in the chicken runs and the gardens contained cockleshell mounds and cockleshell paths. The cockle carts were seen, when not in use, idling in fields and gardens. The clip clopping, braying and neighing of the donkeys and horses echoed continually around the village. The cockle women travelled through the village to gather cockles in the Llwchwr Estuary. They either walked with their donkeys, or rode on their horse-drawn carts, their feet swinging nonchalantly over the sides of the cart. Cockle gathering was referred to locally as 'going out the sands'.

Joyce Richards remembers the cockle women passing the family home, Manchester House,[3] opposite the Infant School[4] "They used to pass our house, about five carts at a time, very early in the morning. In the dark winter mornings, their carts had two lamps to light the way. When in bed, we used to hear them talking as they went 'out the sands'. During the

155

summer months, when our bedroom windows were open, we could hear them even more clearly."

The cockle women were respected by all in the village. Marian Eaton says of them, "They were the most wonderful, honest, hard workers that God ever put on this earth. These good-looking women were physically strong, with good principles, and strong personalities. They were proud of their physical fitness, and walked erect. They were impatient with talk of ailments, self-praise, and idle gossip."

The work was exceptionally hard, and the money poor. They went 'out the sands' from leaving school to becoming grandmothers, retiring at a late age. Their cockle gathering was governed by the tide, resulting in unsociable hours. It was a way of life that they were born to. Women were regarded as equals. This matriarchal system worked throughout the whole community. In the village, Mary Ann Thomas' son, John, was known as, John Mary Ann. John was more easily identified by his mother's Christian name, than by his surname. In the same context, Griff Rees refers to his brother-in-law, Willie, as Willie Maggie May (Willie, husband of Maggie May).

If the women wanted to be independent, they went cockle gathering, but the money earned was shared within the family. There was a high invalidity and mortality rate in the collieries. Social security did not exist, but the cockle women were financially independent if widowed, during coal strikes, or if their husbands became invalids through accident in their work. Mary Bennett experienced the latter. "My husband was a collier. He fractured his spine when a stone fell on him underground. He was lying on a couch for twenty years until he died in hospital of the miners' disease, silicosis. Smart man he was. He was taken to Swansea General Hospital after the accident. He had a plaster jacket. After they took it off, he seemed as if he had fallen forward somehow. He couldn't help me with the cockles. He couldn't do anything for me. I used to come home with the horse and cart and my hands were swollen badly with the frost. He couldn't even help me by holding the horse for me to strip the animal, before I took him into the stable up the garden."

The cockle women controlled the family finances with iron gloves. Marian Eaton comments, "My father, Henry William Davies, a prominent builder in Penclawdd, had great respect for the cockle women. Before the days of council houses in the village, it was their aim to own their own house. There was a pride in owning your own house. This they were able to do by supplementing their husbands' income through their work. They never owed my father a brass farthing."

Very little impeded their work. Joyce Richards, née Howells, when a baby, was looked after by her sister when her mother, Jane Howells was 'out the sands'. Joyce's sister, being unable to change nappies, used to fetch her mother from the cockle beds, near the village at the time, to perform the deed. Her mother came home, quickly changed Joyce's nappy, and returned to the sands immediately.

The cockle women developed muscles and sometimes hands like men. They sieved the sand from the cockles by hand and then lifted the heavy sacks of cockles onto the donkeys and carts. They washed and boiled the cockles in large containers and later carried them in baskets to sell in Swansea Market and around the houses. During the Second World War years, Mary Bennett went to work in the ICI factory in Waunarlwydd. When having her medical examination by a Gowerton doctor, Doctor Owen, the latter, not realising Mary was a cockle woman, was amazed at her large muscles and inquired of her, "What the hell have you been doing?"

The cockle women were loyal to each other. Bonding developed through shared experience. Mary Bennett recalls "It was a hard life but a happy one. You were your own boss. If you felt like this, I don't think I'll go out today, well, you had nobody to answer to. It was your misfortune if you couldn't go. Then you wouldn't have so much money. We used to go and help if we saw one by herself gathering cockles on a bank. We'd always go and see if she was all right. We wouldn't go off the sands until everybody was off the sands. We clung together like one body.

But we had fun. We made our own fun. Now and again we'd go for an afternoon trip if there was no tide. We'd enjoy ourselves – a busload. We were a happy crowd. It was hard work, but we were a happy crowd."

Their initiation into the industry usually started at a young age, hardening and disciplining them for their future careers. Amazingly, it did not deter them, but actually encouraged them to continue in what was often their mothers' and their grandmothers' footsteps.

When a school pupil, Lizzie May Davies used to help her older sister transport her cockles. At the time, the nearest train station was in Gowerton. Before going to school, Lizzie May accompanied her sister to the railway station, the heavy shell cockles being carried in sacks on the back of the dutiful donkey. They walked along back lanes to Gowerton, the main Gowerton-Penclawdd road not having been constructed. Her sister continued her journey to Swansea to sell her cockles and Lizzie May walked the donkey the three miles home to Penclawdd, and then went to school.

When she helped her sister sell boiled cockles – cockles that had been boiled out of their shells and ready for eating – the girls skilfully carried a *stwc* (cask) of cockles on their heads and walked to Gowerton along the railway track. To balance the *stwcs*, they walked in an upright position, which resulted in them having extremely straight backs. This was no easy task, as the casks were heavy in their own right, without the added weight of the cockles.

Dora Davies of Llanmorlais, reminisced. 'A very important factor in the life of a cockle gatherer was the donkey. One could not achieve much in this business without the poor old donkey. So, at the age of nine years it fell to my lot to fetch the donkey from the fields or woods, or from wherever it had taken a fancy to roam. At early morning tides, I had to go at two o'clock in the morning to look for it. I remember fetching the donkey one winter's morning with a candle fixed in a jam pot, when I saw a light. It came slowly down the Wern and entered the lane near Cwm Cynner Farm. Instinctively I thought, it must be a corpse light. We firmly believed in those days that the spirit of a departed one traversed the road that the cortege would take on the funeral day. I never questioned that it might be someone like myself on the same errand, namely looking for donkeys by candlelight.

Being the eldest of our rapidly increasing family, I had to go and earn my living at the age of ten, and help support the family. I went 'to the sands', and my first job was shoring the cockles. This meant taking the cockles to the shore while the others continued gathering, and then returning for another load.

On Saturdays, I went to Swansea Market with my mother in the trap to sell the cockles. Thus I had put my foot on the first rung of the ladder to become a successful cockle gatherer and seller.'[5]

Mary Bennett's first work in the estuary was not gathering cockles, but helping her father fish with field nets. At low tide, two pairs of hazel sticks, known as fish stops, were placed in the sand some distance apart. A net was strung horizontally between the fish stops, and attached to the bottom of them.

William Rees, a miner in the Lynch Colliery, Llanmorlais, felt the necessity to supplement his colliery wage as he had previously invested and lost a large amount of money in a local mine. He strongly felt the importance of his family being well-dressed, especially for the popular singing festivals in the chapels at Whitsun. In-between his working shifts at the colliery, he fished the estuary with field nets.

At the age of twelve, Mary started accompanying him late at night or very early morning to Cefn Sidan sands, on the north side of the estuary, three miles from their home. Mary held the lantern, while her father collected the fish. She put the fish in sacks and her father placed the sacks on the donkey. Mary was to ensure that no fish fell out of the sacks on the homeward journey. In the afternoons, while her father was working in the colliery, she picked the fish on her own, usually a smaller catch than in the night. Mary competently mended the broken nets – a skill she had been taught by her father – which the fish had damaged the previous night. She effortlessly travelled the six-mile journey on foot each day. On arriving home, she helped her mother prepare the fish for marketing. "My mother and I washed the fish and my mother took most of them to a Swansea fish merchant called Mrs. Coakley.[6] My mother weighed the rest of the fish and tied them together with string through their mouths into one-pound bundles. The larger fish, usually over one and a half pounds, were sold individually. My mother put as much fish as I could carry in a cockle basket. I walked around the houses of Penlan, Blue Anchor and back home to Llotrog, through Cefn Bychan[7] selling the small fish at three pence a pound and the larger fish at one shilling a pound." Being one of the oldest of eleven children, Mary's help was needed to supplement the family income, and so she left school before the age of fourteen years.

Ten years later, after leaving school at the age of fourteen, Mary's younger sister, Ethel, was anxious to follow in her sister's footsteps and accompany her father fish at night. After much persuasion by Ethel, William consented. At half-past twelve in the morning, he brought the donkey from the stable and placed five sacks on the animal's back. Ethel questioned him, "Why are you putting so many sacks on the donkey's back Dad?"

He replied, 'Fisherman's luck. We might have one tonight, or we might have a load.'

Ethel still has vivid memories of that night. "A carbon lantern was used to light our way. The cup of the lantern was filled with carbon and water and lit with a match. The door was closed, sealing and protecting the flame from all weathers. On reaching the first river in the estuary, my father said, 'This is the first river that you will cross and it will be your last river coming back.' The estuary was extremely dark. The only lights visible were at Caereithin Colliery in Three Crosses, the tin-plate works in Llanelli Docks and three lights in Pembrey, the latter still being visible today. 'Now,' said my father, 'we must go to that second light in Pembrey and we will come out on the bank where the nets will be.' As we went along, my father said, 'Look where you are going, and take note of little objects, and study and memorize all the rivulets that are running down from the banks.' We eventually arrived at the bank where the nets should have been, but I could not see them. My father told me to lie down on the dry sand and shade the lamp on the surface of the sand. I could then see the shadow of the net sticks.

We went to them and I had never seen such a sight in all my life. I was catching on my father and jumping for joy. There were loads of all kinds of fish. My father said, 'We must be busy as the tide will be back and we've got to be off.' So I helped my father pick the fish, and put them in the sacks. We had too much for the donkey, so my father tied a sackfull onto the iron bar with the net sticks. We went home and washed all the fish. My mother took them on the half-past eight morning train to Swansea where she sold them wholesale to Mrs. Coakley in Goat Street. I remember the shop before it was bombed in the war. It had no windows, but shutters. All the fish would be on a big slab. Mrs. Coakley was always busy, filleting fish, etc. She'd say to my mother, 'Sue, go in and make me some breakfast and make some for yourself and for Ethel!' We'd come home on the one o'clock train. I did not often accompany my mother into Swansea to sell the fish as I usually fished the afternoon tide for my father."

Ethel learned quickly and it was not long before William was confident that his daughter could fish at night without him. At low tide, anticipating a small catch, Ethel did not 'bother' to go with a donkey. Taking only her lantern and her sack, she walked down the narrow steep lanes from her house in Llotrog, to join her Uncle Heazel, Joe Guy and *Will a Chwaer* (Will and sister) on the main road, by the Memorial Halls. "We called the 'old people' by their nicknames then. Will lived with his sister, hence his nickname." Her father watched her from their garden until she waved her lantern to assure him that all was well. The small group of three men and a girl continued on their way in the 'dead' of night through the west-end of the village, along Salthouse Point, and into the dark, silent estuary. They were helped by the light of their lanterns and occasionally, by the merciful light of the moon. "We all had our stops of nets, but mine was always the furthest out in the estuary. *Will a Chwaer* was the only herring fisherman in the village. His nets were three quarters of the way up the poles as opposed to the other fish nets, which were at the base of the poles. His full herring nets were a sight to see, shining silver in the moonlight. I can't explain what a wonderful sight it was. We'd gather our fish and when full, about forty to fifty pounds, my uncle would put my sack on my back and I would go home up the steep hill to Llotrog. I used to place my sack on the low wall behind Bethel Chapel, and lean against it for a rest. My neck bone would be red hot. I dare not put my sack on the ground, because if I did, I would not be able to pick it up again."

In 1936, at the age of eleven years, Della Williams, née Jones, started selling cockles door to door in the Swansea Valley every Saturday, with her grandmother, Hannah Jenkins. Occasionally, she missed school on a Friday, to help her grandmother. They went by bus from Penclawdd to Dyfaty,

Swansea. Here, they changed buses and continued the two and a half-hour journey to Ystalyfera by James Brothers Buses, an Ammanford bus company. They sold their cockles in Ystalyfera, Cwm-twrch, Cwmllyn-fell and Rhosaman, walking between each village. It took two days. The inhabitants of the area favoured shell cockles, which Della and her grandmother carried in cockle baskets on their arms. The cockles, served with laverbread[8] and bacon, were a popular Sunday breakfast. Although cockles are not seasonal, for some unknown reason, cockles were not popular in the summer months in that area.

In winter, the cockle women worked in freezing conditions. Very thick, warm woollen clothes were essential. They wore two petticoats, a woollen skirt and a thick shawl around the shoulders over a flannel blouse. A smaller shawl was worn around the head with a tight fitting cap on top. The shawl was fastened with a safety pin at the back of the neck in Egyptian style. In winter, on late afternoon tides, the damp air froze their clothes.

Before rubber gloves were invented, their hands became red and swollen from gathering in the freezing sand. They went through the pain barrier until their hands became numb. Only then could they use them to their advantage. The women wore men's nailed boots, with thick grey woollen miners stockings held up by garters. In later years, Wellington boots were worn.

Doris Davies, of Llanmorlais, recalls, 'My mother was considered clever by the villagers for she was one of the very few women to possess a sewing machine, so she was much sought after to make the Welsh costumes, men's flannel shirts and drawers, and women's calico shifts. Welsh costumes were called bedgowns, but as they were not worn to bed I do not know how they acquired that name. Women went to the annual fair at Gowerton and bought yards of white flannel. They brought this to my mother to be dyed red. I remember going with her to the chemist in Swansea to buy alum with which she treated the flannel before dying it. After being dyed, it was spread over the garden hedge to dry. From afar, it looked as if a regiment of soldiers was guarding the cottage.'[9]

Gathering the cockles from the sand was a skilled art, which the cockle gatherers perfected over the years. The implements used were simple but effective. *Y gram a rhaca*[10] was used to lift the cockles from the sand when the beds were exposed at low tide. A hedge-cutting hook was bought from the ironmongers and converted into a *cram* by husbands, fathers, or Jonathan Morgan the ironmonger who owned the local forge. The blade was cut at the thick end and the wooden handle discarded. The blade was put in the fire and turned by hammering it against metal. Its narrow end was sharpened to a very fine point. The blunt end of the blade was bound with cloth to form a handle. This tool was now a *cram*. In the cold winter months, the *cram* was warmed in the kitchen Rayburn oven overnight to make the handling of it more comfortable. The rake had eight to ten teeth and a short handle. The cockle women bent at the waist, and keeping their legs rigid, worked forward. The sharp end of the *cram* was placed in the cockle bed a yard in front of them to their left and scraped through the sand towards them to expose the cockles, and draw water to the surface. It was imperative that the gatherers drew the water from their left to their right. Ethel Coghlan, née Rees, was an expert. Hayden and Della Williams say of her, "Oh! there was a one to draw the water!" The cockles were then raked together and placed in the sieves by hand. The water rinsed the cockles, eliminating excess sand around them when placed in the sieve, resulting in more efficient gathering. If there was no water near the cockles, they were carried in black pails to the nearest supply.

The sieves were bought in Griffiths the ironmonger in Swansea, for the princely sum of four shillings and six pence. Today the same implement is on sale for fifteen pounds. The law stipulated that the square holes in the mesh should measure five eighths and later eleven sixteenths of an inch. Open shelled cockles, and empty cockleshells were not needed. These had to be picked out of each sieve-full of cockles by hand, and discarded. It was discovered that if the sieves were rewired with rectangular holes in the mesh, the closed shelled cockles sieved through and the open shells remained. This was a great asset, speeding the process considerably. The cockles were washed in large black buckets with seawater, and then placed in sacks on donkeys or carts to transport home for boiling. However, the cockle women's work was not finished for the day.

The faithful donkeys' and horses' needs came first. They were stripped, fed, watered and safely housed in their stables in winter and put to graze in fields in summer.

The cockles were then boiled on open fires and in summer, salted. Some cockle women went home to change into dry clothes before boiling, while others boiled first. Says Della Williams "My mother made it a rule that we went home to wash, change into dry clothes and have a meal before we went to boil. Whether you work with your head or your hands, you have to work hard, but there was not many jobs harder than cockling. The only one that I know was in the tin-plate works, where my husband Haydn, worked."

Cockles were boiled in large metal tubs – originally bought from gypsies and so named Gypsy Boilers – on handmade grates of stone and metal, fired by coal. Each grate burnt one hundred weight of coal to boil a gathering of cockles. The boiling took place in various areas of the village – communally on the *Scêr* opposite the Ship and near the Railway, or individually in their own gardens etc. It was imperative to have a water supply at hand to rinse the cockles. Evidence of the boiling areas in the village were indicated by large piles of discarded cockleshells. After her marriage, Mary Bennett boiled her cockles on the marsh in front of her house in No. 30, Chapel Road, Crofty. "My husband made me a big grate and a large Gypsy Boiler which had two handles. I boiled the cockles on a fire in the grate. After they were boiled, I put them into a large bath of cold water. I rinsed them in another five baths of cold water."

In the 1940s, the Environmental Health's governing body introduced a law, stating that it was compulsory to steam sterilize all cockles sold. Factories were built and machinery introduced to accommodate the new legislation. The separating machine steamed the cockles and also separated them from their shells, taking much of the backbreaking work out of boiling cockles. Della and Haydn Williams built a factory 'out the docks'.[11]

Della and Haydn Williams in their factory.
Cockles in baskets ready for marketing.

Joyce and John Davies' factory was in close proximity and Ethel Rees, by now married to Lenny Coghlan, built a factory on Salthouse Point, in Crofty.

Della and Haydn Williams also built a grit factory next to their cockle factory, where the cockleshells were ground into grit for chicken feed.[12] David John Dalimore lost his life when operating the grinding machine in the grit works. It is thought that his sleeve caught in the machine, pulling him in to an horrific death. He worked on his own and so nobody came to his aid.

Ethel and Lenny Coghlan outside their factory.

Most of the cockle-gathering families had sheds in their gardens, situated opposite their back-kitchen doors. The sheds were always warm, having a coal fire – which usually heated an adjacent oven – or a coal-fired stove. They were originally used as a place in which the house-proud cockle women could change their clothing after gathering cockles, thus protecting their houses from the sand and mud of the estuary. But gradually, over the years, the families spent more and more time in the sheds – washing, ironing, cooking and eating. Eventually, many favoured their sheds to their houses, and rarely used the latter for any purpose other then to sleep in.

The donkeys were usually bought from Ireland. It was a common sight to see them grazing on the *Graig* that formed a backcloth to the village.

The cockle women tended to their animals' every need, as the latter were essential in their work. But they grew to love their donkeys and horses and grieved greatly when they were parted from them. Mary Bennett lost her beloved donkey, Bob, to the treacherous estuary, while she watched helplessly. "He was trapped on the marsh in Crofty, by a very high, fast-flowing tide. He tried to swim to safety but was beaten by the strong currents. I was on the marsh road and I could see Bob swimming in to me. I was screaming to him, but he did not make it to safety and was drowned. I was so upset that my family could do nothing with me. I cried for days."

After retiring, Ethel and Lenny Coghlan were forced to sell their much-loved horse, Joe. "When we first had Joe, he was very wild. The owner was not very willing to sell him, knowing that I would be driving him. He ran and smashed the cart two or three times. For a whole week, we walked him 'out the sands', talking to him all the way. Eventually, he was like a human being. He understood us so well. He was a wonderful horse. When crossing a river, if there was a deep hole in it, Joe would not go forward, and so I knew that there was danger there, and so I would stop. I totally relied on him. He was very intelligent." Ethel and her husband grew to love Joe dearly. "We gave him a box of Mars bars a week – two bars on a Friday and Saturday, and one every other day." Joe was unwilling to share his bowl of corn with the other horses in the field, but he befriended two robins who used to come every day to stand on the rim of the bowl and peck at the corn without any interference from him. On their retirement, Joe was kept as a pet, but unfortunately, caused great problems. "He was a demon. When we put him in his field, he would jump out and come home." Joe's owners were afraid that he would cause a road accident and so reluctantly decided that the only solution was to sell him. Neither could bear to see him go to his new owner, so they arranged to have him collected from outside their cockle factory. Here they tied him to a post and bade their sad farewells. "I worried about him. I was so worried that they would not feed him," says Ethel.

Ned belonged to Marged Thomas, known by her maiden name, Marged Meli. Marged was one of the last cockle women in the village to use a donkey. For some unknown reason, Ned bit his mistress' leg. Marged neglected the wound, which never healed properly, and eventually caused her death.

Joyce Richards, when a pupil in the Old School, helped her mother by preparing the evening meal and cleaning the house in her school dinner hour, while her mother went 'out the sands'. On returning home, her

Ethel Coghlan and Joe.

mother left the cockle cart on land outside the front of their house, but took the horse through the house to the back garden. Joyce was not pleased.

One had to be courageous to face the vast expanse of sands with its fast flowing tide. It was an estuary and filled quicker than one could walk. It was particularly hazardous in foggy weather when it was extremely difficult to see the deep pills crossing the sand.

In 1935, the treacherous estuary claimed the life of Della Williams' father. William Jones drowned during an horrific gale, while gathering mussels between Penclawdd and Llanelli. The mussels grew in an extremely dangerous part of the estuary. Before the building of the sea wall in the west-end of Penclawdd in 1937, only wooden railway sleepers laid side by side supported the road bank at the edge of the estuary. Consequently, that area of the village flooded at high tide. Della recalls sadly, "We wanted him to come back, but he didn't. Eight other boats came back but my father's didn't. It was about four o'clock in the afternoon on a day in January and it was dark. They didn't tell us what had happened then but the police came in the evening and told us."

Before the Christmas of 1937, another fatality occurred in the estuary. The cockle women were busy with festive preparations and were late 'going out the sands'. Consequently, they had less time in which to gather the shellfish. Ethel Coghlan recalls, "I was a young girl then and I started with a donkey. We used to go out with the donkeys and walk out and walk back. I remember there was a part you could go to from the cockles to pick mussels. This lady who I met on the way had been in Swansea buying a doll for her daughter for Christmas, and of course we were late going out. I promised, after picking cockles, to follow her to pick mussels. But when I reached the cockle bed my friend Lizzie James, and her husband, Will, said, 'Don't go to the mussels today Ethel, because the tide isn't very good, there isn't much of an ebb on it. We'll go tomorrow'. However, Mrs. Pamp, Mrs. Jenkins and her daughter, Mrs. Anderson and Elizabeth Jane went to pick mussels. It was a freak tide that goes out and in again, straight away. They were down opposite Llanelli. The tide came sweeping in and they never noticed it. When they crossed an area where there were big potholes, Marged Ann Pamp and Elizabeth Jane Dallimore fell in. We could see their coats holding them up in the water, and baskets everywhere. The others had enough time to turn and go back onto the bank. There was a fisherman putting his nets out in the estuary. He endangered his life by crossing a bank to call a boat that was trawling in Llanelli. We ran following the coats. The boat came and picked them up from the water and fetched the others who were still on the bank, but Mrs. Pamp and Elizabeth Jane had drowned. That was a terrible tragedy in Penclawdd. My father never allowed me to go to the mussels after that."

It seems that Mr. Pamp warned his wife not to go cockling that day as there was to be an eclipse of the moon and he anticipated danger. Many villagers feel that the eclipse might have affected the tide, which the cockle women usually knew so well.

At the age of about thirteen, Kathleen Trimm, née Bennett, had a frightening experience in the estuary opposite her home in West End. When helping her brother, Wyn, fish his nets, she inadvertently walked into quicksand. Her Wellington boots filled with mud and she was quickly sucked down to her armpits. How she escaped unaided remains a mystery. "Wyn was lugging some nets and fishing them. The fish he sold for pocket money. He would wait for the tide to go out then fish the nets and lug the hooks for the next tide. One day he asked me to fish the nets for him, as he had to be elsewhere, promising to give me some of his profits. It was a fine August morning about ten o'clock in the school summer holidays. I must have been at least thirteen years of age as if younger, I don't think I'd have been allowed out on my own. I was dressed appropriately, wearing

Wellington boots and carrying a basket. My mother watched me go out down The Promenade wall and over the mud flats. She waved and went in the house. My brother had shown me where the nets were and how to take the fish off the hooks, but I wasn't going to lug them. I was walking quite happily when I came across soft muddy sand. I was unable to take my feet out and could feel myself gradually sinking. As my boots filled with mud, I continued to sink even further down. I can remember trying to pull my body to get out, flinging the basket away. I somehow moved forward and was able to lever myself out, but not before I was up to my chest in mud. I think I managed to get out with one or maybe two of my boots, but I was so frightened that I can't remember certain facts, just relief at getting out. I was crying and covered in mud from head to toe. I looked towards my house on The Promenade, but there was no one to be seen, so I just picked up my basket and walked home. I can't remember having any fish in my basket so I must have walked into the quicksand on my way out. I walked down the driveway to my house shouting to my mother who quickly rushed out to see what was wrong. She comforted me, helped me out of my clothes and I had a very welcome bath. In the evening, my father said that as far as he knew there was only one patch of quicksand in the area, a couple of yards in diameter. This is what I had found. Needless to say, I never went fishing nets again. Even now, many years later, I always avoid walking in mud."

Baskets and *stwcs* were used to transport the cockles for marketing. They were made locally by the men of the cockle women's families. The *stwcs* were fashioned out of special wooden casks with stainless steel bands, through which liquid was unable to escape. The casks were cut into two with two handles carved out of one half. The other half became the *stwc*.

Butter was delivered to the villages from Carmarthenshire farms in tubs, which were suitable for converting into *stwcs*. The empty tubs were collected by William Rees to make into *stwcs* for his daughter, Mary.

Hazel or birch twigs were gathered in the autumn, and in the following spring, when the sap had dried out and the twigs more flexible, were skillfully woven into baskets.

Hilary Edwards, née Durban's maternal *Dad-cu*, Joseph Henry Barnfield, always with pipe in mouth, made cockle baskets and *stwcs* in a shed in his large garden in Penlan. His mother, Ann Barnfield, kept a small general stores in Mill Street, where she sold Canadian apples, which were delivered in wooden casks. When empty, the casks provided a constant supply of suitable material for her son to make *stwcs*. Later, he made Hilary a small cockle basket with an intricately woven handle, more elaborate than the working baskets. Hilary spent many happy hours watching her grandfather working in his warm wooden shed. The men of the village did not supply an adequate number of baskets for the cockle women. Many were bought from blind institutes, the nearest being in Morriston, about six miles from Penclawdd.

Each cockle woman had her own 'patch' for selling her produce, be it in a street in a particular village or town, or in Swansea Market. This she established over a period of time and returned to each week or year. It was an unwritten and unspoken law that nobody poached on another's 'patch'. The understanding was faithfully respected by all. Over the years, the cockle women made many friends amongst their customers.

They often sold laverbread as well as cockles. Laverbread grows on beaches around the Welsh coastline. It was usually fried with cockles and home-cured bacon, and was a favourite meal any time of the day.

Before the commencement of the train and bus services to Penclawdd, cockles were only sold within walking distance of the village, for example, Swansea, Llanelli and the Gower Peninsular. Swansea Market has been famous for its cockle sellers for many years. The cockle women walked the nine miles to Swansea, carrying a basket full of cockles on each arm and a *stwc* full of cockles on their heads. They walked barefoot to *Olchfa* between Killay and Sketty, about seven miles east of Penclawdd, to save wear on their leather soled boots, which they tied to their baskets or waists. At *Olchfa*, the cockle women washed their feet in the stream, donned their boots, and continued walking to Swansea respectably shod. This procedure was reversed on the homeward journey. Their baskets now containing provisions, tea, sugar, etc., which they had bought in Swansea with part of the income earned from selling their cockles. The arrival of the train service in the 1860s made the transporting of cockles easier, enabling the shellfish to be sold further afield. The first passenger service from Penclawdd only ran on a Saturday. The cockle women wore Welsh costumes and close fitting black cockle bonnets with white starched frills under the brims. Their cockle baskets were covered with white cloths. After selling their cockles at Swansea Market, they returned on the 2.30 p.m. train. As their baskets and *stwcs* contained *rhywbeth danteithion* (some luxuries), the train was named the 'Relish Train'. They carried their money received from their sales in bags around their waists, under their pinafores. Their husbands waited patiently outside the station, and only when handed to by their wives, did they dutifully carry the baskets and *stwcs* home.

From 1897 to 1899, at the ages of eighteen to twenty-one, Lizzann McCarthy lodged each summer in Bristol, to sell cockles. Having gathered

Penclawdd Railway Station.
Cockle women carrying stwcs on their heads.

and prepared the cockles in Penclawdd, her mother and sisters sent them on the 6.30 Saturday morning goods train to Temple Meads Station in Bristol. Lizzann collected the cockles, and spent Saturday selling them around the houses from door to door. Through bad health as a child, Lizzann started school at the late age of eight, missing much schooling and as a result was unable to read. She was also Welsh-speaking. The two factors resulted in her marketing of cockles in an English city extremely difficult. She was unable to read the street signs and conversation with her customers was almost impossible. The added misery of being away from family and friends made her naturally extremely homesick. She was a faithful member of Tabernacle Chapel in Penclawdd, and so, attended a local chapel with her landlady during her stay in Bristol.

When twenty-one years of age, she married Joseph Henry Barnfield, of the same age, and left the cockle industry to attend to her family of eventually five daughters, Annie, Rosy, Jane, Elsie and Gwyneth, one having died in infancy. When first married, the couple lived with Lizzann's parents in Band Row, but within two years, Lizzann was to loose both her parents. Her daughter, Gwyneth Durban, remembers her mother talking of the sad time. "My father had gone up the garden to pick peas, cabbage and pull some new potatoes so it must have been summer time. As he looked

Lizzann McCarthy in working clothes.

towards the old docks, he saw a crowd had gathered and realized that something must have happened. Half an hour later they carried my grandmother home. She had dropped dead while sieving cockles. She was forty-one. Two years later, my grandfather was killed in Cwma Colliery, and my parents went to live with my father's parents in Mill Street." Lizzann's siblings were not so fortunate. Now orphans, and with no one

Lizzann McCarthy in 'Sunday Best'.

to look after them, the youngest – Jane, Daniel and William – were forced to enter Penmaen Workhouse.

At the age of thirteen years, the miners' strike of 1915 instigated Mary Bennett to start cockling to earn money for her family, as her father and brothers were miners and so unemployed. She decided to go to Llantrisant where the tin-plate works was in operation, and hopefully money would be reasonably plentiful. It was to be her first journey beyond Swansea. Her father picked the cockles and went with her to the lower Gowerton

172

Station, where his parting words were, "If you can't sell the cockles, throw them and come home." Not knowing where to alight from the train, she was advised by a lady passenger to write her destination on a label on her basket, and where the basket was removed from the train, to follow suit. She took the advice, and arrived safely in Llantrisant.

The road from the train station to the town went through the tin-plate works, where Mary sold most of her cockles. She continued selling around the houses. One of her customers invited Mary in for a rest and some refreshments. Mary readily agreed and was served much appreciated toast and a cup of tea. Mary comments of the lady of the house, "She was a clean little woman." On completing the sale of her cockles, and with two pounds in her pocket, Mary was anxious to contact home. "I went to the post office and I sent a telegram home to tell them to send me more cockles as I hadn't done half the place. My next thoughts were 'What am I going to do now, and where am I going to sleep?' So I thought I would return to my customer who had invited me into her house for breakfast. I asked her if she knew where I could have lodgings. She answered, 'I've got a bedroom here, but I can't tell you until my husband comes home from the tin-plate works.'" When the woman's husband arrived home, both he and Mary were embarrassed. "He had been teasing me earlier when buying my cockles in the tin-plate works. His face went redder than mine." When the husband heard of Mary's predicament, he kindly said to her, "I can't see you on the road. I've got children myself. You can stop here." She lodged in the house for eight happy years until she married at the age of twenty-two years.

A few years after her daughter was born, her husband suffered a disabling accident in the colliery and was invalided out of work. Mary decided to return to her former career of selling cockles. "I thought I'd go back to Llantrisant, so I borrowed a donkey as the rest of my family were using ours." Mary returned to her old 'patch' but extended it further to Cowbridge, Penygraig and Pontypridd.

Mary's sister, Ethel, enjoyed fishing in the estuary with her father, but was soon impatient to gather cockles and have her own 'patch'. She acquired a donkey and started cockling. A neighbour helped sell her cockles by inviting Ethel to accompany her on her 'patch' in Morriston. A little later, Ethel's sister, Mary, helped her to acquire her own 'patch' in Pontyclun, in the Rhondda Valley. "My mother bought me a small pail. One Friday, I went with my sister by train to Llanharan. My sister got out there and told me to carry on to Pontyclun, and when there, to ask the porter to put me on the main road. I got out at Pontyclun with my little tub of laverbread and a basket of cockles, with white starched linen cloths over them. There were beautiful, big houses outside Pontyclun, so I thought, 'here goes!' The first house belonged to a solicitor. I went round the back and knocked on the door. When it opened, I could see silver being cleaned in the kitchen. I asked if they liked cockles. An upstairs window opened and a lady in a dressing gown popped her head out and said, 'Oh! We love cockles.' She came downstairs and bought my cockles. 'Oh! What a lovely tea towel you have.' She said. 'I wish mine were like that.' I used to starch my towels and iron them on both sides. They were stiff. The following week, I took her a tea towel. We became firm friends. She was a lovely lady.

After knocking on every door, I continued the few miles to Brynsadler. I travelled down a little lane to a terrace of three houses. At one of the houses, belonging to Mr. and Mrs. West, I sold the last of my cockles." When the owners realized that Ethel was a native of Penclawdd, they informed her that a minister of Penclawdd, the Reverend Arthur Jenkins, had lived in the vicinity with his sister.

By midday on that first day of establishing her own 'patch' Ethel had sold all her cockles. She met her sister at the train station to go to Penygraig. Mary sold the rest of her cockles there and they ran back to the train station to catch the 5.00 p.m. train home."

A friendship was quickly established between Mr. and Mrs. West and Ethel, and they provided her with a hot midday meal for many future years while she sold cockles in the area. Ethel returned their kindness by inviting their daughter, Gwyneth, who attended the local High School, to spend a holiday with her and her family, in Llotrog.

Gwyneth experienced a wonderful holiday. Ethel's father familiarized Gwyneth with the unique beauty of the Gower Peninsular, of limestone headlands, sandy bays, ruined castles, cromlechs and downs. One of the highlights of the holiday was a visit to King Arthur's Stone, a megalithic tombstone on Cefn Bryn – the limestone and sandstone humpbacked downs that form the spine of the peninsular. Gwyneth enjoyed herself so much, that she persuaded the Rees family to allow her to stay for a week beyond the arranged time. After her return home, Gwyneth's parents, and her sister Blanch, came to visit Ethel's family. Ethel had guessed that they were anxious to discover the living conditions to which they had subjected their daughter. Mrs. West admitted, "Well, Ethel, I wasn't that willing for Gwyneth to come down here, but I need not have worried, as you have a beautiful home." The West family has remained good friends with Ethel to this day.

Ethel was dissatisfied as she felt that her round was too small. "It was enjoyable but I wanted more. I was married at last, and I told my husband,

Lenny, that I was going to buy a van. He was not happy at the thought of me driving on my own, but I insisted. I learned to drive with Fletcher's School of Motoring in Swansea." Although it was obvious to Ethel's driving instructor that it was her first experience of driving a motor vehicle, he was bewildered by her excellent road sense. When he questioned her, "You tell me that you have not driven a car before, but you have been driving something."

"Yes, I have been driving a horse and cart, and I know the dangers of the road." Ethel replied.

She soon passed her test, as did her husband, Lenny, who had been learning to drive at the same time. Ethel bought a van and joined the minority of female driver vehicle owners of the 1930s. Her van enabled her to extend her 'patch' to a larger area in the Rhondda Valley, including Teilas Town and Mardy. As well as her cockles, Ethel, helped by her sister Lilian Thomas, sold laverbread and fresh home-grown produce, which she bought in Swansea Market. When her son, Harold, married, she sold her daughter-in-law's garden produce of vegetables and flowers. At first they sold door to door, but eventually, they parked the van and their customers came to them.

Lenny Coghlan was a miner, as was his father before him. When Lenny was fifteen, his father was killed in the colliery, when a stone fell on the back of his neck while he was taking his food break. When Lenny had a minor accident in his work, Ethel was adamant that he was to leave his dangerous employment. She informed him, "You are not going back. You are coming 'out the sands' with me." Much to Ethel's relief, he agreed. "We built a cockle plant on Salthouse Point in Crofty. We rose together, had food together and did everything together for over twenty years. Mind, we used to have our stormy patches. It was cloudy many days, but it was beautiful when the storm was over. I loved going out early in the morning, about four o'clock. It was as if the world was coming alive. The birds would be singing and sometimes the cuckoo. It was a wonderful feeling. Nobody knows what it is. It was wonderful to be alive. Still dark, we dressed the horses in the fields where we kept them on Salthouse Point, and we'd go down over the sands as happy as anything – both of us together, for twenty-four years, my husband and me."

In 1939, at the age of fourteen years, Della Williams established her own selling 'patch' in Newport, which she took over from her grandmother. Her grandmother spent only one week familiarizing Della with the 'patch', which consisted of many miles, all undertaken by foot. The 'patch' consisted of the following routine:

Monday:	The docks area of Newport in the afternoon.
Tuesday:	Bargoed and Aberbargoed.
Wednesday:	Bedwys and Trethomas.
Thursday:	Risca and Cross Keys.
Friday:	Remained all day in Newport.
Saturday:	Crymlyn, Newbridge, Abercarn and Cwmcarn.

The inhabitants of the area were only interested in boiled cockles. The cockles were carried in *stwcs* on the head and in baskets on each arm. Hannah Jenkins taught her granddaughter the skilled art of 'carrying on the head'. A small towel was folded into a circle and placed inside a flat hat, which when placed on the head, provided an even flat pad for the *stwc*. "It was a different type of selling to the Swansea Valley; selling that I wasn't used to because I had to learn to carry on my head. It was said that they were not Penclawdd cockles if they were not carried on the head. I held my *stwc* for about two months if not more before I could balance it." At the end of the week, Hanah Jenkins left Della to her own devices to find herself a new cockle 'patch' nearby. Unexplainably, the cockle-selling season was during the summer months in this area, as opposed to the winter months in the Swansea Valley. In her first year's selling season, March to October, Della stayed in Newport, her cockles being sent by her mother, Margaret Jones, by train from Penclawdd. Her mother joined her on Saturdays to help her sell cockles. Della was very homesick, and always wished that she could accompany her mother home to Penclawdd at the end of the day. But she thought positively. "When I was in Newport, I used to count myself fortunate, as my grandmother used to take me to the pictures (cinema) every Monday and sometimes to the theatre on a Thursday. My grandmother loved the theatre. Many girls in Penclawdd never went to the pictures and certainly not the theatre." After her first selling season, Della commuted to Newport from Penclawdd three times a week. The rest of the week she spent 'going out the sands'. Della worked this strict routine for fifty-one years.

The 1930s saw the introduction of a public bus service from Llanrhidian to Swansea via Penclawdd. The bus service continued to improve to such an extent that by 1937 the passenger train service terminated.

The goods train service terminated in 1957 and in 1961 the railway lines were removed. A familiar feature of Penclawdd had disappeared forever. Fortunately, the station house was bought by Wynford and Janice Sage, and converted into an attractive dwelling, appropriately named, Whistlestop House. The platform overgrew with grass but has been well tended and retained, so happily the station is still recognizable.

By the 1940s, the United Welsh Transport and the South Wales Transport bus services provided excellent transport for the cockle women, eventually running every half-hour from Llanmorlais to Swansea. The cockle women's baskets occupied much space in the buses, but nobody objected. It was part of life in Penclawdd that everyone accepted, cockle people and non-cockle people alike. The villagers enjoyed each others company while travelling by bus. It was so different from the lonely car journeys of today.

In 1941, Swansea Market received extensive damage during the consecutive three night bombing raid on Swansea, by the Germans. All that remained was a red bricked shell containing mullion window frames. Within these walls were a few permanent stalls, but the cockle women sold their harvests on temporary affairs, usually by the main entrance of the Market in Oxford Street.

Although considered a Penclawdd industry, laverbread was not gathered on the Penclawdd coast. Ethel Coghlan bought her laverbread wholesale from Roch, a Bishopston firm trading in Swansea Market. When the proprietors retired, and the firm ceased trading, Ethel and Lenny decided to 'branch out' into the laverbread industry. They were the first cockle gatherers to do so in Penclawdd, but were soon followed by others. Ethel and her husband built a laverbread factory near their cockle plant on Salthouse Point. They gathered cockles in the week and at weekends, picked the seaweed, travelling many miles around the Welsh coast, from Freshwater West on the north coast of the Llwchwr Estuary, to North Wales. Collecting laverbread was no easy task. The weed was picked by hand on high tides after the sea had washed over it, and put in pails. It was wet, and so very heavy at this stage. The pails were carried to the parked van – in most instances over rocky beaches and steep cliffs – in relays, to make the task easier. At the factory, it was imperative that hygiene was strictly practised. Stainless steel, chrome and plastic utensils were sterilized and windows veiled. Each process was undertaken in individual rooms. The weed was washed by hand in chrome plated baths, with six changes of clean water, and drained in plastic sieves. In the boiling room it was cooked in stainless steel containers over jets fired by Calor Gas. The weed was gradually added to a measured amount of water in the containers, more being added as the previous amount reduced. "It was just like boiling cabbage, only for much longer," comments Ethel. The weed was cooked for eight hours, stirring continually, making sure it did not dry or burn. It was essential to use the correct proportion of water to weed, as this insured the setting of the laverbread. The amount was perfected and used instinctively over a period of time. The hot bubbling laverbread was carried in stainless steel buckets to the mincing room. Says

Ethel, "It went through the mincing machine and out onto trays hot and steamy. It was lovely then. We would eat a little bit. It would fill the trays like a black sea." It was left overnight and by morning was set. The laverbread was put in plastic containers called morns and then taken to market.

Ethel says, "Today, cockling is big business. It's everyone for themselves now. They do not look after each other as we did. We were like one big family." The cockle women worked long and hard hours for little money. Their diligence today would have earned them good wages. Ethel's sister, Lilian Thomas, rightly states, "We were born too early." Despite the extreme difficulties and dangers of the work, the cockle women agree that the attraction of the work was the companionship and independence it provided, as well as the extra family income. But Marian Eaton comments, "It was mainly women's work. It was beneath a man's dignity."

Over the years, new laws have forced the cockle industry to change drastically. The family-firm of Selwyn's – Shell Fish Processors – was established in 1950 and still trades in Llanmorlais as a family business, employing a workforce of twenty. It is now owned by the late Selwyn Jones' son, Brian – great-nephew of Ethel Coghlan – and his wife, Alison. Their son Ashley, daughter Hayley, and son-in-law Paul, are also involved in the business. Alison talks of its growth.

"We started cooking the cockles in the garden and progressed to a Nissen hut, which meant we worked under cover for the first time. Local regulations changed and we built a shed that contained a more automated system of processing the cockles. Brian and I went to the markets and around the valleys selling boiled and shell cockles, mussels, and home produce. We became conscious of more demand for cockles at home and abroad – receiving much interest from Holland. We decided to improve our machinery, which meant that we needed a larger building. This move took us out of the cottage industry and fortunately it paid off. However, regulations kept changing and the only way forward for us was to build a factory that would comply with EEC standards. In our new building everything has been 'hospitalized'. We have white plastic cladding, and we wear white plastic boots, white caps, white coats and white gloves.

We supply ten supermarkets in Wales. So far, we have not ventured into the English supermarkets, as we don't know if our fresh produce will be appreciated there. All our vehicles are refrigerated. We have four mobiles that we take to open-air and covered markets – Carmarthen, Maesteg,

Newport, Ebbw Vale, Talbot Green, and Cardiff. The vans have temperature controls that can be monitored on top and underneath the counters. They give us the freedom of being able to take the cockles wherever we wish to go and so we have expanded our trade considerably. We also take our produce to Slough, Rainham in Kent, and Billingsgate Market and Selfridges in London.

It is surprising how, years ago, the 'old people' travelled as far as Bristol and Bath to sell their cockles. I think they were very brave to travel so far away from home, and sometimes on their own. They were very dominant characters. Where I trade up the valleys, my customers often tell me of how the cockle women used to come there with their baskets on their arms, and their *stwcs* on their heads, wearing white aprons, and their cockles covered with white cloths. They also experimented in pickling cockles. Its amazing how they tried to expand, within their limited facilities. There are only about half-a-dozen woman going 'out the sands' now, and few are entering the profession.

Left to right: Alison, Brian, Mark (helper), Paul and Hayley.

179

In the 1980s, when the mines started using machinery instead of horses, we did the same, as it was labour intensive. We pushed the authorities into allowing us to use tractors and eventually Land Rovers on the sands. To do so, we had to break existing laws, and often appeared in court, until eventually, the Welsh Office conceded, and changed the laws in our favour. For example, the old laws stated that we could only take the vehicles on high water, but the cockles are in low water.

The vehicles are a great advantage over the horse and cart, affording far more comfort and protection. I also think that the animals are happy to be retired. When we fetched the horses in the mornings, we used to tempt them with bits of bread, but, especially on cold and wet days, they would run to the other side of the field. They knew where they were going, to the Wild West, and did not want to go. When we were 'out the sands', all the horses would follow the first horse to leave the sands, even if their owners had not finished gathering cockles. There was no way of stopping the horses as there was no grass there, and sometimes they would run home. We were also limited as to where we could take the horses. They would not venture over the large areas of soft sand that exists in the estuary, as they were very sensitive to danger. This is not a problem with the vehicles.

We still hand-rake the cockles. It is the only thing that has not changed in the industry. We are strongly against dredging in this area, as we are conscious of the necessity to preserve the cockle stocks. Also, dredging leaves broken shells in with the cockles. Our method of gathering is more expensive, but produces far superior cockles.

It is a wonderful experience gathering cockles; working so close to nature. Although we are aware of the danger of the tides, it is still very tranquil out there in the estuary. We can hear the cockles 'singing'. They come to the surface of the sand and all open their shells for water at the same time. It sounds like a melody. When we tread on them, the 'singing' takes on different tones. It's fascinating. A young boy, unable to work because of mental problems, has been advised to gather cockles for therapeutic reasons. It is unusual for the authorities to allow someone taking Social Security to work.

Cockle picking is a lucrative business today, but it had not always been so. My father and mother-in-law often recalled how they use to gather cockles with a spoon, one by one, as supplies were so scarce. The Oyster Catchers and Spatina grass were blamed, but the real reason is not known. Nature has its own way of determining what is going to happen. Fortunately, at the moment, the beds are well stocked.

Cockles are considered a delicacy in some countries. The Spanish love them. We export our canned cockles and laverbread – which are canned by a canning company – to supply the Spanish market.

We are trying to encourage our produce to be eaten cold or heated without fat as opposed to frying and so promoting it as a healthy food. Far better to have the real thing then take kelp tablets. Unfortunately, our produce cannot be labelled organic as organic produce has to have management farming, but it is naturally harvested. We pick some laverbread in Pembrokeshire, but the rest we buy.

Last May 17th (1999) the Queen and the Duke of Edinburgh came to Cardiff to open the Welsh Assembly. They revisited 3M's in Gorseinon, where several years ago they had opened a new part of the factory. They also visited Cefn Hengoed School in Swansea. The school was allocated money as a consequence. The Queen and Duke wanted to see working people in Wales and I think the council thought that the cockle pickers would be ideal because of their heritage. We were asked to house their

Mary Bennett being introduced to Queen Elizabeth.

visit. Robert and Sheila Allen, owners of the Welcome to Town in Llan-rhidian, provided us with delicacies made from our produce – roulades, pâtés, etc. – for the occasion. We were limited in the people we invited, to our close family, and those who had been 'on the sands' all their lives. My mother-in-law, Lynda, suggested that we invite her aunty, Mary Bennett – now in her late nineties – the oldest cockle women and probably the oldest inhabitant of Crofty. So Mary came in her finery. She sat outside the factory chatting away, but as the Queen and Duke were about to arrive, Mary's leg caught in one of the stirrups of her wheelchair. Her leg started bleeding so profusely that we had to call an ambulance, but Mary insisted on waiting until the Queen and the Duke had greeted her before she went in it. The Queen said to her that she believed Mary had been a member of the cockle industry. Mary replied, 'Yes, and if it wasn't for my eyesight, I'd be out there now.'"

NOTES

1. Cockle: An almost circular bi-valve mollusc. Its soft body, which is yellow in colour in this area, is protected by its shell. The baby cockles are called spats. After its brief swimming stage, it settles in the soft muddy sands of the estuary where it grows in beds. When about a twentieth of an inch in length, it lives on minute plants and organisms in the sea-water moving very slightly through the sand by using its strong muscular foot. It adds two rings to its shell in the first year and one in each following year, making it possible to tell its age by its shell. At three years it is about one inch across and can live to six years. Like many plants, the cockles grow more rapidly with sun and rain. The cockles gathered in the Llwchwr Estuary are renowned for their flavour and tenderness and it is said by the locals that they are the 'best in the world'. Although the breeding season is in April, May and June, cockle gathering takes place throughout the year.
2. Mussel: A marine bi-valve, having a dark slightly elongated shell and living attached to rocks.
3. Both the Hodges' home, and Morgan Morgans' living and shop premise were known as Manchester House.
4. Now the Community Centre.
5. Exert from North Gower Heritage Group Letter Number 4. Spring 1996.
6. The firm, established in 1856, still exists today, and is one of the most successful fish merchants in Swansea, trading on a stall in Swansea Market as Coakley Green and Sons.
7. Small areas of Penclawdd.
8. Laverbread: An edible seaweed.
9. Exert from North Gower Heritage Group Letter Number 4. Spring 1996.
10. As the *cram* is an implement invented by the Welsh speaking cockle women, the word is untranslatable. The *rhaca* is a rake.
11. Marshland where Penclawdd Docks had been.
12. Chickens need gritty material to help digest their food. The grit collects in a muscular organ known as the gizzard, which grinds their food into digestible particles. Chickens also absorb the calcium from the cockleshells, which help them produce strong eggshells.

6

Penclawdd at War

Few of Penclawdd's inhabitants remember the First World War, which David Lloyd George referred to as 'This war, like the next war, is the war to end all wars.'

The Allied Powers – Britain and the Empire, France, Russia (left December 1917), Japan, Italy (entered May 1915), Serbia, Belgium, Romania (entered August 1916) and USA (entered April 1917) – and the Central Powers – Germany, Austria-Hungary, Turkey (entered November 1914) and Bulgaria (entered October 1915) – fought from 1914 to 1918 in the struggle to gain territory and power.

The Western and Eastern Fronts in Europe, Italy, the Middle East, the German Colonies in Africa and the Pacific witnessed the ravages of war. It was fought at sea and in the air, but it was the trench warfare on land that incurred the greatest fatalities. Tens of thousands of lives were lost on both sides, leaving horrific carnage on the battlefields – to become known as the Killing Fields.

When the First World War was declared in August 1914, it was presupposed that business would continue as usual, and the conflict would be short-lived. As the war progressed, it became obvious that these assumptions were wrong, and that the government should take control.

In 1915, the Defence of the Realm Act was passed, which gave the government the power to commandeer factories and convert them to any use they so desired. The British Army had experienced a shortage of shells in the Battle of Ypres in April 1915. As a consequence, the government quickly passed the Munitions Act in May 1915, which created the Ministry of Munitions under David Lloyd George. It empowered the state to control all aspects of the manufacture of munitions. By 1918, this Ministry employed over three million people, producing shells and guns at the rate required by the army.

A Ministry of Food was established in 1917 to distribute food, considering both civilian and military requirements. By February 1918, rationing – of meat, butter, bacon, lard, sugar and ham – was introduced when the full effects of the U-boat attacks on British shipping were felt.

The government controlled and directed manpower. The Ministry of

Labour, assisted from March 1917 by the Ministry of National Service, ensured that essential workers were kept at home. Conscriptions from 1916 were carefully monitored to avoid too many skilled men joining up.

Wilfred Tucker, although a small boy at the time, remembers the years of the First World War. "I have some vivid memories of the First World War, because aircraft was in its infancy at that time. I can see it in my mind's eye now. Mother had told me to call in Morgan John's shop to buy something, on my way home from school. I came home through the village. I could only have been about seven or eight years old. I was looking up at Cae Trumpic, above Tenlan, when I saw an airship coming over the hill. They were used to patrol the coast and were kept at Pembrey, where there was an ammunition works. It was very exciting.

The soldiers used to come home in full kit, especially if they were coming home on last leave before embarkation. They carried haversacks, gas masks, rifles and bayonets. A solder living in Blue Anchor came off the train in front of me when I was coming home from school. I followed him all the way home, not taking my eyes off him.

I remember the first military funeral I ever saw in the church. William John, John Fry's son, had been killed in the Battle of Jutland, I think. There were uniformed soldiers, sailors and police. We were thrilled to bits. We were sitting on the churchyard wall on the north side, waiting for the gun firing salute. Anyone in uniform at that time was so exciting. Church members always held an evening of entertainment for the young men serving their country in the armed forces on home leave."

Daniel Rees, now a centenarian, was enlisted into the army, and served his country fighting in the trenches in France during the last six months of the war. "I did not volunteer to go into the services, but when I was seventeen – not eighteen until the following April – the government said to me 'Daniel, you've got to go to the army.' They sent me a letter asking me to come and be examined to join the army. My father thought I was too young. He went to see the gentleman concerned who said to him, 'Alright, if you give me a bit of money, I will keep Daniel out of the war for a while.' They were bad days. My father did not know what to do, as although he thought I was too young, he did not want to do bad things. However, he gave the gentleman the money and so I passed my certificate in Gowerton County School, and then went to the army in the following October. Not many men went from Penclawdd. I was very young. I was in with the English people in the York and Lancashire Regiment. It was a very good regiment." Daniel was shot in the right arm by a bullet, but stayed in France until the end of the war.

Life in Penclawdd during the Second World War is remembered by many.

Audrey Rees vividly recalls the declaration of war at eleven o'clock on the morning of 3 September 1939. "I was in the conservatory in Westminster House with my cousin, Rhidian, and my friend, Dorothy Eaton. Mamma was going into the kitchen to fetch a very large rice pudding, which she had cooked in the oil stove. Suddenly, an announcement came over the wireless that war had been declared."

The Second World War was a 'total war', which demanded the effort of the nation as a whole to ensure survival and ultimately, victory. Unlike the First Word War, the civilian population of Britain was under threat of attack by the German Luftwaffe (German Airforce). The Air Raid Precaution Act was passed in November 1937, coming into force on 1 January 1938, to prepare against attacks, and rearmament commenced. When war broke out, buildings had been sandbagged, gas masks issued, and static water tanks for fire-fighting and air-raid shelters constructed. A blackout was imposed at night. Street lamps were turned off, railway carriages were lit by dim blue bulbs, and house windows were to be covered with thick material so that no light could escape. ARP (Air Raid Precaution) wardens were appointed to supervise specified areas during an attack. Identity cards were issued to everyone. It was all part of the organisation of Civil Defence, which played a vital part during the Blitz.

The government had learned from the First World War that mobilisation of the nation was essential in a 'total war'. The Emergency Powers Acts (1939 and 1940) provided the government with complete authority to direct the lives of people in the interest of the war effort.

Conscription (compulsory military service) was introduced for men aged eighteen to forty during the summer of 1939. On the declaration of war, the young males of twenty years of age were the first to be enlisted into the services. As the war continued, casualties increased. More men were needed, and so the enlisting age increased and decreased by a year. The youngest age halted at seventeen and a half years, but the oldest age continued to rise.

The Schedule of Reserved Occupations introduced in 1939 stated, that men in vital jobs – for example, miners, agricultural workers, munition workers, boiler-makers and teachers – were exempt from the armed forces.

By May 1940, German forces were moving rapidly across France and the Low Countries, and an invasion of Britain seemed imminent. Anthony Eden, Secretary of State for War, called upon all able-bodied men between seventeen and sixty-five years, not in the services, to join the Local Defence Volunteers – later to be renamed the Home Guards. Within twenty-four hours, twenty-five thousand men had enrolled. Their official duties were to observe and defend strategic points in the local areas, such as roads and factories, sabotage enemy movements in the event of invasion, and to attack small enemy detachments.

In December 1941, the Ministry of Labour extended the conscription age of men to fifty-one years, and single women between the ages of nineteen and thirty were also called. The latter were given the option of joining one of the armed forces – WRNS (Womens Royal Navy Service) ATS (Auxiliary Territorial Service) or WAAF (Womens Auxiliary Air Force) – the Civil Defence, or working in factories connected with the war effort – making ammunition, etc. Married women were allowed to volunteer for the forces, or employment, and boys of sixteen were permitted to volunteer for the Home Guards. The Women's Land Army organised women to work on farms throughout the country.

The Local Authority for evacuation organised the evacuation of children and teachers from built up areas to rural counties, and many people left the cities to stay with relatives in country areas.

On 8 January 1940, the Ministry of Food introduced rationing. 'In spring 1942, the rations consisted of 6p worth of meat per week (this worked out at about a pound in weight (450 grams), bacon four ounces (100g), sugar 8 ounces (225g), cheese 3 ounces (75g) tea 2 ounces (50g), butter 2 ounces (50g), margarine 4 ounces (100g). The ration of preservatives amounted to one pound (450g) per month. In addition, there was a 'points' system. Each person was allocated 16 points for a period of a month, which could be spent on items such as tinned fruit, rice and tinned vegetables. Points could be spent at any shop, the snag being that the cost of food in points varied in accordance with supplies (the lower the stocks, the higher the price in points). About 4 ounces (100g) of sweets and chocolates per month could be obtained on the 'personal points' rations scheme. Bread, however, remained unrationed during the war: instead the extraction rate of wheat was raised to 85 per cent so that less grain was used to make flour. The only loaf made was called the 'national wheatmeal'.[1] Each citizen was issued with a ration book. They were to register with a retailer from whom they obtained all their rationed food.

Petrol was rationed at the start of the war, and clothes were rationed from May 1941, as materials were needed for military uniforms. People were encouraged to grow their own food to supplement their diet and 'Dig for Victory' became a national slogan. Farmers were encouraged to produce more by being given subsidies and a guaranteed price for their crops.

The old engine house of Wernbwll Colliery was used as a distribution centre for the Gower butchers' meat allocation. Myfanwy Gronow worked at the centre for nine years.

"I used to love going there although it was only open on Thursday afternoons. All the meat was taken there and hung. The building was freezing. The meat was weighed on a very large weighing machine. My job was to calculate the price of the meat by its weight, which I did on my ready reckoner. The butchers were allocated by price different amounts, depending on their number of customers, and on each of their customer's needs – how many in the family. Each butcher was given a certain amount of fresh beef, pork and lamb and the rest of his allocation – if any – was made up with hard lamb (frozen lamb). The butchers had to calculate how much meat each of their customers were entitled to, which must have been difficult. One butcher, George Francis, was a real comic. 'Do you know?' he used to say, 'I'm sure I've got all the widows in Penclawdd.' A widow's meat allowance was very little, perhaps only a chop, whereas a family would be entitled to a joint. It used to amaze me how quickly George could calculate how much meat he could have in relation to the amount of money he was allowed. But he was used to going to the mart and you train your mind to work in the way that you need it to work. I would have to use the ready reckoner. I left the centre to go to Glanely Hospital in Cardiff, with my leg. George and four other butchers came to visit me. George tried to convince me that he had written me a letter while he had been a recent patient in Swansea Hospital. He said, 'I gave it to Nurse Green and asked her to deliver it to you – my best girlfriend. I'm sure I sent it. I even put a lot of commas and full stops at the end for you to put in the right places.' Oh! He was a real wag. I laughed and laughed and the nurses couldn't wait for them to go to hear the joke."

At the outbreak of war, Bert Thomas built a piggery on the small holding, Caerau, where he lived with his wife, Ceinwen, daughter, Joan (Callow), and son, Wynne. The property was situated between Penclawdd and Three Crosses. Joan, who was a young girl at the time, remembers the business. "My father worked in the engine house of Wernbwll Colliery until its closure in 1937. We were living in Caerau – a small holding about one mile from the colliery. He decided to build a piggery. He built it himself, having read a lot about the design. The pigs were kept in very clean conditions – a place for eating, a place for lying on fresh straw and a place where they went to the toilet. Pigs are very clean animals and adhered to this arrangement. However, I hated the smell of the piggery, and would do anything to avoid walking through it. The buying, selling and breeding of pigs made a decent living in those days, especially as my father had the contract for all the waste food (swill) from the army camp based in the west-end of Penclawdd. This waste food had to be heated to a certain temperature, and the 'boiler' used for this was one obtained from the engine house of the colliery. Every morning, a lorry arrived from the camp with the swill, and every morning, my mother made tea or coffee and Welsh cakes for the soldiers. Many good friends were made, and they often visited us in their free time at weekends. When the base became a prisoner of war camp, my father still had the contract, and so we came in contact with some of the prisoners. Although they were not allowed in the house, my mother still sent food outside for them. I can remember my father making frequent visits to Gloucester Mart. Very few people had cars then. He travelled from Swansea by train – sometimes leaving on Sunday evening and staying in a hotel near the station in Gloucester overnight. During the war years, every farm was allowed to kill two pigs per year for their own use. If you walked into a farmhouse, you always saw hams and bacon sides hanging by large hooks from the ceiling of the kitchen or living room. Neighbours tried to kill at different times, so that they could share the supply of brawn – made from pigs' heads – faggots, and fresh pig steak."

Most villagers had grown their own vegetables and kept pigs and chickens before the outbreak of war. There was now a restriction on the killing of pigs, but few were deterred. Sidney Parkhouse was one such villager, as his son, Dennis, remembers. "Our pig was killed, and Merfyn Gronow was salting the meat in my father's pantry. It was against the law, but everyone was doing it. Two local policemen, Mr. Lewis and Edgar Thomas called, and were having a drink in the kitchen with my father. Merfyn was trapped in the pantry for about three hours, getting hotter and hotter. It was roasting in there."

A system was immediately devised in the Elementary School to safeguard its pupils during a bombing attack. The school staff were forewarned by telephone from a reliable source, and when the sirens sounded, the school was quickly evacuated. The children living in close proximity to the school, who could get home within a short stipulated time did so, while the other children ran to houses near the school. When the all clear was given, all returned to school and lessons were resumed as normal.

However, the declaration of war greatly affected the attendance of pupils in the Infant School. Its Headmistress, Miss I. Mary Price, wrote in her school report after the summer holidays, on 4 September 1939, 'The school did not reopen today owing to the outbreak of war between this country and Germany. My two assistants and I attended school in the morning to await instruction, but as nothing came, we left at ten o'clock.'

On the eleventh of the month she reported, 'School reopened this morning. Only three children were admitted. Several parents have decided not to allow their children to start school owing to the war.' Four days later her report read, 'There are only sixty-six children on the books. All the children carry their gas masks back and forth to school. Gas mask drill is taken twice a day.' Later, the air raids on Swansea understandably had an adverse affect on the attendance, which the headmistress realized. On 2 September 1940, she reported, 'The signal was sounded immediately after marking of registers at 10.15 a.m. All the children were dispersed to their homes. They did not return to school after the all clear signal. There was no warning sounded in the afternoon, but the severity of last nights raid on Swansea is probably responsible for this reluctance of parents to send their children to school.' The three consecutive nights bombing of Swansea during the February of 1941 inevitably resulted in very poor school attendance.

Under the War Charities Acts 1940, a Comforts Fund was established in various areas, to help the young men and women in the services. When a Comforts Fund was established in Penclawdd, the villagers gave generously and the service men and women received a wealth of contributions. Glenys Harry, who was conscripted into the ATS, comments, "It was an excellent organisation. We had many gifts from the fund – gloves, etc." The village was divided into areas and volunteer collectors undertook house to house collections. Individual donations were also received. Funds were raised by entertainment – concerts, dramas, dances, Welcome Home concerts and Variety Days. The women of the village knitted garments, and various gifts were given such as oxo, chocolate, cigarettes and tobacco. In 1940, the first annual report of the fund was issued:

'1940 – First Annual Report of the PENCLAWDD COMFORTS for the TROOPS Fund. (Registered under War Charities Acts 1940)
Chairman – A. J. Jenkins Esq.
Hon. Treasurer – James Wallbey Esq.
Hon. Secretary – Bryn Evans Esq.
Hon. Assist Sec. – Robert Guy Esq.

In reviewing the work of the Penclawdd Comforts Fund for the year 1940, we may well feel proud of the splendid results achieved. This has been made possible because of the enthusiasm and support of the general public to the fund, and the lively interest of each member of the Committee in the work the Organization is now doing.

We would like to express our gratitude and appreciation to the following:

To those who contributed so generously to our 'Gift Day' Collection, to inaugurate the fund, an effort which realised the magnificent amount of £32-5/-. The Entertainment Committee for the organising of Welcome Home and other Concerts and Entertainments. The numerous artistes who have helped to make these concerts popular. The collectors[2] of the fund for faithful and conscientious work. Those ladies and gentlemen who have presided, and made presentations at Welcome Home and other Concerts. The women, old and young, for the large number of garments knitted. The vicar, for the church hall. The Officers and men of the Royal Sussex Regiment for their willing assistance at all times. Our own boys and girls now serving with H.M. Forces for their many hundred letters of appreciation for the work done on their behalf. To all the rest of you who have in anyway helped to make the fund the success it has been, and still is.

We hope that you will give the fund your continued support, and to those who have not yet contributed, may we take this opportunity of appealing to you to respond generously, so that the whole village may be united in this noble work, which will stand as an expression of the pride and affection we have for our boys and girls.

On behalf of the Committee
Bryn Evans, Hon. Secretary.

Woollen articles made and sent to the boys during the period Feb. 1940 to March 1941: Socks 451 pairs, Mittens 43 pairs, Cuffs 24 pairs, Gloves 33 pairs, Helmets 81, Scarves 84, Pullovers 74, Total 790.'

In the late 1930s, it had been realized that future air raids would be accompanied by fires. Before the war, Swansea Borough Police Force had manned and controlled an efficient modern fire brigade. However, under the Air Raid Precautions Act of 1937, the County Borough of Swansea had been obliged to provide an Auxiliary Fire Service (AFS). In 1938, the County Borough had arranged with Gower Rural District Council to establish a reciprocal fire service in the event of war. Steps had been taken to recruit and train five hundred volunteers, to include, firemen, drivers and supporting personnel – telephonists, engineers and electricians. The Swansea Borough Water Engineer had been instructed to provide an adequate water supply for fire fighting, and water, free from pollution, for public consumption. By 1941, there were about forty-six static water tanks in the County Borough. Administrative headquarters were set up in Northampton Gardens. Its 'A' divisional headquarters in St. Thomas served the centre, east and northern side of the town, and Sketty Hall, Sketty, its 'B' divisional headquarters, served the town's western side. The AFS consisting of both full-time and part-time personnel was to provide support for the regular Swansea Police Fire Brigade. Like the police force, it was controlled by the Borough Watch Committee, and under the command of the Chief Constable.

Penclawdd station was one of the substations to Swansea's headquarters. It was housed in a prefabricated lean-to, built behind the stone arch of the old copper works. The station was manned continuously by male and

Members of Penclawdd A.F.S.
Back row, left to right: Glyn Jenkins, Williams Henry Morgan (Forge), Cyril Howells, Leonard Hughes, Lez Jenkins, Herby Jones, Stan Jenkins, Willy Felsted, Dai Henry Davies (Dai Hendy), Trevor Richards, John Henry Howells, Harold Davies, Bryn Thomas (Chloroform), Luther Davies.
Middle row, left to right: Miriam Williams, Kathleen Williams, Howard Guy, Denny Williams, Proth Jenkins, Rosy Morgan, Harriet Williams, Tudor Jones.
Front row, left to right: Ernie Parkhouse, Brynmor Rees, Elwyn Thomas, Moc Morgan Leyshan, Gwyn Morgan, Garfield Jones, ? Hughes, Phil Jenkins.

female volunteers from the village, who worked a shift system. Denny Williams was its chief, and Wilfred Tucker the assistant chief.

Miriam and Kathleen Williams – identical twins – not wanting to leave Penclawdd to work for the war effort, decided to join the Penclawdd AFS. Kathleen has happy memories of their time spent in the organization. "We wanted to stay at home, so joined the Auxiliary Fire Service. Our job was to man the telephone switchboard. We used to go with the men on their practice exercises to Broad Pool at the foot of Cefn Bryn. They towed the pump by the tender (large van). We'd travel in the tender and come out like animals from the ark, two by two. We also helped them on exercises over the old docks. It was better than sitting in the office. When on duty in the evenings, we'd go to the dances in the church hall. If the officers came down from Swansea, the men used to run over and let us know and we'd go back around the grit works. Some of the men used to go to the Workingmen's Club, and we'd do the same for them. We'd run over, open the door and beckon them out. The men were good old sorts and very mischievous. We'd take our knitting on duty. They'd break the wool when our backs were turned and deny all knowledge of it. They taught us to play cards and dominos. They'd send us to John Harry's shop to buy bacon, etc. We'd cook it for them on the promise that they'd cover for us to go to a dance. One day, John Harry said, 'There's a nice bit of haddock here.' When we cooked it at the station, we had to open all the doors, as otherwise it would have smelt the place out. We drove the tender around the grit works. We slipped up in not applying for our driving licence then, as you didn't have to pass a driving test in those days. But we had no time, between working, going to the AFS, and attending all those dances. There were so many soldiers in the village. The 'Aliens' were in the camps. They'd come from everywhere. We went to HQ in Sketty, Swansea, to man the switchboards during the bombing raids on Swansea. We were terrified, but we still went. We were on duty there during the blitz of the town in 1941."

Cyril Howells joined the AFS in 1943, having spent four years in Dursley, Gloucestershire, serving an apprenticeship. "We spent much time reading, playing cards and chatting. The station was very cosy and was fine to sleep in on night shifts. The station had a full-time employer who worked nine to five each day. Every Sunday morning, everyone available took part in exercises 'out the docks'. Wilfred Tucker gave the orders and timed us on how long we took to take out the hose. Our station was used as a standby then. The stations nearer Swansea – Cocket, etc. – would be called out and we would move in and man them. We used to use the tender to transport our members to and from dances in Gower. I can remember returning empty bottles in the tender to the Blue Anchor pub on a Sunday morning, after a celebration on the previous Saturday night. Morgan Leyshon gave a demonstration of how he could drink a pint quickly. He put the glass to his mouth and didn't stop until it was all gone. I'm glad I joined as it was a good experience."

The industries connected with the war effort inland east of the Llwchwr Estuary – Gowerton Steelworks, Gowerton Tin-plate Works, the ICI works at Waunarlwydd – and the ammunition works at Pembrey on the north coast of the estuary, were prime targets for the German bombers. Wilfred Tucker remembers a frightening experience when on duty. "One night, when in the AFS station, we heard a plane coming across. We knew that the sirens had gone and suddenly everything lit up. We saw a string of flames in the estuary river stretching from Llanelli to Loughor. We waited for the big bang that thankfully never materialized. I think they made a mistake. We never discovered what actually happened."

The following articles were published in the 'South Wales Evening Post' newspaper on 8 May 1945:

THE PRICE SWANSEA PAID

Three nights of terror.

'We have excluded mention of the desultory and seemingly aimless raids on vicinities about Swansea – some of the areas with and others devoid of any conceivable military objective; of these, especially in 1940, there were a great many. At one time as many as 90 bombs had fallen in Gower area alone – Bishopston, along the marshy ground near Penclawdd, etc. In Ilston at one time three 500lb. and 400 incendiary bombs fell.

Swansea A. A. Defenses.

The German attack inflicted astonishingly little industrial damage; it seemed often to be weak, erratic and desultory.'

The village ARP Wardens were stationed in the headmaster's study of the Elementary School. Peggy Jones, née Howells, was an active member. "The war years were a busy time in the village. I was a member of the ARP with Mrs. Lord, Edie Evans, Ceinwen Francis and Mrs. Aldman. At first, we only had our metal helmets, but eventually we were provided with a uniform, which consisted of a navy skirt, navy tunic and a navy hat with a red and navy band, and a badge in front. Philip John Davies – a councillor – of Gower Stores, was in charge. Mr. Edwards the postman was also greatly involved. We were on duty day and night, and worked

Peggy Jones with metal helmet before being provided with uniform.

on a shift system. I was on duty two nights a week, and usually with Mrs. Lord. If there was an air raid, we went out assessing the damage, and phoning for the necessary equipment required. All the war organizations in the village paraded in uniform on carnival day."

The WVS (Womens Voluntary Service) opened a café in a hut at the bus stop in-between the forge and the Emporium. It was organized by Carys, daughter of Doctor Hughes. The café was open long hours to provide shelter and refreshments for the service boys and girls in the village. Peggy Jones also belonged to this organization. "We provided tea, coffee, baked beans on toast and toasted tea cakes – which we bought in the Emporium – for the soldiers. They would come of an evening, and sit in the back room, have a drink, a snack and a chat. Sometimes the Home Guards would come in, as, after all, they were soldiers. We were open in the morning, and until half-past nine at night. I worked Tuesday nights, and Thursday mornings." Food rationing and lack of provisions rendered home cooking a difficult task, but the WVS succeeded in supplying the men with a welcome resting-place. John Elliott visited it on the very few occasions that he was home on leave. "While we were waiting for the bus at night, we'd go in and have a cup of tea and a rock cake. They were rock cakes, too. It was always handy to go in there. It was a comfort place."

Major Tom Rees had served his country in the army in the First World War. It appears that he loved the discipline of army life and was 'in seventh heaven' when asked to organize the Home Guards in Penclawdd. An astonishingly high number of village men volunteered to join. A hut next to the WVS café was used as their headquarters and drilling was practised on the marsh opposite the Old Council Houses in the east-end of the village. The volunteers were armed with rifles and bayonets which they were allowed to keep at home. A daughter of one of the Home Guards formed an attachment to a soldier stationed on the Point. The relationship became serious and an engagement was imminent. However, the father discovered that the soldier was married, and threatened the young man with his bayonet. The mother of the girl quickly intervened by arranging with Major Rees to have the weapons removed from the house.

Peggy Jones' father was a member of the Home Guards. "My dad was in charge of armoury. I can remember a Bren gun on the table at home. He had about five Home Guards there at a time to show them how to dismantle it and put it together again. He knew a lot about guns – he used to shoot game – and had learned to repair them. My husband, John, was also a Home Guard. We had a scare one night when a parachute was seen coming down and it was feared that the Germans were landing. There was a rush. We women were told, 'Stay inside and lock the door. Don't open it until you hear the password 'green tiles'.' In a couple of hours the men returned. We asked them if they had found any Germans. They replied, 'No, but why didn't you lock the door? We've been able to walk in without mentioning 'green tiles'.'

Home Guard John Jones with nephew Ken Jones.

Sidney and Ivor Parkhouse belonged to the Home Guards. In later years, they often related humorous incidents of the time to Sidney's son, Dennis. "One evening a message came through that the Germans had landed in Llanmadoc. My father quickly went to the houses of the Home Guards rounding them up to prepare for the invasion. When he called at Geraint's house, Geraint told him, 'I can't come tonight. I'm working mornings.' There was a massive parade 'out the docks' and a general was coming down to inspect them. Graham Jones, a real character, was ready in his uniform but couldn't find his beret. He arrived on parade late, wearing his bowler hat. He stopped the parade as they all collapsed laughing. One of the guards went to Tom's house to let him know that he couldn't go on parade the next day. Tom was not at home so the guard left a message with Tom's wife, Liza. Later, Tom asked the man why hadn't he come on parade. 'But I let Liza know,' he said, 'I let her know that I wasn't coming.'

'Whose in charge of this bloody army?' said Tom, 'bloody Liza or me?'

The guards were in a trench practising rapid firing – six shoots at a target. My Uncle Ivor told Eddie, 'You've only fired five shots.'

'No I haven't.' said Eddie, and got up and fired his gun near the others. There was another bullet in it. All the guards got up and went home."

Tom was awarded the MBE for his services in Penclawdd Home Guards after they were disbanded in 1944.

In 1941, the stack of the old copper works was demolished, as it was deemed a dangerous landmark for incoming German bombers.

In the local industries, the bomb alert procedure was followed diligently. A red alert was sounded to forewarn the workers that the German planes were approaching. Another red alert announced that they were nearer, and all machinery was shut down, and lights switched off. The men used air-raid shelters underground and over ground. Sometimes the alert lasted for six to seven hours.

There were many false alarms. An alert was sounded in Gowerton Steel-works when it was feared that a bomb had landed on the works. On inspection, after all clear, it was discovered that a shell from a mobile anti-aircraft gun, probably fired near the White Gates, on the Gowerton-Penclawdd road, about one mile away, had come through the roof of the works, hit a girder and exploded. Fortunately, nobody was hurt. On another occasion, the Home Guards were called to investigate lights that had been seen on the marsh near Gowerton Steelworks. Their first two inspections proved fruitless, but on the third alarm, they decided to invigilate all night, only to discover that the lights were marsh gas. Wilfred Tucker remembers. "The area was covered with sodden marsh and gas used to come up through it and ignite. What they did about it I don't know, but at least they were satisfied that the lights were not Germans."

Mag, daughter of *Ben-y-Saer*, married William Henry (Will) Harris, of Mill Street, Penclawdd. Will obtained employment at the Eagle Bush Tin-plate Works, in Neath, and the couple took up residence at No. 12, New Henry Street, Neath. Will became partially blinded by the furnaces at the works, and was forced to retire. Mag established a small grocery shop in the front room of their house. She wrote to her sister, Sal Francis, No. 1, The Croft, Banc Bach, of her fears during the war years:

> 'Well, here I am again and thank God we are all still alive and well. I do hope you both are quite well. What a night Saturday night was! We had gone to bed, when two sirens went, so we were from the fire to the pantry all night. We must trust now that He will spare us. We've got a good mind to close up, but where are we safe? Sal, if anything happens to us, you will find three hundred pounds in the Neath Post Office in my name. Share it with Frank and Ben. Don't show this to anybody.
>
> Tons of love to you both,
> Mag and Will.'

Rudolph Ratti remembers the unfair treatment that his parents were subjected to by the authorities. "My father, being a native of Italy, was interned on the Isle of Man. Two weeks later, the local policeman, Sergeant Lord, came knocking on our door. He told my mother that she had to go to live at least twelve miles away from the coast. My grandfather was in the house at the time and said to Sergeant Lord, 'She's as British as you are, so what is it all about?'

'Well,' said Sergeant Lord, 'it's the law of the land. It's nothing to do with me Mr. Collins. It's British law. The wife takes the nationality of the husband.'

'Well what about the children then,' said my grandfather.

'The definition of the word native is to be born of a place and so they are British citizens,' replied Sergeant Lord.

The Collins had relations in Tumble and my mother spent about ten months there with my younger brother, Michael, who was preschool age. My grandparents came to live in our house, to look after my sister and me and to run the shop. My father wasn't away for long, as there were so many people in the village who could vouch for his good name. He'd come over to this country at the age of fourteen, and by then, he had lived far longer here, than in the country of his birth."

In August 1940, *Willie Roberts y Railway* married Ilene Eaton, and the couple bought a flat in Harrow on the Hill, in North London. On her marriage, Ilene was forced to resign from her teaching profession, as was the rule of the time. Willie worked in the docks in London's East End. They experienced the heavy bomb targeting of the Germans on the city, spending night after night in air-raid shelters on makeshift beds, and playing cards to pass away the time, as sleep was often impossible. They were eventually persuaded by their parents to leave London. They returned to Penclawdd and lived with Willie's mother, Ann Roberts, who by then – after the death of her husband – had left the Railway, and was living in Sunny Bank – one of two semidetached properties adjacent to Band Row. Willie found employment in the ICI works in Waunarlwydd and also taught in the Air Training Co. (ATC), which was held twice a week in the Secondary Modern School, Penclawdd. Many young men of the village belonged to the organisation, which was run by a local teacher, David Jenkins (Dai Jinks). Ernie Bond was its drill instructor. Willie Roberts taught Morse code and wireless telegraphy, which he had learned in Conway Wireless College, before entering the merchant navy. After the war years, he lectured the subjects in varies parts of the country – Bristol, Cardiff. He often related with pride how he had taught men much older than himself. Morlais Davies attended the classes. "Quite a lot of my age group belonged to the Air Training Co. It was excellent as not only did

Wedding photograph – Willie and Ilene Roberts, August 1940.

they teach us Morse code and wireless telegraphy, but also maths, English and drill. We learned a lot from it."

Penclawdd hosted evacuees from the Germans' target areas – London and the south eastern counties of England. Children came from Kent – Gillingham, Deal, Dover and Sandwich – and Southend in Essex. Male pupils from the Sir Roger Manwood Grammar School in Sandwich, Kent[3] are well remembered for their school uniform and their good manners – doffing of their straw boaters in passing.

Peggy Jones was on WVS duty in the Elementary School to greet the first arrivals. "The school was used as a distribution centre for the children. They arrived – many in school uniform – in buses from Gowerton Railway Station. We provided them with tea, buns, and sandwiches, and they were then allocated to various homes. Sergeant and Mrs. Lord were in charge of the evacuees in Penclawdd, and Owen Bevan, who lived in Siampa, a boarding house in Port Eynon, was Gower Evacuee Officer.

Each household was pressurized a bit into giving children homes, depending on the amount of vacant bedrooms in the house. The children's parents provided them with clothes and pocket money, and we were allocated so much for their keep."

Joan Callow, née Thomas, has vague memories of Peter staying with her family. "All I can remember is someone coming to Caerau and asking how many bedrooms we had, and not checking whether they were suitably furnished. We were given one boy – Peter. He was from a posh boarding school – a public school. I can remember the evacuees being marched to church, all wearing boaters. They didn't stay very long in Penclawdd. I think they were from Sandwich in Kent. I don't know whether we ever received a letter from Peter's parents."

Furley Spanton on right with brother John and hosts in Carmarthen.

Evacuee, Furley Spanton, has fond memories of his short stay in Penclawdd. "One hundred and eighty Sir Roger Manwood Grammar School pupils arrived at Gowerton Railway Station one Sunday evening at the end of May 1940. We were coached to Penclawdd, tired, but wondering what was to happen to us, having been 'cut off' from our mothers' apron strings some ten hours previously.

We were marshaled altogether in the village and given homes to go to. Those unable to climb the steep hill at the back of the village were driven by car. The car my brother, John, and I were in made a very hard job of the climb up a very bad road.

John and I were taken to a group of cottages overlooking the village and the bay beyond. Here we were introduced to a Mr. and Mrs. Davies, who immediately apologized for the very old home they lived in and told us they (the cottages) had been condemned just before the war. Mr. and Mrs. Davies were kindness beyond one could wish for in the circumstances. Mr. Davies worked on the roads for the council.

My fond memory of our short stay of about three weeks in Penclawdd was the view from the outside toilet, high up at the back-end of the garden overlooking the house and onto the bay beyond. Another thing that sticks in my mind is the cockle-carrying donkeys, because at first, my brother and I could not think what the 'rusty pump' noise was that we could hear on and off during the day. We found out it was the neighing of the donkeys.

Our fifth and sixth forms schooled for the three weeks at Gowerton Grammar School to where they were taken each day by coach. The rest of us – the fourth form and downwards – did part-time in the local chapel and church halls. In our spare time, we played cricket and had compulsory bath periods in the local rugger club clubhouse.

On one or two occasions, we were taken to Port Eynon Bay for a swim. This was before the coastline was mined, and defences erected.

The schooling facilities were so bad that our headmaster, Mr. E. P. Oates, had the whole school moved within three weeks to Carmarthen, where we were again rehoused. We went to the Grammar School that we shared with the local boys and girls. Here I immediately met a lovely girl, who I later married. We have now been together for forty-nine years. Hitler did me a great favour. Not that I approved of his ways though, as I ended up in the army from 1943 to 1947.

I remember in particular the day the Italians came into the war, as the ice-cream bars and restaurants run by Italians were all broken into and smashed up as feelings ran high.

Whilst our stay in Penclawdd was short, I can only say the people of the village did all they could to help and comfort us. I am very pleased to say I have only ever known that in the Welsh people.

My wife, Betty, and I visit Carmarthen every year to see my sister-in-law. She and her husband (now deceased) used to live in West Cross, Swansea. While visiting them there, we passed through Penclawdd on one or two occasions. To me, it seemed to have altered very little, except that I noticed the donkey had been replaced by the tractor for cockling."

Jack Ian Hoppé, also a pupil at Sir Roger Manwood's School, looked forward to his evacuation with great excitement. "I passed the scholarship from Deal Parochial School to Sir Roger Manwood's Grammar School in

Jack Ian Hoppé.
Taken in August 1940 in front garden of Newlands,
1 Monument Hill, Carmarthen, with Trinity College
visible in the background.

Sandwich in May 1939 and was due to start term in September. With the declaration of war on 3rd September, Sandwich was considered a safe area and Gillingham County Boys' School was evacuated from the industrial Medway area to the town, to share the school premises at Manwood's. The result was that term was delayed for three weeks until air-raid shelters were built; each school used the buildings on a half-day basis only. The arrangement worked well, although a great deal of teaching was carried out in venues all around the town of Sandwich.

In May 1940, when the Germans swept through the Low Countries and France and the threat of invasion became real, it was clear that east Kent could no longer be considered a safe haven. The pupils of Gillingham County Boys' School were re-evacuated to South Wales, and this was quickly followed by a seven day warning notice that Manwoods would leave on 2nd June. My recollection of this week is one of immense activity. At this time, I was an only child, (my brother was born at the height of a shelling raid on Deal in 1941) and I remember clearly how very excited I was. It was a great adventure in the making and I couldn't wait to get going. Most of my friends felt the same way.

I do however remember the great concern shown by my parents. My father was in the gas industry, which was a reserved occupation, but this meant he had to stay in Deal throughout the war and my mother would not leave him. She told me subsequently that they, and other similarly placed parents, wondered if they would ever see their offsprings again. It must have been terrible for them.

The week prior to 2nd June was spent in hectic preparation. We were allowed to take with us a small case containing sufficient clothes, etc. to carry us through two weeks, together with our gas masks, and food and drink for the journey to we knew not where. In addition, we were allowed to deposit at school, one large case/trunk and our bicycles, which were to be transported separately in railway goods' vans. We were not to see them again until we arrived in Carmarthen some time after we left Penclawdd.

The summer of 1940 was a glorious one – day after day of warm sunshine – and 2nd June was no exception. I remember walking the mile to St. Leonard's Church in Upper Deal where I joined the others for the six-mile bus journey to the school at Sandwich. At this stage, I have no recollection of feelings other than of excitement. The whole school was assembled and proceeded to Sandwich Station, where we boarded a special train. After what seemed to be a very long wait, we eventually left, with many parents of boys living in the local area waving us off from the platform.

The journey seemed never-ending since we had no idea where we were heading. Eating and drinking seemed to be the favoured occupation and speculation about our eventual destination was rife. It was only when someone pointed out that we were entering the Severn Tunnel that Wales became a low-odds speculation. My main memory of the journey was seeing troop trains at a couple of Kent stations that we stopped at. They were full of weary wounded soldiers, who had managed to get back from Dunkirk. Many were bandaged, with their dressings soiled, but they were still able to give us schoolboys a cheery wave and a smile. I remember clearly thinking at this time that war was a serious business, and was a lot more than playing with pins on maps, which I had spent some time doing before I left home. As the journey proceeded, I remember wondering for the first time, when I would see my parents again, and what would happen to them if the invasion took place across the narrowest part of the channel.

The journey came to an end in the early evening, when we left the train at Gowerton and travelled by bus to Penclawdd. Here we assembled in the playground of the local Elementary School and were provided with tea and buns by some of the ladies of the village. The refreshments were greatly welcomed by the majority of the boys who had long since devoured their sandwiches, etc. which had been packed for the journey. There was still an air of excitement among the boys, possibly a little dulled by being weary. It had been a long day.

The second master, with the local billeting officer, started to allocate boys to billets, with the youngest being those first allocated. All the boys and their masters were billeted by midnight. Michael Brown and I were taken by one of the village ladies to Gower House, which was a general store. Michael and I had been friends from Deal Parochial School days. He subsequently became the chief reporter for one of the large national daily newspapers. The welcome we received was great – clearly deeply genuine, and so affectionately warm. As I remember, there was the father, Mr. Preston, together with a son, Eurfryn, and a daughter, Linda. The latter was responsible for the running of the household.

We were looked after so very well with good food and much kindness. We slept in a double bed in what I think was the front bedroom, and although sleeping on a straw mattress was a new experience for us both, we were comfortable. The one thing I found difficult to come to terms with was the sanitary arrangements. Although from a working class family, I had been used to flush toilets in an indoor and an outdoor lavatory. I did find the bucket arrangement in a little shed at the bottom of the garden a bit tough to take. I think, looking back, that it was this more than anything else that induced my first severe homesickness after about two days.

My main memories of Penclawdd are:

1. The extreme kindness of all the residents living in a small and not terribly prosperous village.
2. The sound of donkeys at five o'clock in the morning as the cockle ladies went off to the sands.
3. The start of lessons after two days when we had classes in the open air in absolutely beautiful weather in the hills behind the village.
4. The school First Eleven cricket match against the village team.
5. Being taken by Eurfryn Preston in his car – I think it was a Morris 12 – over to Port Eynon. To go in a private car for me was both a novelty and a thrill. I remember that as we were en route we heard on a wireless in the car that Italy had entered the war (10 June). By the next day the Italian proprietor[4] of a little shop in the village had been interned and the shop closed – a great pity, as the ice-cream from this shop was terrific!

There is no doubt, however, that my main long-lasting memory, which had the most lasting influence on my later life, was being in a community which lived and breathed rugby. We heard in Penclawdd a story that far outmatched anything we read in the contemporary literature of the day – the 'Hotspur', the 'Skipper', the 'Adventure', the 'Wizard' or the 'Rover'. It was the story of two Grammar School boys, cousins, born next door to one another in Tabernacle Terrace, Penclawdd, who played for Swansea against the All Blacks and who made such a major contribution to the victory by the Welsh club. The story was told and retold to us with appropriate press cuttings, 'The All Blacks beaten by two school boys.' The boys were of course the famous halfbacks, Haydn Tanner and Willie Davies and how proud their village was of them. The story made a deep impression on me and on many other pupils of the school. It did much to increase our enthusiasm for the game that, in my case, in one way or another, has given me so much pleasure in all the years that followed.

It soon became clear to the headmaster that we would be unable to stay in Penclawdd since there were no proper educational facilities available. The nearest possibility was Gowerton Grammar School. Sadly, it was not large enough to host another school.

Thus, on 14th June, the school left by bus for Carmarthen, where it was to remain for the next four and a half years. It returned to Sandwich in December 1944.

I have very clear memories of the sadness of the villagers of Penclawdd when we were to leave. We too felt sorry to go, but realized that we did need a more secure educational base than was to be found with our new friends in Penclawdd. The affection that the village showed towards the school was no better illustrated than by the farewell concert that was organised for us in the Tabernacle Chapel, on the evening before our departure. One of my enduring memories is the absolute beauty of the singing. I can still see a young woman in a black dress coming forward and singing, 'Just a song at twilight'. I had never heard any singing as beautiful as this. The headmaster gave a speech, including a few words of thanks in Welsh, and we left for Carmarthen the next morning. Although our stay in Penclawdd was less than two weeks, it was nevertheless a stay that we would all remember and which would have a positive effect in the shaping of our development. I for one remember the people of Penclawdd with much gratitude and affection.

Looking back such a long time is difficult, but I am sure of one thing. I had an experience in Penclawdd that I could have gained by no other means, albeit as a result of the war. It was a good experience given to me by fine people. I believe that I am a better person because of it."

Peggy Jones and family housed four evacuees during the war years. "My husband, John, and I were living with my parents in the Flat Roof House. First, we had two lovely little boys from a grammar school near London. One day, my father came home from work to find that they had taken it upon themselves to clean his work shed to perfection. They were moved after a short time.

We received two more boys. David was from the Essex coast, near Southend, and Peter was from London. David was a nice boy, but Peter was a little devil. One day my mother had made custard to accompany fruits from the garden. Custard powder was impossible to buy, and so the sauce was a precious commodity. She placed it in the sink to cool and instructed the boys to wash their hands for tea. Peter washed his hands all over the custard, so the fruit was eaten on its own. He used to play pop with David, to such an extent that we eventually asked for him to be taken away. David used to go to church with John, and joined the choir. After he had been with us for about nine months, his mother came to visit him. She stayed with us for the weekend. David wrote for a while, but we lost touch. I often wonder what happened to them."

After the invasion of France on D. Day, the children returned to their homes. Before they departed, a concert was held in Bethel Chapel, during which, the headmaster of the Elementary School, Mr. James, gave a most inspiring speech thanking the people of Penclawdd for their warm hospitality."

The Royal Artillery Regiment was stationed on Salthouse Point – known as the Point – in Crofty, throughout the war years. They used the area as a shell-testing range. The Llwchwr Estuary was ideal geographically for the purpose, having five uninterrupted miles of flat unoccupied land for firing.

In the late autumn of 1939, a company of the Royal Sussex Regiment – consisting of thirty men – was billeted in the church hall; the first of many troops which were to descend on the village during the war years. Due to the lack of bathing facilities available in the hall, Carys Hughes in her capacity as head of WVS, organized weekly baths for the soldiers in the few village homes that boasted bathrooms.

Peggy Jones remembers the men's arrival. "The baby clinic was held at the hall. Annie Jones was the caretaker. One day, some soldiers suddenly marched in, and announced that they were to be based there. Annie informed them that she was unable to hand them the keys without church authority. One of them dumped a large boiler in the kitchen. He cut two cabbages in half, without washing them, and threw them into the boiler, slugs and all. When we asked him why hadn't he wash them, he said, 'It's late and we want our food. The soldiers will eat any bloody thing.' They had bunks in the clubroom and in the main room. We'd have two or three to our house for supper regularly, but they were cockneys, and we didn't understand a word they said. They left Penclawdd to go on manoeuvres and when they returned they marched through the village singing, 'Sussex by the Sea'. They eventually left for active service."

The soldiers were warmly welcomed by all the villagers, and consequently were most reluctant to leave just before Christmas 1939.

Ruby Skinner, née Davies, was clerk to Penclawdd Home Guards. The latter liaised closely with the various regiments that were stationed in Penclawdd and so she had first-hand knowledge of the regiments' movements.

"A few days before New Year 1940, a Scottish regiment was billeted in the hall. During their brief stay of about two months, they experienced the same bathing arrangements as the previous regiment.

During the following months, there was no activity, but sometime in the late summer, there were two other regiments stationed there, who stayed for a short time.

In early 1941, the Pioneer Corps started constructing an army camp of corrugated steel Nissen huts at Graig-y-Coed, in the west-end of the village. These soldiers, although in British uniforms, were German and Austrian Jews. They were mostly professional men – doctors, dentists and engineers – and many musicians, who had fled Germany. While in the village, they formed their own dance band, and weekly dances were held in the church hall. The building of the camp took almost a year. It was quite large and would accommodate about a thousand troops.

The first arrivals were the Royal Artillery, who stayed for several months.

In 1942, several regiments of American troops were stationed at the camp.

The war continued, and, as the Yanks, both white and coloured, came and went, we entered 1945 with the arrival of the Black Watch Regiment. The latter had been sent to reform before departing for the Far East. They were there during the end of the war in Europe, and what wonderful celebrations were held at the camp, which was open to everyone."

Peggy Jones lived in Tabernacle Terrace when the Black Watch Regiment was stationed at the camp. "The regiment used to wake us in the morning with their bagpipes and drums 'beating the retreat' on the tennis courts in the Rec. behind our house. They ruined the courts, practising every morning, but mind, it was wonderful to hear. When they left the village, they 'beat the retreat' on the road from Ship Banc to Mrs. Brenton's shop in West End. They were dressed up in their kilts, etc. I'll always remember. It was a beautiful sight.

They used to have church parade in Tabernacle Chapel. William Jenkins, organist and choirmaster, allowed one of their men to play the organ, having first checked that he was a competent organist. He was very fussy about the organ, as it was very precious. The soldiers took the service, but the minister, Mr. Williams, always took the sermon."

The companies had tanks and also ducks – large amphibious boats. Driving practice of the vehicles took place on the *Graig* in Penclawd, and on the beach at Port Eynon.

The bases benefited the village in creating civilian employment for the villagers. Many worked in administration, and local women provided a laundry service for the men. St. Gwynour's Church Mothers' Union visited the camps to darn the soldiers' socks. Win Walters remembers her mother, a Mothers' Union member, relating to her their astonishment when the soldiers served them tea from a large bucket.

The soldiers greatly involved themselves in village life. They socialized with the locals, attending the weekly dances that were held in the church hall, when music was played by a local band. The dances were extremely popular amongst girls of the village and surrounding areas – Gowerton, Gorseinon and Llanelli – and queues formed early to be assured of entry. The cinema was also a great attraction. On Saturday nights – the busiest night – the queues were often fifty-yards long and many were disappointed in failing to obtain seats. Ilene Foote, who worked at the cinema, remembers one cold winter's night when the Americans were stationed at the camps. "Snow White was showing at the cinema. It was snowing so heavily that we couldn't open the main door for them to come in, so we opened the anteroom door. They were like children, as they hadn't seen snow before. They were skating up the road. Only little black faces could be seen. They were covered in snow. It was so appropriate that we were showing Snow White."

Soldiers reciprocated by holding concerts. Joyce Richards, née Hodges, was a teenager at the time. "The late actor and comedian, Frankie Howard, was one of the soldiers on the Point who entertained us in the concerts. He was a good all-round entertainer and had his audience in stitches. One of his favorite songs was 'Swim little fish, swim on'."

Frankie Howard delivered baskets of laundry to Winnie Jones who provided the soldiers with a laundry service. "When he brought the laundry basket to our house he would lean against the door post, half-asleep. I never understood what he said. He was so dopey. He also provided us with the regiment's stale bread for our pigs. He ran Housey-Housey sessions for the villagers. He was known as Daphne on the Point but I never called him that. But our son Ken, who was a toddler at the time, overheard one of the soldiers telling me what they called him, and when he saw Frankie Howard coming to our house, he would forewarn me with, 'Mammy, Daphne is coming.'"

A friendship developed between Frankie and Madie Jones, née Evans, who worked at the camp. Madie experienced the serious side of the man that others in the village probably never saw. "Frankie Howard (he changed the 'a' to 'e' for his professional career, thinking it would attract a little more attention on a billboard) was a Londoner who worked in an insurance office, before being conscripted into the Royal Artillery in about 1941. He was posted to the Experimental Establishment at the Point in about 1942, where he worked as a clerk in the Administration Office. He was totally unsuited to army life. He couldn't learn drill and was a misfit in the regiment, always getting into trouble. He must have found the transition from civilian life to that of the army very difficult to cope with. I can't imagine how he managed his basic training. He was a real 'fish out of water'. He was quite eccentric and a lonely person. When he started coming to our house he wouldn't let go. He would cling to any life outside the army.

His ambition was to become a professional performer, and he joined an amateur dramatic society in, I think, Gorseinon and took part in plays such as 'Laburnum Grove'. One of the officers at the Point organised a concert party, with a performance given in the old cinema – the Memorial Hall. Frank was one the 'turns' – a stand-up comedian. However, he was a very serious, intelligent man, who enjoyed classical concerts, one of which I remember he took me to in the Brangwyn Hall in Swansea.

His other great interest was to attend the weekly variety shows in the Empire Theatre in Oxford Street, Swansea, where all the famous comedy acts appeared. One I remember was Cyril Fletcher of 'Odd Odes' fame. Frank always took a notebook and pen with him and copied the comedians' material and later used it himself.

He left Penclawdd in 1944, just before D. Day, and was fortunate enough to join ENSA (Entertainment National Service Association) – the entertainment's branch of the army. His experience there proved invaluable in getting him started on his professional career after 1946."

He was very popular in the village and the feeling was obviously reciprocated as after the war, he paid several visits to Penclawdd. Joyce Richards, née Howells, while working as a soloist entertainer in the Blue Anchor in the 1980s, remembers him visiting the public house. "Joyce Davies, the publican, presented him with a gift. He responded with a speech in which he talked fondly of many people in the village that he remembered from the war years, and the happy times he had experienced."

Joyce Richards, née Hodges, remembers the good company of the soldiers, but also the fact that the American soldiers tried to impress the local girls by bragging, "We have a big ranch back home." But they were very kind to the village children, giving them candy and chewing gum, supplementing their meagre supply which was allowed on war rationing.

It seems that the soldiers' behaviour was exemplary during their stay in the village. Although Penclawdd hosted a thousand troops in the camp and a few hundred more at Salthouse Point, there was not one case of rape or assault in all the war years. Ilene Foote says of them, "They were the nicest boys that you could wish to meet. But I didn't like the Texas Rangers. They used to walk down the road swigging beer and you didn't want to be on the road when they were there."

The soldiers were moved with little or no warning. Wilfred and Elsie Tucker suddenly lost two good friends overnight. "Elsie and I became friendly with two of them. They came to supper one night, leaving with the promise to see us in the morning. We never saw them again. We found out later that they had gone overnight to the invasion of France."

The socializing resulted in many of the soldiers marrying local girls, and settling in the village, while others married and left with their new wives to return to their native homes in England, Scotland and many parts of America. Ruby Davies married John Skinner of the Black Watch Regiment. John was stationed away from Penclawdd after their marriage, but some years later, they returned to live in the village. Beatrix Austin, of the Ship, was not so fortunate. "I was engaged to be married to Jack Butler of Penarth, a soldier stationed on the Point during the last world war. I had given in my notice to the Secondary Modern School, where I worked as deputy cook, to go and live in Penarth. Jack was taken ill on duty, and died suddenly of a heart attack. I still have my engagement ring. I look at it sometimes." Beatie has never married.

The army commandeered any empty dwellings to house their officers. Wilfred Tucker and his wife, Elsie, were near victims of the practice. "The house that I live in now went empty in 1941. Its occupants had vacated and moved to Gorseinon. Elsie and I were living at her mother's at No. 20, Station Road. I asked John Fry, the owner, if we could have this house and he said that it was ours. Before we moved in, the local policeman visited us. He told us to quickly put a chair on view in the house, as he had been asked to advise the military the next day of any empty dwelling and just one piece of furniture rendered it occupied. I quickly put a chair in view in the front room, and we moved in soon afterwards."

The Ministry of Defence's use of the estuary for testing ammunition caused much disruption and added danger to the cockle gatherers. A large post was erected in the estuary opposite the Elementary School, on which a red flag was flown everyday between 8.00 a.m. and 4.30 p.m., to warn of shell testing in operation and prohibition beyond. The flag was lowered when firing and recovery were completed – the latter undertaken by heavy, large wheeled lorries.

Consequently, the hours of daylight gathering were greatly reduced. Depending on the tides, the summer hours were approximately 3.30 a.m. to 8.00 a.m. and 5.00 p.m. to 8.30 p.m. In winter, they did not exist.

As ever, Ethel Coghlan thought deeply about her beloved work and arrived at a decision to eliminate the problem of limited gathering. "I decided to go out at night. I knew the way as my father had taught me when we went fishing together. I knew every little inlet, and still do. I can picture it all in my mind's eye now. We were a little clique – Margaret Jones and her daughter, Della, Doreen and me. I led the way, and wherever I went, they followed. They had not been 'out the sands' in the dark before. They were afraid at first. Later, all the cockle women joined us and we were a big gang."

The army was conscious of the disruption they caused the cockle gatherers and cooperated with them at every possible opportunity. When the flag was lowered earlier then usual, Sergeant Major Whetherby, the officer in charge, phoned Mrs. Rees, the postmistress, immediately. The latter informed the cockle women.

Time being of the essence, many donkeys were replaced by flat carts with motor axles and wheels, which were pulled by horses. The horse and carts were much faster and transported more cockles at one time than did the donkeys.

There were many obstacles to contend with. The army had placed high posts in the estuary to prevent the landing of enemy aircraft, and unexploded shells lay hidden in the sand. Because of the blackout regulations, the cockle gatherers were unable to use lamps to light their way. Only torches, covered with black material, were permitted. Moonlight nights were extremely welcome.

It was imperative to stay on the 'safe track' across the sands to and from the cockle beds. Fortunately, the 'track' was unaffected by the ebb and flow of the tide, as it had hardened through many years of use. Inevitably, accidents occurred. One dark night, Mrs. Hinds narrowly escaped death when her horse's hoof touched the side of an unexploded shell. The unfortunate animal was blown to pieces, but his mistress sitting on the cart behind, miraculously escaped uninjured.

The cockle women had many experiences in the estuary during the war years. Ethel Coghlan remembers, "Oh! I'll never forget one night when the German planes and our planes met over the bay. They started fighting in the air. There were traces of bullets everywhere above us. One of the planes came down in the sea that night. I said that I was going home, as it was a bit dangerous. A bullet could come down and hit us. So off home we went.

If we left it a bit late to come home, we would see the army lorries coming out. The sergeant would shout at us, 'You buggers get home, get home' and we'd all run.

Mrs. Webb, who was over seventy, would not budge. 'I ain't got *cocos* (cockles) yet,' she'd tell the sergeant. He'd catch her and put her on her donkey. It was a bit of fun."

When Della Williams returned to Penclawdd after her first cockle-selling season in Newport, Britain was at war. Della considered joining the ATS, but her mother had other ideas. Margaret Jones had bought a second horse, harness and cart, for thirteen pounds and ten shillings, which as Della says, "was a lot of money then." She informed Della that she was to work in the tin-plate works in Gowerton and also go 'out the sands'. Della obediently respected her wishes. "We did not argue or answer back in those days. We did as we were told." Della caught the 6.30 a.m. bus from Penclawdd to start work in the tin-plate works at 7.00 a.m. "It was hard work. Work that I was not used to, and indoor work." After finishing work at 4.30 p.m., Della met her mother at Ship Banc, and together they went 'out the sands'. "I had to learn to cockle in the dark. Mrs. Coghlan was a wonderful woman for cockling in the dark." After working this rigid routine for eight months, Della left the tin-plate works – where she met her future husband, Haydn Williams, a native of Gowerton – and concentrated on cockling.

The shell testing ceased at the end of the war, but in July 1953, much to the cockle gatherers' consternation, the Ministry of Defence announced that it planned to use the area for testing again. Live ammunition of calibre up to twenty-five pound shells would be used. The Ministry gave assurance that interference to the cockle industry would be minimal. The case against the proposals was required within a week. On 16 July, a 'special urgency' meeting was held at Salthouse Point. 'The Gower Society was represented by its President, Chairman, Secretary and Public Relations Officer. The meeting was presided over by an official of the Welsh Office of the Ministry of Housing and Local Government, who described himself as "neutral" and stated that this was a private meeting, not a public inquiry, which would follow later if necessary. The Ministry of Supply was represented by six high officials from London. The following thirteen authorities were represented: Glamorgan County Council, Minister of Agriculture and Fisheries, Carmarthenshire County Council, Llanelli

Harbour Trust, Gower Rural District Council, the National Parks Commission, Llanelli Rural District Council, Council for Preservation of Rural Wales, Llwchwr Urban District Council, Wildfowlers Association of Great Britain, South Wales Sea Fisheries District Committee, the Gower Society, and the South West Wales River Board.'[5] The result was success for the cockle gatherers. The Ministry withdrew their scheme and tested elsewhere. Unfortunately, all shells were not recovered from the estuary during the war and even today, all who work in the estuary, face the danger of unexploded shells.

After the Black Watch Regiment left Penclawdd in early December 1945, the camp was occupied by German prisoners of war. Wilfred Tucker visited the camp. "Gwynfor Jenkins started a choir which he called the Civil Defence Choir. We used to sing in aid of the Comfort Fund. On one occasion, we gave a concert for the prisoners. One of the pieces was an old German folk song, which we sang in English. As we sang, we could see all the Germans in the front row crying. But some were obviously real Nazis, and were not upset."

Myrddin Rees worked at the camp for about twelve months. "I was working underground. I was very friendly with Doctor Hughes as I used to do odd jobs for him. He said to me, 'Myrddin, get out from underground now. I'll have a job for you at the Point.' He kept his word, and I was soon employed there by the Ministry of Works.

One day I was called to the office. I was informed that German prisoners of war were coming to the camps at West End, and asked if I would go and work there. Well, I couldn't refuse, and so the boss took me up to one of the Nissen huts. It was full of tools of every description – carpenter's tools, plumber's tools, etc. and guns vaselined to prevent rusting. I was told that I would be responsible for all the contents of the hut and that it would also be my job to find prisoners who were carpenters, etc. to do necessary maintenance jobs in the camp. They would be paid extra money – a few pence – for the jobs as well as their normal allowance. Four British soldiers would be in charge of each prisoner. I was to check that all was in order on the camp premises including the high barbed wire fence surrounding it.

On one occasion, a prisoner wanted a few tools, including a pliers. When he returned them, the pliers were missing. 'Now listen,' I said to him, 'I don't want to make a bother here, but I'm going to walk around that hut and if those pliers aren't on the table when I come back, I'm going to see the commandant – who was in charge.' When I returned, the pliers were on the table.

The prisoners complained to me about their food. I told them, 'Do you know that we are only having two ounces of butter and two ounces of margarine per week?' They found that hard to believe but never complained to me again.

Only a few of the Germans were aggressive to me. I was in a hut with some one day. The huts were dark inside, as they had no windows. One of them said to me, 'You're lucky you're getting out of here alive.'

'Get out of my way,' I said. I wouldn't show them that I was afraid.

I was taken by a soldier to one of the officers who asked me to buy him a dictionary. His hut was like a palace inside. I was not prepared go to town (Swansea) to do him this favour and refused. He started shouting at me and the soldier asked him if he should deal with me. I was ready for him, but the officer said, 'No. Leave him alone.' I was glad to get out.

The prisoners didn't wear uniforms but had an identification number on their jackets. I was going to the bus stop by the station one day, when a prisoner crossed the road towards me. 'Where are you going?' he asked me.

I said, 'You bugger off back to camp or I'll report you.' He went back, but he was seen walking along the railway line, caught, and punished.

On another occasion, my wife, Marion, and I were going to town and who was on the bus but one of the Germans. I thought, 'Good gracious. I can't go anywhere without seeing a prisoner.' I had to leave the bus and take him back to the camp.

It was, of course, the fault of the British soldiers in charge that the prisoners were escaping. One prisoner escaped and got as far as Europe, but he was captured and returned to Penclawdd. The next day I saw him in a cage surrounded by barbed wire – his punishment. As I passed him I said, 'I warned you. I told you this would happen to you.'

I saw a few in the cinema one evening, but I didn't report them on that occasion. Most of them could speak good English.

Two of them confided in me that they had been called to the forces within a year of qualifying as doctors. They were worried that they would be unable to finish the course.

I organised a prisoner – a sign writer – to paint a sign for the commandant. He worked in my hut but I had to watch him all the time because of the tools. I used to give him a bit of food and became quiet friendly with him. He was a quiet chap. I often felt sorry for some of the prisoners. I used to cycle home to dinner. They often gave me money that they had earned through their jobs, to buy bread for them as they were hungry. Sometimes I bought them goods and didn't have the money. But some of the Germans were hard – real SS men.

The Germans wouldn't believe that they had lost the war. They were convinced that nobody could beat them and would not be persuaded otherwise. 'Our planes are faster than yours,' they used to say to me, and they were right.

But I told them, 'The war is over. We have beaten you in the air: we have beaten you everywhere.'

The British soldiers weren't pleased that I – a civilian – was in charge. The military wanted to run the show themselves. I could see the end coming. A man came to check the tools. It took three hours. A few days later my boss said to me, 'Myrddin, you'll have to go from here boy. The Minister of Works has given in to them. Next Monday go back to the Point.' I didn't mind, as I was happy enough on the Point.

After the war, I went back underground and worked there for thirty-five years altogether. I liked working in the colliery. I then became caretaker of Penclawdd Secondary Modern School and we lived in The Lodge."

After the war years, the Nissen huts were used as extra housing accommodation for the villagers, usually for newly married couples. They were still known as The Camps. In the late 1940s, the occupants were re-housed in council houses built in Llanyrnewydd. The Nissen huts were demolished, and Graig-y-Coed housing estate – the first private housing estate in the village – was built on the site.

Although Penclawdd escaped damage during the war years, the villagers suffered a great loss when their excellent shopping centre of Swansea was demolished by three consecutive nights of intensive bombing by the Germans. The following article appeared in the 'South Wales Evening Post' newspaper, 8 May 1945:

'THE PRICE SWANSEA PAID
Three nights of terror.

When war broke out in 1939, the possibility of an air attack upon Swansea was common knowledge. That the town, both as a great seaport and an industrial centre, possessed legitimate and important objects of attack – some of them, like the Nation Oil Refinery in its vicinity, of unusual importance – was well understood. Nor were Germans, when Germany was actually supplying the machinery for the local new enterprise of military value, likely to ignore them. But it was considered, that, as a result of the town's geographical position, while the allied line held on the Franco-Belgian frontier, it would be difficult of access to enemy raiders.

The authorities in fact, made the neighbourhood a reception area for air-raid evacuees.

France surrendered on 17 June 1940. The surrender terms handed over the French coast to the enemy, and Cherbourg was 20 miles nearer Swansea than London.

On 10 July, a German plane exacted its first toll of civilian life on Swansea in a daylight raid upon the docks.

The most devastating effect on the town was experienced during the three nights of February 19th, 20th and 21st.

February 19th-20th-21st. The three consecutive large-scale attacks by 250 enemy planes which marked the climax of enemy effort, destroying the centre of the town, killing 230 people, and severely wounding about 250.

There were 94 roads hit and 396 shops, 107 business premises and 72 small industries destroyed or damaged.

Only Plymouth and Liverpool experienced an ordeal equally or even more protracted, excluding London.'

Of its splendid departmental stores, only Lewis Lewis, situated in High Street, and not in the centre of Swansea, remained undamaged. The other shops quickly found alternative temporary premises, but since the gradual rebuilding of Swansea after the war, only David Evans now remains trading. However, it is in name only, as in 1978, the stores was bought by the large House of Fraser store chain.

NOTES

1. David Taylor. *Mastering Economic and Social History*. Houndmills, Basingstoke, Hampshire RG21 2XS. 1998, p. 583.
2. Collectors:
   Mrs. E. J. Morgan and Miss Harriet Williams.
   Mrs. D. J. Dallimore and Mrs. M. J. Leyshon.
   Mrs. Edna Williams and Miss Dolly Hazel.
   Mrs. W. Davies and Mrs. M. Humphreys.
   Miss Myra Griffiths and Miss Ethel Williams.
   Miss C. Francis.
   Mrs. G. Williams and Mrs. D. Porter.
   Miss Kate Eynon.
   Miss Elsie Beynon.
   Mr. John Jones and Mr. Gwylfa Williams.
   Miss Teg. Davies and Miss Parkhouse.
3. Sir Roger Manwood Grammar School took in boarders, which gave the misconception of 'Public School' to many people over the years.
4. Ernest Ratti.
5. 'The Penclawdd Business'. *Gower Journal, Volume 6*.

7

Women in the Forces

Many young men and women of Penclawdd were conscripted into, or volunteered for, the services. The majority fought in the various campaigns of the war, a minority saw little or no action and a few remained in Britain throughout the war years.

The Second World War was a war of rapid movement. Major campaigns took place in Western and Central Europe, in the heart of Russia, in Burma and the Far East and in the Pacific and Atlantic Oceans.

In 1919, the Treaty of Versailles had given Poland access to the Baltic by granting her a corridor of land along the River Vistula. Danzig remained a Free City under a League of Nations mandate. Within weeks of the declaration of war, the Germans had occupied Western Poland by the Blitzkrieg[1] method of warfare and the Russians had claimed seventy-six thousand square miles of her eastern region. Polish resistance was heroic but useless. Consequently, Germany occupied Danzig and Poland lost her access to the sea.

Throughout the winter of 1939-40, there was no large-scale military action, instigating American journalists to name it the 'phoney war'. During this period, the small British Expeditionary Force established itself in France. It consisted of the British Army – mostly territorial units – that was not well-trained at the time.

In April 1940, Germany occupied Denmark. Germany was anxious to safeguard her export of Swedish iron ore – which was vital for her armaments industry – from the Norwegian port of Narvik. On 9 April, German troops landed at Oslo, Kirstiansand, Stavanger, Bergen and Trondheim, and although British and French troops arrived a few days later, they were unsuccessful in dislodging the Germans. May saw German occupation of Holland, Belgium and France. From 26 May to 4 June the British Navy played the vital roll of evacuating over three hundred and thirty-eight thousand troops, two thirds of them British, from Dunkirk and neighbouring beaches to the safety of Britain. This was a remarkable achievement in the face of constant Luftwaffe attacks on the beaches.

10 June saw Italy declare war on Britain. Within hours of the declaration, thousands of Italian nationals living in Britain were sent to internment

camps. The policy was designed to prevent potential Italian spies feeding information to Mussolini's government.

Britain supported by her Dominions and Colonies, faced Germany and Italy alone.

In the Battle of Britain – August to October – Hitler attempted unsuccessfully to invade Britain. His failure was mostly the result of the magnificent efforts of the RAF – by the bomber crews who attacked the German airfields, and the fighter pilots who prevented the German Air Force gaining supremacy over southern England.

With the entry of Italy into the war, fighting had spread to Africa and the Mediterranean. In September, Mussolini had invaded Egypt from the Italian colony of Libya. Wavell, with his mixed army of British, Indian, Australian, New Zealand, French and Polish troops, pushed the Italians out of Egypt and back into Libya.

Germany invaded Yugoslavia in April 1941. Churchill's lack of appreciation of the importance of air support in naval operations, resulted in the Germans' easy conquest of the Greek mainland in April and the island of Crete in May.

By April 1941, Rommel had driven the British out of Libya. By November, Britain had safeguarded the Middle East and Italian East Africa was entirely in British hands. British forces advanced for the second time into Libya. A feature of the ensuing fighting was the hammering given to Malta – an important British stronghold – by the German Air Force. For the following three years, British submarines, aircraft and ships, operating from the island, prevented large quantities of supplies reaching the Axis forces in North Africa.

Hitler attacked Russia in June.

On 7 December 1941, Japan attacked the American base at Pearl Harbour and followed by capturing the British territories of Hong Kong, Singapore, Malaya and Burma as well as the Philippine Islands. Immediately war was worldwide.

Rommel had captured Tobruk on 21 June 1942 and pushed British Forces back into Egypt, but the following October saw the 'turn of the tide' when, in the Battle of El Alamein, General Montgomery and his Eighth Army succeeded in driving Rommel out of Egypt, across Libya, and into Tunisia.

The Allies then concentrated on Europe. In July and August 1943, they captured Sicily. They bombarded the toe of Italy and invaded northwards. Bitter fighting ensued before Cassino, in May 1944, Rome in June and eventually Milan in May 1945 were taken, eliminating Italy from the war.

The invasion of France started on D. Day 6 June 1944 when the Allies landed on the sixty-mile stretch of Normandy beaches. Many thousands of American troops who had been stationed in South Wales left from Welsh ports. The Dowlais born author, the late Gwyn Alf Williams, an historian of international repute, was in the only Welsh regiment, the South Wales Borderers, to take part in the first wave of the Normandy landings. In his autobiographical book, 'Fishers of Men', he describes his feelings on arriving at Gold Beach. 'The noise was all engulfing, with aircraft zooming overhead, ships weaving in and out of our path, men shouting. A kind of disciplined confusion gripped us all. What we had to do was get ashore and up that beach – a narrow strip with hundreds of men and vehicles, tanks and transporters burning, the off zip of bullets and inexplicable explosions – up a narrow hill past a church with a great bite out of its roof, a French tricolour stuck into it, along a path over a hill. The whole world narrowed down to that strip, as the craft closed in on it, in a cacophony of noise.'[2]

By September, both France and Belgium were liberated. As a result, inhabitants of London were released from the bombarding – from bases the other side of the channel – of Hitler's 'secret weapons' (from June by doodlebugs V1s – flying bombs and from September by V2s – long range rockets).

Holland was liberated and the Allies continued into Germany crossing the Rhine and capturing Bologne. Simultaneously, in the east, the Russians advanced on Berlin via Poland. Eventually, Hitler recognised defeat and committed suicide. On 7 May 1945, a general armistice was signed at Rheims.

On 6 August, the Americans dropped an atomic bomb on Hiroshima. Two days later Russia declared war on Japan. On 9 August, the Americans dropped a second bomb on Nagasaki. Japan instantly surrendered and 4 August 1945 saw the end of the Second World War.

Fifteen men of the village were killed, and many have since died, but there are men and women in the village, and its surrounding area, who still have vivid memories of their war experiences.

John William, elder son of Jim and Elizabeth (Bess) Howell, proprietors of the fish and chip shop in Glanmor Terrace, known as The Central Bar, was conscripted into the navy in the summer of 1939. In early 1941, his fiancée, Marion, was anxious to locate his whereabouts, as she wanted to send him a recent photograph of herself.

"I had this photograph taken in 1941 to sent to John. We – his parents and younger brother, Leonard – thought he was in Alexandria in Egypt. I wrote him a letter and said, 'We think you're in Alexandria but we don't

John William Howell.

Photograph Marion Jones, née Thomas, had taken to send to her fiancée.

really know. If you would make sure that the last word in your next letter to me is yes, then we will know that you are in Alexandria.' We did receive a letter in which the last word was yes."

HMS Gloucester.

John William was killed in action in May of that year, when his ship, the HMS Gloucester, was sunk in the Mediterranean during the invasion of the island of Crete.

Marion was one of the first village girls to learn to drive, a talent she put to good advantage when serving her country in the WAAFs.

"It was a hoot actually. A bunch of about four or five of us had gone to town to the cinema and to have a cup of coffee, as girls do. I said, 'Let's join the forces.' We went to the YMCA to get the necessary forms and then I rushed back to Jim's place. I filled in my form – wildly excited, as I really wanted to go to the WAAFs – and posted it. A week later, when I saw my friends, I discovered that they had changed their minds, but I wasn't too concerned, as I was going.

I was posted to Gloucester, where I received an introductory training, and given my uniform. I was posted to North Wales, where I was told my job was to be a driver. It suited me, as I had learned to drive before joining up, but I still had to be trained. I learned about engines. I thoroughly enjoyed myself. I really did. I found it so interesting and discovered that I had a natural aptitude for the work.

I came home on leave for a week or two before I went to Bridgenorth, where the weather was wickedly cold. We all developed chilblains on our fingers, and although we were issued with gloves, they were of no use, as they were always wet, and so we abandoned them, and kept them in our pockets.

We were then posted to our serious work. Four of us, Madge, Dora, Eva and I were posted to Marsham Street, Westminster, London. It was a very elegant area. We were told, 'Clear off for the day and try and find somewhere to live.' We paired off and I went with Dora. We finally found a miserable little place in Wilton Street that smelt. We later lived in a better place in Gloucester Street, Pimlico. From there, we could walk comfortably to work. Gordon's Hospital was nearby, which had been converted into a club. It was run by the WVS, who were very kind to us, and made sure that we had a good lunch, but it was peanuts really. We could eat there anytime we liked, and relax and put our feet up. Connie joined us. Connie and I quarrelled with Dora and off she went, and got herself digs somewhere else. We then moved to Saint George's Square, which was rather nice. I had a very grand boyfriend when there, who lived in Dolphin Square. I drove him, and we went for meals and the cinema together. John was still missing as far as I was concerned, and I still wore my engagement ring.

They'd say, 'Come on Thomas! Get your car! Get going!' I had to clean and service it, but fitters were employed to carry out the big jobs. On one occasion, I had to put five new tyres on a standard van. The men were coming and going, and they were having a laugh at my expense. I said to myself, 'I'm going to do this. I'm going to do this even if it kills me.' Putting on tyres was really hard graft, and I had spent most of the day at it. It was about five o'clock. A call came in and I was the only one there, and I was really knackered. I had to drive a fellow up to Birmingham and the conditions were bad. It was a dark winter's night. Use of the large headlights was prohibited, so I could only use small headlights. They were hooded so only slits of light came through, reducing visibility to about ten yards. I think we all learned to have x-ray eyes.

On another occasion, I had a grand tour of Scotland. One man wanted a car for three weeks. His job was to visit airfields to ensure that all seaplanes were well-hidden and camouflaged from enemy aircraft. We would see them on rivers, gleaming white if they had not been painted. He would then stop, and arrange for them to be hidden and camouflaged.

I was to take two gentlemen to Peterborough on a three or four-day trip. One of them was an American Executive of EMI (electronics) – a VIP. He was in our country to inspect the electronics on aircraft. He had an escort with him, Anthony Parsons, who later became Sir Anthony Parsons – British Ambassador to the UN. When the American returned home, he sent me a Dunhill silver lighter – very expensive – with the note, 'Thank you for your incredible driving.' They took me, and another couple, out for lunch to a Corner House, and then to Speakers Corner in Hyde Park. We then had tea in the Grosvenor, followed by the cinema. The evening ended with dinner at the fish restaurant, Prunee's I think it was called, in Saint James'. Parsons had oysters, and when he laughed at a joke, it went all over his beard. It was a memorable thing for them to do, to take me to all those elegant places.

Sometimes naval types would come in the car. I remember driving three of them to Skegness. I had washed the car with a hose. I picked two up in ICI House and then drove down to the Admiralty. Before turning into Admiralty House, we had to stop because of the traffic. I put on my brakes but they didn't work as they had become wet when I cleaned the car. I went neatly into the back of the lorry in front. The lorry was unmarked. My car was damaged, but no harm was done. We picked up the fellow from Admiralty House. He was covered in gold and buttons. It was a wicked morning. London fog was bad then. We drove through a part of London that I was not familiar with, and we had to go over London Bridge. I gave the map to the fellow in gold – he was sitting next to me – and said, 'You read this Sir.' He looked absolutely shocked but he had no choice, and I kept my eyes in front. But he did navigate, and we got to be quite jolly together. 'You went through red lights,' he said somewhere en route. When we came home late that evening, we were all singing 'Roll out the Barrel', as I drove down the embankment.

This was all packed into less then two years. It was an interesting and exciting life. I came from this little village and suddenly I was landed with all these gentry. Oddly enough, I was so naïve that they never overawed me.

I found everyone extremely kind and helpful during my war years. One evening, I was travelling home to Penclawdd in the van. I was very tired, and decided it would be wise to stop somewhere overnight. I walked into what I thought was a small hotel, but was, in fact, a pub, and not residential. However, they kindly gave me a bed for the night.

The service men were very trustworthy and respectful of the female sex. A girl could travel on her own all night in a train compartment – they were lit by two dim blue lights – full of service men, and be confident that she was completely safe.

However, on one occasion, my confidence was temporarily shaken. One dark winter's evening, I caught the slow train back to London. We arrived in Paddington about six o'clock. I waited in Page Street for a bus to Victoria Station, and in no time, a group of us had gathered – soldiers, girls in uniform. It was extremely cold. Every winter during the war years was very cold. A furniture van stopped and offered us a lift. It was black and dark, with hooded headlights. We all got into the back of this huge van that was so pitch black inside that we couldn't see each other. We women sat on the floor, and the men stood. I suddenly felt something brushing my leg. It continued until I thought, 'I'm going to scream. I'm going to scream.' I'd had enough and protested venomously. The driver switched on the lights. I discovered that my offender was the hem of the long coat of the soldier standing innocently next to me.

I developed a wonky back and was eventually admitted to Holton Hospital in Berkshire.

At Christmas, we visited the patients in the other wards. We went to the burns ward where the pilots who had came down in their aeroplanes were being treated. The cases were really bad. One poor pilot had lost both his legs and an arm and had suffered horrific injuries to his face. The memory stayed with me for a long time. There was a saline bath in the ward which contained salted water flowing through it. The burnt pilots were put in the bath when admitted into the hospital as it was discovered that the injuries of the pilots that came down in the sea were not nearly as severe as those that had not.

I was there for a year being treated for a tubercular spine, which I had contracted from drinking milk from an infected cow. I drank an awful lot of milk. Everybody did then.

I was discharged from the forces to Morrison Hospital.

I met Jeff (Jones), married him, and had our son, Paul.

Years later I was strapped for cash, and wondered what to do. I taught Paul to drive much against his will. It is very difficult teaching one of the family. I gave driving lessons as a hobby, and eventually decided to start my own School of Motoring, which I ran for thirteen years. It was great."

In 1943, Morwyn Elliott joined the ATS and trained for six weeks at Queen's Camp, Guilford, Surrey. "Princess Elizabeth had been stationed there the April before I joined in the May. She did not sleep at the camp but returned to Windsor Castle each evening. Princess Elizabeth was employed in driving ambulances.

We women were taught various duties. Those with excellent eyesight were chosen to fire guns at enemy aircraft. Many were trained as lorry drivers, but it was imperative that they be at least five-foot-four inches, to ensure perfect vision when driving the large vehicles."

Her training completed, Morwyn joined the Royal Army Service Co. attached to the camp, where she stayed until the end of the war. "My job was a clerk organizing the lorries which were transporting food to the camps in Normandy as they prepared for D. Day."

Glenys Harry was conscripted into the services at the age of twenty-one years. "I arose one morning to find a buff envelope from Her Majesty's Service waiting for me and I'm not very good in the mornings. I was twenty-one in the January and went in the March. I wanted to join the WRNS but they were fully conscripted. My father told me, 'Don't you dare go to the ammunition works in Bridgend,' so I joined the ATS. I had a very thorough medical examination and was to sit a written exam in the YMCA. My friend and I made a pact. I didn't like maths, so she was to whisper the maths answers to me, and I the English answers to her, as she spoke mostly Welsh. My good friend Teggy (Tegwedd) also joined the ATS. She was a hoot and used to ride a donkey in the donkey derby in Penclawdd Carnivals.

I gave my required three references from Councillor Henry Davies, Mrs. Daisy Rees and Mrs. Evans of the Railway Inn – my last employer – and went to Wrexham for my initial training.

I found it a bit off-putting as we had very strict army discipline. We were taught to quick march, slow march and salute. I often fell asleep in

Glenys Harry, née Rees.

the lectures we had to attend, as it was very tiring marching in the heat. At the end of the six-week training, we had to sit another exam.

I then went to Cardiff. I liked being there as I could nip home on a twenty-four-hour pass. We were taught plotting skills for plotting guns and planes, and mapping and weather forecasting. I worked in the gun operational room. When a plane came over, we'd relay to the gun site the relevant map number and range, and they would shoot the plane. The plot had to be dead on. The man who taught us mapping was from Hawaii. He was a most pleasant little man, with lovely brown skin.

After six months training, I was stationed at Newport, where the gun site was a quarter of a mile up the road from the camp. We went to the church hall first, where our six beds were on the stage. I wrote home and told my parents that I was on the stage at last. We then went to our camp. We were sixteen to a hut and eight on shift at a time, day and night. We all got on well and had no arguments. We were in huts but the officers were in the large house – Belmont House – which belonged to Lady Baenham, who lived down the road. The gun operational room – which was sound-proof – was in Belmont House. The house had shutters on the windows, which was an unusual feature of the time. The battery was in Christ-church overlooking Caerleon. I was there for two years and it was really pleasant but it took about a year to adjust to army life. It was impossible to have a mind of your own. The life was so regimented and your every movement was dictated.

There was a bad raid on Cardiff, and Newport railway was badly hit. The nuns at Cardiff complained that they did not have gun protection, but they didn't understand that we were forbidden to fire over a town.

It wasn't their fault. Newport was easier to protect as the planes approached the town over countryside, but the gun site was hit badly and I think five were killed. One plane came down, and the crew parachuted out.

One morning I nearly 'had it in the neck'. I was on heights plotting for the guns firing at planes at a height. I put out the wrong height and Sergeant Burnstein, who was a real pig, said to me, 'What school did you go to Rees?'

I replied, 'Night school, I can't think in the day.' Everyone laughed and laughed except Sergeant Burnstein.

We were always hungry, as our cook was hopeless. One day we pinched some bacon. We were asked, 'What's that lovely smell coming from your hut?' When we replied that we were cooking bacon, everyone wanted to know where we had got it, but we had prepared our answer and said that one of the girl's parents had sent it to us from their farm in Somerset, where they kept pigs.

I was to be awarded a stripe, become a corporal and posted to Ireland. I didn't want to leave my friends so I howled and cried. They gave the stripe to Doris. Doris had an unfortunate surname – Goodenough – so we called her Doris Badenough. As she had accepted the stripe and was prepared to leave us, we decided to play a trick on her. We had parcels from the Red Cross in America. They were very kind to us. Sheila had received a beautiful tortoiseshell case of Max Factor make-up. Oh! It was gorgeous. Sheila was our officer. Her surname was Crow and when she shouted orders, we used to say to her, 'Stop crowing.' Doris was a very heavy sleeper and while she was asleep, Sheila painted her face with huge red cupid lips, rosy cheeks, large black eyes and thick black eyebrows. She looked a sight. We then shouted 'Raid!' Joan had gone down ahead to report back on the result. When Doris arrived, Captain Bishop, the duty officer said, 'God Almighty, that's Private Rees' work.' But I was innocent really. We had also put a sign on Doris' back saying, 'Kick me.' When Captain Bishop saw it he said, 'I've a good mind to.'

One night we were told that we were to plot a hostile plane and that the guns were on 'stand down'. That was all we were told. We plotted the plane from the south coast to Pembrey. The lights on our plotting blocks showed green for a friendly plane, amber for unknown and red for hostile. Later that night, we discovered that the plane had flown one of our spies out of Germany. He had been there for a long time and the Germans had become suspicious of him. He landed at Pembrey without a hitch declaring, 'I have come to claim Cornwall.' It was a clever operation.

When the area – Swansea, Cardiff and Newport – was no longer targeted by the Germans, the guns were disbanded.

We were sent to Bristol to what we called a Holding[3] and were divided up. It was terrible, as we had been together for two years. Some went to Weymouth in Dorset and I went to a tiny place near Exeter in Devon. It had nothing going for it except a few farms. We were again stationed at a large house. We were on beam operations – searchlights – which was very very slow plotting. While I was in Devon, one of the ATS girls – Daniels – whom I was stationed with in Newport had compassionate leave when her brother, a Bevin Boy, was killed in the colliery. She was shattered when she heard the news. I was sent to Exford in Somerset to relieve her. We were stationed at Edgecot House on the edge of Lorna Doone country. I then returned to Exeter. I was in Devon for two years. By then, the Germans had taken the Channel Islands and we were concentrating on protecting the west coast of England, so the guns were taken there and the searchlight camp disbanded.

All the gun-plotting camps on the west coast were fully manned, so I had to change my job. This meant trying another exam. I was sent to Millhill in London in full kit, as from London, I was going home on leave. When I arrived in Millhill, there was a bombing raid to end all bombing raids, so I went straight to the cellar. The next day, I had my exam, and went to Paddington to catch the train home. There was another raid while I was there, and I was delayed for two hours. They were two very frightening raids.

My mother found my being in the army difficult, as I was the only one of our family in the forces. When in 1943, she learned that my younger brother George was to be a Bevin Boy, she nearly went 'up the wall'. If I was due back at camp, and it was raining, she purposely awoke me too late to catch the bus to Swansea. She'd say, 'Don't think you can go back on the train soaked to the skin,' but she got used to it in the end. Leave was ten days. The troop trains came from Carmarthen and were always full when they arrived at High Street Station, Swansea. We never had a seat and the trains creaked and stopped everywhere – at every siding. One day, I got on the troop compartment of a train by mistake. It was packed with very young Australian air cadets, who had been training at Fairwood Aerodrome. The doors were immediately shut and locked. When I realized that I was in the wrong part of the train, I tried to get off, but it was too late. The sergeant and the boys told me that they were going to board a ship in Southampton. I was only going to Newport. I thought that they were teasing at first, but when I realized that they were serious, there was a panic. When we arrived at Newport, they got me out through a window. I was as black as coal. Those trains were so dirty. I was lucky, as if the military police had seen me I would have been confined to quarters for at least fourteen days.

After leave, I went back to Devon and worked as a filing clerk in the Quarter Masters' Stores. The quartermaster, known as Q, looked after the uniforms, machinery, etc. He was a regular soldier and about forty years of age, as were most of the sergeants. They had been in the Territorial Army before the war and so were called up immediately. I stayed until the battery moved out. It was a very happy time in Devon. We used to go to Honiton – where the lace was made – on our bicycles. One American driver bought her wedding veil there. It must have cost her a fortune, as a small lace corner of a hanky cost fourteen shilling and six pence. The local people were very kind to us and used to invite us to supper. We manned the barrage balloons until the colonel said it was asking too much of us, and so the air force took over. We manned the switchboards instead.

The battery was to be disbanded and I was going home on leave. Miss Phillips our officer was from Pontardawe. She asked me to take her dog, Bundles, to Swansea High Street Station, where I was to be met by her father. She loved Bundles. We all loved Bundles. He only knew army life and was everybody's bundle. Miss Phillips said goodbye to Bundles with, 'Be a good boy darling Bundles.' It proved to be a disasterous journey. It was the journey of my life. I had a train pass and when I asked the ticket officer for a single for Bundles, he asked me, 'A bundle of what my dear?' Bundles missed the steps when he jumped on the train, landed on the rails and could not jump back up. I ran up the platform like Roger Bannister shouting, 'Stop the train! Stop the train! My dog is on the lines!' Bundles and I eventually got on the train where he went to sleep, snoring loudly. When I stopped for a cup of tea, he chased a cat on the platform, upsetting tea all over the poor soldiers and Waafs who were sitting at the table. He was caught and kindly held by a sergeant major while I finished my tea. I arrived at High Street, exhausted, to Mr. Phillips' greeting, 'Hallo darling Bundles.'

I went to Harwich where the boys were doing commando training on the beach. It was only eighty-five miles from the Hook of Holland that was occupied by the Germans. It was a dangerous place as flying bombs – doodlebugs – were dropping there from Germany, where they were catapulted from platforms. The planes had no pilots, and after a certain distance, their tails went on fire. When the fire went out, they dropped. We had a very severe raid one night, and were unable to get out of the cellars. Sometimes, a high wind would send them back into the sea, but they got as far as Colchester and some did reach London. Everyone thought that they were the secret weapons that were talked about, but they weren't. The secret weapons were the V2s. We were not told much in the army incase of careless talk. They had sayings – 'Be like Dad. Keep mum' and 'Careless talk costs lives'. We had an embroidered badge – which we called a flash – sewn on our lower sleeve. It had P for plotter surrounded by laurel leaves on it. We had to take them off eventually, because they were a clear indication that we worked in a plotting station and there were many German spies about. The Germans loved to get radar stations as our radar trapped so many of their planes. The beach at Harwich was heavily mined, as it was so near the Hook of Holland. I never saw a child while I was there. They had all been evacuated – too dangerous. But it was a happy time for me. It was a very pleasant battery.

I was asked to do some plotting again, and although rusty, it came back to me. The V2s would shoot across the channel – and there were a few of them – drop, explode, drop and explode again. They were faster than sound and so could not be picked up by radar. We were sworn to secrecy. The biggest of all the plotting stations was Biggin Hill. While I was at Harwich, the colonel invited men that were on a training ship called the Torrington to join us for Christmas dinner. They were not more than eighteen years of age. The next day their ship was torpedoed and only two survived. The boy sitting next to me was to go on leave the following week to North Wales. We were really shocked. They were so young. It hit us for six. Harwich was a very, very dangerous place. It was later discovered that the V2s were made and sent from an underground chamber in Germany. It had huge iron galleries like those in chapels, and a railway.

We were detailed to see the war correspondents' films such as the skeleton bodies of the Jews in Germany, to make us mad. Many war correspondents were killed as they were in the front lines. I don't think that they had enough acknowledgment.

But there was more laughter than tears. We made our own fun. We had one decrepit old wireless that we had to bang the daylight out of to get it going. We also had a gramophone and one record – Kerri Pipers – that we played over and over again. We all knew the words off by heart. The lights went out at ten thirty. I took a flat (iron) back and we used to take our life in out hands by plugging it into the electric light socket. But it was better then the old 'spit and grab'[4] on the stove.

We were issued with three thick white pants, three long khaki pants with elastic at the bottoms, three shirts with detachable collars, six collars, a straight skirt, a jacket, two pairs of shoes (clonkers), a glengarry for off-duty, a peaked cap and a pair of trousers. We wore the latter on radar duty as we had to sleep in our uniform incase of night raids. We were allowed to wear a watch and ring and no other jewellery.

When I was training, I received eight shilling a week, which eventually increased to twenty-eight shillings. Throughout my service, my father supplemented my wages by one pound every week. On high days and holidays I received two pounds. He also told me that I could send for a money-telegram if need be, but I only once took advantage of this offer to buy a grip (holdall).

The beginning of the end was when we bombed Dresden. That was a massive operation that was kept secret from us until after the event. One morning we could hear a terrible hum. We could hear nothing else. We discovered later that it was the planes – mostly American – taking off from Ipswich. It was a massive bombing raid but they had it coming to them, and we didn't loose a lot of planes, so we were told. Our boys then went into Holland and freed it. I was in the Royal Fusiliers and when they moved out I went to an ammunition dump in Gillingham – a Holding.

When I arrived there it had been snowing. The huts had not been occupied for a long time and the walls were wet. When the bedding arrived it was damp. I had been so warned against damp things, that I slept on a chair. I then went to Windstay Park in North Wales, five miles from Llangollen. I was in an office there and in the office next to me was an administration officer by the name of Stella Gibson. She was the niece of Guy Gibson.[5] She was very offish and ate alone in the canteen. One morning she came into my office and I wondered why she was so pleasant. It transpired that she wanted my help in pronouncing some Welsh words that she found impossible. I could not speak Welsh but I could read and sing it. Cook was not pleased with me because I had helped her and threatened me with a small ration of dinner that night. Stella Gibson was not popular but fortunately we only saw her at meal times. She played a lot of golf and all that caper.

My last camp was in the grounds of Longleat. The American Army was stationed there also and they really lived in style. The men suffering from horrific injuries were recuperating there. The battle-stressed were housed in a building in the woods where it was quiet. I was demobbed from Longleat."

Tegwedd (Teg) Murley was conscripted into the forces at the age of twenty. Teg had not been away from home for any length of time, and was not looking forward to her army service.

"I was conscripted into the ATS at the age of twenty; nearly twenty one. I didn't want to go to the army and told my mother that I might be able to join the Land Army and work locally. My mother said, 'Perhaps

Tegwedd Murley, née Davies.

you won't have to go to the forces. The war will be over soon.' But it continued, and I went to the YMCA in Swansea to have an examination – an IQ test, which I passed A1. My mother had mixed feelings. She was glad that I had passed highly but not pleased that it enabled me to go to the army.

Ethel Williams from Penclawdd and I went to Wrexham together to do the basic training. I was a real tomboy and found the marching easy – left right, left right. One girl always went the wrong way. I hated the sergeant major. He used to shout at her and it was as much as I could do not to shout at him.

We had school lessons. I was terrified at first. I could hear all these girls talking posh and I thought, 'What chance have I got?' But I felt like a million dollars at the end of the course, as half of them had to go back to school, as they could neither read nor write. I could have gone far in the army, but I resented the fact that I had been made to join.

When I left school at fourteen my friends went to work, but my mother encouraged me to stay at home. I had two older brothers, but there was a ten-year gap between the youngest and me, so I think I was a bit spoilt. I was always with my mother and that was probably why I was so homesick when I went away. I cried for a twelve month. I was very self-conscious when I joined up, but the army helped me to get over that.

I made some wonderful friends. They were such a great bunch of girls. I still write to Joey McCay from Sterling. Her daughter is a missionary in Nicaragua. She often invited me to spend leave with her family, but my mother always persuaded me to go home.

We went to Gresford near Wrexham. There had been a big mine explosion there when two hundred men were killed. We used to walk down a hill and were in England. We would window-shop sometimes on a Sunday.

Our training finished, we were posted to a transit camp in Oswestry. The buses were irregular but we had bikes at our disposal, which we made good use of.

Three weeks later, we were told to stay in camp that night, as we were to receive our posting orders. At nine o'clock, our kit ready, we were marched to the train station and given a blanket each. We thought, 'That's funny – a blanket.' We travelled in the train overnight and the next morning we saw nothing but snow. We thought that we had been sent abroad and some of the girls started crying. But we were in the north of Scotland in Iverngordon, near Inverness. We arrived at the camp of Nissen huts. It was all right. We had one stove and a supply of logs. A goods train passed everyday transporting coal. We used to stand at the wire and the men used to throw us big lumps of coal. I used to think, 'What if my mother could see me now?' We'd put the coal on the stove and make toast with bread from the cookhouse.

We were near a small village – a bit like Penclawdd – with a few shops, a picture house and mountains around. The locals had never seen girl soldiers before and when a few girls went down the village they returned covered in blood. The locals had thrown stones at them. They were that clannish, but when we left they were crying. The first film I saw in the pictures was 'How Green was my Valley'. It was not the most suitable film for me at the time and didn't help my homesickness. Some of the audience started laughing at the Welsh accents in the film. There were Welsh boys in the audience who took exception and they started fighting. It was so bad that they had to stop the film.

The lairds used to invite us to their beautiful homes, provide us with plenty of food and teach us to sword dance.

We all had to do guard duty. One dark night, my friend and I were on duty, armed with a gun each, near the men's hut. It was a mixed camp. The area was very remote and the sea was across the road. We'd had gun training but using them was another matter. If I'd have had to kill someone I think I'd have shot the gun backwards. We heard someone approaching mumbling to himself. I thought, 'I wonder who this is?' I said 'Halt, who goes there?' There was no reply. I said to my friend, 'You try this time.'

She said, 'Halt who goes there?' Again we had no answer, only more mumbling. We didn't know what to do. 'Come on,' said my friend, 'let's tackle him.' We pushed him with our guns across the road and into the sea. He was soaking. We then realized that he was our sergeant major. He had been drinking heavily and was quite drunk. We reported what had happened to the office but we heard no more of the incident.

I was there for two years. I had always said that I wouldn't get married unless my boyfriend, Leonard Murley, got stationed abroad. During my time there, I heard that he was going to be posted to Karachi, so we were married.

One of my jobs was a spotter. I had to spot whether the approaching planes were enemy or Allied aircraft and inform the office by phone. I also had to guard a big gun. We all did cookhouse duties.

One evening, about forty of us, including the sergeant major, had a musical contest. I had a good voice then, as I had had singing and piano lessons. I won the singing competition. The sergeant major was a member of the Royal Academy of Music – we were not aware of it at the time – and he was furious that I had taken the veneer off him. He was so angry that he ordered me to do cookhouse fatigues, where I cleaned potatoes for a week. However, by the end of our time together, he was wonderful.

I was 'well away' in the forces. One of the girls was a hairdresser and another was a manicurist. For a packet of five fags they'd do you up like a model.

Some of the girls in our battery – Battery 548 – were terrors, but all in good fun. One Christmas we were caught for doing something wrong – the hairdresser, myself and two others – and as a punishment we were ordered to feather two turkeys. We had no idea how it was done. The hairdresser said that she knew what to do. She tipped paraffin all over the birds and set them alight. Nobody had turkey that Christmas. We had to make do with pork.

The train journey to and from home took two days either way and our leave was only nine days. We never had a seat, but stood all the way in the corridors. On the return journey after leave, an extra engine was attached to the rear of the train at Fort William to help cope with the mountainous countryside. The trains were long and full of troops, but nothing out of order ever occurred.

I was stationed at Nigg in Scotland, South and North Shields, Newcastle, Sunderland and Cumberland. By the time I left the area my accent was the same as the locals. The girls in our battery came from many different parts of the country and so our accents were very varied. At first we found it difficult to understand one another.

Towards the end of the war we were stationed as near home as possible. I went to London. The train was full of service men. A sailor said to us, 'Where are you girls going?' When we replied London he said, 'They've flattened London. I don't know where you are going to stay.' By the time we reached London, we were scared stiff. He had frightened us so much. He was only pulling our legs but we had taken him seriously.

We had to travel by underground to our hotel. We had never been on an escalator before. We all stood with our kit bags at the top of the escalator and said, 'Who is going to go first?' A chap with one leg came along and went down with no hesitation, so we thought if he could do it so could we. We all got on together and rolled down to the bottom. I'll never forget it.

We stayed at the hotel to await our posting. All the girls were posted and at the end of a month. I was the only one left. I was getting fed up so inquired at the desk as to why I hadn't been posted. There had been a mix-up between my name Murley, and a girl called Hurley. That evening I was posted to Westminster, and the following morning the hotel where I had been staying received a direct hit. What a lucky escape!

I was in London when the doodlebugs were coming over. That was quite an experience. You'd hear the plane coming and when it stopped you'd wonder where it was going to fall. Would it be on you?

I was stationed in the heart of Westminster in the quarters of the Abbey choirboys, near Churchill's Club and Westminster Abbey. I found the cockney accent even more difficult then the northern accents. We sold cigarettes and sweets, etc. in the central hall, which was a transit camp. I can remember the food now. It was fish cakes, fish cakes. We had the same food everyday as there were different people coming in everyday, stopping the night, and then posted elsewhere.

When the war finished, we were disbanded, had our cards, and sent home."

Peggy Grove, a native of Cardiff, now lives in the old station house at Llanmorlais. Her daughter, Heather, and son-in-law, Gwyn Jones, have sympathetically renovated and enlarged the building into a desirable dwelling. It was through Peggy's contribution to the war effort that she came to live in Gower.

"I was dressmaking in the departmental store, David Morgan, in Cardiff. I had to keep my hands nice and I was sort of delicate looking. I was coming up to eighteen and as I was working on sewing machines, I was afraid that I would be called to work in a parachute factory, as had many of my colleagues. I'd seen an advert, 'Come in and join the Women's Land Army' and thought I'd join before I was eighteen. When I told the girls at work of my decision, there was a roar of laughter. 'You've never seen a cow in your life. You'll never be able to milk one.'

It was true that my only experience of country life was Sunday School outings, but their mockery made me even more determined. 'I'm going to join today,' I said. 'I'll show you.'

I went with a friend who was seventeen. When I informed the lady in the office that I wanted to join the Land Army, she looked at me and said,

Peggy Grove just before she joined
The Women's Land Army.

'Are you sure my dear?' I was about seven and a half stone and very pale from working indoors. I assured her that I did, as I had no wish to work in a factory. She asked me, 'Have you been on a farm before?' I had not as we went to few places in those days. Nobody had cars. She advised me to go home and think it over. 'Discuss it with your parents. Don't do anything too hasty my dear. I'm sure there's something else you can do. What is your work at the moment?' I replied that I was a dressmaker but not afraid of hard work as our mother used to make us do jobs around the house. I left with the promise to return the next day.

My friend said, 'You're not really going to go are you?'

I said, 'Yes I am.'

I went home, but there was no 'talking it over'. I had already made up my mind. I went back to the office the next day and informed the lady of my decision. She said, 'O.K, but do you realize that you might be sent miles and miles away from home.' I said I was aware of that, as there were no farms in Cardiff, but I didn't mind.

A few days later, I had a letter to go for a medical, which I passed with no problems.

When my uniform arrived by post we had such a laugh. It consisted of a hat, a pair of jodhpurs, thick woollen socks, a green woollen jumper, shirts and a tie like a man's, a pair of big wellies, leather boots with laces and walking out shoes. The boots and shoes were of hard leather and very uncomfortable. I was used to wearing light fancy shoes. I was provided with two pairs of dungarees but could have done with half-a-dozen. The work was mucky and the clothes thick. Washing them proved to be a problem, as there were no washing machines in those days. I paraded in my uniform and my brother laughed and laughed.

My instructions arrived. I caught a train to Bridgend. I knew no one on the train and thought, 'This is it. I'm on my way.' When I got off the train I felt completely lost, but I saw three other girls in Land Army uniform with their cases, looking equally as lost as I was. We were met and told to make our own way to the hostel at the training farm in Coity.

It was June and very hot. The four of us walked to the hostel, and when we arrived, we all had sore feet. We were shown to our rooms. They were small with bunk beds. We were given tickets for our meals for the week and made our way to the canteen. I'll always remember my first meal there. My soup had a spider in it but I fished it out and ate the soup, as I was so hungry. Our meal was followed by a cup of tea but no biscuits. We didn't sleep much that night, just talked and laughed. I slept in the bottom bunk and my friend slept on the top.

In the morning, we dressed in our dungarees, shirts, thick socks and boots and collected our food for the day. We had little choice and I opted for bread and jam. There was no butter. A boy collected us in a Jeep, and informed us that in future we were to find our own way on foot. We were taken to a field and the boy said, 'Right, here is a hoe each.' I had never seen a hoe before. 'Now watch me. This is a field of carrots.' He started knocking out the weeds and thinning out the carrots. 'Now you all have a go and I will be back to take you home at tea time.' We were told to work on one row at a time. Well the carrots tops and the weeds looked exactly the same. After a while, we became hot and hungry. We didn't have a watch but felt sure it was lunchtime. It was a scorching hot day. We went under a hedge and ate our food which, by now, had dried up. We had not thought to bring a drink. We were tired and thirsty. We'd travelled the day before and had not slept much in the night. Before long we were all asleep. When we awoke we had no idea of the time. We saw that we had left all the weeds and knocked out all the carrots, which had dried up in the sun. We had another go but were soon hungry again. Nearby was a field of onions. We pulled a few and attempted to eat them. When the boy returned he shouted, 'You dull idiots! I hope the boss doesn't come out here tonight as you'll be in trouble.' The big boss was a gentleman farmer. He did no work and always wore spats. Well! What a start! We weren't asked to work on the carrot field again.

We cleaned out the cows' muck and put it in wheelbarrows. We wheeled it up a plank on the dump. One day my wheelbarrow and I tipped over. All we could do was laugh. It was not much of a training farm. We helped throw up some hay but it was important that we learn to milk, as the farmers desperately needed help with their milking. We were taken to the dairy where the lady in charge was to show us how it was done. The cow had recently given birth to a calf and so had plenty of milk. The lady demonstrated, and made it look easy. We were to sit on a small three-legged stool and hold the bucket between our legs. The first girl tried, but the cow swished her tail, and the girl fell on her back. She often wet herself when she laughed and so had to make a quick exit. I tried and the same thing happened. Not one of us was successful in getting milk. The lady said, 'Go the lot of you and don't come back tomorrow.' That was all I learned about milking on the training farm. I discovered later that a cow knows when a stranger is milking her and retains her milk.

After being there a month, the course was finished, and I went home for a weekend. The next week I took a train to Swansea, where I was met at the station by a Miss Brooks, who was in charge of all the Land Army Girls in the area. She visited as at the farms to check that we were all right. She was a very nice well-spoken lady, who lived in Pennard and owned horses. She had a car, which was very unusual in those days. Another girl had been taken to the station by her parents and Miss Brooks took her to a farm in Overton and me to Beynon's farm in Penmaen. As we travelled through Gower, I thought I was going to the end of the world.

I met the family. Mrs. Bertha Beynon was there but her husband Tom, who was to be my boss, wasn't. He was probably in the mart. The five-year-old twins, Trevor and Gwyneth had just started school. Joan was a baby of about one-year, learning to walk. Ten-year-old Gwyn was a very intelligent boy. The local school at Parkmill was experiencing few scholarship passes at the time. It was thought that he would benefit from attending Llanrhidian School, which was very good. He stayed with his mother's sister in Llanrhidian in the week, and so I only saw him at weekends and holidays. Bertha Beynon's sister, Alice, was also living on the farm, as her husband was a prisoner of war. She had a baby called Jean, who was about the same age as Joan. I was in my element, as I love children. We had a lovely tea with fresh eggs and cream. They made their own cream and I could have had as many eggs as I wanted. I thought, 'Oh! This is lovely' as eggs were on ration.

I was taken to my bedroom, which had a beautiful view over the bay, but when I tried to find the bathroom I was mystified. I thought that perhaps it was downstairs, but when I asked for the toilet, I was taken outside, around the corner and through an orchard to a little shed. That was the toilet. I didn't live in a posh house in Cardiff, but I was used to a water closet with a chain. I wondered what I was to do in the dark nights, and later bought a torch.

The house had a cold water tap and a wash basin by the back door. The cold tap had to suffice in the mornings, and in the evenings, we drew a jug of water from the small boiler in the kitchen, and washed in a basin in our bedrooms. It was a strict house rule that every jug of hot water drawn off the tank was to be replaced by a jug of cold water. In an outside shed, an old fashioned stove heated a water tank with a tap. Coal, wood and any old rubbish fuelled the stove. It was a good system, as everything was burned away. The water was heated for baths and cleaning the skin of the pigs after they were killed. Baths were taken in a tin bath in the shed.

I didn't sleep very well that first night. I was in strange surroundings and was also wondering what I would be expected to do the next day.

In the morning, I was given a quick cup of tea, and then went with the boss to bring in the cows from the fields, as they were only kept inside during winter nights. There were about eight cows. Each had a name and its own place in the cowshed. They all knew where to go, and if one went to the wrong place, there would be a row. When they were ready for milking, I thought to myself, 'Here goes.' Tom could obviously see my face as he said, 'You can milk I hope?' I had to admit that I couldn't. 'But you went to the training farm,' he said. 'I asked for a girl who could milk.' I explained what had happened and he was quite reasonable. He gave me an easy cow but I couldn't get any milk out of her. I tried again in the evening with a little more success. In a few weeks I was quite good at it and was capable of taking over the milking when the boss was not there to do it. You just had to get on with it. There was no such thing as can't. I found that out. I was surprised how my wrists hurt, and I later bought a leather support, which helped.

The farm had one milk churn. The evening's milk filled half the churn and most of the following morning's milk was added to it to fill it. The rest of the milk was kept for the family and also delivered around the local houses. After morning milking, Tom and I carried the full churn, which was very heavy, up the hill to the stand. The churn always seemed to be carried uphill when it was full and downhill when empty. The Milk Marketing Board collected our churn, and the other full churns in Gower, and replaced them with empty ones. All the containers used in milking had to be scalded with boiling water heated by the stove in the kitchen. A Milk Marketing Board Inspector came out every so often to inspect the cows for TB.

I used to deliver milk in the mornings to Nicholston House. It is an hotel now, but then it was a guesthouse. In the summer months – their busy time – I delivered extra milk in the evening as well. I also carried two cans of milk up the hill to the nearby houses every morning, pouring the milk into the jugs provided, with a pint ladle.

Breakfast was served about half passed nine after milking. I was very hungry by then and would have eaten anything. We had bacon, which I didn't eat at home. I'd never eaten laverbread but it was on my plate and I ate it without a word, as I was so hungry. I was conscious of bacon joints covered with muslin, hanging on hooks from the ceiling. One of my jobs was to feed the pig. I never had much bother with her and after a while became quite friendly with her. One morning, when I was preparing her food, the boss said, 'Don't bother with the pig today. The butchers are coming later to kill her.'

I was horrified and said, 'What for?'

'Well for bacon of course,' said Tom. 'Where do you think your breakfast comes from?'

I said, 'I thought the bacon hanging in the kitchen came from a shop.'

'That was last year's pig,' he said. 'Now we have to kill this pig for next year's bacon.'

Bacon was on ration and all those who kept pigs had to give up their bacon ration, but of course they were still better off. The butcher, and Tom's two brothers, Glyn and Will came from Long Oaks. The pig started howling long before they arrived, and I'm sure she knew what was going to happen. I was told to go to the shed to keep the boiler going for hot water and then come and help with the pig. I thought to myself 'no way' and locked myself in the shed. I could hear her squealing and I stuck my fingers in my ears. When all went quiet Tom told me to unlock the door and bring the hot water. I had to clean up the mess. The pig was on a bench. They poured water over her and I had to scrape the hair off her skin. Oh! It was terrible. At first I refused to eat the meat – no way – but after a few days I was hungry and gave in.

I had become a bit hardened by the time I fed the second pig. I knew that once the bacon was finished it would be killed. The day arrived, and Tom's help didn't turn up. Tom said to me, 'Come on maid, we've got a job to do. It's only me and thee maid.' I knew that I would have to help this time but was unaware of what it would entail. Tom put a thick rope around the pig's neck and took him into a shed. The pig was squealing and squealing. There was a big beam in the roof of the shed and Tom said, 'When I throw the rope over the beam I want you to catch it the other side.' I still had no idea how he was going to kill the pig. I held onto the rope – I was bigger and stronger by now – and Tom helped me pull. The pig was hoisted into the air. As I held on like mad Tom thrust a knife into the pig's throat. The blood poured out all over me. The animal was kicking and kicking and the rope slipped out of my grasp. The pig wasn't dead. I was horrified. The animal ran out of the shed into a heap of manure and died in all that mess. I stood there shaking. It was a dreadful experience. Looking back I think, 'Why didn't I walk away?' But I couldn't. It was my job.

One day the boss said, 'Come on. We have a little field of hay to cut.' He had a Ford tractor and I knew that I would be expected to drive it. After Tom cut a few rounds he said, 'It's your turn now.' I said that I couldn't drive but he took no notice and said, 'You will. There's no such thing as can't.' It was a simple little tractor and I soon got the knack. I found cornering difficult at first but I conquered that as well, and stayed on the tractor, and finished cutting the field. I was quite pleased with myself. The boss let me drive back to the farm on the road, but we met no other traffic. Few people owned cars and petrol was on ration.

The farm had a beautiful grey and white stallion called Captain. I didn't 'take to him' as he was so big. One day, the boss and I were gathering swedes. The boss was in the cart, guiding Captain, and I was throwing the swedes into the cart. After a while he told me to get into the cart and take the reins. I did as I was told and immediately Captain started racing twice around the field and back to Tom. I was terrified and said that I'd never go in that cart again.

They teased me at the farm that horses had only one set of teeth, so I put my fingers in one of the smaller horses mouth to find out. Of course he bit me, and I discovered the truth about his teeth. When they asked where I had bruised my fingers they laughed at what I had done and said, 'How dull can you get?'

On threshing days, Will Harry – from Cilibion Farm – brought his threshing machine around the Gower farms. The farmers would help each other out and the women would bake. They were allowed to kill a lamb for threshing days if they applied. It was the only time that they could. Sometimes the threshing lasted a few days, depending on the amount of corn, and the farmers would stay at the farmhouse. That was the way it was done. The corn would have been cut previously, turned, and allowed to dry out in the field. When it was ready it would have been stacked, either in the field, or nearer the farmhouse. A man would stand on the top of the machine and we would throw the corn to him. I was not allowed to stand on top of the machine as earlier a Land Army Girl had fallen into a shoot with the corn. What a horrible death! As we came to the bottom of the stacks, the rats would run out. They terrified me. The farm dogs would catch them and the farmers would hit them. One ran up the back of Glyn's trouser leg and I had to shout at him, as he didn't know it was there. Threshing was a dirty dusty old job.

I hoed in the fields until I had blisters on my hands. I cleaned out the cowsheds and the hen houses and the manure was taken to the fields by tractor. I stood on top of the manure and scattered it over the fields. The calves were kept in sheds in the winter, and in the spring I cleaned out the sheds. Again the manure was used on the fields. It was very hard work. I can't believe that I did it now. No chemicals were ever used. The smell in the hen house was terrible – much worse than in the cow shed and the pigsty.

There were very few Land Girls living in farmhouses in Gower, as most stayed in hostels. A big house in Parkmill was taken over for Land Girls and also Kilfrew Manor was used. I got to know the girls in the Parkmill Hostel, and they were very nice. I used to walk there from the farm or occasionally go by bus. I walked back in the dark through all those trees, and thought nothing of it. The girls in the hostels were allocated to work on the farms as required. For example, they were needed for potato picking. They were quicker and less clumsy than the men. In one way I was better off staying on the farm because the food was good, and it had a homely atmosphere. However, the hostel girls' working day was finished when they returned to the hostel at about five, which was the house rule. I, on the other hand, would be out the fields until eleven o'clock. During the war, an hour was added onto British Summer Time to help the farmers. I didn't get overtime but that was farming life.

I filled the one hundred weight potato sacks, hoisted them on and off the weighing machine, and then sewed them up with twine. They were canvas bags – the old sacking – which was good stuff. We used to make aprons out of them to use when doing dirty jobs out the fields.

The Americans were stationed in Penclawdd. They took over the Gower beaches with their ducks practising for the Normany landings. By D. Day they had all disappeared.

I only went home to Cardiff some weekends, as if there was a harvest I stayed at the farm. When I did go home, I worked Saturday morning and rushed to catch the one o'clock bus from Swansea. I travelled from there to Cardiff on the N. & C. Coaches, and returned on Sunday evening. The last bus went as far as Sandy Lane in Pennard, and I walked to the farm from there.

Dances were held at the local halls and I soon got to know the locals of my own age. My first dance was in Pennard Hall. I had to walk to the dances, but soon realized that I would have to buy a bike to get around, as did the others. I had ridden to work in Cardiff. There was a lady's second hand bike in good condition going, but I had no savings as all my money was spent going home at weekends. I only earned about one pound five shillings a week. The boss said he'd pay for the bike on the condition that I gave him half-a-crown a week. So that was how I had my bike.

One night I came back from Cardiff and had no intention of going out, as I was tired, but I was persuaded by a friend to go to a dance in Penmaen. I quickly changed and off we went. It was the norm for the girls to go to the dances early, but most of the boys appeared after the pubs closed. As we were late arriving, the hall was full. I knew all the local faces by now, and so noticed a boy in naval uniform, who was unfamiliar to me. I was sitting next to a girl who was an evacuee.

'Oh!' she said, 'Look at that lovely sailor over there. He's looking at me. He's coming over to ask me to dance.' I didn't like to stare as I quite fancied him myself. 'Oh!' she said, 'He's coming. He's coming.'

But he said to me, 'Would you like to dance?'

She was most envious and never forgave me for it. I didn't wear my uniform to dances. I had made myself a really nice dress which I was wearing that evening.

He asked me, 'Where do you live? I've never seen you before.'

I explained my circumstances, and he told me that he had just returned from Canada, and was on a few days leave. He, like myself, had been persuaded last minute by a friend to attend the dance. We danced again and clicked just like that. Llewelyn took me home that evening and we started going out regularly.

The war was coming to an end. He didn't return abroad, and was discharged from Portsmouth. I was able to leave the farm, as the men were coming home. The Land Army Girls more or less had their marching orders after the war, but some of them married farmers. I went to work in a shop in Port Eynon to be near Llewellyn – he lived in Horton. I never returned to Cardiff to live, and we were married on 1947.

When Llewelyn came out of the navy, he only had a demob suit. He had enough money to buy a new suit, but not enough coupons, so my brother in Cardiff arranged for him to buy one on the black market."

Many of the young boys and girls of the village were too young to join the services when war was declared. Some of the boys, anxious to fight for their country, gave inaccurate dates of birth. One young girl, determined to help in the war effort, spent five years nursing in Bristol and London.

"I was in Gowerton County School when war broke out. To a certain degree, it caused a bit of excitement. We didn't know anything about war. All the boys and girls wanted to get involved. I was sixteen in the November, and too young to join the forces, but I did want to do nursing.

Saint Monica's, in Bristol, accepted girls at the age of sixteen as opposed to Swansea, where girls of that young age were not wanted. I thought I was going to work in a hospital, but in fact, it was a home for people in reduced circumstances – a glorified nursing home. It had been built by Dame Monica, who was very wealthy. The building contained the best of everything – beautiful furniture, beautiful china and cutlery, etc. The nurses' home was also very beautiful.

I was in Bristol during the bombing of the town centre. We could see the reflection of the fires in the sky from the nurses' home, but we carried on with life regardless.

When there was an air raid on a town, the trains stopped outside the station until the all clear. There was an air raid in Newport and our train – we were four girls home on leave – stopped for over an hour. Consequently, when we arrived in High Street Station, we'd missed the last buses home. I informed my friends that I was not going to walk to Penclawdd on my own, but was going with them to Gorseinon. We walked as far as Fforestfach. We had to take all our belongings home with us incase the nurses' home would be bombed, and so our cases were extremely heavy. I said I couldn't walk any further with my case and was going to wait for a policeman to appear. A policeman took us to an ARP depot in Fforestfach, where we sat around a beautiful fire, and were given a very welcome cup of tea. There was a wonderful spirit during the war years, and everybody helped everybody else. Having been assured that our cases were in safe hands, we continued walking to Gorseinon, arriving about half-past two. I stayed the night with my friends, and we collected our cases the next morning.

After two years, I went to Hampstead, in London, where I nursed fever patients – diphtheria, chicken pox, measles, etc. I was there when the Germans were firing V1s and V2s. I loved London, and my five years there was a wonderful experience. We were five Welsh girls and one English girl – known as the Welsh Gang. We became great pals. We had an excellent relationship and even swapped clothes.

Like all nurses, we didn't have much money. The girls who smoked – luckily I didn't – were always broke on the second week after pay. The girls who didn't smoke were always broke on the third week. Consequently, the fourth week was grim. We'd empty our purses and pockets and the first girl off duty on the fourth week was given the little money we had. Pennies meant more then. We could take a tube to Tottenham Court Road from Hampstead for thrupence.

We were transferred for a month to nurse TB patients in Colindale. It was situated on one side of the railway line, and Hendon Aerodrome on the other. One day, we decided to walk to Burnt Oak, and when we arrived, we were starving. I had one penny in my purse and my friend had nothing. We looked hopefully in the window of a cake shop, but the rock cakes – there were no nice cakes during the war – were a penny ha'penny each, and so we went without. We often went for walks, but always rushed back to the hospital for lunch and tea. We never ventured far.

Penicillin was so expensive that it was only prescribed to service men and women. It was kept in the lab, and when needed, delivered to us. We were then supervised while injecting it into the patient. They were very strict, and it was never given to civilians. Penicillin would have saved so many lives if it had not been in such short supply. Methods were primitive compared to today. We used rubber gloves that had been worn in theatre, but we did sterilize them first.

We were well-organized in the event of a German attack. We each knew which patient we were responsible for, and as soon as the alarm was sounded, we moved quickly. We had all the patients in the basement of the building in seven minutes. All the staff helped – the maids, the secretaries, etc. I can remember taking one man down who had a bad heart. I can remember thinking, 'You're heart can't be that bad.' as I used to tear down the corridors. The basement was horrible, as it was infested with black beetles, attracted by the hot water pipes.

I returned to Penclawdd at the end of the war in 1945, and married in the same year."

NOTES

1. Lightening war: A swift intensive military attack designed to defeat the opposition quickly.
2. Gwyn Alf Williams, *Fishers of Men*. Llandysul, Dyfed. 1966, p. 34.
3. Holding: A camp where the ATS were stationed in-between batteries, usually for a period of three weeks.
4. Spit and grab: Flat iron heated on a fire or stove.
5. Guy Gibson of 'The Dam Busters' fame.

8

Men in the Army

John Elliott volunteered for the Welsh Guards and spent four years and eleven months away from his home during the war years.

"I was born in 1920, and by the age of five years, was living in Little Hills Farm, Ilston. Farming was poor. There were small collieries opening everywhere so at about seventeen, I went to work in Gelli Gros Colliery – owned by Hopkins of Llanmorlais – so I could then help my father financially. I was banking on the surface and sometimes underground, but I wasn't cutting coal. I had a little accident on my finger, and was on compensation when war broke out.

I thought that the war would only last six months, so I thought I'd better go. I went on 9th December to join the navy. My uncle, William Tucker, was in the navy in the First World War, but he was killed in the Wernbwll Colliery in 1933. At that time, they had called up many men in the militias, so the navy was pretty full. I was told there were no boats and I could go home for six months. I thought that by then the war would be over, so I crossed the landing in the YMCA building to the army room. The man there asked me how old I was. When I said that I was nineteen, he told me to come back when I was twenty. When I told him I was a miner, he said, 'That's finished it.' When I told him I had been a farm labourer before, he said, 'Go outside the door. Come in and tell me that you are twenty and that you are a general labourer.' So on my first pay, it stated that I was a year older than I actually was, and a general labourer. He said, 'You're a tall chap. How tall are you?' I said I was about five feet and ten inches. 'They're looking for you in the Welsh Guards[1],' he said. So within seven days I was in Caterham in Surrey.

We trained in Colchester and Camberley under canvas. We were thirty boys in a barracks room and fair play, that room was spick and span. Every cup and every box was in line. The floor was polished, and rather than scrape the floor with our boots, we'd put our blankets down to walk on them, then sleep on them in the nights. But it was a lovely battalion with a lot of men from North Wales. I speak Welsh, but I couldn't understand the North Walian boys. We had to clean and polish and when we were sitting on our beds cleaning, we'd start singing. There was nothing else to

John Elliott on right.

do. We were only having two bob (two shillings) a day. But *Duw* (God) those boys from the Rhondda and the other valleys had been going to chapel and they knew all the parts of the oratorios. You could swear that we had been purposely put together. The singing was wonderful. They could also play rugby of course.

Then the Germans broke through on 10th May. We were a battalion of Welsh Guards, Irish Guards and a machine gun company called the Manchester Royals. They called us a Whippet Battalion. Whenever there was trouble, they'd whip us in and quickly pull us out. We were supposed to go to Norway, and the Irish boys got on the boat and went, but the Germans bombed the boat and killed everybody above the rank of sergeant, so they came back.

We went to the Hook of Holland to fetch Queen Wilemena out.

About ten days later we were in Tunbridge Wells and Camberley, still under canvas.

The Duke of Gloucester, and Lord Gort who was in charge of the BEF (British Expeditionary Force), were in danger of being surrounded outside Boulogne. They stuck us on a boat from Folkestone, and out we went again. We arrived at Boulogne on the Tuesday. We left everything on the boat, and just ran up and took the town, and held it while the BEF came down through us to the destroyer. They had beautiful horses, but they could not get them up the gangplank of the ship, so they shot them into the harbour and off they sailed. They told us to hold the town and then pull back, and that a boat would come to the docks to pick us up. We were fighting Romel's lot – his armour division – who fought with tanks. By Wednesday we were pulled down to the docks, and had five days of real pummeling there. The boats could only come in on high tide every twelve hours. We waited for a boat from the Wednesday until the Saturday. We had little food and water, and nowhere to bury our dead. We were in a deuce of a mess. We were eighty-six Welsh Guards and only thirty-six uninjured. We had an officer with us called Windsor Williams and Major Lewis. The Major was the most highly decorated officer in the army. He took our names on the last day when we were running out of supplies – ammunition food and water – and said, 'My kneecap is off, so they'll probable take me and put me in a hospital. I know France and Belgium like the back of my hand – he had money and had been often on holiday – and I will probably get away. I don't know what's going to happen to you. Because we've shot everybody with white flags, you'll probably get shot into the docks, but if you give me your names and addresses, I'll tell your parents where I last saw you.' There was a padre there and hundreds of French. I had been hit in the leg. It was a flesh and not a bone wound. I didn't know I'd been hit until I felt my sock pulling. When I took my gaiter off to have a look, I found that the blood had dried in my sock and was pulling the hairs on my leg. A stretcher-bearer took the bit of shrapnel out with a type of scissors.

On that Saturday afternoon, 25th May, the Germans hit the town with everything they had. We were near the boat that had come in for us, but the Germans were up on the hill shooting down at us below on the docks, and so we were unable to board it. They set the docks on fire to get light. We had a Major Jones Mortimor from North Wales. He said that he would take our company – Number Two Company – and try and drive the Germans out. We went up the hill, but we got pulverized there again, and the boat sailed during the time we were up there.

We were captured at about half-past two on the Saturday afternoon. It was not until four years and eleven months later that I was to come home.

The front line boys – Rommel's lot – were tidy men. We'd had little to eat and drink, so they sent a couple of boys to buy us pop and food. There was a little German there who spoke fluent English. I can see him now, with his tin hat hanging on his bayonet. We were sitting on the steps of a chapel. Sergeant Robins said to us, 'I don't want a photograph in the German papers of the Welsh Guards with their hands up. Don't put your hands up. They'll probably shoot you into the docks, but it won't be long.' We were walking along the docks where the horses had been shot. We walked off the docks and we felt we were living hour by hour. The Germans hadn't seen British soldiers before. They were travelling along on their bikes and when they discovered that we were British they pulled out their cameras and started taking photographs of us. We were a peep show. One of them said, 'Do you know the song 'Roll out the barrel'? We've heard it on the wireless. Sing it.' So we did sing it. We'd have done anything to save being shot. They marched us to a football field and put a couple of machine guns around in the grandstands, and there we stayed until the next morning.

They walked us through Holland, doing about twenty-five kilometers a day. We lost the front line troops, and then the German SS men took over. They were terrible. They were even killing their own troops if they deserted. We were about thirty-six in number, and a couple of our boys were wounded and failed on the march. Once the Germans knew we were wounded they shot us, so the poor boys were afraid to say that they were wounded. We carried them for a long while. When we got very near to the border they brought lorries to transport us through Strasbourg and Alsace into Germany. We got out of the lorries in a little town on the German border and walked to a railway station. All the German flags and swastikas were there. We had our hands on our hats. They were gobbing on us because we were the first British they had seen. There was a mess on us. The Americans had not entered the war then, and they were there with their movie cameras taking photos of us – the first British prisoners caught by the Germans. I was one of the first six thousand caught. My number was six thousand three hundred and forty one. The Yanks shouted at us, 'You will be in the 'Picture Post' in America next week!' The rest of the men there were mostly sailors who had been captured in the ports when the Germans took over Norway. We were given a rye loaf of bread each in front of the cameras, but when we went around the corner to the train – cattle trucks they were – they took the loaves off us and put them back in the baskets. That taught us a lesson. In future, whenever we were given a loaf of bread by the Germans, we'd eat it straight away so that the buggers couldn't take it back. It was hard eating a whole loaf without anything to drink, but we did it, as we had learned our lesson.

We were roughly about eighty prisoners in two cattle wagons. We were in them for four days without food and drink, and some dead amongst us. We were taken to the River Vistula in Poland. The Germans were cruel with no feelings for anybody. All the towns in Poland were surrounded by little forts to protect them, as being a buffer state, they were always fighting. We were put in Fort Eleven underground in the dungeon that had a floor of cobbled stones. It wasn't too bad as we were only a few there. A little later we were taken nearer the town to the camp Stalag XXA, known as Stalag Seventeen. There I stayed for over four years."

Arthur Harry of Mill Farm, Reynoldston, although not a native of Penclawdd, spent many hours in the village in the room above Jim's shop, where the youngsters of the village gathered. It was there that he met Glenys – Rees as she then was – before the outbreak of war, when they were both fourteen years of age. They corresponded regularly throughout their years in the forces.

Arthur was conscripted into the army in January 1940, at twenty years of age.

"I had worked my trade as a mechanic for five years before I was called up. After three days of REME test in the workshop, it was acknowledged that I was competent in my trade, which was an advantage in the army, and needed no further training in that field. I spent two months in Clay Cross, and was then posted to Harrogate where a couple of dozen of us joined a militia unit. I spent my war years in the Royal Signal Co. in charge of transport, where I became a corporal.

I was supposed to go in an advance party to Norway, but fortunately I didn't go. They never returned.

I went to the Middle East first. We sailed around the Cape to Ceylon.[2] It was a terrible trip. I was seasick for the nine weeks on board the liner. The only way I could manage was to make a bed on deck, and stay put. If I moved, I was buggered. At Ceylon, we were unloaded onto troop ships, and I was seasick again as we sailed up the Red Sea and the Suez Canal to Port Said.

Arthur Harry, second from right, in Port Said, Egypt.

We were issued with thick green army shirts, thick khaki shorts with turn-ups and a pith hat. The uniform was inappropriate for such a hot climate, and we were later issued with a lighter weight uniform. At a beer café in Port Said I ate a free meal of beautiful crabs. They were as white as snow. I probably ate too many after not having eaten properly for weeks, as I was violently ill for days afterwards.

We then travelled to Palestine, where we did a bit of training.

We went to Egypt with the First Bush – Wavell's lot – when the Italians were there. It was before Rommel and Monty's time. I went up the desert in June 1940. The first piece of bread I had was the following Christmas Day. We bathed in the sea when possible. We had no fresh water and made tea out of seawater. We used to have a couple of sips and use the rest to shave. There was so much desert. We could travel for hundreds of miles and whichever way we looked it was the same. If we left camp and did not return before dark, it was wiser to stay put until the morning, as it was impossible to find the way back. We were at Tobruk on Christmas Day 1940. It was a little landing place at the head of Hell-Fire Pass. The troops had filled their kit bags with presents. They were too heavy to carry, so they buried them in the sand at the top of the pass, planning to pick them up on the way back. The Arabs probably found them, as we never returned. We quickly pushed the Italians back into Libya and went to Greece.

There was a mess out there. It was an impossible task to get the Germans out. We had good troops – British, Australian and New Zealanders – but no air force protection. I only saw three of our planes and I only saw them once. We could see the Gerry bombers looking out of the plane as they fired at us on the road. We hid in the hay fields and under trees. It was terrible. I was lucky to get out of there – very lucky. We had to make a swift retreat by foot. There were thousands of us on the road making for the coast. At night, the navy cruisers took us to the troop ships, which we boarded the quickest way possible – many of us climbing up the side nets. As soon as it was daylight, the German planes started bombing us. The troop ships were firing their anti-tank guns that were strapped in lines at the side of the ships' railings. They were firing like hell, but the Germans were sinking our ships as fast as they could get out there. There was as many men left behind, and taken prisoners, as got out. It was an unnecessary waste of good men. Our troops landed in Crete and the same thing happened – no air support. Before we went into action, we were ordered to cut off our stripes, pips, etc. The ranks of our prisoners were undistinguishable, to safeguard against leaking information.

I spent my twenty-first birthday in Cairo, on 9th November 1941.

There was an air raid on, and I spent the day in bed, and didn't move. I didn't care if I was bombed, as I was so fed up.

In 1942, we spent about eight months laying oil pipelines in Iraq and Iran. The countries were very similar with no obvious frontiers. All we saw was sand. We experienced extreme contrasts in temperature. The winter was very cold but summer in Baghdad was the hottest I have ever known. We never stopped sweating even when resting. We quickly became tired of the red-hot sun day after day. We were thankful when it set at night thinking, 'Thank God it's gone.'"

While stationed in the area, Arthur kept a diary.

1st January.

'Got drunk in canteen on New Year's Eve. Bad head today. Having half-day off. Playing football against 59. Weather very cold. Received photo of Glen five days ago. Everything going OK.'

5th January.

'Freezing very hard. Very busy with lorries every morning. On guard all night. Had letter from home. Camping forty miles inside Iran border.'

2nd February.

'Billet in Khorramshahr. People very poor and dirty.'

4th February.

'Weather becoming much warmer. Everything same as usual.'

10th February.

'Received three air graphs from Glen. Very pleased to hear of her getting my mail OK.'

17th February.

'Rain stopped but very muddy. Feeling tired after fitting two springs on three-ton lorries.'

"The Arabs were the biggest thieves imaginable. They'd steal from our lorries while we were stationary at the villages. We had to keep going like hell, otherwise they'd pinch everything. The buggers even used to pinch the wooden seats of our home-made toilets. At night, we chained our ammunition to ourselves and put them in trenches under our beds. The Arabs still managed to steal it. Our camps were guarded but they were so smart that we never saw them. We lost so much ammunition that we contacted their headmen – they didn't have police – and demanded its return, threatening to take their village if not obeyed. Our ammunition was returned. A pipeline ran on the sand from Yafo to the oil wells at Baghdad."

11th March.

'Getting lorries ready to move 59 Sec. to Baghdad. Lovely day. On guard all night. Got blind drunk. Missed drinking wines.'

12th March.

'Too bad to get out of bed until dinnertime. My mate and I giving drinking up until after war.'

"We followed the line for about a week and were stationed at Baghdad to protect the oil well. It was a hell of a place. The Arabs stole our telegraph wires. We had to be careful as they carried knives and would kill us."

20th March.

'Wrote green envelope[3] to Glen. Very busy with transport. Feeling very fed up with this life.'

31st March.

'Getting very hot. Sweating to death. Very busy with lorry.'

12th April.

'Half-day off. Very hot. Received air graph from home saying Glen had to join ATS.'

13th April.

'Dull day. Very heavy weather. Thinking of Glen all day. Feeling fed up to the teeth. All out working on line.'

17th April.

'Everything quiet. Feeling fed up with army. Looking forward to war finishing. Building pipeline in Kjamaqin city.'

"I met Hedley Clement, from Mumbles, when stopping overnight at a camp in Baghdad. We saw little beer, but in the camp there were piles of beer cans stacked up to the roof. Nobody was buying it. We thought, 'this is bloody funny' and decided to have a can each. On opening the cans we realized why. The temperature was so high that the gassy beer exploded. The beer spouted out with tremendous force. We couldn't stop it and it blew sky high. We managed to drink very little."

28th April.

'Last day in Baghdad. Awful sandstorm all evening. Packing up ready to move in morning.'

9th May.

'Camping on hill thirteen miles outside Musayyib. Country very green, just like Gower.'

27th May.

'Everything same as usual. Writing letters all evening. Very hot in day. Fighting broke out in Libya.'

22nd June.

'Lovely day. Very cool. Plenty to keep myself busy. Bad news from desert. Tobruk falls.'

28th June.

'News very bad in desert seventy miles from Alexandria.'

16th June.

'Very hot and feeling half-dead. Looking forward to getting back to Blighty again.'

24th September.

'Received air graph from Glen saying she had volunteered to go abroad. Felt rotten when I read the awful news.'

9th November.

'Birthday. Laying on the bed all day feeling awful.'

"We travelled to Basrha from where we sailed to India, and travelled to Poona. We were there with Mountbatten. He was very popular with the troops and, unlike Monty, did not stand on ceremony, demanding no formal parades. I remember standing sweating in incredible heat on parade with one officer.

We then flew up into Burma. It was all jungle. We didn't see anything but jungle. There were bulldozers working day and night pushing down trees to make a road through the jungle to transport ammunition. One of my jobs as a corporal was to take my turn at night guard duty. It was particularly dangerous in the jungle. I'd sit in the guardroom without light, usually on my own, and every two hours phone the other sentries to inform if all was well. If I was attacked what hope did I have? I'd go to the phone in the dugout, in the pitch dark, my bayonet in front of me, incase there was a Jap waiting for me. My nerves would be on edge. It was a hell of a job. After the war, when walking along the road, if a bird flew out of a tree, I'd jump off the ground.

We were advancing everyday. The Japs broke through and surrounded our troops in Imphal and took Kohima. A handful of us were flown to Dimapur as the advanced party, while the heavy ammunition came later. The first couple of nights we were only ten miles from the Japs. We always knew where they had camped, as they left trails of rice – bags of it on the ground. If we saw dead Japs, we dare not go near them incase they had been booby-trapped. We used to throw a tin of petrol over them to put them on fire. We were at Imphal for a while freeing our troops. A boy from Llangennith, who worked on the buses, was at Imphal. After the war, he often related how we had come in to free them.

We then advanced to Kohima, which was situated on top of a hill. As we travelled, we were looking down on the clouds in the valleys. Some of the trucks went over the top and plunged to the bottom of the valleys, but we were unable to help them, as it would take too long to walk down. Ahead, we could see the sky above Kohima white with our parachutes. The Japs had dug well in. They had constructed a warren of cement bunkers underground. The Second Division – all British – couldn't get them out and had lost a lot of men there. We were standing by to reinforce. We eventually got them out by throwing flame-throwers off the tanks into the bunkers. The Japs ran out like rats. The Nagar tribe – natives of Kohima – were very much like the Japs in stature, short and thick set. They were muscular fellows, probably from walking up and down all those hills. The Nagar were keen to attack the Jap prisoners, so we had to guard the Japs to keep the buggers out.

By then I had completed my five years, and was due to come home. I found that the regular soldiers were as cunning as hell, and dodged everything. We Welsh were always chosen to go on dirty jobs, but they wouldn't pick the regulars, as they were a lazy lot of buggers. The dozen or so of us left came down the river in a duck to the nearest aerodrome. We flew to Calcutta and travelled to Bombay by train, where we waited a week for a ship, and then home.

After a couple of years of fighting, you get so browned off that you couldn't care a hell for your safety. The bombs would drop, and the bullets fly, but you wouldn't bother to move. One fellow from Swansea called Davies, wouldn't even wear his tin hat, and would walk through the middle of flying bullets. He'd volunteer for everything, and never got hurt while I was there. I don't know if he survived, as he didn't come home with us."

The words are said, which are inscribed on a headstone in Burma, reminding us of all who fought and died there:

> 'Let us remember before God,
> and commend to his sure keeping:
> those who have died for their country in war:
> those whom we knew and whose memory we treasure;
> and all who have lived and died in the service of mankind.'

Arthur recalls his travels through serving his country. "I travelled a hell of a lot during the war, and went to many countries. I was so glad that we called in Cape Town, in South Africa, as I thought it a lovely place. The climate was beautiful, and everything was green. I went to Egypt, Palestine, Greece, Iraq, Iran, India and Burma. I remember the mud huts of Nazareth, and the oranges of Palestine. We ate bananas in Beirut, and as we slept on the ground, we stretched out our hands and picked handfuls of grapes.

I came home for two months, and spent the last twelve months of the war in Germany. That was a holiday. When our troops first occupied Germany, they could make a fortune. A packet of ten cigarettes sold for ten pounds. They were able to send home as much as one hundred pounds a week. By the time I was there the regulations had tightened, but it was still a profitable time.

I didn't bother to send for my medals.

I didn't see Glenys for the five years that I spend abroad, as I had no home leave. There were hundreds of broken romances in the forces, but Glenys and I stuck it out. We were married in 1946, after I was demobbed from Germany."

Idris Jones on right at Kinmel Park, Rhyl, North Wales.

Idris Jones was called up on 31 October 1939.

"Elwyn Gwyther – who lived by the old lead works – and I had been into Swansea with the idea of joining the Welsh Guards, but we didn't carry it out. I had a choice of which service to join and chose the army, but later wished that I had joined the navy.

My training started in Kinmel Park, near Rhyl, in North Wales. We were there until the following May (1940), training in the Royal Artillery with twenty-five pound guns. We were taught square bashing (marching) and drills.

I was then posted to Ascot which was a distribution centre, sending detachments to different places. Thomas John Bennett – Station Road – was with me. He was a bit of a comedian. He went to Malta on the anti-aircraft guns and was there all through Malta's worse time.

I went to Shropshire – to the Seventy-Fifth Shropshire Yeomanry – where we were stationed in a large country house called Shavington Hall and later in Aderley Hall.

I was in Oswestry in 1940 after the Battle of Dunkirk. We were digging trenches at the sides of the roads, expecting German troops any minute. Anyway that passed over and I was stationed at a little place in Cheshire called Tattenhall. A nice little village it was, and we didn't have a bad time there. From Tattenhall we went to Tarpoley where we stayed for six to seven months. Wrentham, in Suffolk, was our next stay, where again we were in a big country house. We went to church parade on a Sunday to a Congregation Church in Southwold, which is a little village on the east coast. It's Nelson's birthplace, and has a small memorial on the beach in his memory. We used to watch the Norfolk fisherman, wearing big black jerseys, bringing in small sprats and lying them on the beach to dry. We often had some. Oh! They were lovely. After church service, we used to go to a café for tea. The locals milled their own flour and their cakes were delicious. It was a very interesting place and we used to look forward to our Sunday outing. In 1942, we had orders to travel to Liverpool to board the huge liner Cape Town Castle.

We sailed up the Irish Sea and took in oil at Scotland on the Firth of Forth. We sailed around the Irish coast and out into the Atlantic. We sailed to The Azores and down the west coast of Africa, heading for Free Town. It was one of the roughest seas I have ever been on. The big liners were bobbing up and down like small rowing boats. The liners, carrying our troops, travelled in convoy. They were escorted by British warships, which were protecting them from German submarine ships. At the beginning of the war, the Germans were sinking many of our merchant navy ships. They were so daring that they would sail in-between the warships and sink the merchant navy ships in the middle of the convoy. But as our use of asdic[4] improved, the subs began to have a rough time, and they had received a bit of a bashing in the Atlantic before we were there.

The climate was wonderful. We called in Free Town in very steamy heat. The Negroes were coming out to our ship in small canoes. If we threw a copper out, they might dive after it, but if we threw a sixpenny bit, they'd definitely dive for it. We sailed around the Cape to Durban. It was a marvellous journey. It was like a four-week holiday – the best time of my war years. It was better then working underground. I'd have never done that. We continued up the Indian Ocean and took in oil at Aden. There were mines in the Indian Ocean, but they did not bother us, and it was not as dangerous as the Atlantic. We sailed up the Red Sea towards Egypt. We passed Ethiopia and the Arabian Desert. It was very brown barren country – horrible. I was glad to get to Egypt.

We eventually arrived at Cairo. We were stationed in a big camp where we attended lectures on the events of Monty's Battle of El Alamein. We could see the pyramids nine miles away in the distance. I worked in a party that took goods off the railways. The Arab peasants worked for us, helping us with the big cases. At night, a big gang of them would suddenly diminish to one or two as they slunk off to sleep under the trucks. They didn't want to work and had very little food. The taskmaster – A British Army Sergeant – would whip them. They also had their own taskmasters who would appear with whips – grinning.

Monty's Eighth Army had gone ahead to Tripoli on the north coast of Africa. They had chased Rommel out, and by then, he knew that he had been beaten, and put up no fight. We gradually followed them, going through Tobruk, and into Libya. We slept on the sand, and when we awoke in the morning, we'd find scorpions in our blankets and see chameleons in the trees. Water was very scarce in the desert. Fourteen of us would wash in the same bowl of water. By the time the last one had washed, the water was like oil. A purifying chemical was mixed with our drinking water to stop bacteria. It was horrible stuff. We ate the same food all the time – biscuits and bully (corned beef). They were the most horrible biscuits. It was like eating pieces of timber. I'll remember their name until the end of my days – Arnotts biscuits. I discovered years later that they were made in Australia. When in Italy, we went to the Yankee positions. Their biscuits were as good as the ones in our shops today. The Yanks had everything except beer and spirits. They were always chewing gum and smoking. We used to collect the Italian farmers' eggs until the Americans came. They could give big money for them. The Egyptian peasants would fill whisky bottles with weak tea in an attempt to sell it to us as whisky. They'd run by our sides with one hand outstretched to take our money. Some of our boys were taken in, and would then chase the peasants over the desert. The Egyptians used to dig up the graves to get the boots from the dead soldiers – they were so desperate. We encountered Italian immigrant farmers who lived on practically nothing – a few watermelons. Crops had to be watered continually. There was machinery scattered over the desert. We'd have been left there if Montgomery hadn't attacked when he did.

On our arrival at Tripoli, we boarded a Liberty ship – the Americans used to build one in a week – to invade Sicily. As we landed in Siracusa, the German planes came over but they didn't drop any bombs on us. We were thrilled to be in Sicily after Africa. The almond trees were fruiting by the side of the road. We picked them as if we'd never seen a nut before. We went through orange and lemon groves and picked loads of lemons to mix the juice with the wine. We gradually travelled through the Messina Straits of Sicily – the Americans were on the west side – passing the temporary grave of Hedley Verity, the Yorkshire cricketer, near the roadside. We reached Messina, and started bombarding Reggio di Calabria, situated on the toe of Italy. The invasion of Italy had started.

We travelled northwards with Monty's Eighth Army through Italy from the Adriatic Sector to the Central Sector. We didn't have too bad a time, experiencing only spasmodic firing from the Germans, but when we arrived at Monte Cassino, we came to a dead stop. Monty had been instructed to return to England to prepare for the Second Front – D. Day. He was replaced by General Leese. The Germans had retreated north to the heights of Cassino from where they could see for miles around. They could easily direct shellfire on any of our activities. We hitched a gun onto a big vehicle in daytime, which was very foolish. I don't know if it was done on purpose to give the Germans the impression that we were drawing the gun away from Cassino. When we left the position, the shells were raining on us. They were eight-eight millimeter, high muscle, velocity shells – not big but could kill. There were a lot of holes in the area in different directions. Someone had placed a name there – Clapham Junction. The Germans were in the monastery and *Duw* they were holding on for grim death. We had a perfect view of them. They were German parachutists – terrific fighters. A plane came over one morning dropping a bomb on the monastery, but with no effect as the walls were ten to twelve-feet thick. The bombs kept dropping, but the Germans remained until 11th May 1944. A big attack went in to take Cassino. The Poles received the most deaths and injuries as they were ahead in the infantry and we were behind in the artillery. Thousands of Poles were killed.

Two days later, we were in action in the advance party in front with the infantry, going towards the German lines. It was pitch-black and a problem to know where we were as we had never been in that area before. The artillery was sending shells ahead of us and we were following. We were directing the gunfire via the wireless by map reading. It was the first time I had to map read as I was normally on the guns in the artillery. The officer in charge of us was a duke – the Duke of Bradford. Oh! He was a mean devil. He was one of the meanest men I've ever met. He suddenly disappeared. Unknown to us, a sergeant in charge of wireless control had been slightly injured and decided to go back with the Duke, taking our wireless with him. It was essential for us to have the wireless to send back messages to the gun. Without it we had no contact. We carried on through flying shells and rocks, oblivious of what had happened. When we became aware that we were without the wireless, we approached an officer and explained our situation, and asked his advice. He suggested that as we could not contact our guns we had better go back. We gradually retreated through shell and mortar fire and we thought we'd had it. I dived into a shallow ditch as clods of earth flew in the air and covered me. A mortar bomb had landed nearby and it was a miracle that I was not killed. We slowly marched back to the gun. On the 13th May, we arrived where the gun was situated near a village.

I was given orders to rest and to have plenty of sleep, as I'd just come back from the front. I was sitting quietly and the boys were playing cards nearby. The tannoy rang. It was then that I had it. After the gunners had received firing range instructions from the infantry, a message had to be relayed back to inform as to whether or not their instructions had been carried out. As I went to the tannoy to convey the message that the gun had been fired, it blew into smithereens. The shell and the ammunition to drive it out exploded before they left the barrel. It was a 555 gun with a hundred pound shell charge which could send it about eight miles. I can't remember how many were killed. Everything went on fire. A premature, as it was called, had more disasterous results than a German shell. It was the nearest thing to hell upon earth. The experience was so frightening that in those circumstances the gunners were given the opportunity to get off the guns, as it shattered their confidence, and they were always afraid in future that the same would happen. I went down and somehow dragged myself out of the gun pit. The tannoy was on the sandbank wall surrounding the gun. If I had stayed outside the wall I would have been alright, but I went through the opening in the wall to speak into the tannoy. I was put on a Jeep and taken to a nearby hospital.

You knew all about it then when you lost a leg. The first week was the worse. The medical profession has improved so much on amputations today. I discovered after the war that I was operated on by a Welsh surgeon. What a coincidence! I was transferred to a hospital in Naples, and later to Liverpool. I was out of the war. I went to Bradford for a week and then to Chapel Alerton in Leeds – the biggest British Military Hospital in the country. I was there until July, and was then transferred to the war casualty Rookwood Hospital in Cardiff, where I started writing to Aurwen. She later became my wife.

I received about five medals. When I went for an interview with the military before I left hospital, they asked me if I wanted to stay in the army. They informed me that I could work in the stores. 'No thank you.' I said."

Morgan Guy of Llotrog, Penclawdd, joined the army in 1938, at the age of eighteen.

"I left school at fourteen. I'd like to have been a mechanic, but Jeffries Motors of Morriston was the only option, and I thought it too far to travel from Penclawdd.

A fellow from Penclawdd by the name of Josiah Thomas had a shoe business in Portland Street, Swansea, but on my applying, he told me that he had no work for me. It was a dark old-fashion shop even then, and had boots and shoes hanging up on the ceiling. There was a shoe repair business in Wind Street, Swansea, called Smith and Sons (SOS), which was far more modern. It was a large business, having about twenty-six employees. I learned my trade there, and had one year left to finish when I was called up. The firm tried to defer my entry into the services until I had completed my apprenticeship, but failed.

I was called up on my eighteenth birthday in April, and was unhappy, as I would miss the haymaking.

When I signed up, I met a boy called Groves from Swansea, who advised me to volunteer for the Welsh Guards, as he had done. We travelled to Caterham together.

Morgan Guy.

As we went through the gates, we saw the guards' chapel on our right, and the booking-in office on our left. We walked up a long drive through an avenue of trees, which opened into a large square – similar to the Horse Guards' Parade – surrounded by buildings. This was the barracks, the training depot of the Five-Foot Regiments of the Brigades of Guards – Grenadiers, Coldstream, Scots, Irish and Welsh. The Welsh was the youngest of the Foot Regiments. The officer said – he had a voice like a bull – 'That tall building is the hospital and that's the lunatic asylum.'

One fellow said, 'We have come to the right place.'

We did our eight-week training there – marching and spit and polish. Oh! Everything was spit and polish. We had a kit inspection. Some of the boys were nearly crying and my heart was in my boots. But, funny thing, I wasn't actually homesick. I had been when I left home, but I was in good company, and the twenty of us in our platoon were all together for eight weeks.

We passed out and had our distinguishing badges – flashes – and hats with a leek. We were very proud. We were allowed time off at weekends and spent a few hours in Croydon.

We then went as a Holding Battalion[5] to North Africa. It was stalemate for a long time out there. We pushed the Germans back and then they pushed us back. The Germans held Long Stop Hill, outside Algiers, for a long time before we took it. We held until the Americans came, and then left. The Germans attacked in the night and pushed the Americans out, so we, the Five Brigade of Guards, returned.

They asked for volunteers, you, you, and you, to make a composite battalion to reinforce the newly formed Long Range Desert Group.[6] The volunteers, including myself, were companies from our battalion, the Coldstream Battalion and the Irish Battalion. We belonged to nobody and wore no distinguishing flashes. Our main task was to gather information, such as where there was a concentration of enemy troops and where the enemy ammunition dumps were, etc. We went out at night raiding and blowing up German depots in the desert. I was driving a Bren gun Carrier. There was no fighting, unless of course if we got caught. I was with them for about ten months.

Then the push was coming from Monty. We returned to our battalion and joined the Eighth Army in Algiers and went through Tunis to Cape Bon. Meanwhile, Monty was coming through Libya to Cape Bon where the war in North Africa finished.

We stayed in Cape Bon for months and months. It was a marvellous place with beautiful beaches. We could see the distant city of Tunis in the hills. It was the best time of my war years.

We were reforming and went by amphibious boats – ducks – to Italy, calling en route in the island of Lampedusa. We bypassed Sicily, and landed at Salerno, on the west coast near the foot of Italy.

As we travelled northwards, we saw a most spectacular sight in the distance. The sky was on fire, as our troops were bombarding Pompeii. I shall never forget it.

We went to Naples and then through mountainous countryside to Cassino where we spent months and months. Mules were used there, and in the mountainous regions, to carry equipment. It was outside Cassino that Idris lost his leg. The country was boggy and as we went into Cassino by night, we could hear the huge frogs that lived in the boggy ground croaking. It was really eerie." John Retallack, in his book 'The Welsh Guards', describes the experience vividly. 'No Welsh Guardsman who served in Cassino will ever forget the place, or the strange underground, nocturnal existence they led there. Entry into the town was in itself a weird business. The ground was flooded, partly because the bombing had destroyed the banks of the Rapido, and partly because the Germans had blown the dam higher up the valley. The marshy swamp gave off a swirling mist, and from the sullen waters thousands of bull-frogs lent their harsh voices to the chill night air.'[7]

Morgan continues, "We went to Anzio. John Richards of Penclawdd – he was on signals – was involved in the fighting trying to capture the town. I left him there and later, when I was on the Adriatic coast, received a letter saying that he had died. I was probably one of the last to see him alive.

We bypassed Rome and went to Venice. I had a great time there. I had contracted yellow jaundice and spent some time in hospital. Medication was non-existent for the complaint. I was given a low-fat diet of chicken and vegetables. Confirmation of the disease' cure was the disappearance of pink circles that formed in the urine. I went by boat from Saint Mark's Square to a convalescent home on an island about half a mile away. I had a good time, and enjoyed the three weeks I spent there.

A Royal Welsh Fusilier came to convalesce and said to me, 'Hi! Listen! Your lot's gone back to the bottom of Italy to re-establish. I think they might be going home.'

So I made my way under my own steam to the Adriatic side of Italy. I found my battalion, and there we stayed for months and months.

We eventually went by boat to Marseilles and then Dover. From there I went all the way up to Hoyke in Scotland.

I did sentry duty at the Horse Guards' Parade, Saint James' Palace and Windsor Castle. I went to Great Missenden and while I was there waiting to be demobbed, Captain Buckley, of Buckleys Breweries, Llanelli, who had been my platoon officer, invited me to go to India with him, as his batman. We had been together all day and everyday, so he knew me well. However, I had had enough of the army by then and refused. He was promoted to a major when in India. I was demobbed from Guilford.

I played a lot of rugby before I went abroad, and at the end of the war, while I was waiting to be demobbed. While I was in Great Missenden, I played at Richmond Park for the Welsh Guards in the positions of wing and centre.

At the Victory Celebrations in London on 8th June 1946, I was proud to be on sentry duty lining the route at Marble Arch.

I didn't apply for my medals but they were sent to me from the regiment just after I was demobbed. I received five – the 1939-45 Star, the African Star, the Italian Star, the Long Service Star as I was in for seven years from 1938 to 1945 and I think the British Expeditionary Forces medal which I have lost.

I played rugby for Penclawdd after the war but unfortunately my career came to a sudden halt when I contracted shingles.

I returned to SOS and finished my apprenticeship. In the mid-1950s, I opened my shoe shop in London House, where Mrs. Rees had been postmistress."

John William Howell's younger brother, Leonard, received the telegram informing the family that John was missing.

Leonard Howells.

"I went to the door to get the telegram from Mrs. Rees, the postmistress. My mother never recovered from my brother's death, and died when she was only forty-four. She couldn't accept the fact that he had gone. John was an excellent swimmer, but he didn't have a chance, as the Germans bombed the men who had been swept overboard. My mother dreaded me going into the forces, but we all had to go. We didn't know what we were going into.

I was working in the sheet mills in Gorseinon when I was conscripted into the army at the age of eighteen, in January 1942. I was posted to Prestatyn, a place I hadn't heard of. I asked so many people where it was, but nobody knew.

I went to the training camp in North Wales with Glasnant Preston from Penclawdd. We were in the Royal Co. of Signals. The training was intense. We ran from telegraph pole to telegraph pole for ten miles, with our kit on our backs, alternating between running, quick marching and 'on the double'.

Our training of ten weeks completed, we were split up into divisions and sent abroad. Glasnant and I parted company there. Our division went to Egypt, via Free Town and Cape Town, to pick up lorries. In Egypt, the division was split; we stayed in the Middle East and the rest went to India. We took the lorries over the Sinai Desert to Jordan and Palestine.

We then went to Iraq to protect the oil fields from German attack. I was on signals. The telegraph wires ran from the Divisional Head Quarters to the brigade and from the brigade to the battalion. We were in charge of a certain number of lines. My job was to drive the lorries taking the technicians to the communication lines, to mend them, and keep them operational.

Our diet was very limited. We always had porridge for breakfast, and at midday – tiffin – we had about two slices of bread with cheese and marmalade. The rest of our food was from tins. In the winter, we were given a ration of emergency chocolate. It was so hard it had to be cut with a hammer. I grew to like cheese and marmalade sandwiches and still eat them. My wife, Audrey, was horrified when she first saw me make them, but she grew to like them herself eventually.

Nine months later, we were sent back to join the Eighth Army and Monty on the north coast of Algiers, near Tunis, in North Africa. As we travelled to the front line, we passed the old division coming out. They said to us, 'Where are you going? Where are you going? The war is nearly over.' We didn't half have it from them. In three weeks it finished, and we were sent to Tripoli, to sail for the invasion of Italy.

Our trucks were waterproofed for the two landings. We invaded Salerno from where we travelled northwards to just south of Rome. We were shipped out, reformed, and invaded Anzio. We travelled across Italy, and then went northwards. We went as far as Trieste, on the Yugoslavian border, crossing the River Po en route. The weather conditions were grim. The summers were all right, but the winters were terribly cold, with very heavy rainfall. We parked the vehicles in fields, under trees, for camouflage, and often had to stay put for six weeks at a time, as the wet conditions made movement impossible.

My mother died while I was there.

I came home when the war ended in Italy in 1945. My father, Jim, owned a fish and chip shop, and I had lived on chips. When I entered the army I was sixteen stone, with a forty-two inch waist. When I left the forces, nobody in Penclawdd recognized me. I was ten and a half stone.

I didn't bother to apply for my medals. I just wanted to get out.

We were all given a demob suit in a box. When we left the train at High Street Station, we took any box. We were that disinterested in wearing the suits.

I had been friendly with Audrey before I joined the services. I had been away from home for three years without leave, and when Audrey and I were reunited, we were like strangers at first. However, we soon became at ease with each other again, and married in 1945.

Sergeant Lord, who was in charge of the recreation ground, employed many of us young fellows who had been demobbed, to work on drainage and fencing, etc. Audrey and I were anxious to have a business, and after much financial negotiation, bought a coal business from Morlais Rees of Llanmadoc, which we ran for forty-three years."

Arthur Hopkins.

Arthur Hopkins, a native of Crofty, enjoyed his war years.

"I was called up in June 1939. We were only to be there for six months, but it was a lot longer than that. I was told to enlist in the army, and had no choice. I was in the First Militia. I trained at Brecon. It was a rude awakening – up at six o'clock in the morning and it was freezing cold that winter of '39. Our great coats became frozen solid with the moisture from our breath. But as long as I could get out in the nights, I was happy. We were up at six, and out until twelve at night, only having six hours sleep, but we were young and could take it.

I was sent to Essex University and later to Fords for six months, to learn about the V8 engine. My first job in the army was a tank driver and later became a company commander driver.

At first I was posted to Port Tennant, Swansea, as they thought the Germans were going to parachute down to the oil refinery at Llandarcy. That was the cushiest number I had during my service.

When I was stationed in Dorset, I met Joan Taylor, a Land Army Girl. The hay smelt sweet there when I was on the hay with her. We used to go drinking in the Swan Pub. They were happy times. We were young and full of vigour. Joan didn't mind being in the Land Army and I think she liked the uniform. She was stationed on a dairy farm. She used to milk the cows and did something else which made me laugh. They used to castrate pigs in those days, and Joan used to do it, and throw them to the dogs to eat. The girls were unique as they came from large towns – Joan came from London – and yet they adjusted easily to country life.

Later, I did medical training in Catterick. I did a course on learning to plug the soldiers wounds to try and save their lives. I also attended a course in York on venereal disease.

I was stationed in the Orkneys, from where we went straight to France. They had just made the D. Day landings, and we went in as reinforcements. As we went through Normandy, my friend, Arthur Nurse, cousin of Edgar Nurse, was killed in a platoon, while crossing the River Seine, north of Paris. When I was in France, my friend, Elaine Jones, used to send me two hundred cigarettes every month from Wolverhampton, where she was teaching at the time.

In Holland, a friend and I killed two SS men. They came along on motor bikes and we opened up on them with our sub-machine guns. They were riddled with bullets. I was sorry afterwards, but they might have shot us. We jumped on their motor bikes – BMWs I think they were – and went into Winterswjk in Gerlderland. The Dutch hadn't seen any British soldiers before, so they gave us a wonderful welcome. The cameras came out, and I wrote to the burgomaster after the war, and he sent me four of the photographs. They threw a party for us that night. It was a party I'll never forget. There was plenty of everything. We put the mother and father in the cellar and shut the trap door. I spent the night with the girl of the household, and have never seen her since. We had had girls in France on and off, but that was the 'real McCoy' as we used to call it.

We had good times in the army. It wasn't all bad. We arrived in Germany

Arthur Hopkins on right in Winterswjk, Gerlderland.

and had a whale of a time there. I met a German girl who told me that she had not seen a young man for ten months. 'Well,' I said, 'I'm young,' but a bar of chocolate was all I wanted. We made love in the toilet as the 'non frat ban' (which prohibited service men fraternizing with the Germans) was on. It was a court marshal offence, but I couldn't resist it. Despite the 'non frat ban', all the British soldiers had a German girlfriend. We were young and might have been killed the next morning. Quite a lot of us were.

Every battalion trained about two or three stretcher-bearers. I was a stretcher-bearer who also attended the wounded. My job was to go out after every battle and transport six bodies at a time on my Jeep. We made the German prisoners dig the trenches, and we buried the bodies. I put a bottle in with them containing their name, number, rank and regiment. I buried so many that eventually, it became like burying dead pigs. I put pads on the wounded, primarily to stop them bleeding to death. I spent six months in charge of the boys arriving from India suffering from venereal decease. I pumped them with penicillin. I was by then a full medical orderly.

We went through Reichwald Forest where we experienced 'Monty's Moonlight'. They shone searchlight over the trees. It was like daylight. We were bringing in a wounded chap outside Bremen. His stomach was riddled with bullets, and the blood was spouting out. Whether he made it or not, I don't know. Unlikely I'd say. It was then that I got bumped. It caught me in the temple, and I could see the blood pouring down my face. The Ox and Bucks (Oxfordshire and Buckingham) Regiment picked me up, and I was flown to Brussels. It was three weeks before the end of the war."

The following article was published in the 'South Wales Evening Post' on Tuesday 1 May 1945:

'Penclawdd parents see wounded son.

On April 13th Fusilier Henry Arthur Hopkins, of the Royal Welsh Fusiliers, was shot in the head while with Montgomery's forces attacking near Bremen, and within a few days, his father and mother, Mr. and Mrs. John Hopkins, of Crofty Nurseries, Penclawdd, were at his bedside in a Brussels hospital.

Fusilier Hopkins was carrying a wounded soldier back to the British lines when he was shot by a sniper, and as he was dangerously ill, his parents were invited by the Red Cross to visit him in hospital.

The first intimation they had of it was from the police at Gowerton, and they decided at once to avail themselves of the invitation.

Mrs. Hopkins told an 'Evening Post' reporter today that all arrangements for the trip were made by the Red Cross, and it did not cost them one penny.

"We travelled up to London, she said, "where we were met by a Red Cross lady representative. After spending a night at a hostel, where we were made most comfortable, we were driven to Croydon, and then began the exciting part of the journey.

Neither my husband nor I had ever been in an aeroplane before and, of course, we were very nervous, but we were made at home and we thoroughly enjoyed the experience."

At Brussels, they were taken to another hostel and then driven to the hospital to see their son.

By that time Fusilier Hopkins had been operated upon for the wound in his head and the first thing he said to his mother and father was, "Major Elwyn James, of Sketty, performed the operation on me."

Their son is now recovering from his serious injury although it is feared that he may lose the sight of one eye, and much to the surprise of Mr. and Mrs. Hopkins, he was back in hospital in this country before they arrived home.

Mrs. Hopkins said that they saw little of the signs of war, but spent the time when they were not visiting the hospital on a tour of Brussels.

They came back by boat from Ostend, but their adventures had not ended, for it was a troopship with hundreds of soldiers coming home on leave as well as many released prisoners of war. There was an ENSA party on board, and Mr. and Mrs. Hopkins had the time of their lives.

On two occasions they were approached by soldiers in the city and questioned about their Welsh accent. One soldier came on to them and asked, "What part of Wales are you from?" When they said "Penclawdd," he replied, "I'm from Llanelli."

The same day another soldier stopped them in a bazaar and asked very much the same question and he said he lived in Oxford Street, Swansea. "I did not think of asking his name. I was too excited," said Mrs. Hopkins.

They visited the King's Palace and the Garrison Chapel while in the city.

"It was a great adventure," she added, "and I would like to thank the Red Cross for their kindness to us and the local police for their help."'

Arthur was flown to Brize Norton Hospital. "I was taken to Wakefield, what for I don't know. I then went to Morriston Hospital, which was a military hospital then. I had four or five medals. I didn't collect them. I can't be bothered with medals.

Looking back it was a wonderful era. They were adventurous days and we didn't know what was around the next corner. I finished up in York, in the demob centre, and had seventy-five pounds demob money. They made me a corporal. I'd have signed on after the war if I hadn't been wounded and lost the sight of my eye."

Morlais Davies joined the army at the end of the war. He had excellent employment, working as a shift chemist in Gowerton Steelworks, but was restless. "A friend of mine went to the air force. There was nothing much to do in the village, only the cinema and the famous Ratti's shop – a meeting place of the young of the village. I wanted to go into the air force to learn to fly and had been on many courses with the Air Training Co. However, it was the end of the war, and nobody was wanted. I thought I'd fly for the army, but that was being disbanded, so I didn't get anywhere. I eventually joined the army, and was stationed in Lancashire for my initial training. Four of us were selected to go to Cromer, and from there we sailed to Dieppe. We took forty-eight hours to go through France, and were then shipped to Egypt, where I spent my eighteenth birthday. I spent two years in Egypt, but saw no action. Father was playing the devil. 'Why did you join the army?'

Suddenly they wanted policemen. I said, 'Okay. I'll go for it.' It so happened that my police interview clashed with a three-day-officers'-training exam. I remember the Major General saying to me, 'You have made your decision to join the police force, and leave the army.' So all of a sudden I found myself out of the army, and in the police force." Morlais had intended to make the army his career, but doesn't regret his decision.

NOTES

1. The Welsh Guards started officially on 26 February, 1915, when a royal warrant, signed by King George V, authorized "The formation of a Welsh regiment of Foot Guards, to be designated the 'Welsh Guards'." They joined the other four existing regiments of Foot Guards – the Grenadiers, Coldstream, Scots and Irish.
2. Ceylon: Now Sri Lanka.
3. Green envelope: Members of the forces were allowed to send one uncensored letter a month; the rest were censored.
4. Asdic: A devise for locating submarines or other underwater objects, by electrical impulses.
5. Holding Battalion: To which men who had completed their training were posted.
6. On 23 June 1940, Major Ralph Bagnold of the Royal Signals, who had spent much time and money exploring the deserts of North Africa, was instructed by General Wavell to form the Long Range Desert Group in six weeks. It was a specialist force raised chiefly for the purpose of gathering information about the enemy behind his lines, and capable of moving across generally unknown expanses of desert.
7. John Retallack. *The Welsh Guards* (Great Britain 1981), pp. 75-76.

9

Men in the Navy and Air Force

Davey John Hughes and his good friend John William Howell were conscripted into the navy in the summer of 1939.

"We signed on in Gorseinon, and when war was declared on the 3rd September, we were called up two weeks later.

We trained in Skegness, but left when Butlins took over the camp, and continued training in Plymouth. I missed some of the training to attend my grandmother's funeral. She had brought me up.

John and I sailed on the same ship to Ceylon, but we were then split up. I went on the battle ship the HMS Rodney, and he went on the HMS Gloucester. The Rodney was a large ship, with one thousand and seven hundred men. It carried extra men because of casualties. I was on the guns supplying them with ammunition. The guns were sixteen inches – large enough for a man to crawl through.

The Japs over-ran Malaya and we surrendered. They were very cruel. So many men saw their mates being executed. They could never forgive that.

I had a couple of leaves before I went to Malaya. We didn't expect leave when we were all the way out there. Leave was about fourteen days. Dances were organized in the church hall and concerts were given for the troops. It was heartbreaking to go back after leave. I didn't like the life, but I had to go." At the end of one leave, Davey John obtained a medical paper from Doctor Hughes for extended leave through illness. On returning aboard the Rodney, the officer in charge questioned Davey John on the authenticity of the paper as the doctor's initials and surname were identical to Davey John's. The latter was unable to convince his superiors that he had not forged the paper, and it was not until confirmation was received from Doctor Hughes, that Davey John was believed.

"After staying in Malaya for about twelve months, I came home to discover that John's mother had received a letter to say that he was missing. His ship had gone down with only a few survivors out of over eight hundred men. I met one of them in Plymouth later. He told me how their ship had been blown up when they went to Crete to rescue some of the troops. The Jerrys had dive-bombed them giving them little chance. It's sad when you loose a good mate like that. We were about the same age, and had gone to school together. There was only one month between us. John was in October, and I was in November.

I saw the aircraft carrier, the Courageous, go down in the Mediterranean, with my friend John Austin from Mumbles on board, but he survived.

I served on the Malta convoys – small control boats patrolling the coast from the Rodney.

We were there on all the landings – South Africa, Sicily, Italy and D. Day.

In May 1945, I finished in the navy. I was given many medals – different ones to depict each landing.

After the war, we were sent letters inviting us to be put on the reserve list. I refused, as if there was any trouble, I would have to go back to the navy straight away.

The industries were instructed to give us our jobs back, but after six months, they sacked us. I went back to the building trade, and then to the ICI in Waunarlwydd. There was plenty of work around in those days, especially in Gowerton and Gorseinon."

Phil Foote chose to join the navy rather than continue his employment in Penlan Colliery, Three Crosses, owned by W. Henry Davies – a reflection of colliery working conditions.

"I was working underground as a drammer in the colliery when I had my call-up papers. I had the choice of staying in my work or going to the services. I was to join up on the Wednesday. On the previous Tuesday night, a meeting took place in our house between the colliery manager, my grandfather who was an important man in the colliery, and my father who was a mechanic. As a result, I was given a green card, which deemed me exempt from joining the services. But I said, 'No way. I'm going to join the navy.'

I joined in 1941. I'm glad I went. I enjoyed it. I spent two weeks training on the HMS Raleigh, in Devonport, Plymouth, and later joined the battle ship HMS Rodney, at Liverpool, in 1942, after it had fought in the Battle of Bismarck. I had been on a gunner's course, and my job was to follow the officer's orders and direct the guns on course.

We went on the Malta convoy taking food, ammunition, oil and petrol, in control ships from the Rodney to the troops on the island."

It was known as the Malta Run and incurred many casualties. Because of its position, Malta was an important British stronghold and so was well protected. Planes landed on the island en route to various destinations. In a sense, it became a floating aerodrome. 'Malta made an epic contribution to the outcome of World War Two. Throughout a three-year ordeal, while the RAF and the army fought continuously to defend the islands from air attack, submarines, aircraft and ships operating from Malta, prevented vast quantities of supplies from reaching the Axis forces in North Africa. During April 1942 alone, more bombs fell on the Islands than on the whole of the United Kingdom during the worst month of the Battle of Britain. Ships of the Royal and Merchant Navies fought desperate convoy battles to deliver the vital supplies that enabled a starving Malta to hold out and continue the offensive. The supreme effort of civilians, servicemen and women contributed significantly to our final victory."[1]

Phyl will never forget the experience. "It was a hell of a convoy that year of '42. It was the only time I cried. I was scared, and I admit it. We saw the HMS Eagle being torpedoed. I remember it was a beautiful day. It went down in about seven minutes, and the sun shone as we watched the bodies falling off the deck into the sea.

We had four hours on duty and four hours off duty. Often we had no time to eat and lived on vitamin tablets. But some times were good. We used to swim in the Mediterranean. It was better than being under-ground in the colliery. The colliers worked in terrible conditions. Penlan colliery had a two-foot seam, so the colliers cut the coal as they lay on their stomachs. When home on leave, we'd occa-sionally have ten shillings comfort fund from our former employees.

The Rodney was re-fueled with oil at sea. The oil tanker came along the side of our

Phil Foote sporting his 'lovely set.'

ship, passed a line over, which we attached to a hose, and then refilled our tanks. It sometimes took up to an hour, depending on how much oil we needed.

I had grown a moustache and a beard, and on arriving home on leave my mother didn't recognize me, and said, 'Who is that?'

I said, 'Its me, your son Phil.'

She told me to go to Arthur Jenkins the hairdresser and have them shaved off. It was impossible for me to carry out her wishes at home as I'd had to obtain permission from my captain to grow them, and likewise, would have to have his permission to shave them off.

My mother insisted, 'Tell your captain that I'm saying that you've got to shave them off.'

When I returned on board, my captain, on hearing my request said, 'It's a shame to cut that as it's a lovely set you have. Why do you want them removed?' I had to tell him that my mother didn't like them and off they had to come.

HMS Rodney bombarding the island of Alderney.

We went to Russia: from the sun to the ice. It was very cold up there. We then patrolled the Atlantic.

Our next destination was Free Town, in West Africa, followed by South Africa. We went on the Malta Run again and then returned to Russia.

We bombarded Sicily and Italy and were then ordered to France. We were there on D. Day, having been to Milford Haven for ammunition. We bombarded Caen a few days later, and then bombarded the island of Alderney.

We patrolled the Mediterranean and I left the navy in April

1946. When I joined up I was on two shilling a day, and I left with sixty-four pounds thirteen shillings and a suit."

Phil received an exemplary report on his service in the navy concluding with, 'Has worked very well showing keenness and energy in all tasks given him.'

Phil was rewarded with the Atlantic Star, the Africa Star, the Italian Star, the 1939-46 Star for services rendered, the Russian Convey and the Malta George Cross Fiftieth Anniversary Commemorative Medal.

In recognition of the bravery of its people, Malta was awarded the George Cross in 1942. It was not until 29 May 1992 that a memorial was erected in Malta to those who lost their lives during the long and bitter siege there.

> 'Thanks to the initiative of the George Cross Island Association and with the wholehearted support of the Maltese and British Governments, a magnificent memorial, designed by Professor Sandle, R.A. has been erected on the Bastion Walls of Valletta, overlooking the Grand Harbour. The memorial consists of a stone cupola in which is hung a ten-ton bell and, on the promontory of the bastion, a large recumbent bronze figure lying on a stone catafalque, representing the fallen. The memorial was dedicated in the presence of her Majesty Queen Elizabeth and His Excellency Dr. Censu Tabone, the President of Malta, on 29th May this year.'[2]

In the same year, the Malta George Cross Fiftieth Anniversary Medal was awarded to the service men whom had served in Malta in 1942. It was purely a commemorative medal and not to be worn, but Queen Elizabeth overruled, and granted permission for it to be worn.

In the Suez crises of the 1960s, Phil informed his wife, Ilene, "I'd rather declare myself a conscientious objector and go to jail, than to go to the navy again."

Edgar Nurse spent some years in the ATC, but when conscripted, joined the navy.

"I was working on the road widening on Cefn Bryn. A good many men came from the labour exchange to work, and I made quite a few friends. I was called up while working there. Phil Foote and I went on the same day, 15th October 1941.

Phil and I went to the HMS Raleigh in Plymouth for our training. Afterwards, we went to HMS Drake in Plymouth for our drafting. There was an overflow on the ship and no room for us. We were sent to HMS

HMS Tarter.

Cabot in Bristol, where we stayed at Mullers Orphanage. A draft came for us to be posted on the battleship HMS Rodney. I took ill with flu and missed the draft. We parted company there, and Phil later teamed up with Davey John Hughes. Having recovered, I went to Hull and joined the destroyer HMS Tarter, a Tribal Class destroyer.

Tribal Class destroyers were built before the war. They were named after various tribes – Nubian, Zulu, Maori, Sikh, Punjabi, Ashanti, Bedouin, Eskimo, Somali and Tartar. Only two survived and the Tartar was one of them. I was to remain aboard her until I got demobbed in 1946. A commission usually lasted about two and a half years. I don't know why mine lasted so long. I must have been extraordinary – an extraordinary sailor.

I became friendly with Jimmy James – Taff James. All the Welshmen were called Taff. I was Taff Nurse. Taff James was a marvellous artist and painted the Malta convoy in action on ship's canvas, which he gave to me. I still have it.

In August 1942, we were on the Malta convoy. The fourteen merchant ships had a vast convoy of about thirty destroyers, ten to twelve cruisers, and about five aircraft carriers. But despite the size of the convoy, the German U-boats went in and only two merchant ships arrived at Malta.

We left Gibraltar at night, sailing through the Straits of Gibraltar under the cover of darkness. The next morning, our first sight was our aircraft carrier, the HMS Eagle toppling over and sinking. We were bombed day and night. We took the damaged HMS Foresight on tow, but it impeded

Edgar Nurse, first on left.

the manoeuvrability of our ship and the remainder of the convoy. Our captain, Commander St. J. Tyrwhitt, son of the famous Admiral of the Fleet, Sir Reginald Tyrwhitt of the First World War, took it upon himself to sink the ship. He was court marshalled for it, but was acquitted, which he was overjoyed about.

One day, when I was on watch on the quarter deck, a shout came from able seaman Tong – a Londoner, who was on the deck above me – 'Torpedoes! Torpedoes!' The sea was calm, like a blue millpond and I could see two torpedoes travelling to the stern of the ship in a fork shape. Tong shouted, 'Torpedoes!' to Commander Tyrwhitt, and our captain, as cool as a cucumber, ordered the ship to, 'hard to starboard' and the torpedoes just passed us. Oh! I thought the end had come. The Commander received the DSM (Distinguished Service Medal) for his action. He was mentioned in 'Dispatches' and in the 'London Gazette'.

The Siege of Malta was a terrible thing. A chap from Penclawdd, Thomas John Bennett was there. I think he lost his life because of it, although it was not given as the cause of his death. He came through it all right, got demobbed, and came home. But after that, something took him. When he was supposed to be in work, he wandered around the old Berthlwyd Colliery area all day and then went home. It must have affected him badly. He left Penclawdd and went to London. The next thing I heard was that they found him in a park, dead. He was such a gentleman.

When we were being bombed we could hear the planes roaring down but could not see them, as they dived out of the sun. We were young, with no previous experience of such things, and it was very frightening. After the war, I was often hysterical in the night. My wife would say, 'What's the matter? What's the matter with you?' She was frightened as well.

The weather was sweltering in the Mediterranean. The following month we came back to the UK and then went on the Russian convoy – PQ 17.

After Hitler invaded Russia, the American ships were supplying Russia with ammunition, etc. We joined their convoy to help escort them through. We had a pretty rough time there too. We experienced the two extremes – from the hot to the cold. We were near the island of Spitzbergen refueling our ship from an oil tanker there. We were issued with big coats and chipped ice off the guns. We saw lots of icebergs and imagined them to be U-boats surfacing – especially in hazy conditions. As we sailed further north, the darkness lessened. We weren't based in Russia but were off the coast of Murmansk. I'd have liked to have landed on Russian soil.

We were in the North African invasion in November 1942, which was followed by the invasion of Pantelleria, an island off Malta. We had a rough experience there. One of our hospital ships was hit. It was lit up and so was a sitting target, but being a Red Cross ship, the Germans were not supposed to have attacked it. We could hear the hysterical screams of the nurses on board. We did our best and managed to pick up a few survivors.

We bombarded Siracusa in Sicily and sailed through the Straits of Messina to Salerno, where we stayed for about a month.

I went home and we then took part in the invasion of Normandy in 1944, and were there for a while. Our new captain was Basil Jones, a Welshman living in the south of England. After the war, he wrote a book on his war memoirs. We sailed around the French coast on sweeps – intercepting enemy shipping on the coast – by night. We were hit once and the ship went on fire. We lost a good many boys and many lost arms and legs. It was heartbreaking. We were a small ship with only about two hundred and fifty to three hundred on board and so had got to know each other well."

Basil Jones describes the attack in his war memoirs. 'Four shells burst about Tartar's bridge, starting a fire abaft her bridge, cutting leads to her Directors, bringing down the trellis foremast and all radar, and cutting torpedo communications to aft. The wheelhouse was also hit killing the Assistant Coxswain, and on the bridge the PCO and torpedo control ratings were killed and a number wounded. As the mast fell over, the call-up buzzer from the Aloft look-out position jammed on, and splinters pierced the upper deck of No. 1 Boiler Room causing loss of air pressure and reduction of speed. The conditions of fire, noise, smoke and casualties were distracting, but with our immediate enemy silenced, I pressed on in Tartar.'[3]

Edgar continues, "We were then sent to Ceylon where we did more sweeps. Then the news came through of the bombs dropped on Hiroshima and Nagasaki, and that the Japs had given in.

We landed at Singapore and did a bit of marching after the war ended.

I have always looked on the black side of life. When we left harbour, we weren't told where we were going, but rumours would spread. 'There's going to be a tough battle ahead.'

'Oh!' I used to think. 'I don't think we'll come back from here.'

I had a couple of jobs. I was a tanky – issuing food allocations – and I did a bit of butchering. Each mess was allocated so much food each month, and at the end of the month, any discrepancies were amended. It was known as canteen messing. We cleaned the ship in daytime.

The ship was divided into four parts, forecastle, quarterdeck, maintop and foretop. For watches, the ship was divided into first to port, second to port, first to starboard and second to starboard. We had four hours on and four hours off. My position on action station was on a 4.7 Y gun on quarterdeck.

There was a quartermaster on watch every day. Any orders during the day, he would first blow a Bro'un whistle and then give the orders over the ship's loud speaker system – 'Chefs to the galley! Hands to dinner!' At eleven thirty each morning, we were issued with our tot of rum. We would hear 'Up spirits!' and a man from each mess would get the quota for the mess (about twenty men). Some didn't draw their tot and had thrupence instead.

We always broadcasted our birthdays. We'd have a drop from each tot and afterwards would be flat on our backs.

It was terrible going back after leave. Actually, I wasn't too bad, but my mother would be awfully cut up. Coming home was good. I was on top of the world, but going back was a different matter.

I finished in 1946. We were demobbed sooner in the navy than in the army.

The only thing that I have to show for it are my war medals: Italian Star, Burma Star, African Star, Atlantic Star, Malta Cross, Russian Convoy, French Star, War Medal and 1939-43 Star."

Jacky Evans belonged to Penclawdd ATC and the Home Guards, but when he was conscripted into the forces, the navy was his preference.

"I was called up at the end of 1941, at the age of eighteen. I wanted to join the navy, and when I went to the YMCA for my medical, as luck would have it, I was asked which I wanted to join, and so had my choice.

Like Phil and Edgar, I trained on the HMS Raleigh in Plymouth – the training place for South Wales. I was there for twelve weeks.

I was drafted to the HMS Leopold, and then went to the big camp for combined operations in Inveraray, Scotland, to train as coxswain on landing craft.

I was drafted to the HMS Bulolo. It was an Australian ship that had been taken over by the Royal Navy. It had a crew of Australians (six engineers) New Zealanders and Newfoundlanders – the League of Nations. When I joined, the ship was an armed merchant cruiser on convoy duty, but it was later transferred to combined operations as a landing craft – landing troops on the various raids.

We landed troops at North Africa – Casablanca and Algiers (the main port).

The Med. was our next destination, landing troops on Malta. The island had a rough time, being bombed night and day. At one time, only a Welsh ship – a mine layer – could get through as it was a fast ship, and could get away on its own.

We landed troops for the invasion of Sicily, Sorrento, Anzio and Naples.

We had a couple of weeks of shore leave in Bombay, when our ship went to India for repairs. While there, a few of us had tattoos. I had my right arm tattooed below my elbow. It was something to do as we had time on our hands. It cost one rupee – one and six pence in our old money. It's faded now but it depicts the Crown and Anchor, the White Ensign, the Union Jack and has the name India at its base.

We were at the Normany landings. On the second day there, the Bulolo was bombed, killing seven of our crew. One was a boy from Pontarddulais.

You either liked the services or you didn't, but we had no choice. I only suffered from seasickness at first, and that was on a calm day. The rougher the weather, the better I felt. I wasn't a great lover of rum, and an older chap who had been in the navy for years used to follow me around when our ration was given. I used to give him my tot.

We were in this country when the war finished. We had been abroad for two years without home leave. We were stationed at Westcliff-on-Sea at Southend, where the navy had taken over a housing estate. There were big cockle factories there, but they were closed during the war years. All the east coast was shut down. We were in the rescue squad on the doodlebugs and the rockets night raids on London. Luckily they didn't last long, and it gave us something to do.

I thought that I'd have to have gone to the Far East, but fortunately I was spared that. I was very glad. I was demobbed from the navy in 1946.

I was awarded the Italian Star, African Star, Atlantic Star, Malta Cross, Russian Convoy, French Star, War Medal and 1939-43 Star."

Denzil Sambrook left Penclawdd to work in London, just after the outbreak of war in 1939. He served five years in the Royal Air Force during the war. It was not until fifty years later when he read the book 'Through Darkness to Light', written by P. M. MacDonald,[4] in which the author describes the operations in Romania that Denzil was involved in, did he start to talk of his war experiences.

Denzil Sambrook.

"My trade was in the aircraft industry, converting spitfires into sea spitfires in preparation for their going on the Russian convoy. The sea spitfires were catapulted off the aircraft carriers. We attached two spools onto the aircraft to enable them to catapult off the ship, and an arrester hook to enable them to land on the aircraft carrier. In 1942, at the age of twenty, I decided to volunteer. There was no need for me to join the forces, as I was in a reserved occupation, but I wanted to. I tried to join the navy, but when they discovered my occupation, I was refused entry. A friend of mine, Bill Watts informed me that we could join aircraft crew, which we both did.

I started my training at St. John's Wood in London with John Jenkins. John and I were from Blue Anchor, and had grown up together. I can remember taking him to school on his first day. John's mother and father doted on him. Whatever John wanted he had. They spoilt him but he's as good a friend as you could ever wish for – unassuming, cracks a joke and a bit of fun. He's great.

We went to Torquay and then to St. Athens where we had a whale of a time, as we both played rugby. Most of the PTI (Physical Training

Instructors) were first-class rugby players, but John and I were good enough to play for St. Athens. We went to one of the valleys to play. We palled up with a sergeant – an ex-copper. After the game we went to a local restaurant. After the meal the sergeant said, 'Right boys, we don't have to pay for this.'

John and I looked at each other and said, 'What do you mean?' He had a piece of glass in his pocket, which he intended putting on his plate and making a complaint. We told him that he could do it, but we were certainly not going to back him up.

Although there was a very serious side to our war years, funny things happened as well. There was a bloke from Swansea by the name of Musgrove on the same flight as me. He suggested that we went home for the August Bank Holiday weekend. When I pointed out that our passes only allowed us to go as far as Cardiff, he assured me that there would be no problem. We went to Swansea and came back on the Monday. As we were going through the main gates of the camp, we were stopped by the SP (military police). They asked to see our passes and when they realized that they were not valid for us to go to Swansea, they took our names and numbers. When the SP booked anyone, they had to proceed with a prosecution. We forgot all about it, but a month later we were summonsed over the tannoy to report to Number Five Wing Headquarters. We saw Sergeant Evans from Llanelli. When we explained why we were there, he asked us to return on the Tuesday evening when the Old Man – our commanding officer – would be present. We returned the next three nights in vain. On the Friday evening, Sergeant Evans informed us that he was in a quandary. He said that he didn't have a guard. It was decided that Musgrove and I would take it in turns to be the guard for each other when presented to the Old Man. However, the Old Man seemed uninterested in our charge. He said that he couldn't be bothered to prosecute us and ripped up our charge forms. It was just like Dad's Army. Sergeant Evans became a great friend of ours, especially John and me, and he often granted us passes to go and play rugby in places such as Stradey Park, Llanelli.

After qualifying as flight engineers, we were posted to Topcliffe in Yorkshire. I joined a Canadian aircrew, who had been flying the Wellington – a two-engine job. The crew had been transferred to fly a four-engine aircraft – the Halifax. The latter flew much higher then the Wellington, and being a four-engine aircraft, needed an engineer, hence my joining the crew. We trained until we were all proficient, especially the pilot, the bomber and myself. We flew to Newmarket where we landed on the racecourse, which had been taken over by the RAF.

I was posted to Italy. We were the first crew to take out a Halifax with

H2S – radar – which was situated underneath the aircraft. Our crew consisted of Flight Sergeant Caldwell-Wearne RAAF (pilot – an Australian), Flight Sergeant Jones (wireless operator), Flight Sergeant Collins (bomber), Sergeant Cote (rear gunner), Warrant Officer (WO) Harry Bath (navigator) and myself – Sergeant D. Sambrook (flight engineer). The normal procedure was to fly from Hurns Airport, Bournemouth. Before we took off, the plane in front of us crashed. What a scare! We thought, 'Well. This is a good omen.' Our plane was so choc-o-block full of spare parts for planes in Italy, that you had to walk sideways down the fuselage. It was the procedure for planes not to fly out empty. We were unable to land at Gibraltar to refuel as planned because the Germans were across the bay spying on oncoming planes, and we were anxious not to disclose that we had radar. We continued to Rabat in Morocco, but were unable to land there either because of thick cloud. My pilot was informed over the intercom to divert to Fez. He asked me if we had enough petrol and I said that I thought that we could just about manage it. That was enough of a scare in itself apart from the plane crashing in front of us at the airport. We stayed the night at Fez and eventually landed at Foggia, where I was stationed.

We were the 614 Squadron. Our main target was the oil fields at Ploiesti in Romania where the Germans were getting most of their oil. Ploiesti was the third most heavily guarded city."

'The target was the Romania Americana refinery just east of Ploiesti, which despite persistent attacks was still believed to be in full production. It was a most important target. As a result, the defences had been greatly strengthened and this was a most costly operation. Fifty Wellingtons from all three wings, twenty-three Liberators and eight Halifax were dispatched and eight Wellingtons, one Liberator and two Halifax failed to return. In addition, five Wellingtons returned early.'[5]

"The Pathfinder Force flew from Britain over Germany. They took flares to light up targets for the Bomber Force. We did the same job from Italy to Romania, but we were called Target Markers. We carried forty-eight flares of one million-candlepower each, so if we got hit – which we did – we would be a ball of flame.

We were approaching Ploiesti when our plane shot up in flames. Our pilot told us all to parachute out."

'J.P. 110 I Item flown by Flight Sergeant C. P. Caldwell-Wearne crashed at Ciocanesti, crash site 18, and all but one of the crew survived. Hardly possible in the battle which Norman Lord described. Indeed, it is known that a J.P. 110 was hit and set on fire by a J.U. 88 which continued to sit behind the burning aircraft firing into it. A Wellington apparently dived into the German and opened fire from its nose turret. The guns had apparently previously been loaded with a day tracer (as this turret was not normally used – or even manned – on night operations) and the ensuing firework display so unnerved the fighter that it broke away leaving the Halifax crew to bale out. Caldwell-Wearne was about to jump – the last to go – when the aircraft blew up and he was rendered unconscious. He came to, hanging under his parachute, having no recollection of pulling the rib cord.'[6]

Denzil landed alone in a field of sunflowers. "I was hit by flak on the fingers of my left hand, it took a chunk out of my shoulder and my left arm was full of flak. For years afterwards I was taking flak out of my arm. Flak is bits of anti-aircraft shells, but we were hit by ammunition from a German plane I think.

It was dark. I buried my chute. We all had a small escape kit sown into our jackets. It contained about forty-eight dollars, bandages, a compass and water purifying tables, etc. I tied my arm with the bandages and started walking. I walked for miles. As I was walking through a field I saw a cart. The carts there had four wheels. I thought I'd have a kip in it, but as I walked towards the cart, I could hear someone snoring. I was afraid there might be a dog there, so I beat a hasty retreat. As I sat under a tree, dawn broke, and I saw a scout plane looking for us. They knew that they had shot us down. I walked down a lane that had bushes on either side about five yards apart. There were two men there. They looked at each other and then at me. They realized who I was and I realized who they were. They stood either side of me and took me to a large country estate not far away. It must have been the headquarters of one of the armed forces of Romania. Some of the men had braid halfway up their sleeves. They put me in a slit trench with a guard over me. They gave me food and treated me well; I must say that for them. A young fellow of about twenty-five, with perfect English, appeared. His parents had sent him to school in Hazelmere in Surrey. He said to me, 'You realize that your war years are over.' I agreed with him and asked him for some medical aid for my fingers, etc. 'Yes,' he said, 'we'll see to that,' which they did. He returned in an hour to tell me of my fate. 'We're going to send you under guard down to Bucharest to a prisoner of war camp.'

We went to a level crossing and waited for a train. When it arrived we couldn't see it for people. There were people on top of it, at the sides of it and in the engine – people everywhere. My guard went into a compartment and cleared seats for us. As we sat down, all the people were staring at us. One of them must have inquired of the guard as to whom I was and when he replied, 'Parachutist,' you never saw anything like it in all your life. Whenever we stopped, which was quite often, they crowded to see the parachutist. I was a celebrity for about five hours. It was quite overwhelming. All of a sudden there was a commotion in the corridor, and an officer from the Africa Corps came in. He was about six-foot-two and dressed in his desert uniform. He said, 'Out out' to the passengers, and they quickly scattered. He sat next to me and we chatted. He had a smattering of English. He asked me questions about myself. I told him that I had been flying but I gave none of my particulars, as it was not allowed. He produced a cigarette case from his pocket with two cigarettes. I used to smoke then. When he offered me one. I refused saying, 'No, you only have two and they are very hard to get.'

'You would do me a favour if you took one,' he said.

He told me that the passengers were serfs. He was under the impression that all that flew in the RAF were sons of lords and ladies, and I didn't disillusion him.

The guard and I eventually arrived in Bucharest. There had been a big raid on Ploiesti that night and about twenty of us had been shot down. All my crew was there except WO Harry Bath who had been killed, and the pilot who had gone to the officers quarters. We were lined up outside the prison compound. We could hear some men singing, 'Put your money in your shoes. Put your money in your shoes.' Our money was the dollars in out escape kit. We put it in our shoes but not knowing why. We were then ordered to strip off all our clothes, except our shoes and socks. Our clothes were searched but not our shoes. Of course, the boys behind the wall who had warned us knew the procedure.

I was there for about a month. The food was atrocious. We had a piece of black bread and a cup of coffee – it was a coffee substitute made out of ground pine needles, or so we were told – for breakfast, a bowl of soup for lunch and a bit of bread and coffee for tea. That was all. But when the Swiss Red Cross came to the camp, they were shown a decent meal menu – for example, tea, bread and salami for breakfast, soup for lunch and roast lamb for dinner – but we never had it.

My fingers were so bad that a gold ring I wore, given me by my uncle, had to be cut off. My uncle, John (Jack) Williams, was stationmaster in Penclawdd. He was a lovely man: a real gentleman. I had always admired his ring – not many men I knew wore rings then – and he had promised me that it would be mine after his days. My fingers healed eventually.

I can remember the Americans flying over. They flew by day but we flew by night. We would go out into the yard and shout 'Hooray, hooray!'

The camp commandant – a short tubby man – would point his gun at us, and shout 'I'll shoot! I'll shoot!' But we only did it to annoy, as the Americans couldn't see us.

We had guards patrolling outside the barbed wire fence, which was about six inches from the ground. Most of them hadn't worn boots before they joined the army, and when patrolling up and down, often used to take them off. We had a long piece of wire with a hook on the end, and we'd hook their boots under the wire. We'd hold them up and bribe them with, 'Two cigarettes for your boots.' Unfortunately they became wise to us eventually.

We had been made sergeants when we passed out of training camp. It stated in the Geneva Convention that sergeants were not to work and they adhered to this rule in the camp.

Then the Russians came through.

Our prisoner of war camp was near the railway line that ran between Bucharest in Romania and Sofia in Bulgaria. When some of the boys tried to get out of the compound, the German snipers shot at them. We didn't really know if they were shooting at us or at the railway line. They were also bombing us. We dug trenches and hid in them to protect us from flak. We nearly copped it a couple of times. We were covered with the earth that the bombs threw up. We were that close to being annihilated. We were there for two to three days. It was impossible to escape.

Eventually the Americans came in and flew us back to Foggia.

We had to do three Tour of Ops (operations). The first was thirty flights, the second twenty, and the third ten. Being shot down counted as one Tour of Ops. After the first Op we had a nine months resting period.

From Foggia, I returned to Blighty. It was 1944. We were flown to St. Mawgan in Cornwall. By now I was a warrant officer. A train coach was reserved for us on the Paddington train. We were to go to London to be debriefed. As we stopped at the stations on route, such as Exeter, the platforms were crowded with people, many anxious to come into our compartment. But they were stopped entry as we were forbidden to speak to anyone until after our debriefing.

I was tired of travelling and regimentation and wanted to settle down. I had met Doreen in London before I joined up, and we decided to get married then.

I was expecting to be posted to the Far East, as the war was still being fought there, but it was coming to an end, and I was sent to Morecambe.

It was a transit camp in the Midland Hotel. I requested Christmas leave but I was told that as I was the senior officer, I was to be in charge over the Christmas period. I was offered leave over the New Year instead, which I accepted, as it was useless to argue.

I was under the impression that being a transit camp, posting did not take place there over the weekend. I confidently went to London on the Friday to see Doreen, and returned on the Monday morning – instead of the Sunday night – eight hours late. On my return, my landlady told me that I was to report immediately to the orderly room. The adjutant – the administrative assistant – asked me, 'Where have you been? You were due back on Sunday night.'

When I explained that I didn't think it was important as nobody was posted over a weekend, he told me, 'You were posted last Saturday to Brackla in the North of Scotland.' I was severely reprimanded, and had three-days pay stopped. I spent an extremely severe winter in Scotland.

During the nine-month resting period in-between Ops, one had to take an occupation. I took a course at Cosford and passed out as a PTI. I went to Great Massingham in Norfolk. There I was to be signed in, once by various people and twice by E. L. (Ted) Horsfall – he later had his cap for England – to whom I had been posted. When I asked him for his second signature he said, 'Oh no I'm not. I already have three PTIs and they're all lazy buggers. I do not want a fourth.' As I was leaving the room he said, 'Excuse me. You sound Welsh to me.' When I assured him that I was, he wanted to know if I played rugby. When I informed him that I had played for Swansea, he said, 'Give me that bloody form. I'll sign it for you.' I stayed and he and I and another officer called Paddy Logan – he had a trial for Ireland – became the best of pals.

We used to go out together. It was embarrassing, as lower ranks – which I was – were not supposed to mix with officers. We went to Kings Lynn and caused mayhem there.

Our rugby team played against teams from other stations. The CO (commanding officer) was a rugby fanatic, and every Friday afternoon he'd ring down to Horsfall and ask him, 'Who's the team tomorrow?' He'd then contact that team's CO and have a five-pound bet with him that our team would beat their team. He'd stop good rugby players going on leave if a match was to be played. It happened to one boy – Jones – from the Swansea area. He was furious but Wing Commander Walker – the Chief Technical Officer – arranged for him to be flown to Fairwood Aerodrome immediately after the match. He probably arrived home sooner than if he hadn't played in the match and travelled by train. We had a very good side, and by the end of the season our CO had won fifty pounds. 'Right,' he said, 'we'll go down to Hunstanton near Sandringham and have a good 'do'.' And we did. It was a very happy posting.

I'd hurt my leg, and we had an important match to play. Horsfall told me, 'You'll have to play Sambrook. The Old Man will go crackers if you don't play.' When I expressed my doubts, Horsfall insisted, 'You'll be better than some even with one leg.

It was a fatal mistake. I got into a tackle and snapped the ligaments of my right knee. I was sent to Ely Hospital in Cardiff, where I was put in a cast from my toe to my thigh and my torso to my chest. I was to be in it for nine months. I went to the RAF Remedial Hospital in Loughborough. Later, the college reclaimed its premises from the RAF who then transferred to Plymouth. When I travelled home to see Doreen, I had many sympathetic looks. As I was in my RAF uniform, they probably thought that my injuries had been incurred in an air-crash, not on a rugby pitch. I didn't enlighten them.

It was eventually decided that my knee was going to improve no further and so I was discharged from Plymouth in 1947.

I was awarded the 39-45 Italian Star, but didn't collect it.

Doreen and I went to live in Putney and I worked in London.

My uncle owned an off-licence and a chemist shop in Tycoch Square in Swansea. He intended to sell the chemist shop, but invited me to run the off-licence for two years with the understanding that after that time, it would be mine. I always yearned to come back, and when you were in the services all those years, unless you had a qualification, you were

Penclawdd ATC RFC 1941-42.

nothing. It was 1959. We accepted my uncle's offer and Doreen and I went to live in Tycoch and ran the off-licence for twenty-five years."

John W. Jenkins had belonged to Penclawdd ATC for a few years, before volunteering for the RAF at the age of nineteen, in 1943.

"I was just a young lad when I joined the Penclawdd ATC. One of the most interesting things that happened while I was there, was the forming of the 360 Squadron ATC rugby team. It consisted of representatives from Penclawdd – of which I was one – Gorseinon, Loughor and Pontarddulais. Rugby has always been an important part of my life.

I was in a reserve occupation, and had recently completed my apprenticeship as an engineer when I volunteered to join the RAF. Only volunteers were given specialized duties such as RAF crew and submarine crew, etc. When in the ATC, I had visited Pembrey Gunning School and saw a certain amount of procedures that were used in air force drills. I was also trained in Morse code – an essential knowledge for anyone in aircraft crew. The ATC training gave me the basic ideas of what to expect in RAF training. My engineering apprenticeship was also an asset.

I did a three-day test course in Penarth, and then went to St. John's

John W. Jenkins.

Wood for basic training. We were stationed at Stockley Hall, owned by Alva Lidell the newsreader. We trained – square bashing, etc. – and had our meals in London Zoo, opposite the house. I had many tests, including a medical. They filled all my teeth, and I still have many of the fillings. Torquay was my next station, where I underwent my ITW (Initial Training Wing). We were fortunate in being billeted in the Regina Hotel, which was rather posh. A six-month course followed at St. Athens. St. Athens was great – near home and plenty of rugby. We had school five days a week. We had workshop in the morning and classes in the afternoon and vice versa. Classes were held on Saturday mornings and we were free after GST (General Service Training) on Sunday mornings. One weekend, I went home after Saturday morning school, having previously arranged for someone to sign me in on the Sunday. He forgot, and as a result, I had seven days jankers (extra duties) in the cookhouse. Fortunately, I managed to get off by being chosen to play rugby for Treorchy. The RAF gave one a long training before getting anywhere near an aircraft, but I was now, at last, a flight engineer, and awaiting my call up.

My instructions were to go to Ricol Station, in Yorkshire, where I was introduced to the rest of our crew of seven. They had met previously, and I was the last member to join. I had been trained on an aircraft that was unfamiliar to the rest of the crew, so I was supposed to be the expert on everything on the aircraft: a tall order. We practised flying there for a while across country, and getting familiar with the planes.

We were then posted to 158 Squadron Lissett, from where we did our operations – bombing France and Germany, mostly on night raids. We flew Halifax four-engine bomber planes. All the planes had to be on hard standings as they were so big and heavy. We were a crew of seven, which consisted of a pilot, a flight engineer, a wireless operator, a navigator, a bomb operator, a mid-upper gunner and a tail gunner. The tail gunner and the mid-upper gunner had four 303 Browning machine guns. One of the tail gunner's jobs was to judge the distance of the approaching enemy plane and inform the pilot. The target was not fired at until within eight hundred yards of the Halifax. He'd say, 'It's coming; it's coming; corkscrew,' and the plane would dive and twist. Those were evasive tactics. We were never shot up badly. I was positioned in the astrodome immediately behind the pilot. I had all the instrument panels in front of me. I used a sexton to give a reading to the navigator to plot the course. Once I got really scared. A stream of bullets came whizzing up in-between the wing and me. I said, 'Good God! Did you see those tracers?' They called me Tracer for a bit after that, so I thought I'd say nothing in future.

The 158 Squadron became very famous. It had the highest percentage of men in any squadron that was successful in evading capture and returning after being shot down over enemy lines. We had a Halifax – a four-engine bomber called Friday the 13th – in our squadron that did one hundred operations. It's the most operations any plane has done. A roommate, Bill Calvert, and another engineer went to collect a new plane that had cost a quarter of a million pounds to build. When flying a new plane, or a plane that had received major works, for the first time, the aircraft had to pass an acceptance test. The crew decided to carry out the test before landing. They feathered one engine and flew on three engines. They feathered another engine and flew on two engines. They feathered another engine and flew on one engine. It was just about possible to maintain flight on one engine, but when they attempted to unfeather the engines, they pressed all the buttons simultaneously, overloaded the circuit, blew a fuse and consequently could not unfeather any of the engines. The plane crashed into a pea field. The crew escaped uninjured, but the plane was a write-off – all one quarter of a millions pounds of it, with only two and a half flying hours on it. Bill Calvert and the engineer received red endorsements on their logbooks, and they were lucky to get away with it so lightly.

There were many bomber planes stationed at aerodromes in Yorkshire and Lancashire as their inland geographical position gave the planes their needed distance to gain height before flying over the North Sea. Fighter planes flew from fighter-domes situated on the south coast of England. They needed less mileage to gain height than did the heavier bombers.

We had a couple of nice little daylight trips over France from where the Germans were launching doodlebugs – V1s – flying bombs. They were camouflaged in woodlands, where we were to try and locate, and bomb them. They would not fire at us because they didn't want their positions to be known. So those trips were all right. But going down the Ruhr – known as Happy Valley – where there were thousands of guns, we could guarantee a hot reception.

When we finished operations, the crew split up, and we didn't see each other again for ages and ages. We didn't even keep in touch – just Christmas cards I think.

I was posted to Flying Training Command, where we trained army bods – army personnel – to fly gliders. The gliders had been towed by Alabama two-engine planes, but these planes became underpowered as the gliders became bigger. We taught the Alabama's crews; Sprog pilots – inexperienced pilots – to fly the Halifax. We flew Halifax planes, towing the gliders in Elsmoor up in the Humber.

My next post was in Oxfordshire at Brize Norton, which was a famous station. I hadn't played rugby when I was flying, as that was out of the question, but when I was at Brize Norton, if granted permission by the CO, played quite often. We were there for a long period of time, and while resident there, I was picked to play rugby for Oxfordshire against the Kiwis. It was a big honour. My position was wing's three-quarter. I also played for the RAF and Flying Training Command. It was a big thing to play against other commands.

Sport was very important in the forces. I achieved the goal of becoming Champion of all Events of Sport. I rubbed shoulders with group captains, etc. who were fanatical about rugby. I could get away with murder. On one occasion, when I was home on leave, they sent a plane to Fairwood

Common to come and pick me up to play for Little Risington. I had an extra day's leave, and was flow back to Fairwood.

I could have remained in my reserve occupation but I'm glad I went into the RAF. It was a marvellous experience and I achieved many things. I was about nineteen when I joined the air force. I finished the Tour of Operations and had my Commission before I was twenty-one. It certainly set my on the right road for a rugby future.

The following article was published in the 'South Wales Evening Post' newspaper on Tuesday 1 May 1945:

> 'Pilot Officer J. W. Jenkins, DFC,[7] Penclawdd, received a presentation from members of Penclawdd Flight, Llwchwr (360) Squadron ATC. He is the first ex-cadet to be awarded the DFC. Joining the ATC in 1941, he became a corporal in the Penclawdd Flight and went for training with the RAF in 1943. The presentation was made by Warrant Officer E. Bond, and addresses were given by Flight Officer J. D. Jenkins, Flight Commander; Mr. W. C. Roberts, civilian instructor, and cadet Sergeant Clifford Alcock.'

When I came out of the RAF, the people of Penclawdd knew more about my exploits in rugby than I did, so I was in a bit of demand. I played a few games for Llanelli, but they had international wings at the time. I had a game with Swansea mid-week and I then played for Swansea for three years almost without missing a game. That filled a big gap, as for me to have left the air force and not to have been involved in anything, would have taken some settling down."

John Elliott remained in Stalag 17 until 23 January 1945.

"Stalag 17 was a rough joint. A lot of the boys died there. There was a Scotch dance band entertaining the troops in France called the Barmorals. The drummer and the trumpeter of the band were caught and they were in the camp. Guardsman Nichols of the Grenadier Guards – later to be awarded the VC (Victoria Cross) – was there as was Sam Kid, a television actor. After his release, Sam wrote an excellent biography of his war experiences.

In the summers, we worked on the farms. The Germans would commandeer a house in a village, put barbed wire around it, and stick us in there. The Germans occupied the farms. They killed many of the Polish farmers, and the rest worked on the farms for their enemies. It was particularly hard for those Poles working on their own farms.

I learned German and Polish as I was with them for nearly five years.

It's the best way to learn a foreign language. I was working on a farm that had been occupied by a German family by the name of Velker. I was used to farming, so they treated me pretty tidy. However, I had my meals at a table in the corner of a room while they ate together at another table. I was not allowed eggs, sugar, butter or milk, but they had three daughters and sometimes they would slip me a bit of something.

A little evacuee called Annie Lowery, from Cologne, had been living there for a number of years. She was about eleven years old, and her hair was in a centre parting, with two thick plats either side. While I was working, she spoke to me, laughed at my replies in German and corrected my mistakes. She taught me German, despite the old woman shouting at her not to speak to me. She was not happy being away from her family, and when she saw the photograph of her new baby sister, she longed to go home. Four weeks later, her parents arrived. She said goodbye, and off she went. I can see her now. She was a pretty girl, with dark black eyes.

Four months later, I was harrowing; working a field close to the farm-house. I saw the postman arrive and all the family congregate. When I asked them what was the matter, the old woman shouted at me, 'Go away from here. Your lot has killed Annie Lowery.' Annie was in school, when a plane came down and machine-gunned the children playing in the yard, and killed most of them. I never found out whether the plane that had gunned Cologne was British or American. Naturally, I felt awful about it. We were all upset, but Mrs. Velker was wringing her apron in grief. She would easily have knifed anyone if necessary, but she loved that girl. I knew that I had to keep out of her sight for a while.

The old woman thought that Hitler was God. I once told her that she was wasting her time planting potatoes, as the Russians would be eating them and not the family. 'No, no,' she said, 'Hitler was sent to us by God to get rid of the Jews.'

We worked on the harvest, and in the winter we went back to the big camps. The Polish winters were cruel. It was not unusual to have thirty-five degrees of frost. We cleared snow off the runways for the big bomber planes to fly to Russia as by then the Russians had entered the war. Twenty-five thousand Russians died within ten days. They were coming off the trains frozen stiff. It was hard to believe what the Germans did to people. The Russians were not in the Geneva Red Cross, so they did not have identification discs. We all had discs, and so if one of our boys died, we would take half of the disc and sent it to his family. We had one around our necks and one around our wrists incase different parts of us were blown away. The Germans sprayed the bodies of the Russians with quick-lime and acid from a knapsack sprayer before we buried them in trenches measuring six, by six, by six. Sometimes Red Cross parcels had oxo or marmite tins, and we used to write in them, for example, twenty Russians, and leave the tins about two foot below the surface. It was the only form of identification we could manage.

The Germans' attitude started altering when they were chased out of Africa and the boys got to Sicily and into Italy. We then started bombing Berlin. The Germans in the thirty to forty age-bracket started asking themselves 'What is it all for?' But the young ones – the Hitler youth – did not change.

On 23 January 1945, I was by Danzig when the Russians broke through in Konigsberg."

John's parents received the following letter from the War Organisation of the British Red Cross Society and Order of St. John of Jerusalem, Prisoners of War Department, St James Palace, London S.W.1 on 28 March 1945:

'Dear Mrs. Elliott,

Guardsman W. J. Elliott

Thank you for your letter of March 22nd. Although a number of prisoners interned in the camps in eastern Germany and Poland have been liberated, following the advance of the Russian Armies, the majority have been moved westwards by the Germans.

We do not yet know you son's new address and it is probable that you will be the first to get the news direct from Guardsman Elliott himself. The most recent information about the prisoners from Stalag XXA is that on February 25th they were collected in the Ukermark region and were moving westwards (this is in square E.3 on the prisoner of war map). We cannot, of course, be certain that this applies to every individual prisoner who was in that camp.

We hope you will soon have news: but we think you will realize that as the fighting gets farther and farther into Germany delays in the mail service must be expected to occur and unfortunately, we know of many relatives who have now been for some time without a letter.

When you hear from your son giving you a new address we should be grateful if you would let us know what it is and the date on which he wrote. In the meantime, owing to the number of men involved, we regret we cannot undertake to ask the International Red Cross Committee to make inquiries about individual cases.

Until you receive a new address you can send letters to his last known camp, as they should be forwarded: and may we draw your attention to the information in the enclosed leaflet PW/300/45?

Yours sincerely,
p.p. E. M. Thorton,
Director.'

"The Germans made us start marching. We marched eight hundred and fifty miles to within sixty miles of Berlin. It took us three months. We couldn't take our boots off, as our feet would swell up. We couldn't shave. We were wearing Balaclavas[8] and our beards grew through the stitching. When we reached the Rhine on the way home, we had to pull the Balaclavas off from the back of our heads, hold them away from our faces, and cut our beards off with a scissors. We were lousy with head lice and body lice. It's a strange fact that body lice will never go into the hair, and hair lice will never go on the body.

Our boys had bombed Magdeburg – where there was a large marshalling yard – for five consecutive nights. We were about four hundred of us. The Germans put us in cattle trucks again, and left us in the middle of the station so if the British or Yank planes bombed that night, they would blow us up, and the Germans would not take the blame. All through that night we could hear the planes diving down on the station, but they never dropped a bomb. Now, somebody must have told them that the train was full of British prisoners and not ammunition. The experience was out of this world. Every time a plane came over, we stooped down, waiting and thinking, 'This is the bugger that is going to have us. This is the one.'

At eleven o'clock the next morning, they opened the train and let us out again and marched us about eleven kilometers down to Halberstat. They put us – we were then about two hundred – in an attic of a massive hotel that had been a sports arena before the war. It contained bikes on the lower floor. That night our boys came over and they blew that place. They hit the gas works and the whole roof of the hotel came off. We were looking at the stars. It was hard to believe that the roof hit nobody. It lifted in the air in one piece and none were injured.

Next morning was a beautiful Sunday morning, and at about eleven o'clock, the American planes came over. We could see something silver coming from the planes and we wondered what the devil it was. It was bombs dropping from the planes that were flying in formation and precision bombing. We had not seen this before. They blew the place to bits. They hit a cigar factory, and we never had so many cigars in our lives. They were everywhere. It was raining cigars.

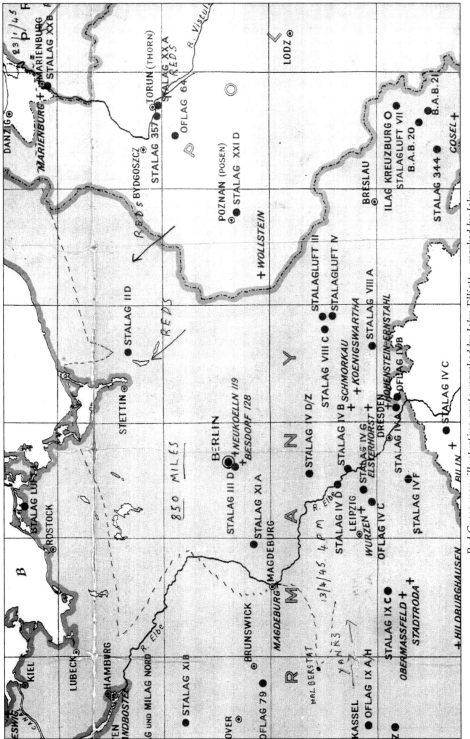

Red Cross map, illustrating route marched by John Elliott – marked by John.

We ran – Frankie and myself – outside the town to where there were woods. We came to a churchyard where we sat looking down over the town. We could see seven churches burning at the same time. They bombed the station, and the railway engines rose up from the rails and landed on the platforms by the bookstalls. The Americans were tremendous.

Frankie and I decided that the Germans did not know where we were. The guards had been killed, so we started walking and didn't stop. We knew that we were not far from the American lines. The Russians were coming behind us, and the Americans were in front of us. It took us from the Sunday, to the Friday 13th April, to get back to the British lines. General Pattern's army was making for Berlin. We could hear the shooting each side and the planes were back and forth, but we were lucky in having taken a part of the line where there were not many troops. The latter were using the valleys, and we were up higher. Before we knew it we were in a village and through our lines."

John sent a letter home to his parents informing them of his situation:

13/5/45[9]
'Dear Mam,

Well, I have just got back through the line to the British boys.

I do not know how long it will take us to get back but I am free from the Germans. Tell you how in a few weeks. I can not believe it that I shall be seeing you again.

All the best for now. Keep your chin up. I am on the way.

John. Xxxx'

"We saw three American tanks, and when we told the Americans that we had been out there for four years and eleven months, they couldn't believe it. They gave us their Red Cross parcels with eighty fags and chocolates.

We experienced a bit of action the next morning – Germans in the woods – but eventually petrol lorries arrived with cans full of petrol. There were two coloured boys driving who informed us that they were going back fifty miles to fetch more petrol. We had a lift with them so far and then with somebody else. We crossed the Rhine in a Jeep. Our Red Caps (British Military Police) picked us up on the road thinking we were spies. They took us back to a unit where we were interrogated by a padre. I remember the weather was very misty. We were put in a big camp run by the Red Cross. Some boys from New Zealand, suffering from shell shock, were there for a rest, and to have their fate decided. A decision was to be made as to whether they were capable of going back to the line or go home. The air was full of Dakotas[10] taking the wounded home. There was a little field with RAF planes taking emergency wounded cases to hospital. By this time we were nineteen prisoners.

They fired a flare if they wanted a Dakota to land. They all flew past except one plane which turned and landed. It was flown by a Canadian pilot who had been dropping ammunition over Germany. He asked us, 'Where are you going? What have you got?' We told him that we were going to Brussels and we had nineteen prisoners who wanted to go home as they had been there for five years. He said, 'O.K. I have never taken off from this field before. This plane is a Dakota and everything red in it is for emergencies, so if you all pull the red things together, we might be all right.' We got in it and all the boys piled on top of each other to get the weight on the wheels so that it would take off quicker. Two to three hours later we were flying over Brussels.

They were bombing Germany at the time from Brussels. I discovered later that Arthur Hopkins from Crofty was lying injured in a Brussels' hospital at the time with head injuries. We flew round and round and round the airfield. It was the first time that I had flown. There were large Stirling bombers[11] waiting to land. They fired flares to indicate that they had wounded or dead on board, which gave them landing priority. Eventually we all landed. It was 16th April.

The next morning we wondered how we were going to get from there to England. An officer informed us, 'We have wounded here and are flying parents out to their dying sons. I don't think there's much hope for you; have some money and go and enjoy yourselves.' So I rose five pounds, left Frankie and went to Brussels Market where the naughty boy of Brussels was. I bought a pound of apples and a pair of black gloves for my mother and my five pounds was gone. Somebody had done me in the process.

Frankie and I met up again, and an officer suddenly said to us, 'If you want a spin to England get in that Jeep and get yourselves to the airport.' At the mobile canteen we watched the Rear Gunner bombers – Tail End Charlies[12] – taking off. They were so brave. They took off in fives with less than fifty yards between them. Another Jeep drew up with five or six boys in it and asked us if we wanted to go with them to England.

We went down to the far end of the runway to an old bomber. It had been blown up over Berlin, and all its bits were hanging off, and the electrical parts were not working. They told us that they were taking it back to England for a refit. We asked them, 'Will it fly?'

They said, 'Well we are going to fly in it.' So we climbed in this old thing and it eventually took off. The Germans were still in Dunkirk. Rather than fight them and loose men, our boys had surrounded them, to try and starve them out. Our pilots knew that the ammunition from the German guns could only reach about sixteen thousand feet, so they flew at eighteen thousand feet over Dunkirk, which they knew would be a safe distance.

It was a lovely day. The English Channel looked like the Llwchwr Estuary. We could see both sides from that height. We were to land in Amersham, by coincidence the town where Frankie lived. While we were cruising, waiting to land, petrol was needed from the reserve tank. The electrical pumps were not working so we took turns in turning the hand pumps that were like bicycle pumps while the pilots teased us, 'Quicker boys, or we'll be down.' After all that time we had to work our way through.

The airport had been forewarned that the first escaped prisoners were arriving home. When the plane landed, Waafs ran down to the plane. I was the first out. I had never seen Waafs before, and the first thing I did was to 'kiss the field'. They asked us if we were walking, and we told them that we were crawling. They shoved things saturated with DDT up our sleeves, up the legs of our trousers, and down our jackets. They rubbed DDT in our hair. They had laid out a lovely meal for us in the aircraft hanger, but we were too excited to eat. Everybody wanted to hear our stories, and the cameras were going.

We went down to an army camp by lorry. There were loads of ladies there in their sixty's – WVS. They informed us as to what medals we were entitled to – the Victory Medal, the 1939-45 Star, the Somme Medal, and the Prisoner of War Medal. I later had the Dunkirk Veterans Medal. They took our tunics and sewed the medals on them while they listened to our stories.

We were then told to shave all our body hair off to get rid of the lice. I put my hat on my head and my belt around my waist but wore nothing else. I was starkers. There were tents in the field, but I had no idea who was in them. I walked down to the medical unit where they were going to give me new clothes, and a medical examination. I heard laughing and some women were peeping at me from the tent. I discovered later that they were New Zealand Red Cross women, helping the boys come around after the bombing. When it was my turn to go in the tent, their faces were red and my face was red also, but I didn't care too much. When I had my medical, the doctor said, 'How do you feel?' I said that I was great. On assuring him that I would visit my own doctor on my return home, he gave me my warrant, and I was soon on the train for Swansea.

I arrived in Swansea on 19th April to see that it had been bombed out of all recognition. Frankie had gone home after we shook hands and wished each other all the best. I had become friendly with another boy on the train. He told me that his father was a milkman, and would not be home until about nine, and suggested that we find the YMCA. It was about half-past four in the morning. We knocked on the door, and some elderly ladies with nightcaps on answered it. They said, 'Who are you?' We told them that we didn't know exactly where we were. They found two sausages and a frying pan full of yesterdays' spuds, and cooked us a fry-up. They all sat around the table while we ate and told our stories. They were so interested. My friend then went to find his father in Townhill, and I went to find the bus garage. I discovered that it had been blown everywhere, but I eventually found a bus about twenty-past nine.

I hadn't heard from my parents for six months, so I didn't really know how they were, but I had a sneaky feeling that they would be all right out in the country. It was hard on the boys living in towns when they heard news commentaries that bombs had been dropped on their hometowns. A few weeks later, when I was in Swansea obtaining tickets for new clothes, I met my friend from Townhill. He told me that his father had died six weeks before his return home from the war.

Nobody knew where I was. I had sent a telegram from Brussels – 'Got away from the Germans. See you soon.'

As I got on the bus I met Will Harry and said hello to him. He didn't recognize me at first. 'Who are you. Oh! John Elliott. God, boy, how are you?' He was so highly delighted to see me. I didn't have the guts to ask him how my parents and sisters were. But he said, 'Funny thing, I was talking to you mother and father a few days ago.'

That was all I wanted to know and quickly said goodbye to him. I got off the bus at the bus shelter on the common. My house was half a mile away. I didn't want to shock them, so I stood there waving a towel. Apparently my sisters were looking out of the window – one was married and had had two children while I was away – and asked each other who the tall bloke was waving something. Betty – our second – said, 'I'm sure that's our John.' There was a house near the bus shelter where a couple known as The Pairings lived. They were town people who had come out there to do a bit of farming, and they were 'cards'. They realized who I was and ran down the common towards me. Then my sisters ran to meet me. They told me that my mother and father had gone to Swansea Market in the car. They had bought an old Austin 12 car – like a gangster's car – while I had been away. Somebody must have seen me in Swansea that morning, or Will Harry could have mentioned it to somebody.

A customer said to my mother, 'That's funny to see you here today Florrie with your John home from the war.'

They gave their produce to a friend to sell, jumped in the car, and were home in about two hours after me. We waited for the car – my sister had the baby in a shawl – outside the house. We were all so excited. As we heard the car coming, our postman, Old Paddy, came. He had a clubfoot and had been gassed in the First World War. We always had milk and mother used to give him a fresh cup every morning to help him.

He came up to me and said, 'Good God John. I've got this to give to you.' It was my telegram from Brussels to say that I was on my way home. I had arrived home before it.

I was unlucky, because as I was an escaped prisoner, I was treated as a regular soldier. Later, when the camps were repatriated, the soldiers were flown home to a camp in High Wycombe and given special nourishing food and medical attention. They were sent home to await instructions, but they did not return to the army. The local boys who had come home three months after me, were presented with wristwatches by the Lord Mayor, and invited to a large banquet in their honour. My mother was really annoyed, and played pop that I had missed out. But I was happy because I was home, and I loved the army.

Living on a farm we had ham and eggs, and I lived well. The war had finished in Germany but the Japanese war had started. After six weeks, I was in Newcastle with the Recy Regiment (Recognizance Regiment) doing jungle training to go to Japan. I was hoping not to be on the front line but just to get out there to see a bit more. I wasn't brave but it was the only answer. I ended up with plenty of money. I had five years army-pay of three hundred and ninety pounds. I had been made up and I was on two pounds and five shillings a week. It was good money. It bought a lot of beer, which was excellent for recuperation.

I finished the training and went home on embarkation leave, but I dare not tell my mother. I kept it quiet. But the Japanese war had finished, and I went to London to Sandown Park where I did public duties – Guard of Honour. I was Guard of Honour when King George the Sixth and Queen Elizabeth came to Swansea. The Welsh Guards were given the Freedom of the Town of Swansea.[13] I was very proud. I remember being on duty when Heilie Salasie came to Swansea, and when the two princesses – Elizabeth and Margaret – came down from Edinburgh with their corgies to Swansea High Street Station.

We were on parade at Sandown Park about two months after going down there. We were on the Swank parade. On a Friday everyman – cooks, barbers, officers, etc. – in every battalion turned out, and we did the trooping of the colour in khaki. The sergeant major shouted, 'Turn to your right and dismiss but all the soldiers that were in Boulogne with Major Jones Mortimor in Number Two Company, stand fast.'

When we all dispersed, there was a smattering of a few left. Major Jones Mortimor was the last officer that we had had in Boulogne. He took us to the Caernarvon Hotel in Hampton Court where he treated us to a slap-up meal and four pints of beer each. He then took us into the palace. The ceilings were beautiful. We went inside the purple cords and laid down to see them properly. There was a row of Welsh Guards lying on the floor looking at the ceiling. It was the best way of seeing them. We then got lost in the maze and a fellow had to fetch us out. Oh! We had a good day.

Major Jones Mortimor shook our hands and said, 'Goodbye boys. Thank you for everything,' and went. We did a few public duties like sweeping up a few leaves, and then we were discharged."

In 1945, John married Morwyn Roberts of Glanmor Terrace, Penclawdd. He wore the suit that he had bought in Weaver and Wearers in Swansea in 1939. He had sent it home on receiving his Welsh Guards uniform in training camp. Morwyn says, "It was pointless buying a new suit as the suit John bought in 1939 had never been worn."

John suffered with frost bitten feet – a legacy of his war years in Poland. It entitled him to obtain more petrol than was rationed, which he gave to his father to use in his car.

'War is mud and blood and stench,
And all that hell can be:
Yet there are men among us still
Babbling of victory.

War is Horror on foul fours,
Creeping along the plains,
And where e'er the filthy fiend goes
The earth is left with stains.

War is nether of all things,
The vilest of all strife –
'Tis humanity slashing across the face
The Prince who gave His life.'[14]

On the north wall of the nave of St. Gwynour's Church, is a memorial tablet, depicting the men of the parish who lost their lives in the First World War. The tablet was unveiled by Colonel Helme, and dedicated by Reverend D. Thomas on 16 May 1926. It reads:

301

'Sacred to the memory of the men connected with Llan-yr-newydd Church who gave their lives for their country in the Great European War 1914-1918.

> Rfm. Samuel Davies.
> A.B. William Fry.
> Pte. Howell Griffiths.
> Pte. Arthur J. Humphreys.
> Pte. William Morris.
> Pte. William Prickett.
> Cpt. Richard Southern.
> Pte. Fred Wilkinson.
> Pte. Sam Geo. Williams.

Their names liveth for evermore.'

There seems to be no record in the village of the men unconnected with the church who were killed in the First World War.

The fifteen Penclawdd men who lost their lives during the Second World War were: Leonard Beale (Army), Cyril Davies (RAF), Eifryn Davies (Army), Garfied Davies (RAF), Gwilym Davies (RN), John Henry Evans (Army), Penry Guy (RAF), John William Howell (RN), Glyndwr Howells (Army), Harold Hughes (Army), Arfryn Jenkins (RAF), Harry Lewis (RN), Arthur Nurse (Army), John Richards (Army) and Danny Webb (Army).

A few years after the Second World War, a plaque was hung in the Small Memorial Hall, commemorating the men who lost their lives in both wars. In the 1980s, a memorial garden was planted on the site of the Big Memorial Hall, which Penclawdd Community Council pledged to tend. A memorial was erected on which the plaque was re-sighted. The plaque reads:

> 'In honour and grateful memory of the Sons of Penclawdd who fell in the First and Second World Wars. 1914-1918. 1939-1945.
>
> They shall not grow old
> As we that are left grow old,
> Age shall not weary them nor the years condemn,
> At the going down of the sun and in the morning,
> We will remember them.
> *Yn angof ni chânt fod.'*
> (Will not be forgotten).

Originally, a memorial service was held in the garden on Armistice Sunday afternoons, but later, it was decided that the mornings were more appropriate.

'O valiant hears, who to your glory came
Through dust of conflict and through battle flame;
Tranquil you lie, you knightly virtue proved,
Your memory hallowed in the land you loved. [. . .]

Long years ago, as earth lay dark and still,
Rose a loud cry upon a lonely hill,
While in the frailty of our human clay
Christ, our Redeemer passed the self-same way.'[15]

NOTES

1. Contents of a letter to Phil Foot from the George Cross Island Memorial Siege Bell Trust.
2. Ibid.
3. Basil Jones, *And So To Battle*. (Tollgates, Battle, East Sussex), p. 84.
4. P. M. MacDonald was commissioned from Sandhurst into the Suffolk Regiment in 1951, then in operations in Malaya. This set the pattern for the next active thirty years. His career took him to a wide variety of places – Treest, East and West Africa, The Gulf, Aden, Germany and Boneo. The highlight of his service however, was a tour as Military Attaché at Warsaw – 1975-77 and later Defence Attaché in Bucharest 1979-82. Since retirement in 1983, *'Through Darkness to Light'* became a leisure obsession.
5. Patrick MacDonald, *Through Darkness to Light* (Upton-upon-Seven 1994), p. 209.
6. Ibid.
7. Distinguished Flying Cross.
8. A Balaclava helmet is a close fitting woollen hood that covers the ears and neck as first worn by soldiers in the Crimean War.
9. 13/5/45: Probably should have been 13/4/45.
10. The Dakota – or Dak to all its crews – was the doyen of all RAF transport aircraft. It carried a crew of three and accommodated twenty-eight passengers. Nearly two thousand Dakotas were supplied to the RAF and these served faithfully in every theatre of war, starting in April 1941, when twelve aircraft were received by No. 31 Squadron RAF, in India. These were Douglas DC2 transports later supplemented by DC3s and eventually C47 Dakotas, military developments of the DC3 civil transport first flown in 1935.
11. Stirlings were heavy night bombers and also transported, with a crew of seven or eight. The Stirling is historically significant as the RAF's first four-engined mono-plane bomber to see operational service. The first prototype flew in May 1939 and the type entered first-line service with No. 7 Squadron in August 1940.

Due to official restrictions in the original 1936 specifications, the design of the Stirling limited its operational ceiling leading to undue casualties in service. By mid-1942, Stirling 1s were beginning to be replaced by Lancasters in many units, but an improved version, the Mark III came into use by early 1943. In that year too, production Stirlings for glider tug, paratroop carriage and heavy transport of goods and personnel emerged tilted Mark Vs having all gun turrets dilated and internal redesign. Other variants were allotted to radio counter measure squadron while from 1943 many Stirling bombers were employed extensively on mine-laying sorties. The ultimate Stirling sorties with Bomber command were flown in September 1944 but Mark IV and V transport versions continued in use until the end of the war. Total production of Stirlings of all Marks were two thousand three hundred and eighty-one aircraft for the RAF. Of these one hundred and sixty were mark Vs while six hundred and forty-one Stirling bomber versions were lost to enemy action.

12. Rear Gunners – Tail End Charlies – were bomber planes that carried a crew of seven or eight. It included a pilot, a second pilot who was an engineer and a navigator who sat behind. On the top of the plane was a bubble, known as a blister, in which an air gunner was situated. Underneath was another blister containing an air gunner and a bomb aimer. Underneath the tail was a glass case that could be swiveled in different directions by the use of a peddle. A tail gunner operating four machine guns was positioned here and was usually the first to be hit when the plane was gunned. He was known as the Tail End Charlie.

13. Entitlement of soldiers to enter a town without wearing bayonets.

14. Idris Jones. *War*.

15. Hymn 305. Ancient and Modern Hymn Book.

10

Rugby and Music

Rugby and music were as synonymous with Penclawdd as were religion, coal and cockles.

Rugby

John W. Jenkins remembers his happy childhood in the village – governed by rugby and religion. "I was brought up on rugby. My father played, his brother played – Joe Jenkins played for Swansea and captained Penclawdd. When they got together, that's all they talked was rugby. They were wonderful days as a youngster in the village before the Second World War. I played rugby for Penclawdd, went to Bethel Chapel and Sunday School in Capel Isaac. They were wonderful times.

I was a young upstart of about seventeen. I had a motorbike of my uncle's. He was called up in 1939. The bike was so big, that I could hardly pick it up. I used to drive around the village and when they heard me coming, they used to scatter saying, 'There's a madman coming.' But that was youth. No fear and no sense probably."

Penclawdd Rugby Club (the Reds) was officially formed in 1888. However, it seems that rugby had been played in the village since 1880-81, the same year as the founding of the Welsh Rugby Union.

In its formative years, the Club had no permanent pitch, but played on suitable available ground in various areas of the village. It initially used Dunraven Field, later *Cae Dono* (Dono's Field) on top of the *Graig*, and during the years preceding the First World War, a field at Graig-y-Coed was favoured.

Joe Austin, scrum half, became one of its first members to play first-class rugby, representing Llanelli (the Scarlets) and Swansea (the All Whites). He was the Club's captain during the 1905-06 season.

In the same year, Penclawdd was unsuccessful in its application to join the Welsh Rugby Union. Despite the failure, the players were not discouraged and continued to improve their standard of play.

The Club was disbanded during the First World War years.

The Club was immediately reformed after the war and quickly resumed its strength. It was so successful that it was asked to withdraw from the Swansea and District League as it was gaining a monopoly of cups.

In 1922, the Club obtained its own pitch for the first time. It leased the Welfare ground, known as the Rec., situated at the foot of the *Graig* behind Tabernacle Chapel. A pavilion was built on the land for the use of Penclawdd Rugby and Cricket Clubs.

1927 saw Penclawdd receive Welsh Rugby Union membership, twenty-two years after its first application.

The achievement was followed in 1929 by the Club becoming one of the founder members of the West Wales Rugby Union. The latter enabled local clubs to play each other in competition and subsequently became a breeding ground for promising players.

On 4 February 1933, a Penclawdd player was capped for Wales for the first time. Bryn Evans, scrum half, and Penclawdd captain in 1929-30, won international fame by winning his only cap against Scotland at St. Helen's, Swansea.

In the 1933-34 season, Penclawdd experienced another first, when it was victorious over Ammanford United at Pontarddulais, winning the West Wales Rugby Championship.

In the team were Haydn Tanner and William Thomas Harcourt Davies. The two cousins, and friends, living in Tabernacle Terrace, were grandsons of David Evan and Elizabeth Austin, tenants of the Ship. On Saturday, 28 September 1935, while still pupils at Gowerton County School, the boys played for the All Whites against New Zealand's international team, the All Blacks. Thousands of rugby fans came from Wales and even England to see the game at St. Helen's ground, at Swansea. 'Special trains from all parts of the Principality were running from early morning, and soon after midday, Swansea presented an 'international' day appearance. Hundreds of enthusiasts chartered a special P.&.A. Campbell boat, the Waverley, to bring them from Ilfracombe, Minehead and Lynmouth to the Mumbles, where they entrained for Swansea. An official of the P.&.A. Campbell Company told the 'Evening Post' that it was the first time that a boat had been engaged to carry people from Devonshire to Swansea for a football match. [. . .] All the West Wales bus services had duplicated on all their routes. [. . .] The All Blacks spent a quiet morning, a few walking around Swansea to view the shops, but most of them rested at the Hotel Metropole.'[1]

In 1905 and 1924, the All Blacks had beaten the All Whites. The forty thousand spectators came to the match in the hope of seeing the Swansea Club take their revenge. They were not disappointed. A report of the match appeared in the 'South Wales Evening Post' newspaper that evening.

W. T. H. (Willie) Davies.

Haydn Tanner.

'HISTORY MADE AT ST. HELEN'S

1905 and 1924 Defeats Avenged.

Forty thousand wildly enthusiastic spectators saw the All Whites make Rugby history at St. Helen's this afternoon by beating the New Zealand touring side by eleven points to three. It was a memorable game. [. . .]

The brilliant Swansea schoolboy halfbacks sent their admirers almost delirious with joy [. . .] for Tanner and Davies made those perfect openings which are the joy of a Welsh Rugby football crowd. [. . .] Haydn Tanner and W. T. H. Davies were playing brilliant rugby. It was they who laid the foundation for Swansea's third try.

Final score – Swansea, 1 con. goal, 2 tries (11pts.)
New Zealand, 1 try (3pt.).'

Tanner and Davies' amazing halfback partnership bordered on the telepathic and they were to become one of the most famous rugby communications of all times. So successful was the schoolboy partnership, that after the match, the All Blacks' captain, Jack Manchester, was reported to have said, 'Please do not say that we have been beaten by two schoolboys.'

In December of the same year, while still only eighteen years and eleven months old, Haydn won his first cap against New Zealand at Cardiff.

Willie was not chosen to play for the team as the selectors favoured Cliff Jones. However, he won his first cap against Ireland the following year but as centre. It was his first of six caps. He was to partner his cousin on only five occasions at international level. After playing a few games for Llanelli, Willie joined the All Whites where he stayed until 1939. He turned professional in the same year with Bradford Northern Rugby League Club. He was to became a Great Britain International and holder of the Lance Todd Trophy – best player at a Rugby League Cup Final (held at Wembley Stadium).

In 1938, Haydn toured South Africa as a British Lion.

During the post-Second World War years he was to play for Cardiff, Wales – which he captained thirteen times – and the Barbarians.

Haydn was to play his last international against France on 26 March 1949.

Many charity matches were held in the village when local dignitaries such as Doctor Hughes (President) were invited to 'kick off'. The matches were well attended as the stars of the Penclawdd team – Haydn Tanner and Willie Davies – attracted many spectators from outside the village, such as Llanelli, Loughor, Pontarddulais, Gowerton, Swansea etc. as well as from within the village.

On Boxing Days, Bilo Rees, a local character, picked his own team. It was known as the All Gower Team. He asked Willie and Haydn to persuade good players to join his team, which played against Penclawdd. Bilo kicked off wearing plus fours and a Welsh cap borrowed from Gwyn Lewis. It was a 'big day' in the village.

1939 saw the Club being disbanded again

The war over, rugby enthusiasts were anxious to recommence the game in the village. Mel Jenkins and David (*Dai*) J. Evans discussed the possibility. Both men were natives of Loughor, but had come to live in Penclawdd on marrying local girls. They were great friends and team-mates. Mel had first been introduced to Penclawdd rugby whilst playing for the Loughor schools. He had become a member of the Penclawdd team in 1937-38.

A meeting was held in the cinema premises, attended by fourteen people including prewar officials – Major Tom Rees, Albert John Jenkins, Tom

Leyshon, Harry Howells, Ernest Davies, Willie Howells, Tom Stock and Les Jenkins. As a result, the Club was reformed with Albert John Jenkins (chairman), Walford Jones (secretary) – to be proceeded by *Dai* Evans – and John Rees (treasurer). The first team was captained by Joe Jenkins. However, the Club had a wealth of problems. Its pavilion and ground were still under military control and it had neither equipment nor money. Undaunted, and with great determination and ingenuity, the Club was re-launched. The soccer goalposts were replaced by rugby goalposts. Permission was obtained for the players to bath at the military camp at West End. Mel Jenkins, *Dai* Evans, Arwyn Harry and Ernest Davies begged clothing coupons from the villagers to purchase jerseys, rugby balls etc. Obsolete wartime blackout material was used to make shorts. When the team played RAF Fairwood only the captain sported a jersey. The rest of the team wore ordinary print shirts. The Club was fortunate in receiving a donation of ten pounds from Granville Davies on behalf of Penclawdd Workingmens' Club.

Katie Hagan, who lived in the Barracks, was employed as team laundress. She charged five shillings for washing and drying a set of jerseys. The Ladies Supporters Club was formed under the chairmanship of Carys Hughes. They proved to be extremely hard-working ladies undertaking many tasks, such as sewing torn jerseys and organizing rugby dinners.

On returning from the forces, the rugby players of the village resumed playing their beloved game.

Morgan Guy played for the Welsh Guards in the war years, before he was stationed abroad, and also while waiting to be demobbed. After the war, he played for Penclawdd. "Penclawdd was a cracking team then. We played Loughor, Gowerton, Neath etc. The games were of a very high standard."

Mel Austin – cousin of Willie Davies and Haydn Tanner – remembers such a game. "Loughor were down here playing and it was a sixpenny gate. We took over one hundred pounds which was a lot of money then, and over four thousand spectators."

Phil Foote has been described as 'speedy and powerful – one of Penclawdd's most consistent forwards.' He had played for Penclawdd twice in 1939. In early 1945, Penclawdd were to play an away match at Tumble. Phil was chosen for the team. "I was still on the HMS Rodney in the port of Rosyth, in the Firth of Forth. I received a very official looking letter from *Dai* Evans asking me to play. I took the letter to my captain and when he saw the letter heading, West Wales Rugby Union, he was very impressed and said, 'You'd better get your kit and go quick.' But we lost the game. After the war, Penclawdd had no money. We were playing Loughor. Out they came on the field with brand new jerseys, socks and shorts and there we were with patches on our jerseys. Before the game, we had a pep talk from John Sambrook and Phyl Williams, showing us on the blackboard the moves we should make. But on the field, our captain, John Jenkins said, 'Now boys, forget all they said and play our own game.' We did, and won by twenty points to something.

We were a good team then. We beat Llanelli twice and Swansea. The teams and their fans came to Penclawdd in buses, which were parked in front of the Ship. Depending on the wind, the spectators could be heard all over the village.

The Penclawdd Rugby Committee met in the Ship to pick the team for the forthcoming Saturday. On the Monday night, the chosen players' names were displayed in the windows of Jim Howell's chip shop, Mrs. Harry's chip shop and Robert John Davies' shop. We had training twice a week –

PENCLAWDD R.F.C.

The following have been selected to play against *LOUGHOR.*

on *Sat.* *MAY 10TH 1947* at *PONTARDULAIS.*

Kick off at *4-0 P.M.*

FULL BACK

Howard John

THREE-QUARTERS

Jno Rees   *Cyril Davies*   *Jno Hughes*   *J. Wm Jenkins*

Morgan Guy, L. P. Howells.

HALF BACKS

T. J. Hopkins + *D. J. Rees.*

Selwyn Jenkins

FORWARDS

Em Howells   *Thos Howells*   *Gwyn Lewis*

T. G. Guy   *T. M. Francis*

Jno Jenkins (Capt.)   *S. Foote*   *Danny Davies*

L. G. Howells,

RESERVES   *Referee - T. H. Phillips*   *Neath.*

Bus Leaves at *3 P.M. SHARP*

Penclawdd RFC team to play 10.5.47.

on Tuesdays and Thursdays. If I was working afternoon shifts on those days, I'd train by running on the roads on my own. I was very fit then.

They were marvelous times. After the game we had a singsong – a concert – when everybody did a 'turn'. We sung hymns, popular songs, and arias from operas and operettas. There were many good singers in Penclawdd, but we all sounded wonderful after a few pints. We finished at 'stop tap' and all went home together on the bus. At the end of the season in May, we had a dinner in different venues – Llandeilo, etc. when the team captain for the next season was chosen. The dinner was attended by the Committee members and the players."

During the Victory Internationals, J. Eifion Davies and Elwyn Gwyther played for Wales.

1947 saw Penclawdd win the West Wales Championship for the second time.

Phil Foote was captain of Penclawdd Club in the 1950-51 season. 1951 saw the end of his playing career when, during a match between Penclawdd and Seven Sisters, he received a kick that resulted in his having a kidney removed.

In 1963, David Parkhouse played for Swansea against the All Blacks, scoring all his side's nine points. David, although small in stature, was a rugby 'giant'. Sadly, he died in his thirty's, robbing Penclawdd and Welsh rugby of a great sportsman.

Doug Rees, fullback, won three caps in 1968 and was proceeded by J. P. R. Williams. Doug played for Swansea but had captained Penclawdd in 1966-67.

The Centenary Captain, Ken Lewis, captained Penclawdd for the first time in 1967-68. He holds the all-time record of being captain for ten seasons.

The Club won the West Wales Cup in 1968-69. The following year they won the Cup again and the West Wales Championship for the third time.

In the 1970s, hooker Roy Thomas played for Llanelli and was unfortunate in never wining a cap although being reserve for Wales on over twenty-five occasions.

In the 1946-47 season, Penclawdd Rugby Youth (PRY) was formed when the local Youth Club and Rugby Club combined under the direction of D. G. (*Dai*) Howells, with Stan Howells as trainer. Morien Guy was its first appointed captain. Mel Austin was one of its members. "If you lived in Penclawdd then, you wanted to play rugby for Penclawdd. I played in the position of prop-forward front row for the first Rugby Youth team when it was formed after the war. I was about eighteen. The Youth was not so organized then as it is now. The team didn't play the whole season, just a few games."

Penclawdd Secondary Modern School Rugby Team in front of
Penclawdd Secondary Modern School.
Back row, left to right: Ioan Stock, Ifor James, Thomas John James, Dennis Parkhouse,
Peter Jones, Keith Long, Mel Harry, Denny Williams.
Front row, left to right: Elwyn Thomas, Dudley Rees, Clive Eaton, Major Tom Rees,
Denzil Evans, Myall Davies, Donald Williams, David Howells, David Jenkins.
Seated, left to right: Derrick Jones, David Parkhouse.

Within three years PRY became the first winners of Swansea and District League. They repeated the performance in the next two consecutive years together with the Glamorgan, and the District Sevens.

David Parkhouse and W. R. C. Davies gained caps for the Welsh Youth against France in March 1953 – David captaining the side.

1956 saw David Evans win a cap against the German Youth. He progressed to Llanelli before joining St. Helens Rugby League side.

Alan Parkhouse emulated his brother David in 1964 when he gained his Youth cap. It was a great disappointment to the Club when, in 1967, after losing in the District Final to Swansea at St. Helen's, one of their outstanding players, Roger Hyndman, failed to win his cap, despite having the better of his opponent, Phil Bennett. He was later to play for both Swansea and Llanelli.

In 1973, Clive Griffiths gained Secondary School honours. He was to obtain a senior cap when he replaced the injured J. P. R. Williams against England in 1979.

The Club won the District Cup in 1973 against Swansea in an exciting finale. Within two years, the Club was winner of the District League Trophy with Steve Long as captain, the Sevens Cup at Waunarlwydd, and the Alcoa Shield.

1976 saw David Humphreys – cousin to David and Alan Parkhouse – win his cap against England at Stradey Park. Flanker, Glyn Hyndman, brother of Roger, won his cap against France.

Penclawdd Rugby Youth Club has an extremely distinguished record. One hundred and seventy of its members have represented the District side and over fifty have played for first-class clubs.

The Club was served loyally by Major Tom Rees for many years, earning himself a Life Vice-Presidency. By the mid-1960s, Dennis Parkhouse was in the helm. He served them faithfully for over thirty years; an experience that has given him great enjoyment and satisfaction. "I was a member of the Youth team that won in 1952 and '53. I became involved in the running of the team when I was still playing rugby for Penclawdd Seniors. I was wondering what position to hold on the Committee when Major Rees suggested that I take over the Youth. He said, 'Take over the Youth, boy. That's where all the great pleasures are.' And it was true. Boys of seventeen, eighteen, nineteen, think you're God if you help them. They still come back to the village and talk of their happy years in the Youth team.

I became secretary and District selector. The latter enabled me to choose good players from Penclawdd to play for the District – the cream of all the area – and then hopefully to have a Welsh trial. I took them to training sessions on Sunday mornings with the District team: the team that I had played for myself.

I was answerable to the senior committee and councillors for the boys' so-called bad behaviour. It is true that they were boisterous, and some criticized their noisy behaviour, but it was nothing dreadful: only singing after 'stop tap', and I couldn't stop that. They were certainly not as bad as many youngsters are today – stealing cars, etc.

At one time I held a squad of thirty-four boys, all under nineteen. I took them on tour. They practised twice a week and played on Saturdays. It was important for them and the village to have rugby to channel their energy into. A couple of them had problems with the police, but they eventually developed into lovely boys and were very appreciative and helpful. They became the best in the squad. It was very pleasing for me. I used to think, 'That's what I'm here for. I can be of more benefit to boys that are bad than the good boys.'

As well as my involvement with the Youth, I have been captain of Penclawdd senior team, senior coach and trainer.

It was a great relief when the playing fields were built at Graig-y-Coed. The Rec. had to accommodate the First, Second and Youth teams as well as the Secondary Modern School's rugby. The pitch was in a terrible state."

Penclawdd Rugby Club's Roll of Honour reads as follows:

Senior Internationals
Bryn Evans, Haydn Tanner, W. T. H. Davies,
Doug Rees, Clive Griffiths.
Victory Internationals
Eifion Davies, Elwyn Gwyther
'B' Internationals
E. R. Thomas, C. Griffiths
Schoolboy Internationals
Gwyn Lewis, Hugh Bevan
Barbarians
E. R. Thomas, Haydn Tanner
Secondary Schools Internationals
Denzil Sambrook, Jim Dark, Haydn Tanner,
W. T. H. Davies, Clive Griffiths
Youth Internationals
David Parkhouse, David Evans, W. R. C. Davies,
David Humphreys, Eirwyn Lewis, Denzil Evans,
Glyn Hyndman, Alan Parkhouse.

Over the years, Penclawdd Club has been served by dedicated administrators as well as talented players. Both have shared a great love of the Club and of the game of rugby. D. J. (*Dai*) Evans was player and administrator (secretary and later financial secretary) for Penclawdd for over fifty years. His good friend, Mel Jenkins, also served the Club well as player and treasurer for over forty years. Together, with Major Tom Rees (chairman) and Dennis Howells (secretary), they were the stalwarts of the Club. Major Tom Rees' son, David Francis (*Dai Bach*), followed in his father's footsteps, and after his playing days, became the Club's chairman, and later, in its Centenary Year, President. As Mel Austin comments, "You can have as many committee members as you like but you have to have a back bone. A ship has to have a captain."

These hard-working disciples of the game must have possessed exceedingly patient and tolerant wives. D. J. Evans said of his wife, "My wife, Elaine, who has threatened divorce on many occasions, still claims to be the oldest fully paid-up member of the 'Rugby Widows Association'."

After their playing days, Davey John Hughes and Phil Foote joined the Committee. Between them, they have served the Club as players and committee members for over one hundred and twenty years.

The Club, having tried unsuccessfully to purchase the Ship from Trumans Brewery in the early 1970s, built its own clubhouse on a site behind the Ship in 1975. It was opened by Cliff Jones.

In 1980-81, the Club's Centenary was celebrated with special events and matches. During the celebratory dinner, which was attended by many of the 'big names' of rugby such as Gerald Davies, *Dai Bach* Rees – small of stature with a high-pitched voice and ginger hair – gave a speech on the origins of the Club. He related how Penclawdd men had crossed the Llwchwr Estuary at low tide and had stolen a rugby ball from the Llanelli Club. He was to be proceeded by Max Boyce, the famous Welsh singer-comedian. But *Dai Bach* had so entertained his audience that Max Boyce stood up saying "I can't follow that," did not, and sat down.

An excellent brochure was published giving a comprehensive history of the Club. Cliff Jones was invited to write its foreword. 'I recall with personal pride and abiding pleasure opening the new modern clubhouse in 1975, and being impressed not only with the warmth and generosity of that welcome (I can taste those delicious cockles even as I write) but also with the quality of play that day against such powerful opponents as Newport, one of the premier clubs in Wales.

As president of the Welsh Rugby Union for our Centenary Year, may I congratulate the Club on this very special occasion, and thank them for their outstanding contribution to Welsh Rugby. May they still be celebrating it, as amateurs, in the centuries to come. *Ymlaen* (keep going) Penclawdd!'[2]

The famous cousins contributed to the Centenary Booklet.

Haydn Tanner wrote 'One did not realize it at the time but there is no doubt in my own mind that the fundamentals were established in Penclawdd. My father was at every possible match, whether it was for Gowerton School or later Penclawdd. [. . .] The foundation was laid in Penclawdd. [. . .] Then of course the war came, after that Cardiff and captaining Wales and the Barbarians. Yes, a long way from being a small boy training with the Penclawdd first team. Nevertheless, the commitment and enjoyment was as great as subsequently.'

Willie Davies' contribution reads, 'I have always had a great affection for my home club, having been born in and played for Penclawdd with my cousin Haydn Tanner. We were destined to play rugby, as our grandparents were the tenants of the Club's headquarters, the Ship and Castle Inn, and we were constantly in the dressing rooms watching and listening to great players. I owe a great deal to Penclawdd RFC for supporting me in my rugby career. They always encouraged me.'

During Penclawdd Rugby Club's Centenary Year, it won the highest accolade. On Saturday 15 November 1980, the Club, coached by Roy Thomas, beat Newport 4-nil in the Welsh Cup competition. An article in the 'South Wales Evening Post' the following Monday read:

'What a famous victory!

Penclawdd's victory in their Centenary season made them the first second-class club to beat one of the major clubs. [. . .] So Penclawdd, one of the cornerstones of West Wales rugby, carved their name with pride on the Cup competition. It was a victory for Cup rugby.'

This major achievement of a small club's win over a first-class team resulted in Penclawdd being awarded the Rugby World Magazine Phillishave Award – Team of the Year. It was presented to them in London by Dennis Thatcher, husband of the then prime minister, Margaret Thatcher.

The plaque in the clubhouse reads:

'This plaque was presented to Penclawdd RFC by a jury of sports journalists on behalf of Rugby World Magazine in recognition of their defeat of Newport RFC in the Welsh Cup.'

In the early 1990s, Trumans Brewery placed the Ship for sale. The Club tried again to purchase the property, thinking it appropriate to return to its original venue and also favoured the more substantial building. But it was not to be. Its offer was rejected, and the Ship was demolished to give way to a small housing development. It is one of the many landmarks of the village that has disappeared.

Music

Before the nineteenth century, few of the working class had accessibility to pianos or other musical instruments. Consequently, as well as being illiterate, they were unable to read music – old notation. Many were gifted vocalists, but their range of compositions was impaired by their circumstances. In the nineteenth century, the problem was addressed when tonic sol-fa was designed to overcome the difficulty of singing at sight from printed signs. It is a modification of a medieval notation used for vocal music. 'The first use of it in England is attributed to a Norwich schoolteacher, Miss Glover. From her beginnings, the system was elaborated by John Curwen (1816-80). It employs every person's instinctive knowledge of the 'feel' or 'flavour' of any note of the scale, i.e. its 'mental effect' determined by its position among other notes of the scale. These mental effects are given names from the ancient gamut of Guido d'Arezzo (ut, re, mi, fa, sol, la) which are derived from the initial syllables of the lines of a Latin hymn. The forms adopted in English being, doh, ray, me, fah, soh, lah, te, doh.'[3]

In the early nineteenth century, tonic sol-fa was taught in Penclawdd Elementary School. It was favoured in the village as opposed to old notation, and was used in the *Gymanfa Ganu*, oratorios, concerts and Band of Hopes.

The wealth of musical activities in Penclawdd immersed its youth in the genre. Coupled with the fact that the musical gene is strongly inherent, it is not surprising that Penclawdd has produced sons and daughters who have attained great eminence in the field of music.

Maureen Mitchinson, née Guy, lived her formative years in West End, Penclawdd. From an early age, she showed a great interest in any kind of performing. The concerts, oratorios, etc., which she attended regularly, were a great source of enjoyment to her. Her first public performance was as a child elocutionist. However, it was as a mezzo-soprano that she was to enjoy worldwide renown.

"I was the youngest of six children. My father was a miner and unfortunately died in his early 50s. My burning ambition as a youngster was to go on the stage and perform, and I was taken to the various concerts at Bethel Chapel where my parents were members.

I started singing lessons and was later advised to enter for a major Glamorgan Scholarship in which I was successful. This Scholarship allowed me to study at the college of my choice – the Guildhall School of Music in London. Here I won many major prizes, and was awarded

Maureen Mitchinson, née Guy.

317

the much coveted Worshipful Company of Musicians Silver Medal, which is bestowed on the foremost student of the College.

During my time at Guildhall, I was performing regularly all over the British Isles, and was often heard on BBC radio and seen on many television programmes.

On 16 February 1956, I sang in a concert – a performance of 'Elijah' – at Tabernacle Chapel, Penclawdd. I met my husband, John, there who was also a soloist. We were married thirteen months later in Bethel by the then minister, Henry Hughes.

On leaving Guildhall, I auditioned for Sadlers Wells Opera Company and was offered a Principal Mezzo-Soprano contract. With that Company I sang many important roles including Delilah in 'Samson and Delilah', Olga in 'Eugene Onegin', Madalena in 'Rigoletto', and Dryade in 'Ariadne auf Naxos'.

I was then asked to join the Royal Opera Covent Garden as Principal Mezzo-Soprano where I worked closely with many of the finest conductors, coaches and producers in the world, singing such roles as Azucena in 'Il Trovatore', Suzuki in 'Madam Butterfly', Erde and several other important roles in the famous 'Ring Cycle' conducted by the late George Solti, the then Music Director of the Company. During this time, I was extremely busy with my concert and recital appearances all over Europe, and made a tour of Australia and New Zealand, where I sang Amneris in 'Aida' in addition to many concert appearances.

After some time, I left the Royal Opera and took up a similar contract with the Frankfurt Opera where I appeared as Adiano in 'Rienzi', Eboli in 'Don Carlo', Azucena in 'Il Trovatore', Orfeo in Glucks opera, and continued my concert career both here and abroad. I appeared in the National Eisteddfod as a performer or as an adjudicator and at major music festivals throughout Europe. A memorable event was the performance of Oedipus Rex in 'Herodus Atticus' (Athens) by Stravinski, the performance being conducted by the composer.

I undertook visits to Scandinavia for concerts, as well as appearances in Israel with both the Israel Philharmonic Orchestra and the Jerusalem Symphony Orchestra. Here I worked with such conductors as Carlo Maria Gulini, Antal Dorati, and Zubin Mehta. I made guest appearances in Budapest, singing Eboli and Amneris, in London with the ENO (English National Opera) singing Eboli, and for the Handel Opera, singing Cornelius in 'Gulius Caesa'.

I also appeared as Fricka with the Scottish Opera, and sang Mrs. Sedley in 'Peter Grimes', and the She Ancient in 'Midsummer Marriage' with the WNO (Welsh Nation Opera).

I have always been grateful to have had tuition and guidance from Ellis Keeler, my singing teacher at Guildhall, Hans Oppenheim, with whom I studied Lieder, Boriska Gereb, my teacher on leaving college, my coach Vida Harford, my teacher in Geneva, Maria Carpi, and the coach Luigi Ricci – former accompanist and coach to Benjamino Gigli – with whom I studied Italian repertoire in Rome.

John and I have been so fortunate in travelling the world together and sharing work as we did so. This was a rather strange phenomenon as I was steeped in opera, and John was more inclined to the world of concerts and oratorios. Nevertheless, it worked out very well in lots of interesting places. In Australia and New Zealand I was singing Amneris in 'Aida' whilst John was touring with concerts. Jointly we appeared in Australia, New Zealand, Portugal, Spain, Israel, Scandinavia, and all over Great Britain and Ireland. We always looked forward with great excitement to our many concerts in Penclawdd as, not only did we see so many relatives in the audience, but our friends as well, giving us wonderful opportunities for post-concert family chats and village gossip.

We have two sons, Mark and David. One works for an engineering company and the elder one is employed in Digital Terrestrial Television Development – two careers diametrically opposed, but both of our sons are extremely happy. Neither are practical musicians, but both have a love of music in general.

During the past ten years, John and I have turned our attention to passing on our wide experience to young singers. I was appointed Vocal Tutor and John, Head of Vocal Studies at the Welsh College of Music and Drama. We retired in 1998.

We are now regular visitors to Banff and Calgary in Canada where we are involved with the new 'Kidsop' organisation which promotes operas for the young. In 1999, we produced 'The Raven King' by Mervyn Burtch. I was the official vocal coach and John sang the tittle role. We shall return there in August this year (2000) and again in December, and January 2001."

Maureen and John now live in St. Maughans Green, Monmouth, where Maureen teaches privately. In April, they plan to move to Carew, near Tenby in Pembrokeshire. Maureen has not lost her love of her native village and comments, "It is always lovely to hear from people in Penclawdd."

Nancy Guy, née Davies, is also a daughter of Penclawdd of whom the villagers are extremely proud. Unfortunately, Nancy's musical career was terminated prematurely by ill health – a fact greatly bemoaned by the inhabitants of the village.

"I was taught to sing by Mr. Gwynfor Jenkins. He was a brilliant

Nancy Guy, née Davies.

musician. During the war years, Mr. Jenkins taught and conducted the Penclawdd Youth Choir and the Penclawdd Male Voice Choir. The men rehearsed in the schoolroom at Tabernacle Chapel on Sunday afternoons after Sunday School. I used to sing at the Welcome Home concerts in the church hall. Frankie Howard used to amuse the packed audience. At this period, I was given the leading parts in the Band of Hope productions, which were held for a whole week in the Penclawdd Memorial Hall – the cinema. I also competed in local *Eisteddfods* and won the prize for the Soprano Solo in 1948 at Bridgend. I was then invited to sing all over Wales at annual oratorios, in chapels, Miners' Welfare Halls and even in the Capitol Cinema at Cardiff.

In 1949 I went to the Royal Academy. In 1957, I won the Kathleen Ferrier Competition for soprano and as a result of the scholarship, I studied at the Royal Opera School. My tutor was Joan Cross. During the same year, I won the 'Golden Voice of Wales'. I continued to sing at local concerts and was the guest artist at the National Eisteddfod in Ebbw Vale. I also broadcasted on radio from Cardiff.

My career was cut short because of ill health."

Penclawdd has always boasted families of gifted musicians, in which the talent, enthusiasm and love of music have been handed down from generation to generation.

Two families by the name of Jenkins, held prominence in this field.

William Jenkins, 1 Penlan Terrace, was one of seven children – Tom, Joe, Daniel (Beach House), Hannah, Elizabeth and Annie. Tom's daughter, Gwen, married Alfryn Jenkins, brother of David Jenkins, thus joining the two Jenkins families. The Jenkins musicians held the majority of musical rolls in Tabernacle Chapel for over half a century.

In the chapel's formative years, singing was unaccompanied, as organs were looked upon with disfavour by the elders, and on the occasion of a concert etc., a piano was hired. However, in about 1894, the chapel purchased a reed organ and William Jenkins was appointed organist.

William earned his living as a music teacher. He had many connections in Gower through his work in the vicinity. He recognized the need of the Gower people to have a musical festival and consequently, through him, the Music Festivals of Gower were born in Tabernacle Chapel in 1909.

With the building of the new Tabernacle Chapel in 1911, a new pipe organ was installed of superior quality to its predecessor, which resulted in raising the standard of singing considerably.

On the death of the conductor Daniel Jenkins in 1933, his brother, William, consented to undertake both duties of organist and conductor.

William provided lessons in piano, organ and vocals to pupils of all ages. He was a strict teacher and often rapped his young pupils' fingers with a pencil when the wrong note was played. His sister, Hannah, entertained the children in the kitchen at a table by the fire, with pencils and paper, while they waited their turn for their music lesson. Griff Rees remembers, when passing William's house on his way home, hearing one of the villagers having vocal lessons. "I can remember passing his house at night and inside would be Tom Coffo (Davies), brother of Johnny the Blue. Tom had a lovely voice. Willie was training him to sing, but Tom could not read music, so Willie had to go over it note by note. *Duw*, it was a pleasure to stand outside listening to Willie teaching him."

Daniel's son, W. Gwynfor Jenkins, proceeded William as Tabernacle Chapel's organist and later was its conductor when David Jenkins became organist. After Gwynfor's death, David Jenkins became the chapel's con-ductor, and Glanrhyd Austin was appointed organist. Gwynfor's son, Leighton, also a musician, was organist of Bethel Chapel, the position being filled at Tabernacle. The musicians often changed rolls for concerts, oratorios and the *Gymanfa Ganu*.

Karl, son of David, and Lilly Jenkins, née Pamp, lived for the first years of his life in a house on the sea front in Penclawdd. After his mother's death, Karl and his father went to live in Benson Cottage with his aunt, Evelyn Hopkins. Karl's early life was greatly influenced by his father's eminence in music.

Karl is one of the world's most successful living composers. He has experimented in the most popular musical sounds of our time, creating a universal music that cannot be categorized. It has its roots in the classical tradition but it is not wholly classical. Karl uses vocals that do not sing in any language, but are used as instrumental sounds. His music has been described in many variants – having a spiritual new age quality, sexy, raunchy, esthetic, ethnic, religious, ecclesiastical and sensual.

In the field of advertising, Karl has won a Creative Circle gold award and the D & AD 'Best Music' prize twice. He composed music for the well-known commercials, Delta Airlines, Cheltenham and Gloucester Building Society, Renault Clio, Levi Jeans and De Beers Diamonds

Karl Jenkins.

April 1995 saw the release of Adiemus: 'Songs of Sanctuary', which topped both the classical and pop charts in Europe and Japan. His album, 'Diamond Music', features his Concerto Grosso 'Palladio'. Performed by the London Philharmonic and the Smith String Quartet, the album includes his 'Passacaglia', 'String Quartet No. 2' and 'Adiemus Variations for string quartet'. Adiemus II: 'Cantata Mundi', the follow-up album to the hugely successful Adiemus, was released in February 1997, and was performed live for the first time at the Royal Albert Hall. Adiemus III: 'Dance of Time' followed. Karl composed 'Eloise', an opera for children and 'Praise', when he was commissioned to compose for male chorus by BBC Songs of Praise. 'Barocco' No. 1 was composed for saxophone quartet, and 'Bri' for chorus and orchestra commissioned for the opening of the Rugby World Cup. His composition 'He Wishes for the Cloths of Heaven' for soprano and chamber orchestra was commissioned by BMG Classics for Lesley Garrett. 'Imagined Oceans' was composed for female voices, recorder, strings and percussion and 'Love's Fool' is a ballet score for mixed ensemble, commissioned by the Royal Ballet.

Karl's wife, Carol, is also a composer, and his son, Jody, was Principal Percussionist of the National Youth Orchestra of Great Britain, and is now at the Royal Academy of Music.

Karl lives in London, but he has retained the family home in Penclawdd. "I think one's roots are important. My emotional and musical roots are in the village, as my father started me on my career here.

When I was about five or six, I started piano lessons with my father. I suppose I was never meant to be a pianist. I wasn't by any means a child prodigy or anything remotely approaching that. It was only later when I went to Gowerton Grammar School and began to play the oboe that I found an instrument that I was better at. But the piano has always been important to me as a compositional aid.

Music-wise, Gowerton Grammar School was excellent. C. K. Watkins (Cynwyd King Watkins) was the music master. He had what I considered at the time to be a very peculiar life style in that he lived in Bridgend, and stayed in Gowerton all the week. He went home on Wednesday nights and at weekends. It always struck me as odd. I think his wife was headmistress of a girls' school in Bridgend. However, he ran a very active music department.

The Welsh composer, Alun Hoddinott – a contemporary of Leighton Jenkins – had been a pupil at the school. He was subsequently one of my music lecturers when I went to Cardiff University to do my degree. He later became Professor of Music there. Gowerton was a good school, as anyone who wanted to learn an instrument could do so for free, which is not the case nowadays. There was a comprehensive range of instruments and a very vibrant school orchestra. It had a strong choral tradition, with lots of concerts and music for various plays which Gilbert Bennett – English teacher – used to put on.

So the school gave me a fantastic grounding and from there I went to the Glamorgan Youth Orchestra and the National Youth Orchestra of Wales, where I eventually became Principal Oboist.

From school I went to Cardiff University, where I did my initial degree, and then to the Royal Academy of Music in London in my postgraduation year.

I started being interested in, and playing jazz when I was at school. As I played the oboe, I fancied playing the saxophone as the fingering is similar. I think it was at university, rather than at school, that I bought my first saxophone, and got into that to a certain degree. When I was at the Academy, I worked initially as a jazz musician.

I worked with Ronnie Scott and that was the first stage of my professional life after the Royal Academy – working in jazz.

My father was thrilled with my music, but sadly, he and my Aunty Ev – she died four years ago – missed my relative success. My aunt brought me up after the death of my mother when I was about five. The loss of my father was quite a blow. I was in the South of France playing in my first jazz group, Graham Collier, in the Nice Festival. My father had had a heart attack the previous year. I was in a beach café with the rest of the band when a phone call came through from the consulate in Nice asking for Karl Jenkins. I knew immediately what it was. My father had died. It was 1967-68. I was about twenty-five.

My father greatly encouraged my music, but he was a bit dubious about jazz, as then it didn't have the respectability that it now has. It's now a bona fide kind of musical language and is acknowledged as such. But in those days it had a stigma attached to it. It was almost considered the devil's music!

It never occurred to me to be anything else other than a musician, but it was mostly a question of elimination. I did 'O' levels, including music, and 'A' levels including music. It seemed appropriate to read music at university.

I never wanted to do anything else, apart from when I was about eleven I wanted to go to sea. There was a strong seafaring tradition on my mother's side of the family. My grandfather, Carl Gustav Pamp, was a Swedish sailor – an engineer on a Swedish merchant ship. His coming to Penclawdd is quite a romantic story. His ship used to sail to South Wales, and while in Newport, he met my grandmother who was selling cockles there. They married and he settled in Penclawdd, and died here. A few previous generations had been sailors. One, a ship's captain, sunk with his ship in the Atlantic. I was named after my grandfather, but my parents preferred Carl spelt with a K. I remember him quite vividly. He was quite a clever man. He was also a great hoarder. When I was in Penclawdd Junior School, we were making models out of matchboxes. When I asked my grandfather if he had any, he produced about fifty or sixty. He also used to pickle onions!

I still have a feeling for Penclawdd although nearly all my contemporaries have left. The only close friend of my generation that I have here now is Tony Small. We see each other quite often, and when he comes to London, he stays over. I also know his sons, Ian and Gareth. The latter is such an amazing trumpeter.

I suppose I lost touch with the village to a certain degree, apart from my Aunty Ev, after my days when I was touring Europe with Soft Machine – a jazz-rock group. I lost touch with Tony until the last few years.

My musical life since university days has been divided into three phases. The first was my jazz-rock days with Ronnie Scott and Soft Machine. During the next ten to fifteen years, I wrote media music, mainly for television commercials and a few films. The last phase is concert work – commissions and the Adiemus project. In musical terms, I've had quite a varied career.

I had some extra lessons with Leighton Jenkins when I was in Grammar School. I went to Tabernacle Chapel three times a day – Sunday School in the afternoon. My father became organist there after Gwynfor Jenkins died. I was in many of the Band of Hope concerts. I can remember being a robin and crying because my tail had fallen down and everybody else's was sticking up straight!

My father taught in Llanmorlais Elementary School in the 1930s, and later in Penclawdd Secondary Modern, teaching art, craft and pottery, etc. in the latter. He took the school productions of the operettas (although he was not officially the music teacher but was deputy head).

He was very active and when I was a child he was out almost every night. He helped with the Youth Club. He accompanied Penclawdd Mixed Choir, run by Glanrhyd Austin, choirmaster. They were very good and won many competitions. My father was organist for the oratorio concerts at Tabernacle Chapel, which Gwynfor Jenkins conducted. Subsequently, after Gwynfor's death, my father conducted and Leighton played the organ.

I remember the oratorios well, as they were my first exposure to orchestras. Morgan Lloyd of Swansea, who used to teach violin around the schools, supplied an orchestra for the concerts. I remember playing an oboe concerto in the second half of the concert when I came down from the Academy, and my father conducted. The first half was an oratorio, and the second half, miscellaneous – soloists sung arias, etc. The orchestra was quite small, with a few strings, but it was good. It gave the concert a certain atmosphere along with the organ and the choir.

My father transcribed the whole of the Fauré Requiem into tonic sol-fa for the choir, which was quite a task. Earlier this century, the working class in Wales learnt tonic sol-fa and not old notation, which was the traditional way of writing music. I suppose my father's musical activities when I was young must have affected my life very much. At the moment (March 1999), I have been commissioned by the BBC Welsh Orchestra to write a piece of music for the millennium on the life of Saint David, (*Dewi Sant*) our Patron Saint. The text is based on some of his sayings – 'Be joyful,' 'Keep the Faith' and 'Do the Small Things'. It is a musical composition for the youth choirs of different parts of Wales. It's to be recorded in November of this year, in Saint David's Cathedral, in Saint David's, Pembrokeshire, and will be broadcast next year. The composition will be performed at a live concert at Saint David's Hall, Cardiff on 1 March 2000."

On Saturday, 4 March 2000, 'The Western Mail' newspaper reported:

> 'The world premier of *Dewi Sant* by Karl Jenkins on Wednesday was sensational and utterly appropriate for the Saint's Day. [. . .] This ambitious new work for large chorus and orchestra confirmed that he has an absolutely unmistakable and memorable sound-world and an innate ability to stir the soul.
>
> If you can recall the sheer theatricality of Bernstein's Mass and the helter-skelter joyousness of Janacek's Glagolitic Mass, you begin to glimpse *Dewi Sant*. Written in seven movements, to reflect the precept of *Dewi's* final sermon, this was an inspiring journey, punctuated by barnstorming brassy and drum-heavy crescendi and climaxes overlaying music of often sexy softness. The valedictory penultimate movement was particularly brilliant.
>
> Jenkins was wonderfully served by the NOW (National Orchestra of Wales) and the fine massed youth choir, all showing a clear affection for the man and the piece.'

The millennium saw the further commissions, 'The Armed Man: A Mass for Peace' performed at the Royal Albert Hall and 'Scenes of Wales' written for the National Youth Orchestra of Wales and premiered at the *Eisteddfod* (2000), held at Llanelli. Also in the year 2000, Adiemus IV, 'The Eternal Knot' was released.

Today, Penclawdd has a brass band of which it is rightly proud. In a sense, its roots were planted in 1873, when William Dennis, great-grandfather of the present band founder, Tony Small, formed a band in Loughor.

Brass bands started appearing in Britain in about the 1820s. The Great Industrial Exhibition of 1851, held in the Crystal Palace in Hyde Park, London,[4] attributed to their growth. Until then, wind groups consisted of a variety of instruments – bugles, cornopeans, ophicleides, French horns, baritones, trombones, clarinets flutes, etc. There was a need for uniformity and standardization. The Sax family of instruments exhibited at Crystal Palace by Adolph Sax of Paris, satisfied that need.

The 1860s and 1870s saw the formation of many new brass bands, and by 1895, there were over forty thousand of them in Britain.

Bands were formed from a variant of working class groups – in mills, collieries, villages, etc. The employees did not have the finances to buy their own instruments, and the latter were often supplied by their employers. Owning their own instruments was advantageous to the bands as it safeguarded against loss of instruments when members left. Soon the cloth-cap image hung over brass bands, and was to stay for nearly a hundred years.

By the 1920s, Robert Parkhouse had formed a band in Penclawdd. Harold Brenton, who played in the Second and Third Brass Bands, has vivid memories of the original band.

"I became aware of this band as a boy of seven years of age, having just moved house from Brig-y-Don, West End, to the house next door to Ratti's shop. The band rehearsed in the upstairs room of the church hall.

The only conductor I ever knew was a Mr. Herbert Suttcliff, who was a Lancashire man – the manager of Gowerton Gas Works. Living next door to the church hall, I attended almost every practice, when I used to plague the players to let me blow their instruments, and they always did. On hot Sundays in the summer, Mr. Suttcliff would take the band over to the old lead works to practise.

One of its members I particularly remember. He was Mydrim Howells, the band's Solo Cornet. Although self-taught, he was a very competent player indeed. He later had music lessons with William Hopkins and became competent in reading music. During the summer, Mydrim used to play out in his garden, and as he lived halfway up Llotrog, he could be heard down to the village.

William John (*Cetch*) Davies was the band's drummer. He was one of Penclawdd's many characters. It was a very large drum and Cetch was a short tubby man.

The band's greatest achievement was to qualify at the Area Band Contest to compete at Crystal Palace in 1928. The bands were graded then, as they are now, into three sections, A. B. C. and D. – A. being the top section. Penclawdd was in section C. Although they did not win any prize, it was a glory just getting there.

The instruments and uniforms – of blue serge and gold braid – were stored at the church hall, and when attending Sunday School, we boys never failed to go upstairs to have a blow on the instruments. I always chose the cornet, which was the instrument I played in the reformed band after the first band disbanded probably in the late 1920s.

I was thirteen years of age when, one day in 1934, Mr. Gilbert James, our headmaster in the Elementary School, came into our classroom to inform us that, anyone wishing to join the band, was to report to the church hall on a given date.

I think about twenty-five to thirty excited boys turned up that night, including John Jones and Ivor Ronald Fry. We were received by the committee members of the original band. They were James Hayes, Robert Parkhouse, and Ivor Fry – to name a few. We were lined up to be allocated with suitable instruments. Their method of doing this was to look at our lips. The boys with thin lips were given small instruments and the boys with thick lips were given big instruments. This was, of course, a heap of rubbish, but there was not a qualified musician amongst them.

Old members started returning to the band, so some progress was made. Our conductor at this stage was Mr. William Hopkins, a violinist. He remained our conductor for the lifetime of the band. We rehearsed at the pavilion on the recreation ground. Sadly, we never reached the competition stage. Our main function, apart from practising, was playing in local carnivals and at community singing on the Rec., on Sunday evenings, in the summer months. Nevertheless, I really enjoyed it.

Unfortunately, with the coming of the Second World War, the band collapsed again. But in 1973, a bright young man – Tony Small – with his professional musical qualifications, gave birth to yet another Penclawdd Brass Band: the best of course."

D. Anthony (Tony) Small belongs to a family of brass instrumentalists. "My great-grandfather, William Dennis, was the first to form a band in West Wales – in Loughor in 1873. It was exactly one hundred years before I formed Penclawdd Brass Band in 1973. My father was a self-taught trumpet player. He played in many dance bands and won medals for solo playing with the famous Roy Allan Band in the Melody Maker National Competitions, which were held in different venues, e.g. South Wales, Western-Super-Mare: the finals were held in Belle Vue, Manchester. I started playing the trumpet at about eleven years of age, when a pupil at Gowerton Boys' Grammar School. Before then, I used to have a little blow on my father's trumpet without him knowing, when he was at work.

He used to work with Mr. Cliff Ward, the very talented conductor of the Pontarddulais Brass Band. They had a chat in work one day and the next thing I knew I had joined the Band. I travelled there and back, by bus, as my father had no transport. It meant changing buses at Gowerton and often Gorseinon as well. Sometimes the buses waited for the connecting bus, and sometimes they didn't. I often walked home on a Sunday night from Gorseinon to Penclawdd if I missed the connection.

When I started with the Band, I was given an instrument. All I could play was the scale of C Major. I used to watch what valves the other players were pressing, and tried to follow suit. That's how I initially picked it up. The advantage of a brass band is that if you enter as a cornet player and learn to read music as such, you can play any instrument in the band – apart from the trombone – as they all use the same clef and fingering. I graduated as a third cornet player, from total beginner, to playing in the British Championship Finals in London – which we won – in six months, which was quite a remarkable achievement really.

Eventually, I had music lessons in Gowerton School where Mr. Vince Hanney (a clarinet player) was the woodwind and brass teacher. He played for the famous Hanney Band, based in Morriston, which was named after one of his predecessors. The Band competed in Paris where it won the World Championship at the end of the nineteenth century.

Whilst still at school, I became a member of the Roy Allan Band and learnt so much from my father, a truly talented jazz trumpet player. This was wonderful experience for me. I also played for the Morgan Lloyd Orchestra and the Glamorgan Youth Orchestra.

I studied at Cardiff University, where I was taught by Mr. Aaeron Trotman, Principal Trumpet of the BBC Welsh Symphony Orchestra, and conductor of the famous Cory Band from the Rhondda. One of my music lecturers was Professor Alun Hoddinott, the famous composer, who now lives in Three Crosses.

Maureen, Mezzo-Soprano, as 'Delilah'.

I then went to the Royal Academy of Music in London, for a postgraduate year. Whilst there, I went to hear Maureen Guy (from Penclawdd) perform Delilah, in the opera 'Samson and Delilah', for the Sadlers Wells Opera Company. The gentleman sitting next to me was an Australian businessman and an opera enthusiast, who had travelled the world. He told me that Maureen's Delilah was the finest that he had ever heard.

I lived in Wembley, and Maureen and her husband, singer John Mitchinson – a great tenor – lived in Collingdale, which was about one mile up the road. Maureen used to come down to fetch me every other Sunday, or so, and take me to their home for lunch. John was an excellent cook.

I remember when Maureen passed her driving test she asked me if I fancied a trip home for a few days but would I mind being a guinea pig, as she had not driven that distance before. She had a little Morris Thousand car and it was an eight-hour trip then – before the first Severn Bridge was built – through every traffic jam in every town. Maureen and John looked after me well. I'll never forget that.

London was brilliant. My friends wanted me to stay on as a professional trumpet player, but due to throat trouble after a bout of glandular fever I went home to be employed by Glamorgan Education Authority as a peripatetic music teacher with the intention of returning to London when my throat condition cleared up – but I stayed in Wales.

They say Welsh people do things in threes. My father was offered a job with Geraldo – a famous bandleader – in London, but my mother wouldn't move from Penclawdd, and I was also offered a professional music career – with the BBC Scottish Orchestra. My wife's father, Sid Matthews, had a very bad accident in the steelworks in Gowerton five weeks before we were to be married. He was badly crushed and his pelvis was shattered. It was touch and go whether he would live. Gillian and I had bought a house in Gowerton, and we both went there the night before our wedding to deposit some presents. Whilst there, I received a telegram inviting me to play with the BBC Scottish Orchestra as First Trumpeter. Gill said, 'You can't go there; we're getting married tomorrow.' Because of Gill's father's condition, I couldn't 'rock the boat', but if circumstances had been different, I might have considered it. My elder son, Gareth, the third generation, has done it. He plays professionally with the Hallé Orchestra[5] in Manchester – one of the very few instrumentalists to gain a position in a professional orchestra whilst still a college student. He has been full-time with the Hallé since 1993.

In 1848, a man called Charles Hallé formed the orchestra, and was its first conductor. He also formed the Northern School of Music, which later became the Royal Northern College of Music, so he did a lot of good work for music in the Manchester area.

My younger son, Ian, could have been a professional musician, but works for an American Investment Bank in London. He is an excellent cornet/trumpet player and occasionally comes home to play for the Penclawdd Band.

It's a hard life being a musician, especially it you have a family. It involves much travelling and very anti-social hours. When I returned from London, I taught two days a week at Gowerton Boys' Grammar School, one day at Gowerton Girls' Grammar School, and the other two days at Secondary Modern Schools at Penclawdd, Loughor and Pontarddulais.

In my spare time, I played in:

(a) Pantomime in the Grand Theatre, Swansea.
(b) The Dragon Hotel's resident band.
(c) The Morgan Lloyd Orchestra (later to become the City of Swansea Orchestra).
(d) The BBC Welsh Symphony Orchestra.
(e) Off stage trumpet work with the Welsh National Opera Company (in Bristol, Cardiff, Birmingham, or Swansea: wherever I was needed). That job involved travelling to the opera venue, performing my trumpet call at side stage, which might only last about thirty seconds to a minute, and then sometimes travelling back to the Dragon Hotel to play in a Dinner Dance getting home between 1.30 and 3.00 a.m.
(f) And other orchestras – e.g. London Festival Ballet, Bristol Sinfonia, and Gwent Chamber.

Basically, it was from necessity that I did all that extra work. We had little money then and only bought what we could pay for. We had no plastic cards, and bank loans were hard, if not impossible, to obtain.

In the summer of '64, I did a summer season with Arthur Askey for twelve weeks, as First Trumpeter. By the end of the season I had saved some money towards a deposit for a house and I bought an old second hand car. The money I had earned for one week's work was more than a month's salary as a teacher, and I thought, 'this is ridiculous,' but stuck it out for the love of a woman!

Apart from all my musical work in the evenings, I also played rugby for Penclawdd. How I managed it all I don't know. I suppose I burnt myself out.

Meanwhile, I had a good little band in Penclawdd Secondary Modern School. The children were there for three years in those days, leaving school at fifteen. I had started teaching there in the September of 1964 and it was January/February '65 before instruments arrived. We played at Christmas, End of Year concerts and Saint David's Day, etc. The children loved it, and many went to Ogmore-on-Sea on residential music courses. The experience 'fired them up' and they were 'full of it'. However, the 'big crunch' came when my older and better players left school. They had to hand the instruments back; fifteen and sixteen year olds were reduced to tears. It meant that they had to give up playing. The nearest band was in Pontarddulais, and parents did not wish their children to travel on their own by bus at night, which would have been the case, as very few parents had their own transport in those days.

It was suggested to me that I had a band class once a week in the Youth Club, which was held in the Secondary Modern School. The Club had excellent classes in many subjects then, as well as its social side. I ran classes there for a couple of years and the Band won its first ever competition in the Glamorgan County Eisteddfod held at Porthcawl, in 1972. The Band was now going strong, and we extended the classes to two nights a week.

The Band's Principal Euphonium, David Knight (sadly killed in a road accident in July 1973) lived in Cefn Golau[6] with his parents – his mother, Winnie, was the Band's secretary – and grandfather, Edwin Thorton. The latter was from Yorkshire, and a former euphonium player. Winnie – a very gifted artist – was a member of the Swansea Arts Society, and offered the Band an opportunity to play in public for the first time outside Penclawdd, providing carols at a Christmas exhibition of paintings in her house. It was a very successful event.

In May 1973, with the help of some enthusiastic parents, which incidentally included my father, Terry, I formed the Penclawdd Brass Band, which operated separately from the Youth Club. We had the first business meeting in the Workingmen's Club.

So the Band came from simple beginnings with no instruments and no music (they belonged to the school). We worked hard to raise money to buy instruments, performing concerts and Christmas Carols, etc. I used to drive carloads of youngsters to play carols in Bishopston, Gorseinon, Llanmorlais, etc. It was hard slog."

The Band went from strength to strength. On Friday, 24 April 1998, the Band presented its Twenty-fifth Anniversary Concert in the Brangwyn Hall, Swansea. A programme was issued, giving the history and all the relevant information of the Band.

Gareth Wardell, its president, contributed the following:

'The Band has become very much part of the culture of the area and provides the opportunity for the development of musicianship to the highest standard. Many of the Band's members have made considerable contributions to the world of music. Maintaining such high standards of achievement is a credit to the dedication of everyone involved, particularly to those who have been with the Band for all of the twenty-five years. In this regard, a special 'thank you' to Tony Small, Musical Director.

Any organisation depends on the people who give their time to make it a success. Certainly the musicians, officers, committee, patrons and supporters who have contributed to Penclawdd Brass Band over the twenty-five years, deserve our gratitude. We can all be justly proud of what the Band has achieved.'

Tony Small wrote: 'On a sad note, I must pay tribute to former individuals who rendered great service to the Band:

David Knight	Principal Euphonium, who was tragically killed at the age of sixteen, in 1973, just after the Band was formed.
Philip Stock	A very talented horn player, who also played for the county band and the NYBBW, who died of leukemia at the age of seventeen and a half years.'
My parents:	
Terry Small	Vice-chairman and Patronage Secretary.
Muriel Small	Always worked hard selling tickets and getting involved in bazaars and fundraising in general.'

Tony took the opportunity to thank his wife, Gillian, for her many years of support. "I must thank my dear wife, Gillian, for her tremendous support. I wish to thank her publicly for allowing me the endless hours I have devoted to the Band – for without her support the formation and development of the Band would just not have been possible. When the Band started, our two sons were mere babes in arms, but she had to endure regular evenings of my absence whilst raising the children, qualities which may well be a rarity these days."'

The programme listed the many achievements of the Band and its members, which has been updated (November 2000) by Tony.

'In 1983, the Band celebrated its tenth birthday in style by winning the prestigious title of National Champions of Great Britain (Second Section) at the Royal Albert Hall, London. This was followed in 1986, by becoming the only band from West Wales since the Second World War to win the Welsh Regional Title (Championship Section). The Band has qualified eleven times to compete in the National Finals, held annually in London.

Penclawdd Brass Band has undertaken overseas tours to Mannheim, Germany, in 1982 and Cork, Ireland, in 1990. They have produced two recordings to date; in 1984 an LP 'Sounds Welsh' and in 1991, an audio cassette – 'Aspects of Penclawdd'. The Band has often broadcast on Swansea Sound and on BBC Radio Wales. They have appeared on television on a number of occasions, the highlights were being featured in Welsh situation comedy, 'Bois y Bledren' in 1981, and more recently, last autumn, starring in 'Brass Cheek', an impressive documentary on the history of Welsh Brass Bands, which was transmitted on BBC 2.

The Band is proud of its link with the West Glamorgan Youth Brass Band, which was founded by Tony in 1974. Penclawdd Band has provided the County Band with a large number of players, some of whom have returned as tutors to the County Band.

It is worthy to note that during the County Youth Band's particularly successful period in the 1980s, two cornet players, Gurnos Rees and Gareth Small, distinguished themselves by winning the supreme award of Best Soloist in the National Finals held at the Royal Albert Hall – 'The Eric Bravington Memorial Award' – in 1984 and 1987 respectively.

To date, fifty-four of the Band's members have had the honour of being selected to play for the National Youth Brass Band of Wales, since its formation in 1982. Penclawdd's contribution has been staggering when one considers that a normal brass band consists of twenty-five players! To date, four members of Penclawdd Band have occupied the Principal Cornet Chair of the NYBBW.

The Band is also very proud that twenty-one members have been selected to play for the National Youth Orchestra of Wales. Three former members have played for the National Youth Brass Band of Great Britain, and a further four members for the National Youth Wind Band of Great Britain, and one for the National Youth Orchestra of Great Britain.

Several members have gone on to further education at colleges, universities and music conservatories and continue to take an active part in music making throughout the British Isles. One former member, trombone player, Keith Richards – brother of John – is playing with a band in Australia. Tony still has contact with him. "Whenever Keith visits Penclawdd, he never forgets his roots, and always looks us up during a rehearsal night – playing his trombone as well!" Over the years, many former members, who no longer play instruments, recall with fond memories, the wonderful times they experienced as playing members of Penclawdd Brass Band.

This exceptional record reflects the quality of opportunity and training young musicians receive at Penclawdd under the watchful guidance of its Musical Director, Tony Small, who continues to devote his energies to the cause of the Penclawdd Brass Band. The Band is extremely grateful to him for his time, effort and considerable skill and musicianship, and also to his patient wife, Gillian, for her fantastic support.

The Band is particularly proud of its fundraising support of many charities over the past twenty-five years, and especially its association with Barnardo's and Leukaemia Research (Wales).

Penclawdd Band is grateful for grant aid received from the Welsh Amateur Music Federation and the Arts Council of Wales Lottery Unit, which assisted in the purchase of a new set of instruments. The old instruments are being passed down to the Junior Band. The Band is particularly pleased that its very own protégé, Gareth Small, is able perform tonight, given his demanding schedule with the Hallé orchestra.'

Tony's personal musical achievements were honoured in the programme. 'Tony was a National Eisteddfod winner at Llanelli in 1962. He has gained wide experience as a freelance musician having performed with several London Orchestras, the Welsh National Opera Orchestra and TV and radio broadcasts with the BBC Welsh Symphony Orchestra. He has also performed with many other orchestras including much work in theatres, Variety shows, Jazz and Big Bands, etc.

Tony has gained considerable success as the conductor of Penclawdd Band, and also the West Glamorgan Youth Brass Band. He has conducted both in a total of twenty-one British Championship Finals in London. West Glamorgan Youth Band's achievements were pioneered by Tony when they were crowned British Champions on three occasions in 1984, 1986 and 1989. In addition, they were silver medallists in the 1990 European Championship held in Scotland. Tony took the County Youth Brass Band to Switzerland in 1978, Denmark/Sweden in 1985, and Australia/Singapore in 1988. He also took the Big Band to Germany in 1992.

In 1996, his work with young people was recognised when the High Sheriff of West Glamorgan presented him with an award, which reads:

> 'Under his leadership and inspiration tremendous opportunities are available for any young person in Penclawdd and the surrounding areas of West Swansea to realize their own self worth and ability through music. The award recognizes his dedication and outstanding work, and also the appreciation of the residents and people of the High Sheriff's Bailiwick for activity and contribution in enhancing the life of the community.'

Tony was one of four founders of the National Youth Brass Band of Wales in 1981 and was Principal Advisory/Music Teacher for West Glamorgan, Musical Director of the County Brass Band for eighteen years, as well as Musical Director of the County Big Band for eleven years. He is an examiner for the Guildhall School of Music, London, a Mentor Teacher for the Associated Board of Music, and has successfully taught brass in this area for thirty-six years.

Following a period of rebuilding after several players had moved away to universities, music colleges and new employment, Penclawdd Band has had a good year in 2000. It won second prize at Ebbw Vale in May, and improved upon this in September with an excellent win at Ammanford, where its accomplished Principal Euphonium player Alun Evans won the Best Soloist prize (the Vincent Richards Memorial Cup). Alun is a wonderful role model for aspiring young players, and was a very successful competitor in his younger days, winning the National Eisteddfod nine times, the Welsh Championship three times, and being placed third in the British Solo Championships – an outstanding series of results. The Band finished the competitive season at Treorchy in November by being proclaimed runners-up of the First Section and was presented with a handsome cup.

Bands are promoted or relegated on the strength of their competition results over the previous two seasons, and since Penclawdd Band head the First Section table for 1999 and 2000, they are now promoted back to the Championship Section having been three years in the First Section. The Band had been in the Championship Section for fourteen consecutive years prior to this – a feat unsurpassed by any other West Wales Band. The brass band system has five sections and the Championship Section in Wales is comprised of the nine best bands.

Further success was gained at the Royal National Eisteddfod of Wales held in Llanelli in August, when a group of ten instrumentalists, conducted by Tony Small, won the Open Instrumental Ensemble Competition. Also, talented young trumpet player, Rhydian Griffiths, won the Brass Instrument Solo for the 'under nineteen years' and was selected to perform in the Blue Ribbon Instrumental Play-Off Competition, which was won by a harpist.'

Tony's busy schedule is against his composing. "I dabble with composition, but have never been taught. I would love to do more if I had the time. The Band has played some of my arrangements – as has the Hallé Brass Ensemble."

In Penclawdd, as in all villages, strong friendships were formed in childhood. Through circumstances in later life – higher education, employment, etc. – many 'lost touch' with their peers. Such was the friendship of Tony Small and Karl Jenkins. Fortunately, through their mutual work in music, they have regained contact and rekindled the friendship. In the Band's Twenty-fifth Anniversary Programme, Tony thanked Karl for his contribution to the concert. 'I am delighted that my good friend, Karl Jenkins, a native of Penclawdd, and now a highly successful international composer, has been able to find the time in his extremely busy schedule, to compose for the Band a most charming piece of music, to commemorate our Twenty-fifth Anniversary Celebrations. On behalf of the Band and myself, thank

Penclawdd Brass Band in front of Brangwyn Hall, Swansea.
The Welsh Regional Championships 2000/Pencampwriaethau Rhanbarthol Cymru.
Front Row, left to right: Paul Lewis, Anthony Salter, Alun Evans, Stuart Davies,
Tony Small (Musical Director), Alex Salter, Rachel Thomas, Richard Phillips, Colin Jenkins.
Kneeling in front: Liam Ascough.
2nd Row, left to right: David Danford, Matthew Gibbs, Karen Harry, Anthony Oates,
Steven Lloyd, John Richards, Adam George, Gareth Griffiths, Graig Mathewson.
3rd Row, left to right: Ryan Matthews, Gale Lewis, Rhydian Griffiths,
Colette Stanford, Dawn Devonald.
4th Row, left to right: Lewis Gibbs, David Hopkins, Owain Harries, Gurnos Rees, Emrys Hopkins.

you very much Karl for your gift and kind gesture – we hope you will enjoy our performance!'

Although not peers, Tony and Mark Thomas are also friendly through their work. Mark wrote a piece of music entitled, 'Salthouse Point', for the Band's Twenty-first Anniversary Concert at the Brangwyn Hall. He invited the Penclawdd Band to perform – with several Welsh stars – his special arrangement of the Welsh Anthem on S4C, at the stroke of midnight, to herald in the year 2000.

Mark Thomas has been hailed as one of Britain's most diverse and exciting composers. He spent his preschool years listening to the village gossip in Penclawdd post office, where his parents, Ambrose and Olive Thomas, were postmaster and postmistress.

Mark Thomas.

Olive is sensitive to her younger son's early love of music. "Mark was interested in music from a very young age. One day I started to worry as he had been away from the house for a long time. He eventually returned in the evening. I was naturally relieved, but also annoyed. The Salvation Army used to come to the village and play standing opposite the cinema. Mark and his friend, Paul Davies, had listened to the Band and then followed them to Blue Anchor and Three Crosses and had come home via the *Cwm*.

Mark told me of how they had found an old chapel, I don't know where, and inside an organ, which was still in working condition. Mark had played the organ. They were all alone but totally unafraid. When they arrived home, they were not in the least aware that they had done anything wrong and had caused me all that worry."

Mark recalls his early interest in music. "We lived in the back of the premises that housed the post office in Sea View. From my house, I could hear the Gower Concert Orchestra practising in the Small Hall (Memorial Hall). When I was about seven years of age, I persuaded my father to take me to hear the orchestra. I had a violin but I could hardly play it." The orchestra members were old age pensioners of the village, including brothers Bryn and Evan Evans. Ambrose eventually persuaded the members to allow his son to play in their orchestra.

When Mark became a pupil at Penclawdd Junior School, he told his parents of his intense desire to be in Standard Two. Olive recalls, "Mark couldn't wait to go to Gwen Jenkins' class. Ambrose and I couldn't understand why, until he went there: Morgan Lloyd gave her pupils violin lessons on Wednesday afternoons."

In time, Mark felt that school violin lessons did not suffice, and persuaded his parents to arrange for him to have private tuition. "We organized lessons for him with Morgan Lloyd, in his home on Gower Road, Uplands. It was very convenient as the Penclawdd bus passed Gower Road on its way to Swansea. Mark also had theory lessons with Morgan Lloyd's wife, Dilys. Mark asked if he could have a new violin if he passed the Grade One, music examination. We agreed, never thinking he would. But he passed with honours and so he had his new violin.

While a pupil at Gowerton Grammar School, Mark attend the musical courses – three a year – at Ogmore. Tony Small was one of his tutors. At the end of each week's course, the pupils performed a concert on the Friday night. We went to all of them. They were marvellous.

When about twelve, he joined the National Youth Orchestra of Wales. The summer courses at Ogmore were followed immediately by the NYOW's courses held in North and South Wales alternatively. Mark used to come home from Ogmore, only to collect a suitcase of clean clothes and then go straight to the NYOW courses. One year he didn't even have time to come home between courses, so we took his clean clothes to Ogmore and collected his dirty ones. When the courses were in South Wales – Swansea, Carmarthen, Ammanford – we used to attend all the concerts, but North Wales was too far for us to travel. When in Swansea, the members of the orchestra were housed in the old Swansea Teachers' Training College in Townhill. At the end of each course, the orchestra held a concert in the Brangwyn Hall.

The games' teacher at Gowerton School wanted Mark to play rugby, but although he loved the game, he cared for his violin playing more. He told the teacher that he would only play if he could hold his arm behind his back."

Mark studied music at Cardiff University. Alun Hodinott was professor of music there at the time. Mark was taught composition by Dr. David Wynne – a contemporary of Ralph Vaughan Williams – whom he greatly admired and respected. He obtained a B.Mus.Hons degree and went to London as a freelance violinist. Mark recalls the start of his professional career. "In 1980, I auditioned for Co-Leader in the orchestra for Sadlers Wells Royal Ballet, sometimes playing at the Royal Opera House, Covent Garden. I met Mary while on tour in Plymouth. We married and have been together ever since. There was much touring involved in the job – it being a touring company – which wasn't very pleasant for us being newly married. In a sense, it was like an apprenticeship job. I started looking for work in London. The Ballet Company went on tour to the Far East, but didn't take the orchestra with them, and so, I was faced with about two months out of work. Mary suggested that I go freelance, which I did – for the London Symphony Orchestra, the Royal Philharmonic Orchestra, among others.

Within a few weeks, I found myself playing on James Bond films – 'A View to a Kill', 'Living Daylights', and 'Licence to Kill' and the films 'Batman', 'Willow', and 'Highlander'. It was there that I got a flavour for film music. I met the composers, John Barry and Jerry Goldsmith – my favourite. The latter did 'Basic Instinct', and more recently, 'The Mummy'. He's phenomenal. He's in his sixties but he's still doing them. It was a wonderful for me to have first-hand film experience. The idea of composing for films and television really appealed to me. I became a member of the original orchestra that accompanied the first performances of Andrew Lloyd Webber's musical, 'Phantom of the Opera'. A few years ago, we went to the musical as a birthday treat for our daughter Rosanna. I took the children to see the orchestra. It was remarkable that over fifty per cent of the members were still there, fourteen years on! I only stayed six months. It wasn't possible for me to stop playing in the orchestra and be a composer overnight. There had to be a 'dove tailing' period. I had been composing for a long time. When our elder daughter, Imogen, was a baby, I made use of the sleepless nights by composing. But I then started writing film music professionally for Welsh television – HTV, S4C – and some American companies.

I composed music for Penclawdd Brass Band's Twenty-first Anniversary Celebrations in 1994. During The Year of Literature held in Swansea in 1995, I was commissioned to compose a musical score for Dylan Thomas' 'Return Journey'. The BBC Welsh Symphony Orchestra performed the piece in the Brangwyn Hall and at an open-air concert in Singleton Park. The American Ex-President, Jimmy Carter – a great fan of Dylan Thomas – attended the concert, and we entertained him during his stay. I composed and conducted music for Gowerton Grammar School's Centenary Celebration (1997).

When I worked for the Royal Shakespeare Company in Stratford – the first-ever Welsh composer to compose for the RSC – I was provided with a cottage for me, Mary, and our children, Imogen, Rosanna and Tristam. We spent quite some time there. In fact, we felt so at home, that when Tristam saw our cottage on the television news featuring flooding in the Midlands, he said, 'Look Dad. There's our cottage,' as if we owned it. We all enjoyed our stay there. It was great: a fantastic experience. My work was to score 'Two Gentlemen of Verona', directed by Edward Hall, son of Sir Peter Hall. I was asked to write new music for the old song of Shakespeare's words, 'Who is Sylvia? What is she'? It was quite a daunting experience.

Working in the theatre is very different from working on films. To me, the former is a much slower process, as the score has to come together while the play is being rehearsed. When I score a film, I usually come 'on board' after the film is completed; when I'm given the 'fine cut'. It is in film and drama-composing that I am most at home – working to pictures."

Mark's work for film and television is prolific. His scores for television include, National Lottery (HTV)', 'Southern Eye', 'South of Westminster', 'Raging Planet, the Wonders of Weather', 'The Mysteries of Magic', 'A Mind to Kill', 'The Marshal', 'Night of the Hunter', 'The Jazz Detective' – an entire score using jazz musicians – 'Wild Justice', 'Old Enemies', and 'Moses, the Animated Old Testament'. He was asked by Sally Burton to compose music for the film 'A Christmas Story' for which he received a BAFTA Nomination. Richard Burton's diaries had been used to write a film on his boyhood, which was televised in both English and Welsh.

Mark encounters many coincidences in life. "In 1995, I was working in the film editing, cutting room, 'Soho Images', in Dean Street, Soho. Most of television editing is done in that area. De Lane Lea is another editing-room there. I was working on the lovely film, 'Daisies in September' – a Hollywood film shot in this country (HTV/Hallmark) – starring Jean Symonds and Joss Ackland. Work had stopped through a technical hitch, and I decided to have lunch in the famous Indian restaurant, the Red Fort, before returning home to Swansea where we then lived. I saw Sir Peter Hall through the window – a tall man of regal stature and easily recognizable. I have a great admiration for him. He's the famous theatre director of the Royal Shakespeare Company – which he started in the 1960s. I thought nothing of it at the time as one often sees famous people in Dean Street. However, when I arrived home, Mary greeted me in a state of high excitement. It transpired that Sir Peter Hall's company had phoned my home at what must have been the very time that I had seen Sir Peter Hall in Dean Street. He had heard my work and wanted me to pitch for the music of a film starring Antonio Banderas. As it transpired, I did not get the job, but about a year later, worked for him in 'The Final Passage', a drama series for Channel 4. It was shot in the West Indies, about a West Indian family in the '50s being brought to Britain to work. It was my first taste of working for a famous director. He's phenomenal. I work a lot now for his son, Christopher Hall – a television and film producer. I was pleased to work again with Sir Peter Hall scoring Shaw's 'Man and Superman' – with Judi Dench, Ralph Fiennes, Paul Merton and Juliet Stevenson – for Radio 3, to commemorate fifty years of drams on Radio 3 and also last Christmas Day (1999), scoring 'Rumours of Angels', starring Thora Hird. In 1999, I wrote the score for the television series 'Jack of Hearts', and I composed, orchestrated, and conducted, the music for the period BBC television series 'The Aristocrats' set, and filmed mostly, in Ireland. It was a long series and a big job."

Mark's film scores include, 'One Full Moon' (BAFTA Nomination 1994), 'The Making of Maps' (BAFTA nomination and HUGO Award 1997), 'Chameleon', and 'The Sea Change'. 'Twin Town' saw Mark receive an Ivor Novell Nomination, and win a Bafta *Cymru* (Wales) 1997 award, for best original score. It was filmed in Swansea, featured Pontarddulais Male Voice Choir and was directed by Kevin Allen, now living in Hollywood, but originally from Gorseinon.

In 1998, Mark experienced another coincidence. "I was asked to score the film 'Up 'n' Under' by the distributor, as he knew my work. It had been written by the play write, John Godber, who had written many well-known plays such as 'Bouncer'. Godber had promised the actor, Brian Glover, that he would produce his first feature-film for him. (Glover had been in the original cast of the play in the West End). Sadly, Glover died after the filming of 'Up 'n' Under' finished. The film was a big success, and was number two in the Top Ten British film charts for three months.

After having written some music for the film, I met the producer in John Godber's house in Hull. They listened to my tape, said they liked it very much, and we discussed it further. Suddenly, John Godber turned to me and said, 'Do you like rugby?' As we were so involved in the music, the question was completely unexpected. I told him that I had always followed rugby, and, as a student, had gone to Cardiff Arms Park, but I was not a great sports' enthusiast. But his question immediately reminded me of the following story, which I told him there and then. 'When I walked to the Junior School in Penclawdd, I used to pass a man who was always leaning over his garden gate. I often stopped to talk to him. He told me of a rugby player who had lived in Tabernacle Terrace. He said, 'He used to kick a ball in the front garden, 'up and under' over the house, then run through the house dodging the furniture, and catch the ball in the back garden before it reached the ground.' The rugby player was Haydn Tanner and the man, his uncle, I think. Haydn, and his cousin, Willie Davies were as famous in their day as are Gareth Edwards and Barry John, etc. today. That was the way Haydn Tanner used to train, and it became a legend. John Godber's asking me the question was a strange experience: as if it was meant to be. Sometimes fate lends a hand.

I went to Hollywood to compose music for the Warner Bothers film 'The Big Tease' and worked again with its director, Kevin Allen. When we worked together on 'Twin Town', he said he would take me to Hollywood one day. I thought he was joking at the time. The film starred Craig Ferguson, Francis Fisher and David Hasselhof. It's a very funny film about a gay Scottish Hairdresser. I also scored for the Warner Brothers film 'Je M'Appelle Crawford', again directed by Kevin Allen. I wrote the score for Sara Sugarman's film, 'Mad Cows', starring Joanna Lumley, Anna Friel and Prunella Scales, with a cameo appearance by Mohammed Al Fayed. I like Hollywood as in a sense it is like Penclawdd and Swansea. It is not as large as most people think, and one can always meet someone Welsh there. I have an agent in Britain and one in Hollywood.

I rearranged the music of the Welsh National Anthem for the Millenium Celebration, which was recorded on S4C, starring Ioan Gruffudd, Max Boyce, Bryn Terfyl, Bonnie Tyler and Michael Ball.

This year (2000) I have scored 'Merlin the Return' starring Rick Mayall and Patrick Bergin. My latest finished work is the score for the film 'The Testimony of Taliesin Jones' – a Hollywood film with a Welsh subject, shot in Wales with American money. It's a spiritual film with scenes of high emotion. It stars the young Welsh actors Griff Rhys Jones, Jonathan Price, and Mathew Rhys. It also stars the Irish actor, Ian Bannen. Sadly, it was his last film, as he was killed in a car crash soon afterwards. I'm currently working on 'Hooded Angels' – a Western – with Amanda Donaghue, my fourth feature film this year.

I've worked with many famous names – Ennio Morricone, Alan Silvesta, James Horner, Paul McCartney, Queen, Johnny Dankworth, Kate Bush, Tony Bennett, Andre Previn, and John Williams. I adjudicated music competitions with the famous Welsh composer, and friend of Dylan Thomas, Daniel Jones. I find that most of the people I meet in my job are very charismatic, as was Morgan Lloyd, and help to 'fire one up'.

It's a good life. I'm my own boss most of the time, and I can kind of choose when I work, but it does get hard when there is a deadline to be met. Some films – usually of ninety minutes – have virtually continuous music, so that's a lot of music, which has to be composed in six weeks to two months. However, some television programmes have little music, such as comedy programmes that have about thirty seconds of signature tune, small bits of incidental music throughout, and about one and a half minutes at the end. Adverts, which I do a lot of, are even shorter. I compose – in my studio – using modern technology, which is continually being updated, but for the sound track of the films, etc., I favour full orchestra. When my sketched-out score is approved by the directors and producers, I orchestrate the music by preparing all the different parts for the orchestra. It is at this point that Mary becomes involved. She hires the studios and the orchestras for me."

Mark's children have inherited his musical talent. All have won musical scholarships to Millfield School, Rosanna having obtained the newly intro-duced Choral Scholarship (Music scholarship specializing in singing).

Mark and his family moved from Sketty, Swansea, to live in Somerset

– a base easily accessible to his work in London and conveniently situated for visiting directors and producers.

And so, at the turn of the twenty-first century, Penclawdd continues to produce young musicians. Gareth Small, Assistant Principal Trumpet with the famous Hallé Orchestra, was influenced by his father, as was his father before him.

"When I was a pupil at Penclawdd Infant School, an open-air pageant was held to commemorate the Queen's Silver Jubilee in 1977. Months before, the headteacher asked in assembly one morning if anyone played a musical instrument. I put my hand up and said I played the trumpet. Well, I had been allowed to 'have a go' at blowing my father's trumpet when he practised at home! I was told I could perform at the pageant, so my father had to teach me to play 'God Save the Queen'. This I managed to do and

Gareth Small.

344

duly performed at the pageant dressed as a beefeater. I was only six years old then and I have been playing the trumpet ever since. My brother, Ian, and myself were taught to play by my father, Tony, and we often played duets in Bethel Chapel and in school concerts.

We both started attending Penclawdd Brass Band rehearsals when I was nine and Ian was eight years old. Within a few months we played in our first band competition, which was at the Royal National Eisteddfod of Wales held in Gowerton in 1980. We were so excited when we won first prize. A 'normal' week for us consisted of Penclawdd Band rehearsals on Tuesday and Thursday evenings, West Glamorgan Youth Brass Band rehearsals on Saturday mornings and from the age of eleven, West Glamorgan Youth Orchestra rehearsals on Friday nights. Every school holiday was filled with residential music courses in West Glamorgan, and each summer, further courses with the National Youth Brass Band of Wales and the National Youth Orchestra of Wales, some featuring tours to Europe, the USA and Australia.

Looking back, these times were brilliant – both musically and socially. Playing the trumpet became more of a career than a hobby. I joined the Hallé Orchestra following four years of study at the Royal Academy of Music in London.

The two questions I am asked the most are:

1. 'What made you want to play the trumpet?' Well, its definitely in the genes, because my grandfather, Terry, played the trumpet in local dance bands, and my father was greatly influenced by him, playing alongside him in Roy Allan's Dance Band when still a schoolboy. My father also studied at the Royal Academy of Music and still plays the trumpet with various orchestras. They both played the trumpet to a very high standard, so being brought up in this environment was very helpful to me.

2. 'It must be great playing for the Hallé Orchestra, so what's your day job?' Fortunately for me, it's a full-time, salaried position. The Hallé Orchestra plays to audiences all over the country, and makes extensive tours throughout the world. It is a fantastic way of earning a living, doing something I've always loved. I owe it all to the tremendous support I've received from my parents, and the grounding I received from Penclawdd Brass Band and West Glamorgan Youth Music. My father, being Musical Director of Penclawdd Brass Band and West Glamorgan County Youth Bands, was a wonderful mentor, and had a great influence on my development."

NOTES

1. *South Wales Evening Post* newspaper, Saturday, 28 September 1935.
2. Foreword by Cliff Jones, Centenary President of the Welsh Rugby Union, to the booklet published on the centenary of Penclawdd Rugby Club.
3. *Chambers Encyclopedia, Volume 9*, p. 633.
4. A giant glass-and-iron exhibition hall (designed by Sir Joseph Paxton) in Hyde Park, London, that housed the Great Exhibition of 1851. The structure was taken down and rebuilt (1852-54) at Sydenham Hill, at which site it survived until 1936. In 1849, Prince Albert, husband of Queen Victoria and president of the Royal Society of Arts, conceived the idea of inviting exhibitors from all civilized nations to participate in an exposition. Plans were developed, and the necessary funds speedily raised, with Queen Victoria heading the list of subscribers. The exhibition opened in the Crystal Palace on May 1, 1851. [. . .] For a number of years, the Crystal Palace was the site of show, exhibitions, concerts, football matches, and other entertainments. On the night of November 30 – December 1 1936, it was virtually destroyed by fire; the towers that survived were finally demolished in 1941 because they were deemed a dangerous landmark for incoming German Bombers. *Encyclopedia Britannica*, p. 770.
5. Charles Hallé founded his orchestra in Manchester in 1848, making The Hallé the oldest professional orchestra in the country. From the very first concert, The Hallé wanted as many people as possible 'from every type, class and background' to be able to hear the great music of the time. He wanted the prices to be affordable, and the atmosphere to be relaxed and informal. His aim was to present the best conductors and soloists from around the world playing the great classical and romantic master-pieces. But from the outset, The Hallé has also been associated with innovation, championing new performers and composers, often giving local and national premieres to works that have now fond their way into the mainstream repertoire. www.hallé.co.uk
6. Cefn Golau: Originally known as 'Y Plas', home of D. D. Williams, owner of Caereithin and Wernbwll Collieries.

11

Hiraeth

The Welsh word *hiraeth* has no real English equivalent, but roughly translated means longing. The Welshman is bound to *Cymru* (Wales) by bands of unbreakable loyalty as expressed in the Welsh National Anthem:

> *Gwlad, gwlad, pleidiol wyf i'm gwlad;*
> *Tra môr yn fur i'r bur hoff bau,*
> *O bydded i'r hen iaith barhau.*
>
> Ieuan ap Iago – Evan James (1809-1878)

One of the more poignant translations has enjoyed considerable popularity among the Anglo-Welsh:

> Wales, Wales, my mother's sweet home is in Wales:
> Till death be pass'd, my love shall last,
> My longing, my *hiraeth* for Wales.
>
> Translated by Eben Fardd and Owain Alaw

Hiraeth is the emotion of separation; separation from the homeland – Wales. The distance is irrelevant:

> 'To live in Wales [. . .] Is to be told
> of the incredible agony
> of an exile
> that can be at most
> a days travel away.'[1]

Wynford Vaughan Thomas (1908-1987) author and broadcaster, described the intensity of the feeling in his poem *Hiraeth in N.W.3:*

> 'The sight of the English is getting me down.
> Fly westward, my heart, from this festering town
> On the Wings of a Dove – and a First Class Return –
> To the front room of 'Cartref' at Ynys-y-Wern.

347

Swift through the dark flies the 5.49,
Past Slough and past Didcot and derelict mine,
Past pubs and Lucanias and adverts for ales
Till the back-sides of chapels cry 'Welcome to Wales.'[2]

Hiraeth can attack suddenly and acutely as Dylan Thomas (1914-1953) related in a broadcast on 23 June 1949:

> 'Before I came back to live in Wales, a very little time ago, I was travelling on a morning train from Oxford to London when, suddenly, the desire to live neither in Oxford nor in London, or to travel between them came very near to knocking me down, which would not be difficult. [. . .] There, all about me, chastely dropping, with gloved and mincing, just-so finger, saccharine tablets into their cups of stewed Thameswater, or poising their cigarette-holders like blowpipes, or daintily raising, the little finger crooked, a currant bun to the snapping flash of their long, strong teeth, tall and terrible women neighed: women inaccessible as goat crags. [. . .] There, all about me, long thin accents with yellow waist-coats and carefully windswept hair, one lock over the eye, bleated and fluted. In a drawl of corduroy at the tea-urn, vowels were plucked and trussed. [. . .] And then and there, as I watched them all, desire raised its little fist.
> I did not want to be in England, now that they were there.
> I did not want to be in England, whether they were there or not.
> I wanted to be in Wales.'[3]

Over the centuries, many Welshmen have been exiled from their native land. They were driven out by the Romans, the Saxons, and the Normans in the Middle Ages. In more recent years however, the prime motivation to leave Wales has been ambition for material success. The latter has been the reason for many inhabitants of Penclawdd distancing themselves from their village, be it for a period of time or forever. Through their self-inflicted exile, they have experienced a *hiraeth* for Wales, but even stronger, a *hiraeth* for Penclawdd and its people.

In 1870, William F. Thomas (carpenter), brother of Benjamin Thomas (*Ben-y-Saer*) emigrated from Penclawdd, with his wife, Francis Hooper, and their two-year-old daughter, Annie. William was twenty-six years of age, and his wife, five years his junior. They settled in Niles, Trumbull, Ohio.

William F. Thomas.

Francis bore another daughter, Helena (Lena) in 1873, and a son, William, in 1874.

William became an extremely successful building contractor and businessman, building and owning many properties that he leased out to various businesses, such as The Great Atlantic and Pacific Tea Co. William and his family lived in a large, imposing house, situated in spacious grounds at 415 Robbins Avenue. He owned a car, which, unlike Penclawdd, was the norm in America at the time. He became a pillar of society in Niles, and enjoyed serving in the office of mayor.

It seems the family visited Wales in the early 1880s, as their younger son, Frank Hooper, was born in the country on 15 February 1884.

In November 1893, their daughter, Annie, died at the age of twenty- five.

Sixteen years later, William and Francis lost another of their children. On 12 August 1910, Frank was admitted into hospital to have an operation. It seemed to have been a success and Frank was recovering, but on the nineteenth of the month, he died unexpectedly of heart failure. On 22 September of that year, William wrote a heart-rending letter to his brother, Ben:

Left to right: William F. Thomas, Francis Hooper Thomas, Lena Thomas,
outside 415 Robbins Avenue, Niles, Ohio.

'It has been very hard on us to lose our dear boy. Such a fine bright young man as he was with such good promising prospects ahead of him and to be taken away so sudden in his young manhood. [. . .] We had, as usual, called up the hospital that morning. The nurse said Frank was fine so I felt he was on the road to recovery and was planning a trip with him to the Old Country as soon as he would be able to travel. But that was not to be, for in just six hours he had started on that great long journey from whence no traveller ever returns. Yes, my dear boy had passed away from us forever. [. . .] His was the largest funeral ever seen here. There were over fifty floral pieces sent here from distant cities seventy-five miles away – Pittsburgh, Cleveland, Youngstown, Warren and Alliance, etc. They were all very beautiful but, oh! if we could only have kept our dear boy it would be worth to us more than all that could be sent from all the wealth of the country.'

Although it seems that William had no intention of returning to his native village to live, he never lost his love of Penclawdd and his relatives there. He wrote constantly to them of his family news in Ohio, but the largest percentage of his letters consisted of enquiries of life in the village. In his letter to his brother on 6 October 1910, William made reference to the new Bethel and Tabernacle Chapels:

'I am very glad to hear that your chapel (Bethel) has been completed. How do you like it? Is it as good as you expected? Do the people like it? I suppose you had a great day there at the dedication. Mag (his niece) sent me a picture of it the other day but she thought it was not a very good one. Will be glad to get another if it is good.

How are they getting along with the lower chapel (Tabernacle)? Did they spoil that when they changed the plans? I was sorry when I heard that the Penclawdd boys failed to secure that job. Wish I had been there to help them.

The weather here has been very dry and warm. Scarcely any rain for five or six months until now when we have had two or three days' rain. The crops through this section suffered greatly.'

On 20 March 1913, William informed Ben of his wife's death:

'I am very sorry to have to inform you of the death of poor Fanny (Francis Hooper) which took place on the tenth of this month after just one week's illness. [. . .] The doctor pronounced it tonsillitis but whatever it was it seems to have gone through her whole system and caused blood poisoning. [. . .] I was taken very ill myself suddenly on the fourth day of her sickness and had to be removed to Lena's house (535 Robbins Avenue) under the care of a nurse so that I was kept informed as to Fanny's condition until after she passed away nor was I allowed to see her after.'

Yet another tragedy was to befall William when, in October 1916, his remaining son, William died.

In the 1911 National Eisteddfod held at Carmarthen, G. E. Gordon donated one of his maps of the South Wales coalfield, issued in 1905, as a prize to the winner of the Male Tenor Vocalist Competition. The successful candidate was G. Edgar Thomas, son of *Ben-y-Saer*. On the strength of his success, Edgar was invited to join his uncle, William, in America in the hope of furthering his singing career. Edgar was born the same year as William's son, Frank.

Edgar sailed to America on the HMS Arabic. While on board, he sent a postcard to his sister Mag, and his brother-in-law, William Henry Harris (Will). One side of the card depicted the HMS Arabic embroidered in silk. On the other side Edgar wrote:

'Enjoying ourselves fine so far. Don't worry. I'm writing this in cabin. 9 o'clock. We are four in our cabin. Breakfast at 7. Dinner at 11.30.

G. Edgar Thomas.

Tea 4. We are doing alright with Stewart. We are having supper as well. No one else. Trusting you are quite well. Your loving bros. Edg.'

Soon after his arrival in Niles, Edgar stayed in the home of his cousin, Helena (daughter of William) and her husband, William Taylor, at 535 Robbins Avenue. He sung at the local chapels where he was well received, as the articles in the local papers that he sent home to his family reported:

'A special musical program was enjoyed by a large congregation at the Methodist Church on Sunday night. G. Edgar Thomas, a noted singer from Penclawdd, South Wales, who helped the male chorus win the grand prize at the Pittsburgh Eisteddfod, and who for several days had been the guest of his uncle, W. F. Thomas, at the home of Mr. and Mrs. Will Taylor, sang several numbers.

His voice is strong, mellow and dramatic and is declared by those who have heard him equal to that of the famous Evan Williams. [. . .] The choir of the church sang an anthem that was much appreciated. Following the concert, Mr. and Mrs. Taylor gave an informal reception for Mr. Thomas at their home in Robbins Avenue during which the Methodist Choir again had the pleasure of hearing him sing.'

'Mrs. William B. Taylor and Mrs. George Wheeler entertained yesterday afternoon at the home of Mrs. Taylor at an informal musical, in honour of Prof. G. Edgar Thomas, who is their guest.

On the program were; Prof. Thomas, Miss Vera Morgan of Youngstown, Miss Totterdale, Mr. C. E. Gaither and Miss Martha Dane. [. . .] The program was a delightful one. Guests from out of the city were: Miss Vera Morgan, Mrs. Creahan of Youngstown, Mrs. W. H. Daugherty, Pittsburgh, Mrs. J. E. France, Lamona, Pa. and Mrs. A. G. Bohenkamp, Cincinnati.

In the receiving line were: W. F. Thomas, Prof. Thomas, Mrs. Taylor and Frs. Wheeler.'

'At an evening service in St. Luke's Episcopal Church yesterday evening Rev. L. P. McDonald preached an eloquent and instructive sermon on 'The Trial of Baalam.' and Prof. J. Edgar Thomas sang the beautiful difficult composition of Stephen Adams, 'Babylon' as an offertory number. This composition is considered Mr. Adams' masterpiece and it was sung with much feeling and pathos by Mr. Thomas, whose excellent voice was particularly suited to the number. A large congregation were in attendance at the services.'

After the outbreak of the First World War, Edgar wrote to Mag and Will on 20 September 1914. He was by now living at 512 Rebecca Avenue, Wilkinsburg, Pennsylvania, and employed in the Westinghouse Electric and Manufacturing Company:

'Longing to see you all but I don't know when though. I suppose I had better wait until this dreadful war is over. Don't worry about me. I feel fine. Well, what do you think of this Mag? What is going to become of it? We don't much talk about it in this part. It seems to be quiet around here about the war but everybody seems to be anxious to get the evening papers just to see how things are getting along, but I don't know whether we get the truth or no. There seems to be a lot of difference in these papers here and ours back home. I thank you very much Will for your kindness in sending me those papers. They are very acceptable. I'm not the only one that's reading them as they are passed from one to the other in this town. I send them on to Uncle in Niles. [. . .] I'm still holding the same position at the Westinghouse. Boss, as you have heard I suppose, but for how long I don't know. It looks pretty bad around here. There's a good many men been stopped in our shops and there is no sign of them coming back. They have no orders. This war has affected them. I hope it won't last very long.

Let me know Will what you think of the war. Do you think the

Allies will win? That's the feeling of most of them in this part but it looks rather dark sometimes. They don't seem to be willing that the British Army is so slow and allowing the Germans to do so much damage to their army.

Some day I might tour this country before I come back if all goes well. Don't trouble about me. I feel quite at home here and have very nice friends, but of course, naturally, it's not as good as home.
Love to both of you from your loving Bros. Edg.
Xxxx thousands.'

Edgar continued to assure his family of his good health and happiness in America in a letter to Mag and Will dated 15 January:

'I'm as happy as the day and feeling fine, thank God. Trusting that you both are of the same feeling. I'm sorry I don't write often but I have to write to so many and I haven't much time to spare. I believe the hours are shorter here than with you.

This is the 15th January, the commencement of another year. Trusting that this year will be brighter and more prosperous than all that have gone before. May peace soon come and reign the whole world, down with militarism. I'm no fighter and am no believer in fighting. Hoping the Allies will soon be victorious under the able leadership of the great Lloyd George – the little Welshman. Wishing him every success. He has not failed in anything yet. Hoping he will prove to the world what Welshmen or the Welsh people are able to do. Put to the task, may the Lord help him and his family. [. . .] It has been said by the most prominent men here that I am the greatest singer in Pittsburgh; ha, ha. The reason why I don't come to the limelight more is because I haven't enough cheek necessary to push myself and you have to have it here in USA. Father told me many times to trust to providence and I intend to.

The church I sing in at present pays me two pounds eight shilling for a Sunday – a few hours in the morning and evening. Rehearsals are on Saturday evenings for a few hours, so I can't grumble. There are hundreds of voice teachers here so it's a graft for them all. My position at work in Westinghouse is all right in comparison. The worst part of my job is that I have to get up so early. I rise at six and start work at seven and finish at five. On Saturdays, I work seven to eleven thirty in the morning. But I'm not working very hard and have no worry after I leave the factory. I earn thirty cents an hour – about eighteen pence an hour – so I can't grumble. But I can't save anything as my rent is two pounds sixteen shilling a month for one room a little larger than your sitting room. It's a pretty good-sized room with two French windows but there is no heat. Of course, most houses here have large furnaces in the cellar to heat the houses during the winter and believe me they need it. In my room I have a little gas stove and this evening is below zero. Br.r.r.r.r. It's twelve below zero in Niles at the moment.

They sent for me to try for a church position two weeks ago. Of course there are several trying for it but they told me that I had the best voice. I sang Pugh Evans' 'Lead kindly Light'. I felt in pretty good form, so I just gave them a little of the 'Welsh Spirit'. They said that the rendition was perfect. But they also said that I was too powerful and too dramatic. The usual style in these churches is the Legato style – the English style. They want you to sing as straight as you possibly can. They do not want to know what you are singing about. I couldn't do that. I forget myself when I sing solo. I don't want to lose the dramatic powerful feeling for the sake of a church position but it's a rich church and they'll pay me one thousand and two hundred dollars a year – two hundred and forty pounds.
Happy New Year from your loving bros. Edie.'

In July, Edgar wrote a letter to his father, his sister Sal and her husband Frank, his sister Lizzie and her husband Henry William, and the latter's daughters, Marian and Sis:

'Fancy you having frost in June. These last few weeks we have been having excellent summer weather. Yesterday was 4th July, the great day in this country – Independence Day – and of course it was a general holiday. We had a lovely day. We went down the river in the morning just for a little while. Four of us – three Welsh and one Irish man – and then we went to hear the great socialist speaker, Eugene Debs.[4] Henry William, I guess, knows him. He was really great. We went to the park in the evening to see the fire-works. I guess there would have been a crowd of twenty to thirty thousand there. [. . .] I had a new summer suit last week. I guess you would make fun of me if I wore it in Penclawdd. It's what they call Shepherd's Plaid. It cost twenty-five dollars so you can guess

where your money goes in this country. You have to dress here. [. . .]
I have been packing my grip to take a trip to Niles for the month if
all is well and my money will last out.'

Edgar fulfilled his wish to tour the country, combining work with
pleasure. On 18 July 1918, he wrote to his brother and sisters:

'Here I am at Dubious, Pennsylvania. I guess you know that I'm
touring this country with three other fellows. We have been here
for five weeks and we have about eight weeks more to go this
summer but we are booked for twelve months with about two
weeks rest in all. The concerts are held in large tents that can hold
two thousand and we have an audience every day of about one
thousand to eighteen hundred. We commence at two thirty and
we give about one and a quarter-hours in the afternoon and one
and a half-hours in the evening. After we are through with our
evening programme the lecturer comes on and gives an hour
lecture. We are in a different town every day. These concerts are
held for seven days with different attractions everyday for the
seven days. The work is delightful, the audiences are great, the
weather is lovely, and the travelling is fine. We are four jolly fellows
going around all the time and the lecturer is with us everyday so
there are five of us travelling together. We have travelled over five
thousand miles already. We have two more concerts to give in this
country and then we go on to Canada and we have about eight
weeks there. We may have a little trouble crossing the border as
there are different laws in the two countries. I'm finishing this
letter in a town called Ridgeway. [. . .] Well I hope you are all quite
well. I hope the Eisteddfod will be a success. I hope your party will
win Will. Go to it boys. I wish you were singing with us fellows. It
has been great in the past and I hope it will be in the future.
Health, wealth and happiness to you all.
With love from your loving bros. Ed.'

On the twentieth of the next month Edgar was in Canada. He wrote to
Mag and Will. The letterhead of his writing paper depicted The Union
Station flanked by Walker House Hotel – The House of Plenty, and the
Carlsrite Hotel – the House of Comfort. They boasted to be Toronto's two
famous hotels and stated that 'We pay particular attention to the comfort
of ladies and children travelling alone':

'Here I am at present in Toronto waiting for my train so I thought I'd drop you a few lines to let you know that I am feeling fine and enjoying the work immensely. We have two more weeks in Canada. We are on our way to a town called Georgetown. Canada is a lovely country and the weather has been glorious. The people are fine and we are treated just fine here. [. . .] I hope your National Eisteddfod will prove a success – musically and financially. [. . .] I'm sorry to hear of Mar, Sis and Ben's illnesses. [. . .] I expected to see Uncle this week in Canada. He did come up to meet me but he had to go back on business before he reached me.

We see thousands of soldiers in Canada. Some ready to go and some just returned sick and wounded. It's a dreadful sight but I guess it's nothing to what will be before this war is over.
Heaps of love
From you loving bros. Ed.'

It was probably the last letter that Edgar wrote to his family.

In March 1918, the Spanish Influenza Epidemic – which is more precisely called a pandemic because it affected populations – broke out in Camp Fuston, Kansas, USA. It occurred in three waves. American troops that arrived in Europe in April to participate in the First World War are thought to have brought the virus with them. By July, it had spread to Poland. A second more severe form of the disease emerged in the August. The next winter saw the third wave. By the spring, the virus had run its course but not before it had spread to nearly every inhabited part of the world. There were ten thousand fatalities in Wales and altogether more than twenty million persons throughout the world died of Spanish Flu.

Edgar fell victim to the disease and died in America in December 1918. He was interned in Niles Union Cemetery with his aunt, Francis, and his cousins, Annie, Frank, and William.

In 1916, William F. Thomas and his daughter, Helena Taylor, had both found themselves living alone – Helena having been widowed in 1915 – and so William had gone to live with his daughter at 535 Robbins Avenue. He continued to write to his family in Penclawdd and in Neath. Although having only one close relative surviving in America, it seems he had no intention of returning to live in South Wales. He wrote to Sal, Frank and his brother on 17 February 1923:

'Yes, both your letters reached me all safe and so glad to get them as both are so lovely, interesting and newsy.

Wish I could write like you Sal, so easy and fluently expressive. Unfortunately, when I was young, writing letters was a rare thing so I missed the advantage of that part of my education.

I remember when a boy working with my father. We walked to the Old Colliery every day for over two years and had to be on the job by six o'clock in the morning and till six in the evening. It certainly made long days compared with the present.

It will be only a short while until you'll have such good roads in every direction that we shall hear of you riding in your cars back and forth to your work the same as they do here. [. . .] Please remember me to all especially the doctor and Reverend Jenkins (Bethel).'

William corresponded with his nephew, Frank on the nineteenth of the next month:

'I take it that you must be helping on the new road to Llanrhidian, which will be, when finished, a great boon to Penclawdd. Then you and Sal can get a motor car of your own and drive down Gower whenever you feel like it.

I'm glad to hear of the prospect of a new colliery to be started in the Wernbwll Valley. It will be a great thing for Penclawdd.

Sorry to hear of Tom Harry passing away and also Bob Guy. Some great man has predicted that after 1925 we shall all live on forever, but I rather think the old saying is true still – 'The young may die, but the old must die.'

I just got a letter from Scotland this morning from Jack Adams' (Gorseinon) sister saying her husband is coming to this country next month. He is Scotch and a very nice fellow. Of course, I only met him once, but he left a very favourable impression on me. I think the fellow might do well here. He is a steady man, and I shall do all I can to get him a job, and am pretty sure of success because I am acquainted with all the mill proprietors. At present, there is a scarcity of men in nearly all industries, especially iron and steel. [. . .] You can tell the children (Marian and Sis) that I often think of them when I'm alone here in the evenings playing solitaire.'

Mag received a letter from her uncle early in the New Year of 1924:

'Your wonderful letters and cards have been very gladly received with all their contents. As welcome to me as the flowers in May. [. . .]

Two of William F. Thomas' stores.
The Grand Atlantic & Pacific Tea Co., and Park's Pharmacy.

I told you before that I was building a store room or what is generally called with you a shop. Well I finished it six weeks ago and rented it to a grocer, but he has not moved in yet. [. . .] I do hope this will find all well and your dear father fully up to the mark of expectation. Tell him I am thinking of him night and morning and praying to God to help and comfort him in his suffering.'

A few days after his birthday in April 1925, William describes his birthday celebration to his nice, Sal:

'Your very welcome letter with birthday card enclosed just received today. [. . .] Well dear, we had quite a party of twenty-five and everybody enjoyed it. We had a five o'clock dinner, then music, dancing and cards until after eleven. We then had a midnight luncheon when the party broke up with everybody happy and promising to come again. [. . .] I received cards from Scotland, Wales, New York, Philadelphia, Pittsburgh, Cleveland and other neighbouring towns too numerous to mention. And what do you think? I have had a very pressing invitation from many of our leading citizens to stand for mayor again next November but I have concluded it will not be wise of me to accept it.'

In his letter dated 19 November of the same year, William makes many inquiries about Penclawdd:

'Have the boys finished their road contract yet? I read of it in the papers how Penclawdd contractors secured the job. [. . .] That's an excellent idea to open up a road from the Hendy (farm) to Penlan Cottage. It's something I have thought of a thousand times when sitting alone here in the evenings. I suppose that new road was figured out by Gordon so he can lay out his property for building purposes.

Has the Llanrhidian Road been finished yet? No doubt it will help much to bring traffic from Gower through Penclawdd to Gowerton and the neighbourhood.

How is the colliery by Blue Anchor (Wernbwll Colliery) doing? Are they getting out much coal there and how is it shipped out?

Am sending a picture of one of my stores. Business is improving and generally looking better.'

William wrote to Mag and Will during the last days of the coal strike of 1926:

'It is to be hoped that the great coal strike is finally ended but I fear not finished as it should be. It is too bad that working men should listen to radical leaders who draw big salaries and look after their own interests more than the poor men's interests. To me in this case, they were not looking after the welfare of the working men, but were trying to bring about a state of Bolshevism and ruin Great Britain with its wonderful trade by driving that trade to other countries which has nearly been accomplished. Wake up now and do all you can to regain what you have lost!

Well dear, I suppose you all enjoyed the great Eisteddfod but lost the first prize, which came to Cleveland, which is less than sixty miles from us. Well, I rather see it coming here than any other country outside of Wales.'

On 26 April 1927, Mag and Will were informed of William's birthday celebrations. He was obviously extremely pleased with his guests of professional men, and was confident that his niece and nephew would be impressed:

'We had a very nice party of some relatives of my late wife's and old friends. Had place cards for sixteen among whom were two lawyers, two druggists, our doctor and a couple of businessmen to a one o'clock luncheon. We had a few short speeches, lots of smokes of different kinds of cigars and a jolly good time all the afternoon. Everybody enjoyed themselves greatly declaring that they had never sat down to a better meal.

The following Sunday (Easter), we had another party of half-a-dozen or more that failed to come on Thursday. One of those brought a beautiful rose bush in full bloom and a lily, both nearly three-feet high. The gentleman who brought them is manager of the estate of two very wealthy bachelor brothers, millionaires, living fifty miles from here. They call here often.'

In William's letter to Mag and Will on 15 February 1929, it seems that he had no intimation of the Great Wall Street Crash that was to take place the following August:

'Business seems to be looking up here slowly and all are hopefully looking forward to the inauguration next month of our new president (President Hoover – Republican). I see by the papers that there is likely to be an election over there soon. Let us hope it will be for the best and both masters and men will get together into better understanding between them. We have listened in on the radio the past two weeks to the Westminster Chimes and Big Ben London striking the midnight hour every evening at seven o'clock which is five hours later than your time. It is wonderful to think we can count every stroke plainly five thousand miles away. Have you heard it at Neath?
God bless you both is the wish of your far away uncle.'

On 16 May 1930 in his letter to Mag and Will, William compared America to Wales:

'I am glad to say that I feel very well considering age and condition without any close family tie in this country. I naturally would feel better if there were a few of my own near me but it can't be helped.

I enjoyed my birthday a month ago and had a very nice party of about a dozen – all men. Among them were a preacher and a lawyer so you see we were well blessed with good company.

Times are not so good in this country as they were. The same complaint as you have. Lots of unemployment. It was reported recently that we have over six million here that have to be helped but not on the dole system. Here we have Community Chest with headquarters in each town, which take in collections and ration it out. They think the dole sounds too poor. Nevertheless, both to me look like they are paying men for doing nothing. Have been very surprised that so much has been paid out over there to men for doing nothing when so much could be done in improving the country roads and building new ones where needed. It could be done and paid for with the dole money and it would help keep men in fit condition for work whenever it would start. Excuse me for writing all this stuff so will quit now or it will tire me writing it and also you to read it.'

By May 1931, unemployment was still a serious problem in America as Mag and Will hear from William:

'I see by letters and papers received from over there that improvements in trade and business is still very slow. I'm sorry to say it is and has been quite as bad here the past year. I am sure it will surprise you to know that there have been eight to ten million unemployed in the United States which is more in number according to proportion of population than you have in Great Britain. [. . .]
With all good wishes to you both with lots of love from Uncle.'

This is the last known letter that William wrote to his relations in Wales. He died in Ohio in the 1930s, and was laid to rest with his family in Niles Union Cemetery.

Margaret Ann (Maggie) Austin, eldest daughter of David Evan and Elizabeth Austin of the Ship, lived with her husband, Evan John, and their six children, in the Dolphin Inn in Llanrhidian. Encouraged by a relative, Evan John decided to resign his tenancy of the pub and go to Massachusetts, America, to improve the family's financial situation.

Although Maggie was pregnant with their seventh child, she did not inform her husband of her condition, as she was sure that the knowledge would prevent him leaving her, and she was anxious for him to fulfil his ambition. As Maggie was determined not to join her husband, his intention was to stay in America until he made his fortune, and then return home.

But sadly, it was not to be. Evan John went to Massachusetts, and Maggie went to live in Penclawdd to be near her family. Evan John was extremely disappointed with America as the work was not good, and the wages poor. He contracted pneumonia and died within seven years. Through lack of finances, he had been unable to return home to see his family and his new baby. Maggie was left to raise her children without her husband's help and support.

After Daniel Rees had served his country in the First World War, he became a student at Aberystwyth University. "I went to Gowerton County School where I stayed until I was about eighteen and then, after the war, I went to the university in Aberystwyth where I trained to become a teacher." Daniel Rees obtained a teaching post in Llanmorlais School. He travelled from and to his home in Penclawdd every day by train.

As a child, Daniel had been taught by Mr. Jenkins in Penclawdd Elementary School. Mr. Jenkins' son had travelled the world while serving his country in the navy in the First World War. He had informed Daniel of the opportunities in Australia – an abundance of work with high salaries.

Daniel decided to discover Australia and after his marriage to Violet, the couple emigrated and stayed for ten happy years. However, Violet suffered poor health and her father persuaded them to return to Penclawdd. "My wife and I got married in 1923 and we went to live in Australia, where I taught for ten years. I was earning good money. I had plenty of money but my wife was not very strong. She was a weak woman. She was very weak. Her father said, 'Come home. You have been out there long enough.' My wife went home first and I followed later. I sailed in a big liner to Portsmouth. My wife came to meet me in London. We had a holiday there."

Although Cyril Howells worked in Dursley, Gloucestershire, for only four years, he experienced the heartache of living away from Penclawdd.

"I was anxious to obtain an apprenticeship as a fitter and turner, but was unsuccessful locally. I needed a forty-pound premium, and my father just didn't have the money.

I left on Whit Tuesday in 1939. I was fifteen, not sixteen until the July. I had not disclosed my true age, as I was so desperate for employment.

I remember leaving Penclawdd on the South Wales Transport bus, and mother crying her heart out watching me go. I didn't think at the time of the trauma she was going through. My two older brothers had already left home – one to Birmingham and the other to the police in

Essex. Only John and I were at home and now she was losing the third – all in a year.

I went by train from High Street Station, in Swansea, with Vernon – the son of a Crofty policeman – and arrived at Colley Station, on the main line between Gloucester and Bristol. It was a very old train, with only two coaches, called the Dursley Donkey. There was a large factory there which had instigated the train service.

We were met on the platform by Mr. Montgomery, the manager of the Exchange. He was a gentleman; a Christian from head to foot; a wonderful man. He took us to our lodgings in his Hillman Minx car. He had thoughtfully arranged for us to stay with a Welsh family.

We went upstairs wearing our shoes. When we came down our landlady was waiting for us with, 'Now boys, you'll have to take your shoes off when you go upstairs.'

A few weeks later one of the men in work asked me what part of Wales I came from. He returned with a fellow wearing a brown smock. If you had a brown smock you were somebody. When I discovered that the fellow was from Penclawdd I started crying like a baby. His name was Dan, older brother of Luther Davies whom I knew well. He had been living there for twenty years. Dan asked Vernon and I to catch a certain bus the next night at six o'clock to go to his home in Cam. His wife, Sissy, was from Crofty. When we arrived, the table was full of everything. We went there regularly afterwards.

Vernon had a telegram to go home, as his mother was desperately ill. I thought to myself that if he was going home, so was I, as I was so homesick. When his car arrived I packed his and my cases in. We had to go to Mr. Montgomery at the Ministry of Labour to inform him of our movements. He told Vernon that he was allowed home on compassionate grounds. However, I was informed that I would be breaking my contract in going and would be unable to return. Mr. Montgomery added that if I didn't come back, perhaps Vernon wouldn't either, and that I would be spoiling it for him as well as myself.

I decided to stay. But how God guides you. If you believe in Him, let Him work for you. I went out of the town for a walk in the country on my own. I met five or six boys in a lane. When they saw me crying, they asked me my problem. 'Oh! Come with us,' they said. From then on I was right. I think they were placed there to meet me. One can't say 'God does not work.' God does work.

A week or two later, Mr. Montgomery – he was a Mason – informed me that his Lodge was going to the Wye valley and would I like to go with them. I would have loved to have gone to Wales, but I was so shy that I felt I couldn't possibly go with a group of businessmen. I refused, but how nice of the manager to think of me – a young boy. He was a true Christian.

After completing my four-year apprenticeship, I went to the army for a short time and then returned to Penclawdd."

Jack Ian Hoppé had not returned to South Wales for over forty years after his evacuation there from 1940 to 1944. But early one morning, he experienced a sudden acute *hiraeth* for Wales.

"I awoke one summer morning and felt an intense desire to visit South Wales and in particular to visit both Penclawdd and Carmarthen. My wife and I got up, threw a few bits into a couple of bags, and were on our way by five-thirty. We approached Penclawdd just before eleven o'clock.

The railway station and level crossing were long gone, but as we bore right, 'Yes,' I thought, 'that's Gower House where I was billeted in 1940.' We parked in the small park at the bottom of the road on the seafront, and walked back. I peered over the back fence into the garden and exclaimed in amazement, 'Good heavens; the old privy is still there!' At that moment the door of the privy opened and an elderly man appeared. I didn't recognise him but felt that there was something familiar about him. 'I'm going round,' I said to my wife, and away I went to walk along the garden path. The man and I met halfway.

'I'm sorry to trouble you, but have you lived here for a long time?' I said, trying to sound as harmless and polite as possible.

'All my life,' came the slightly terse reply.'

'Were you here in 1940?' I asked.

'Yes I was. Why?'

'Do you remember two little evacuee boys who came in 1940?' I inquired.

'Yes, Jack and Michael,' came the reply.

'Well, I'm Jack.'

The elderly gentleman's face lit up with pleasure as he shook my hand and invited us into the house. It was of course Eurfryn, who had married Vi after his war service. His sister, Linda, was also still living in Gower House.

What a lovely reunion we had. The warm welcome had not changed, and we had some hours in reminiscing. It was good to meet Vi who seemed to have heard much about the two evacuees, although of course, I hadn't met her in 1940. Apart from the warm and affectionate welcome, my main memories of the reunion were the existence of an indoor loo and the discussion we had about rugby. I talked of my great admiration for

Haydn Tanner and I recounted the games I had seen him play in after the war. 'Oh! You should have been here last week. He was sitting in that chair,' said Eurfryn. 'He was best man at my wedding.' I was a week too late to have been introduced to one of the 'Greats' of rugby football. Just my luck!

We received a lovely letter from Eurfryn after we arrived home and were delighted to receive a copy of the 1980 souvenir book celebrating the Centenary of Penclawdd RFC.

We kept in touch although sadly both Eurfryn and Linda died a couple of years after our visit. Subsequently, Vi moved from Gower House. We always hear from her at Christmas."

Janet Jones, née Davies, niece of Gwynfor Jenkins, has spent the last thirty-four years of her life living in Canada and North America.

"I was born on the 26th of March, 1943, in Penrhiewtyn Hospital, Neath, one month later to the day than Howard Tucker. There were wounded miners in the maternity ward because a local coal mine had been bombed. I was probably born in a corridor.

In September 1953, I started in Gowerton Girls' Grammar School, together with the thirteen other pupils from Penclawdd Junior School who passed the iniquitous Eleven Plus Exam, the largest group ever from the village. (One of Elaine Jones' 'good years'.)

Sadly, on 21st December 1960, my mother, Elsie Jenkins Davies died, just prior to 'A' levels.

In 1965, I earned my BSc. (Hon's), majoring in botany, with a minor in zoology, at Cardiff University. There I met John, who was doing a PhD. in chemistry.

In 1965 to 1966 I did my Postgraduate Certificate in education, at King's College, London. Meanwhile, John had left for Edmonton, where he did postdoctoral work in chemistry at the University of Alberta – went to redress the balance of the Brain Drain.

I sailed to Canada in 1966, and taught biology at McNally Composite High School. John left in November 1967 for the USA to work in research for DuPont Company in New Jersey. In the fall of 1969, I was reunited with John, and we survived the Edmonton winter of '69, where for forty days, the temperature did not get above 0 degrees centigrade.

We left to get married in Tabernacle Chapel, Penclawdd, on Saturday, December 20th. We flew into New York on New Year's Day, 1970.

From September 1970 to '79, I taught advanced biology in Matawan Regional High School, receiving the Outstanding Science Teacher of the Year Award in New Jersey, from Princeton University in 1976.

*Janet, John and Meredith Jones
on Meredith's Graduation Day.*

By then, I had received another great loss when, my father, Richard George Davies, passed away in Penclawdd on December 29th 1973.

I received MSc. in education from University of Delaware after John was transferred to Wilmington by DuPont.

In October 1981, our daughter, Meredith, was born.

Since 1990, I have been teaching at Middle School, science and biology in Wilmington Friends School, which Meredith had attended since kindergarten. I was awarded a Woodrow Wilson Fellowship to study Middle School Life Science teaching practices at Princeton University in the summer of 1994.

This month – June 2000 – Meredith graduates from WFS, attending Brown University in the fall. John and I retire from DuPont and WFS respectively. There is to be a big life change for all!"

Inevitably, Janet has experienced a *hiraeth* for Penclawdd, but thanks to progress, America is not as distanced from Wales as it was for past generations of village emigrants.

"My emigration to Canada and the USA occurred in the last thirty years of the twentieth century when the world became more of a 'Global Village', as John Kenneth Galbraith called it. Thanks to the marvels of modern technology, telecommunication and transportation, I have never been further away from my family and friends than a telephone call or an eight-hour plane ride. And now, I communicate via e-mail with college friends, my cousins, Howard Tucker, and Geoffrey Nicholls who lives in the 'new' houses in Penlan, although his mother, Dulcie, still lives in the Benson Street house, Tŷ Clyd.

I have always carried my feelings of 'home' and my Welshness with me. Lydia, my stepmother, emerged from the loo last week (she was over for Meredith's graduation from High School) and said, 'This house is so Welsh!' In some ways, you have to be Welsh to recognize the signs – water colours of Rhossili and The Worm, Mumbles and Swansea Bay; Welsh tapestry mats under the china, and *carthen* (Welsh blanket) on the beds; a Nantgarw plate in the hall and an old oak dresser from Pembrokeshire, bursting with copper lustre jugs and blue-willow china. And then there are the obvious signs – old maps of Wales and Gower; prints of Welsh castles, Cardiff University, rugby matches and Michael Powell's 'Welsh Terraces'; a pennant celebrating the centenary of Penclawdd RFC; brass miners lamps on the hall table and a veritable plethora of books on Wales, its poetry, literature, language and culture, in the den.

John and I have been very fortunate in that we have been successful, both professionally and financially. These circumstances have allowed us to return to Wales from North America every other year since 1966. In her Senior Project book on her heritage, Meredith cited twenty-two crossings of the Atlantic, just to and from Wales, not including journeys to Finland, Germany and Australia in her eighteen years. We are blessed.

Perhaps *hiraeth* has been the driving behind my desire to maintain communication and connection with folks in the old country. My father and I maintained a regular stream of letters when I lived in Edmonton, Alberta, which continued after my marriage and subsequent move to New Jersey. John developed the same routine of letter writing with his parents in Pontllanfraith, Gwent. John and I maintain more contact with our school and college friends than they do with each other, so, we end up telling everyone how the others are!

I have never been ashamed of my background. When people ask me about my accent, I tell them that I was born in Wales 'to the left of England, and not on the right on a map of Australia.' This has become an almost automatic reply over the years. But I do think that growing up in Penclawdd, and specifically in my family, was the best thing that could have happened to me. The nature of village life, with its sense of belonging and security, gave me the self- confidence to leave, and yet feel comfortable in just about any place on Earth.

It seems very Welsh growing up with a special sense of one's niche in the community. Throughout my life, whenever I have returned to Penclawdd, I have been identified as 'Elsie Jenkins' (teacher) daughter and her father is/was Dick Davies who lives/lived in Foam-Edge (on The Promenade).' Howard Tucker will always be 'Elsie Fry and Wilfred Tucker's son.' It gives us our 'place' in the village, which is oddly re-assuring.

My Penclawdd was never that 'Dark and Pagan Place'. I still remember lying in bed listening to the early-rising cockle people, clip-clopping their horses and carts out to the Whiteford Sands. My Aunty Martha (Guy) who lived in Westville, next-door to Foam-Edge, used to boil cockles at the top of her garden. To this day, the only way I can eat cockles is to boil them in their brine and eat them hot out of their shell, with brown bread and butter.

When my mother went to Swansea Training College, she specialized in music and botany. Summer time meant walks with her up Hermon and down Crofty lanes. The dry stonewalled hedgerows fascinated me, as she showed me pennyworts, tongue-ferns, primroses, ragged robins and foxgloves. Of course, ever the teacher, my mother went further then simply identifying the individual plant species, she also grouped them into their families and taught me how to distinguish between them.

Music was as necessary as oxygen. Each chapel choir would put on a 'book' (oratorio) every year. When I was thirteen, I was alto in Tabernacle's performance of Handel's 'Messiah'. It was a very special performance, as my mother and father were also in the choir, my great-uncle, William Jenkins, conducted, and Uncle Gwynfor was the organist. The Morgan Lloyd Orchestra accompanied us. Morgan Lloyd was also the instrumental music teacher at Gowerton Girls' Grammar School, and an old family friend. He and his musicians always had high tea at Foam-Edge before every oratorio.

The Band of Hope was another staple of Penclawdd's musical life for me. Marion Lane, Mary Jones, Betty Evans, Pat Davies, Ann Hughes and I, sang and danced our way through the chorus of forgettable musicals, dressed as tea picker, gypsies, fairies and heaven knows what else. We also acted in the Good Friday dramas, under the passionate direction of Ifan Williams, the minister of Tabernacle's son. Later on, our paths crossed again, as Ifan was the headmaster at Penclawdd Junior School when I did three weeks of preparatory student teaching there, before going to London for a year of postgraduate study in education.

Do they still have the Whitsun Monday Walk through the village? It started at the Ship and Castle. The Bethel folks were always the largest contingent (a fecund bunch those independents), Tabernacle a smaller, sedate second, and the Trinity Baptists, a distant third. All of us wore our new best clothes, even the boys, whose trouser-leg length reflected their age; short trousers gave way to long, as the boys grew older (and taller).

Whitsun Tuesday was always the day of the Gower Festival at Tabernacle. Preparation for this hymn-singing extravaganza started months before. After Sunday evening service, just about the entire congregation stayed on for rehearsal and Uncle Gwynfor was a hard taskmaster. For the older girls, being asked to join Mary Myfanwy Davies' Choral Speaking Group was yet another time-consuming honour. All these activities left me with a profound respect for anyone brave enough to specialise in the performing arts. For a small village, Penclawdd was culturally rich. Even now, I can sing the first verses of most of the old Welsh hymns from memory, and I can still recite large chunks of the Bible.

I know the cockle ponies still come in from the marsh with the tide, because if the people on The Promenade forget to close their front gates, these bold horses graze on the front lawns. When I went to Cardiff University, I couldn't get to sleep at night for a long time, because I missed the lapping of the tide up against the seawall.

As a former teacher, I do hope the barbaric practice of publishing the old 'O' and 'A' level results in 'The Western Mail', has ceased. Howard Tucker still remembers meeting my father outside Arwyn's Shop[5] on 'O' level morning, and under my father's orders, having to look my results up before his own, because my father had forgotten his reading glasses! When I taught biology in New Jersey, my Jewish kids complained about their parents' drive for and high expectations of their children's academic achievement. I used to tell them that it was nothing to that of the Welsh, who had the students' test grades printed in the national newspaper! The practice horrified them, but it formed a bond between us, as they saw me as a fellow sufferer, who related to their angst.

Teaching kids biology has always been a source of profound joy to me. I have never wanted to do anything else, ever since I took over Aunty Mary Gwen Jenkins' class – Standard Two – when she fell ill during my student teaching. It gave me a 'high' that I have never lost. Indeed, even in retirement, I know that I will have to be similarly occupied, even if I am just an unpaid teacher volunteer at the Delaware Nature Center.

America is now my home. John and I have been given, and have taken advantage of, every opportunity offered to us here. Americans are great that way. I still enjoy coming back to Wales, but Penclawdd is less and less my old home. I still think that Foam-Edge is in a great location, but it is its current and past inhabitants that I miss, not the house itself. I know that when Lydia decides to give up the house, there will be less of an incentive to come down to Penclawdd, as Howard has realised, after his father's passing.

When in Penclawdd, I walk up the village a lot, popping in to see the family and friends with whom I still keep in touch. They are Dulcie Nicholls, Audrey Rees and Olwen Newton. Of my peers, there are Carol Jones (Angel's sister who now lives in 'I Penlan Terrace, Great Uncle William

Jenkins' old house), Mary Jones and Marion Lane Eynon Jenkins, who still lives at Rose Cottages with Tony, her second husband. I have the closest relationship with Marion. It is with these folk that *hiraeth* is palpable, but it is always the past that is remembered with fondness; we are not part of each other's daily lives. When I leave, I have learned never to say goodbye. The farewell is always, 'See you next time I am over.'

Teaching has helped me realise that my students, like my daughter, will always take a piece of me with them, as I now carry a part of them with me. We are all products of our environment, reflecting our surroundings and the people with whom we interact. I have left Penclawdd, but my life in the village will always be a part of me. Without it, I would not be who I am. This is the legacy I will always carry with me."

NOTES

1. Peter Finch, *A Welsh Wordscape*.
2. *The New Oxford Book of English Light Verse*. Edited Kingsley Amis. W. U. P. (1978), p. 273.
3. Constantine Fitzgibbon. *The life of Dylan Thomas* (Dent 1965), p. 299.
4. Eugene Victor Debs (1855-1926), a railroad labour leader, was for many years the standard-bearer of socialism in the United States. In 1893 he founded the industrial American Railway Union, the nation's largest union. He helped found the Social Democratic Party of America in 1897, the Socialist Party in 1901, and the Industrial Workers of The World in 1905. He was presidential candidate in 1900, 1904, 1908, 1912, and 1920.

    An effective orator famous for his altruism, Debs summed up his philosophy in the slogan "I am for socialism because I am for humanity." He opposed all war except the international battle for socialism. He was given a ten year prison sentence in 1918 for violating the Espionage Act, but was pardoned by President Warren G. Harding in 1921.
5. George Harry's fish and chip shop, Station Road, was then run by his wife, and son, Arwyn, as a fish and chip shop and a newsagents.

Bibliography

David Taylor, *Macmillan Master Series. Mastering Economic and Social History.* (Houndmills, Basingstoke, Hampshire RG21 2XS, 1988.

George Eaton, *Neath and the Spanish Civil War.*

Dorothy M. Bayliffe & Joan N. Harding, *Staring Benson of Swansea* (Cowbridge and Bridgend, 1996).

Helena Barrett and John Phillips, *Suburban Style. The British Home 1840-1960* (Boston, Toronto, London, 1993).

Gower Journal. Volume 17.

Gareth Elwyn Jones, *Modern Wales. A Concise History. 1485-1979* (Cambridge 1984).

Penclawdd Elementary School Reports.

Penclawdd Infant School Reports.

Mary Owen, *Sue Gronow's School. Memories of Penclawdd, Crofty, Llanmorlais.* (Produced for the year 2000 by the North Gower Heritage Group).

R. N. Cooper, *Higher and Lower* (The Lodge, Park Road, Penclawdd, 1998).

Kim Collins, M.A., D.A.S. *A Guide to the Collections* (The West Glamorgan Archive Service, 1998).

J. Vyrnwy Davies, M.A. *A History of Tabernacle Calvinistic Methodist Chapel, Penclawdd 1836-1936.*

'Philas Bidder'. *Gower Journal. Volume 1.*

Geoffrey R. Orrin, *The Gower Churches* (Swansea, The Rural Deanery of West Gower, 1979).

David Egan, *Coal Society. A History of the South Wales Mining Valleys 1840-1980* (Llandysul, 1992).

F. H. Wynne, D.Sc., HM Deputy Chief Inspector of Mines. *Report on the causes of and Circumstances attending the Explosion which occurred at Wernbwll Colliery, Penclawdd, on 28 November 1929.*

R. N. Cooper, *A Dark and Pagan Place* (Cowbridge 1996).

Stewart Williams, *Glamorgan History. Volume 6.*

W. Gerwyn Thomas, *Coal Mining Industry in West Glamorgan* (Cowbridge, 1969), p.206.

Don H. Howells, *Elba Colliery Disaster.*

Vernon Watkins (1906-1967). *The Collier.*

Idris Jones, *Gwalia Deserta.*

J Geraint Jenkins, *Cockles and Mussels. Aspects of Shellfish-gathering in Wales* (National Museum of Wales (Welsh Folk Museum, 1984).

North Gower Heritage Group Letter No. 4, Spring 1966.

'The Penclawdd Business'. *Gower Journal. Volume 5.*

Gwyn A. Williams, *Fishers of Men* (Llandysul, Dyfed, 1996).

John Retallack, *The Welsh Guards* (Great Britain, 1981).

Chez Bowyer, *The Encyclopaedia of British Military Aircraft* (2-6 Hempstead High Street, London W3, 1982).

David Taylor, *Macmillan Master Series. Modern British History* (Houndmills, Basingstoke, Hampshire RG21 2XS, 1984).

J. R. Alban, *The Three Nights' Blitz. Selected Contemporary Reports relating to Swansea's Air Raids of February 1941* (Swansea, 1994).

Basil Jones, *And So To Battle* (Tollgates, Battle, East Sussex).

Patrick Macdonald, *Through Darkness to Light* (Upton-on-Severn, 1994).

Idris Jones. *War.*

Hymn 305, Ancient and Modern Hymn Book.

Brochure – *Penclawdd R.F.C. Centenary (1880-1980).*

Encyclopedia Britannica.

Chambers Encyclopedia, Volume 9.

Programme – *Penclawdd Brass Band. Twenty-fifth Anniversary.*

The Macmillan Family Encyclopedia, Volume 6 (London and Basingstoke, 1987).

Newspapers:
The Cambrian. The South Wales Evening Post. The Western Mail. The South Wales Daily Post.